THE GENESIS
OF
CROWN COLONY GOVERNMENT

THE GENESIS

OF

CROWN COLONY GOVERNMENT:
TRINIDAD, 1783–1810

JAMES MILLETTE

WITH A FOREWORD
by
LEWIS E. BOBB
Lecturer in Government, U.W.I., St Augustine

MOKO ENTERPRISES LTD.
14, Riverside Road,
Curepe, Trinidad, W.I.

THE GENESIS
OF
CROWN COLONY GOVERNMENT
Copyright 1970 by James Millette

*   *   *

printed in trinidad by
quick-service printing company, limited,
42 & 53 observatory street, port-of-spain.

THE GENESIS

OF

CROWN COLONY GOVERNMENT:
TRINIDAD, 1783–1810

JAMES MILLETTE

WITH A FOREWORD
by
LEWIS E. BOBB
Lecturer in Government, U.W.I., St Augustine

MOKO ENTERPRISES LTD.
14, Riverside Road,
Curepe, Trinidad, W.I.

THE GENESIS
OF
CROWN COLONY GOVERNMENT
Copyright 1970 by James Millette

*   *   *

printed in trinidad by
quick-service printing company, limited,
42 & 53 observatory street, port-of-spain.

To

Saville and Dorothy Millette
my parents
Whose faith and perseverance
over many, many years
Made this and more possible.

AUTHOR'S NOTE

This is a book about the history of Trinidad between 1783 and 1810. It is also a book about colonialism and imperialism, about revolution and counter-revolution and about the conflict between conservatism and change in the West Indies. It is, too, about the early struggles for autonomy and rationality in a British colonial society. Accordingly it focuses on the very contemporary problem of administering a conquered colony with non-British peoples and institutions in the late eighteenth and early nineteenth centuries. And as such it is much more than a simple book about Trinidad.

In its broadest sense the book is concerned with the exercise of authority in government, in particular of a special kind of authority in government. It is about the exercise of imperial authority over white and non-white subject and dependent peoples at the tail-end of the early empire, and about the means by which the *laissez-faire* theories of overseas government applicable to the white communities of the First British Empire gave way to the authoritarian conceptions of the Second. The transformation from tolerance to authority was prompted by many factors but, perhaps in the long run, particularly by two: the need to blunt the savage edge of imperialism by engaging in humanitarian reform even against the wishes of the entrenched white minorities in the colonies, and the necessity to cope with the rising 'menace of colour' and particularly with the threat of black or coloured people in government.

The ramifications of this programme of transformation were many in number. The problems raised were problems which were presented in sharpest focus in Trinidad but which were also part of the experience of St. Lucia, of Guyana, and at times of Martinique, Guadeloupe and St. Domingue. And they were problems which were worked out against a background of contemporary slavery and the existence of a substantial free coloured population which sought, unsuccessfully, to straddle two worlds the one black and the other white. It is not surprising therefore that the decision of 1810, a centrepiece in the ensuing analysis, should have been taken in a gush of humanity which came in the fulness of time to reek of racism and reaction. Thus it was that 1865 was 1810 writ large, except that the free coloured view of himself in 1810 was different from that which obtained in 1865; and that precisely was the point. In 1810 Lord Liverpool could be suspected of acting with some generosity; in 1865 the panic surrender of representative institutions by the Jamacian Assembly, and thereafter by many others, was quite clearly motivated by a desperation to keep the machinery of political control out of the hands of the rising black and coloured peoples.

I

It is the theory of this book that the period 1783 to 1810 in the history of Trinidad witnessed the genesis of the system of government known later as the Crown Colony system. That system was fated in due course to become the day by day experience of nearly all the British West Indian islands, Bermuda, the Bahamas and Barbados excepted. Between the 1860's and the 1960's Crown Colony rule became nearly completely ubiquitous. But the near ubiquity of the system in the hundred years of absolute dependence following on the Morant Bay uprising in Jamaica in 1865 belies the very unsure nature of its origins. It may be that it would have developed nonetheless; but the historical fact is that it developed only gradually as a result of a very precise set of factors existing in Trinidad and nowhere else in the West Indies in the late eighteenth and early nineteenth centuries.

The story begins in 1783. Even so, in terms of the larger theme, there already existed, as will be seen from the book, some useful predisposing developments particularly in Grenada after 1763. By that time it was clear that the presumptions of the Westminister pattern of colonial government were fast becoming unworkable. The consequence of Grenada's experience between 1763 and 1790, as evidenced in *Campbell vs Hall* and in the struggle for civil rights by the French whites of that Island, and the legal decisions handed down as a result of those conflicts, was momentous. The trauma of North American independence was, of course, another powerful episode. Thereafter the constitutional relationship existing between the metropolis and the colonies became less conventional and more contractual a relationship. *Campbell vs Hall* and the problem of the French whites led to the development of an attitude of cautious watchfulness on the part of the imperial government. Given the new awareness of contract the metropole had at least to be careful not to alienate its rights too completely by the precipitate grant of traditional concessions. Moreover, it was also true that issues of colonial management were developing which made it increasingly desirable that the metropolis should maintain for as long as it could its prerogative rights for manipulating the internal affairs of newly acquired, and particularly, conquered colonies with foreign white and slave populations.

The history of Trinidad in these years was crucial too in determining the general applicability or inapplicability of the 'Westminster model' as it was then known in the colonies. Till then colonial government was a pale imitation of metropolitan parliamentary government. The question was whether the imitation should be perpetuated. On this crucial and sensitive issue there were few to be found willing to speak out with the hostile forthrightness with which Lord Brougham spoke in the House of Commons in 1811. For him there was no question but that the 'Westminster model' had no place in the colonies, and for good reason too.

"When we talked of English law, we talked of it by reference to English judges, to English juries, and to English feelings and principles. .. It was a mockery to talk of transplanting the English law to the West Indies when only the name was carried thither, and all the true English feeling was left behind. Then the law of

II

England served only as the engine of fraud and oppression, rendered doubly disgraceful, because carried on under the pretence of law and justice. This was under the pretence of justice to the whites, to load the other miserable wretches with oppression unbounded... to substitute oppression and injustice for benevolence. The British constitution was to be found in no other part of the world but in this country." [1]

Brougham was ahead of his time - in the light of our experiences since then clearly very much ahead. But it was the conflict which derived from believing the opposite to be true that contributed to the particular significance of the constitutional struggle in Trinidad after the British conquest.

In the light of later developments the conquest of Trinidad in 1797 was obviously an important date not only in the Island's history but in the history of British imperialism itself. In sum it ushered in a period of intensive reform particularly concerned with the peculiar problems of West Indian society. Canada probably apart, Trinidad became the scene of the first sustained attempt at the evolution of a political system suited to the particular needs of a particular colony. To the extent that Trinidad became an area of experiment in constitution making the problems of the Island between 1797 and 1810 acquired a modern and very familiar ring since constitutional engineering was in large part to become the political and social history of later British colonialism.

For Britain this preoccupation with constitutional contriving was a symptom of a more profound metamorphosis. One can almost say that until 1797, and with the exception of the American Revolution, Great Britain had enjoyed the fruits of imperial dominion; thenceforward she was to encounter by slow and excruciating stages the responsibilities of imperial rule. The disbursement of political power between white and non-white subject populations was to become in the long run the most important of those responsibilities.

Also, it must be said that the gales of change blowing through the British Empire in the late eighteenth and early nineteenth centuries surprised the majority of British statesmen. Faced with the problems of a new age it was not surprising that those responsible for colonial affairs dithered and demurred at the complexities with which they were confronted. The first attempt to settle the Island's constitution was made by the harassed and hard pressed Addington administration containing, as a Tory peer remarked with relish, "none of those confounded men of genius". But men of genius were needed to bridge the growing gulf between old shibboleths and new realities. The extent to which statesmen were still bound by the former is indicated by the fact that it took the better part of a decade, 1801 to 1810, for them to decide that the old representative system could no longer be gratuitously granted to a West Indian colony. It was to take another sixty years, and some help from the white planter class itself, to secure the Assembly's eventual abolition. The history of Trinidad between 1783 and 1810 is part of the history of the gradual disappearance of the West Indian Assembly.

III

It has already been remarked that the social and political problems of Trinidad in the period with which the book deals have a very modern ring. This is true. Many of the problems raised have an acrid, modern smell. This is incidental though perhaps unavoidable. The issues of political and economic dependence, revolution, counter-revolution, republicanism, change, stagnation, constitutional reform, justice and injustice, freedom and oppression are echoed in the events of the West Indies of today. One can hardly write about the representative system of government in the eighteenth and nineteenth centuries without reflecting on the curious anachronism of its re-emergence in the Associated States of the Commonwealth Caribbean. Nor for that matter can one ponder on the 'menace of colour' in government without recognising the true political poverty of the masses of West Indian blacks even after the constitutional 'advances' of the last few years. Also, it is to be remembered that Cuba in 1962 was pre-figured by Trinidad in 1797, the threat of republicanism and of ideological 'contagion' being the ultimate sanction for British intervention in that year. Since then the United States of America has supplanted Britain as arbiter between conservatism and change in the Caribbean, but the issues of upheaval at present founded on the grinding dispossession of the ordinary people are certainly not lacking in precedents.

Also, race loomed large. The society of which we speak was a slave society with deep racial divisions. In those days, too, people were much more blatant about race. Whites were the lords of the earth and they alone had political and economic power. Free blacks and free coloureds had no power and they entered the pale of political and economic society, when at all they did, on sufferance. They too regarded race with respect, often themselves acquiescing in the despisement of their own colour and in the veneration of whiteness. It is not for nothing that black and coloured masters were reputed to be among the harshest of slave owners. As M.G. Smith has pointed out, the relations between free coloureds (and presumably free blacks) and their slaves were conditioned by twin influences, the one the legal and conventional distance between slave and free the other the social and psychological confusions engendered by the vexatious question of colour. Nor is it for nothing that in the slave colonies of the West Indies, French as well as English, the free coloured recognition of the link between slavery and their own condition of disadvantage presaged the development of the final internal onslaught on the slave system.

In all things serious and unserious race was the outspoken presumption. And for a long time the acme of racial conflict in the West Indies rested on the confrontation at all levels of the society between blacks and whites, that is to say, in the eighteenth and early nineteenth centuries, between people of African and European descent. Nothing of importance was free from the considerations stimulated by the racial meeting of these "fell incensed opposites". For example, the earliest attempt at introducing a significant Chinese population into Trinidad had one interesting racial sidelight. It was fervently believed by important whites that the significant advantage to be derived from such a scheme was to be found in the extent to which it would

IV

promote the creation of "a barrier between us, and the negroes; with whom they (the Chinese) do not associate; & consequently to whom they will always offer a formidable opposition". [2] The Chinese never came in sufficient numbers to render this signal service to the white community. Later, however, as Donald Wood has convincingly shown in his *Trinidad in Transition* [3], the East Indian population was to be introduced in the anticipated fulfilment of that strategy. In our own time, West Indian politicians in Trinidad and Guyana have been trapped in the racial treadmill created by the fertile imagination of nineteenth century European racism.

The problem quite simply was a problem of numbers. Left to themselves the Negroes, introduced in large numbers as slaves, were sure to take over these societies in which the white populations were becoming absolutely and relatively smaller. To cope with that threat whites resorted to an abundance of stratagems. Habit, law, psychology, religion, education-and when these failed, brute force and ignorance-were pressed into the many spheres of conflict. In time the Crown Colony system came to be the apotheosis of all these proceedings. At first there weren't many who recognized, as Picton did, the invaluable merit of guile for maintaining and perpetuating the inequalities of colour. But it was the Pictons who set the system surely and unfalteringly under way; and so guile came to predominate. The strategy of passing over as *"silently"* as possible the whole question of individual merit while trusting to the invidious assumptions of the system "to leave the free coloureds where they are" was to be re-echoed again and again between Picton's time and ours. The failure to treat race openly as a serious social issue, the obsessive determination *not* to legislate against racial discrimination in societies in which the majority of persons are black and suffer for it, are today residual elements of a subtle philosophy of oppression but too well laid.

In Trinidad in the early nineteenth century black was black, and that was that. But there was a difference. The existence of a class of free coloured and black persons greatly outnumbering the white population of various nationalities gave the problem of colour and race a sharpness not to be found elsewhere in the contemporary West Indies. In Trinidad, within the large mass of persons enjoying the legal status of freedom some of them white, others non-white, race was an issue. And it remained so for a long time precisely because Trinidad had for practical purposes never known a condition in which people of colour were not waiting in the wings to take over. The 'menace of colour' was only too real. The legacy of that situation was such that as late as 1905 the Island's Colonial Secretary writing on the morrow of a report into the riots of 1903 authoritatively expressed the view after "a very careful, very anxious and very deliberate study of conditions upon the spot. . . that in Trinidad the Colour Question is the one, all-pervading, and immensely difficult question that underlies, and affects, more or less vitally, every matter concerned with the administration of the Colony"; so much so indeed that he predicted "that any serious and important breaches of the peace that may hereafter occur in Trinidad will be found, if their causes be sifted to the bottom, to have their origin, direct or indirect, in the Colour Question". [4]

Given the overt racial assumptions prevalent in nineteenth century Trinidad it was not surprising that the entire debate over the constitution was exclusively a debate among whites. It was almost as if the slaves and the free blacks and free coloureds did not exist. It was only in 1810 that the free coloureds in Trinidad, timorously and tremulously, under threat of complete exclusion from the representative system of government that seemed likely to be established, staked their claim for participation in it. They were the first people of colour actually to do so. That claim was denied but on the pretext of protecting the free black and coloured population who stood to benefit from conceding it. In 1810, therefore, as in 1865 there existed two alternatives: either open up the political system and by so doing admit free blacks and people of colour to full and equal participation with whites, or close it completely. On both occasions the decision-makers opted for closure.

Today as in 1810 and in 1865 the selfsame choice re-presents itself: greater freedom or more repression, democracy or barbarism. And today as in 1810 and 1865 race is a unique element. It is not the only element, for the Western political system as a whole stands under the severest condemnation for its failure to promote, even in white countries, the essence of popular democracy. Also, in the black ex-colonial countries the agents of repression are themselves black men. With black men in power, black people are fundamentally without power and still today stand in the wings as they did yesterday. Yet race remains an important element. In all things material black people the world over are absolutely and relatively poorer, less happy and more dependent than whites. Behind this worldwide inequality between black and white stands the historical legacy of an old colonial system which down to our own time has thrown the shadow of the plantation across the face of our world. The history of Trinidad between 1783 and 1810 is an essential part of that legacy.

If morals are to be drawn I suppose the book shows the futility of the attempt by whites to establish a selfish despotism over the political life of the society, and more broadly the futility of racial chauvinism in this plural society of ours. Throughout the nineteenth century political despotism was in fact to be the unceasing objective of Trinidad whites and particularly of those whites who by reason of British descent thought themselves to be particularly fit to administer the affairs of the Island. From this point of view the deprecation and the suspicion with which "French creoles" have always existed in this society have been something of a mystery. Whites of French, Spanish and generally non-British descent were forced into a permanent posture of defence throughout the nineteenth century by reason of the aspirations towards Anglicization which dwelled forever in the hearts of the British. In this sense, the paper unanimity between British and foreign whites in 1810 was brief in the extreme. Students of this period will know of the struggles which ensued between white and white over membership of the Island's Council not too long afterwards. Later other postures were adopted, Britishers keeping up an incessant din for representative institutions, non-Britishers insisting just as consistently that the time was not yet ripe.

VI

The point was though that in all its forms the demand for representative institutions by white society, supported as it was by the view that blacks and people of colour should play a limited part in the political management of those institutions, was a reactionary demand. It is from this point of view difficult to support the oft-repeated view, perpetuated for example in Williams's *History of the People of Trinidad and Tobago,* that demands for representative institutions by Trinidadians (that is to say, largely white, English Trinidadians) manifested a conflict between local liberalism and metropolitan reaction; for they did not. Such demands were in essence part of a continuing search for the establishment of a selfish political despotism through the "liberal" agitation for representative institutions. As already argued, however, this does not quite let the metropole off the hook. The view that blacks and people of colour were "unfit to rule" was a racial assumption made by local white and metropolitan society alike, and to the extent that the metropolis supported that view to that extent was the metropolis culpable. But it is arguable that the main factors which gave rise to the extended sway of Crown Colony government in the West Indies in the late nineteenth century, at the same time that more democratic institutions were flourishing in the metropolis as well as in the white dominions of the Empire, were particularly local in character.

As Lewis Bobb has argued in his *Foreword* there was a sense in which the Assembly system and the Crown Colony system were different sides of the same coin. Metropolitan control was a fact; and if the issues were important enough metropolitan prescription could be made to stick. Particularly was this so when, between Emancipation and Morant Bay, the accumulated problems of the West Indian islands forced upon them a greater and greater political and administrative dependence on the metropole. In other words the nineteenth century Assembly system after Emancipation was an increasingly dependent system. What made Crown Colony government necessary was not the fact that the West Indies had to be made more dependent on Britain. They already were, and seemingly could not help being so; but given the metropolitan view of the desirability of a white privileged class in the West Indies and the hostility of this group to full black participation in local government, Crown Colony government thereby became inevitable. In other words Crown Colony government was in essence a racial adjustment to the ever present menace of "colour in government".

Slowly and perceptibly however the system changed. Numbers were again important, as were other factors. Black political rule was inevitable given the direction of British democratic politics and the hideous outrage of black people in the colonies. Today the threat is a different threat: it is the threat of black political domination based on the assumption that only the establishment of black despotism in politics could lead to the economic rehabilitation of the black, impoverished masses. Such a view seems to be a natural consequence of a historical development by which formal political power has passed into the hands of black people while the power to maintain and manipulate a particularly undemocratic economic system has remained in the hands of whites.

VII

If this book suggests anything it suggests the need for a very cautious approach to such a solution. I take the view that in a peculiar sense history, in so far as it relates to the enlightened progress of men as men, is very often determined by the generosity of ascendant groups. Obviously black people are not yet an ascendant group in the West Indies. But given the fact that a reformed polity can create black ascendancy and that, given the current moods, Black Power - to use the current phrase - can and will be established in the West Indies, the need for generosity remains. The real problem is to induce such generosity from a people who have known very little generosity themselves.

Here the attitude of whites themselves is crucial. In return for generosity they must surrender privilege. They must renounce the traditions of the past, in particular that urge for "a kind of despotism"which today manifests itself in their monopoly of the economic system through which covertly and in association with the foreign corporate interests they continue to influence the political system. They must identify with the legitimate and basically human aspirations of black people in what is patently a black society. In sum they must, like the rest of us, bring themselves to serve and not merely to exploit the community in which they live.

All of this is not new. C.L.R. James has said as much, though differently, in his *Party Politics in the West Indies.* It is still to be done though. It is to be hoped that this book will be further inspiration to the doing.

*   *   *

The Genesis of Crown Colony Government originated as a thesis presented to the University of London in 1964 for the degree of Doctor of Philosophy in History. Over the years, while the thesis was being written, and since, I have accumulated a variety of debts to a variety of people. Professor G.S. Graham, until lately Professor of Imperial History at King's College, London, provided a good deal of patience, guidance and good humour while I researched in London in 1961-64. A similar service he performed for a fair number of West Indians before and since my time, and his contribution to West Indian historical scholarship in this regard is noteworthy. So, too, is the contribution of my colleagues in History on the three campuses of the University of the West Indies. They have been inspiration and help, particularly so the three outstanding academicians Professors Goveia and Hall and Dr. Roy Augier who have done much to create a genuinely West Indian school of history. Roy Augier it was who read and commented on earlier drafts of this work, and who in particular persuaded me, against my own initial judgment, to take a third look at the Picton-Fullarton affair which is such an epic part of the history of Trinidad in the period about which I have written. C.L.R. James, too, read and commented upon an early draft and was very flattering about its significance. That was, as every other author would appreciate, an enormous help. Mr. P.J. Marshall of King's College, London, gave several helpful references on Fullarton at a critical stage. Library staffs everywhere have been helpful. At the British Museum, the Public Record

Office, the Institute of Historical Research, the West India Committee, and at numerous lesser known libraries in the United Kingdom I met a regular and unfailing courtesy. In the West Indies, particularly at the University libraries, the same is true. In this tradition of generous assistance, Mrs. Shirley Espinet, Assistant Librarian at the St. Augustine campus of the U.W.I., distinguished herself by doing a very painstaking job on the proofs. Mrs. Jean Coggins willingly toiled away at typing the numerous drafts and is to be complimented for her efficiency; and last but far from least there is my colleague in Government at St. Augustine, Mr. Lewis Bobb, who wrote a much too appreciative Foreword.

On the production side, I have been frankly very anxious to demonstrate that a job of this kind and quality can be done in the West Indies. Quick Service Printing Company Limited rose to every challenge posed by the enterprise and all the participants at every level in that establishment must be very highly praised. Also to be thanked are the Research Institute for the the Study of Man, New York, and the Institute of Social and Economic Research, U.W.I., for having assisted by giving grants which helped to make publication possible. Dr. Vera Rubin and Mr. Alister McIntyre, respective Directors of these two institutions have my thanks, as does Mr. Lloyd Best for having, in different days, assisted in obtaining the former grant. My colleagues on the Board of Directors, Moko Enterprises Ltd., have put me in their debt by supporting my proposal for local publication of this book under Company sponsorship. Also, I must pay tribute to John La Rose whose own experience in publishing West Indian literature in London contributed to the accumulation of the confidence so much needed for an enterprise like this.

To my parents I have accorded the insufficient testimony of my affection and appreciation by the dedication of this book. In respect of my wife and children and of all others who have helped in any way whatever I acknowledge my innumerable debts which I fear from experience I shall never be able to repay.

1.   *Parliamentary Debates,* Vol. XX, pp. 615-6, June 13, 1811.

2.   C.O 295/17, Marryat : Shee, 3.6.1807.
3.   Oxford University Press, 1968.
4.   F.O. 295/435, *Memorandum on the Existing Condition of Race-Feeling in the Island of Trinidad,* submitted by the Colonial Secretary, Trinidad and Tobago.

FOREWORD

For some time now the History Department of the University of the West Indies has been planning and working at the production of a three-volume *History of the West Indies.* Such an extensive work of information, it is hoped, would provide a basic text on West Indian history as well as material for the study of West Indian society, past and present. Whatever its success, the project is highly significant if only because it has brought into focus two opposed perspectives. It appears to mark at one and the same time a point of continuity as well as of departure.

From the standpoint of publication, the writing of West Indian history has been mainly the work or interest of scholars in European and American Universities. This state of affairs is likely to continue indefinitely for a variety of reasons; some, material, others, idealistic. For while the efforts made by bodies and institutions in the West Indies to collect and collate a variety of source material on West Indian history are commendable, the hard fact is that the bulk of the material to be researched in order to discover all the facts lies in Britain, in such other European countries as Spain, France, Holland, Denmark, and in the United States. Abroad, a bona-fide West Indian scholar is more likely to find convenient access to the records of his past than he would at home. Unravelling the complexities of history, too, is much less easy than the gifted amateur would make it appear; and it is hardly overrating the influence of historical scholarship on human affairs to say that a serious historian can increase our knowledge of the past only by first equipping himself with a strategic grasp of the sources available for study.

It might be true that the West Indian reading public has no stomach for what is called academic history; and, indeed, a tale tricked out in the garb of historical narrative is more likely to entertain the general reader. Such history, however, written from the fringes of the world of scholarship is, in the long run, worthless. If the writing of our history is not to be left in the hands of faculty 'drop-outs' as it were, it must be founded on new research - painstaking, scrupulous, neutral. This means that it will have to be mainly scholars in universities who, in the field of history, use their learning to enlighten.

But in these matters the decolonisation movement with the resultant political independence has posed a serious but much overlooked dilemma for the West Indian historian. While the change in our political circumstances has tended to foster a new and exciting intellectual interest in our history it has also tended to excessive self-esteem and feelings of racial and nationalist grandeur, to the extent that the popular press of the nineteen-sixties has been turning out a kind of court-history to accompany each independence celebration: Morant Bay .(1865) was not the "chaos in a coal-box" that Carlyle, with more malevolence than insight, held it to be. It, says the Jamaican nationalist, was the birth of a nation. In Guyana the Berbice Slave Rebellion of 1763 has been subject to so much re-interpretation as to make the Ogle shootings of 1948 look, by comparison, like a counter-revolution. Capitalism, slavery and British authoritarianism now appear to have bred such an inward hunger for political power that democracy seems out-of-date and irrelevant and must yield to dictatorship which many may feel will do no great harm provided it is home-grown.

It is natural for the West Indian nationalist, brought up on a history written largely from a European standpoint, to have become fed up with the fare of falsification and misrepresentation by which imperialism often sought to maintain itself. To illustrate the nature of one kind of falsification: Aristotle remarked that some men were by nature slaves. About two thousand years later David Hume discerning "no arts, no sciences, no symptoms of ingenuity among the Negro slaves in the colonies as well as among those dispersed all over eighteenth century Europe" suspected that all Negroes were inferior to all whites. Twentieth century research into African culture (mainly the work of Europeans) has shown how little the slavers understood the workings of their trade and the slave-owners the phenomenon of Negro slavery. "How", as one observer puts it, "could they know that the Africans rounded up in the inland countries were largely peasants and illiterate, as crude and illiterate as the peasantry of Europe; peasants who were sold and shipped and sold again, until they were good only for what they were bought for - hard labour?" They could not - what with the lack of evidence to the contrary and such "comforting philosophy to relieve their consciences".

If political independence gives us the opportunity for historical revaluation then our responsibility is to see that the verdict on ourselves by ourselves is not to be faulted because we have used our own prejudices and neuroses to cure these ills in others. What Froude and Carlyle said our historians must not say in reverse; our historical insights must not be theirs turned about, lest our colonial past lead to our intellectual and moral domination by that past.

Here there are two lines of approach. We may follow Lord Acton's advice: "Resist your time - take a foothold outside it." This has been taken to mean that after the historian has presented his facts impartially, even sympathetically, he should step back and deliver judgements based on immutable standards. Or we may think that Acton asks for too much detachment; that it is exceedingly difficult for the West Indian nationalist historian to ignore the context of his own times. He is inextricably in the grip of contemporary events and his view of historical phenomena is irresistibly influenced by his political and sociological experience and upbringing. But the West Indian scholar writing his history may or may not eliminate his personality. He is surely under no obligation to draw conclusions or pass judgement. What, as a nationalist, he should do, is to seek to construct a usable past with which to shape the future. His work should bring high

XII

visions and possibilities into political being. For, to parody Mill: "The historian who is only an historian is not even a good historian; and the same principle applies to other studies."

It is here that we come to the point of departure in the writing of our history. The break is not merely with European interpretations of it or with the confinements of a colonial education. Eric Williams' *Capitalism and Slavery* made that break forty years ago. So has Elsa Goveia's *Slave Society in the British Leeward Islands* and Douglas Hall's *Free Jamaica*. The real departure is in the approach to the study of West Indian history. Here the University of the West Indies has played a major role. Almost from its inception it has sought to free its young historians of the trammels of traditional guide lines in writing history and has encouraged West Indian political scientists, economists, educationists and sociologists to utilise methods of historical inquiry. By fostering an inter-disciplinary exchange between comparative history and comparative social science it has broken through the crust of concreteness differentiating history from social science so that the West Indian political scientist must needs be historical and the West Indian historian is not surprised that he has written sociology. Thus freed, in the words of Professor Shils, "from the bonds of historicism," a history of the West Indies is being created which, in a sense, never existed before.

One member of a young generation of writers to be trained in these new perspectives and techniques is James Millette, who has now produced this revealing study of the constitutional development of Trinidad between 1783 and 1810. Others of this new breed of 'Mona men' have made similar type studies of Barbados, Jamaica and Guyana; and though at the time of writing they have not yet published in book form, it is not to be expected that Millette's book can pre-date others in the field much longer.

The diversity of scholarly literature that is likely to emerge must not be misinterpreted. West Indian history is not to be seen hereafter as the mere arithmetic sum of our several island histories. Nor must such diversity be turned into apologia' for the condition in which, to borrow Ruth Glass' words, "Insular social groups co-exist, separated from one another in insular places." Behind the diversity are political as well as historical realities.

One of these realities is that the West Indies have never been able to achieve any real sense of community. The desire for political independence that suffused the movement towards federal union provided an opportunity for a nationalist type of regional politics to crystallise and to be identified with a will to preserve federation. But that opportunity was missed. West Indian leaders might have been inspired in the nineteen thirties and forties by a sense of a collective national destiny. Their prospect, however, as politicians, depended on their local standing. Insular issues shaped their politics which were part and parcel of an historical experience in which stronger ties developed between themselves and a "Mother Country' five thousand miles away than among themselves spread over a thousand miles of ocean.

XIII

Thus decolonisation when it came was bound, in those circumstances, to multiply citizenships and to provide a rationale for histories that would nurture the particular identity of each new state. However much like England tiny Barbados used to be, little purpose will be served today in building national sentiment by telling Barbadians that their history, a part of the story of the expansion of Europe, began with the landing of Warner in 1627.

In face of these changes it becomes all the more important that our new historians guard against the writing of set pieces on this or that island. What holds historically true for the small human aggregation of each island could be quite untenable in respect of all of them. And, while it is good that our individual histories be studied with greater thoroughness, a too rigorous adherence to an insular line of approach would be sterile and regressive if it were to make each island's history an overblown version of a miniature reality.

This book avoids these pit-falls. Its substance is a description and an explanation of the turn of events in the constitutional development of Trinidad between 1783 and 1810 - a development that grew out of a necessity to accommodate three differing political heritages: Iberian, French and British. But the focus of the study is on change and survival within the political community which developed in the years immediately following the British conquest of the island in 1797.

The conquest marked not so much a 'turning-point', as a 'turning-on'. In a way, everything was there after 1797 as before 1797. Yet nothing was quite the same. The time 'before' and the time 'after' seemed caught up in a kind of historical sleight-of-hand.

Though the island had legally changed hands it had hardly, in important aspects of its political and social life, changed mental habit. Especially the professional character - excessive paternalism cheek by jowl with political partisanship and the practice of corruption - of the administration was noticeably unchanged. The attitude to public office, under Spanish rule, produced as the book has shown, an unadulterated bureaucracy. The need to work in into an alien culture British political institutions would produce disguised authoritarianism. Whatever the Spanish did, the British did in reverse.

Again, the slaves and the masters continued to be there after the conquest; but alone of all the islands of the British West Indies then, Trinidad had a free coloured population much in excess of its free whites. Thus, if the influence of the French Revolution provided ideals of special appeal to slaves and freed coloureds, it also tightened the authority of the Crown. For in as much as republicanists in Trinidad were thought to seek not merely to abolish slavery, but to turn the unfree and the disenfranchised into citizens with rights of representation, the white ruling classes reacted *prima facie* with a strong preference for the politically protective power of the Crown.

The Crown, almost from the start, was free to indulge an authoritarian mood in this newly acquired colony. That was to be the imperial fashion of the day in the predominantly 'coloured' colonies. There was no country willing and formidable enough to make heard a gospel of anti-imperialism;

no Fourth Committee to call into question the actions of the imperial powers; no sense of stewardship to help guard against the fraudulent conversion of trusteeship into partnership. Yet in Trinidad the British seemed to have settled for institutional conservatism of a kind. It was probably easier and less costly to govern through institutions that were familiar to a majority of the population than to set up new ones. Preoccupied with a military struggle conducted at varying degrees of intensity on an almost global scale, it seemed good statesmanship on the part of the English imperialists to avoid costly innovation and possibly bureaucratic confusion in a country that was, as likely as not, to change hands with the fortunes of that struggle. In any case, the way in which it was decided to govern Trinidad did not conflict with imperial interests and involved no surrender of imperial control. The British Governor was in essence the Government. Though responsive to local feeling he was unfettered by it; his actions being subject to the approval of only the Crown's Secretary of State in England. This system of government, Millette points out, lasted with "minor alterations" for the thirty years after its inception in 1801. Such English notions of political culture, namely: that good government is no substitute for self-government and that there ought to be an organic relationship between those who govern and those who pay taxes - were long in coming to Trinidad.

The reason was that in Trinidad the constitutional problem facing the British Government was in some respects unique. The society was not only planter-dominated but also one in which the majority of the planters were French and Spanish. Faced with a nationalities problem the confidence with which representative institutions had been granted by Britain to her colonies of settlement elsewhere in the West Indies gave way to an indecision which delayed their adoption in Trinidad. The more important, it seemed, that a balance be held between foreign and British planter-interests so much the more did 'direct rule' by an official hierarchy appear necessary. The device of nomination to a Governor's Council would have offered some form of constraint on the exercise of official power; but its very success would have relegated the planter classes, both foreign and British, to the role of "participant subject" (using Barghoorn's phrase) rather than of influential citizens actively involved in the making of political decisions.

By 1810 British and foreign planter-interests were beginning to converge and to become 'class' rather than 'caste' oriented. This was partly because of the increasing pressure on the governmental system produced by the presence of the large body of free coloured citizens in the island. Greater in number than the free white population, of some economic substance and anxious to maintain and extend the privileges formerly enjoyed under Spanish rule they were unlikely to acquiesce in any constitutional settlement which ignored or discounted them. The British Government seemed hard put to find a constitution that would reconcile the conflicting interests of the whites whilst delaying indefinitely the enfranchisement of the free-coloureds. Coloured enfranchisement was itself certain to have distracting repercussions within and beyond Trinidad. Indeed, the arguments used by Governor Picton

XV

and others against the introduction of popular institutions reveal how a country made up of a small British merchant caste demanding a social power out of proportion to its number, wealth and social status, white French refugees seeking a haven of security which white French republicans were, in their own political interests, as willing to subvert as aristocratic French and Spanish royalists, in their own economic interests, were ready to support and free-coloured citizens (larger in number than any other of the population groups except the black slaves and indigenous Caribs combined) would produce a society shot through with perplexing delusions and dilemmas which 'government by Commission' could only fail dismally to resolve.

The book reconstructs this failure and its aftermath using a wealth of documentary detail. In a manner that is forceful without being brash, an analysis of the failure is intelligently conducted through the minutiae. It is also compelling because it tries to meet what E.H. Carr calls the "need of imaginative understanding for the minds of the people" with which it deals and "for the thought behind their acts". How historically significant an analysis it is might well be measured by the extent to which Trinidadians of 1803 seem to have come through one hundred and sixty-odd years to establish dialogue with the Trinidadians of 1970. Then as now it appears prudent, at least to the ruling elites, that colour-class questions be "passed over as silently as possible" if only because, then as now, the masses could begin the destruction of the country equipped with power arising "from neglect, carelessness and contempt of them in Government".

The constitutional problems facing Trinidad in the early years of the nineteenth century and the attempts made to solve them have a much wider significance in the political and social history of the West Indies. That they have been studied in depth by a Trinidadian has its own kind of significance in the politics of the island.

To deal with the wider significance first. The failure of Fullarton and his colleagues in 1803 was not merely the first stumble in what must now be seen as a continuing search for political consensus in Trinidad. The failure presented all concerned with a jaundiced view of the future course of political change in West Indian societies. The Trinidad problem of 1803 was both an example and a prefiguration of all the issues that bore down upon the West Indian society after the abolition of slavery. It had all the ingredients (albeit in microcosm) of the Canadian question which it predated by some forty years; but it produced no Durham, and so the chance to become the forerunner to what has been generally regarded as "the greatest state paper in British imperial history" was lost. Instead the Colonial Office settled for arguments which were to become mental pegs upon which every group interest everywhere in the West Indies could hang on to its own peculiar nostrums and thereby obstruct constitutional progress. It is 1810 rather than 1865 which ought to mark the demise in the nineteenth century of representative institutions in the West Indies. For Trinidad might have become a laboratory for a novel experiment in constitution-making in a plural society and so might have moulded the fortunes of a more positively progressive constitutional change elsewhere in the West Indies; but the Fullarton Commission unwittingly, if excusably, worked with assumptions that were untenable, or saw in the existing political institutions relations that had no basis in fact.

To illustrate. The Commissioners seemed over-impressed with the use of law as a means of holding a society together. Not only did they assume that legislation is a legitimate function of constitutions (which it is not) but also that the law (which in practice is unreliable) provides a sufficient limitation on government. In this, they agreed with "Fullartonians" and "Pictonians" alike even when opposed to one or the other faction.

Again, each of the socially significant groups saw in the granting of representative institutions either a means of increasing or a device for diminishing its influence in the governmental affairs of the island. Both the hope and the fear obscured the reality. The fact is that in the representative system then prevailing, there was a complete separation of Assembly and Executive. They were separable because they derived their existence and powers from different sources - the one, from the people; the other, from the Crown. For representative institutions to bestow on the representatives any great political influence in government the proper condition is one in which both Assembly and Executive have at their disposal only the same kinds of political resources upon which to found their positions. This was not so under the regime of the 'Old Representative System'. The differences in the scope and the quality of political resources made the political power of the Executive highly superior to that of the Assembly; and 'Crown Colony' government when it came did not really reverse the democratic power of the people in favour of the dictatorial power of the Governor. It really brought to fruition what was already there in gestation.

Even if the 'Old Representative System' had permitted parliamentary control of the Executive, it was still deficient in an important particular, namely - consensus. Assemblies were elected by a very limited number of colonists. Not all those who could elect could be elected. The representing, statute-making and deliberative functions in the political process thus became the work of a relatively narrow group of interests in the society. This was bound to exclude many who were capable of contributing to an intelligent public opinion and to make it difficult to establish the broadest possible consensus. The weaker the consensual element in the political life of a society the stronger is the need (as Picton's rule indicated) to use force as an instrument of policy rather than as a device reserved for exceptional circumstances. But it would have come perhaps as a complete surprise to those who demanded the representative institutions prevailing in Britain's other West Indian colonies to learn that the system they rejected was, in substance, no better nor no worse than the system they desired - only different, in form.

In one way or another, all these issues which bedevilled the early movement towards constitutionalism in Trinidad have persisted. They continue to hamstring the island's political development, especially in respect of nourishing those sentiments which are of political value in creating a nation out of differing peoples and cultures. The failure of 1810 was an expression of an almost psychic aversion to the search for shared values and ideals.

And so Millette's study comes to reveal an historical experience devoid of what Renan has called a "daily plebiscite" on "a desire to continue life in common". At the same time there is nothing in it which suggests that the West Indian has followed the Frenchman in believing that the development of historical research is such a danger to nationality that "To forget and. . . . to get one's history wrong are essential factors in the making of a nation". On the contrary this study is nearer the thinking of E.H. Carr, a distinguished modern historian. In his book *What is History?* Carr writes that "Great history is written precisely when the historian's vision of the past is illuminated by insights into the problems of the present". So that, "Before you study the history, study the historian. . . . Before you study the historian, study his historical and social environment". Against this kind of reasoning this book comes alive.

It also comes alive for another reason. Millette is, at the time of writing, the leader of a political party. Because of this, he might be seen as an academic who is in love with history but charmed by politics; or the other way round. Whatever is the view, it would be to his future work as historian and politician that we will have to look to see whether he has distinguished which is mistress; which, wife.

LEWIS E. BOBB

University of the West Indies,
St. Augustine,
Trinidad,
July 20, 1970

CONTENTS

Tables are located between Chapters 6 & 7

THE GENESIS
OF
CROWN COLONY GOVERNMENT

PART ONE

THE YEARS OF MATURING

CHAPTER 1

THE POLITICS OF REVOLUTION

The history of modern Trinidad dates from 1783. In that year, Trinidad, discovered by Columbus on July 31, 1498, on his third voyage of discovery, had been under Spanish rule for close on three hundred years. During those years, the Island had been much more the object of the adventurist attentions of foreigners than of the serious concern of Spain. Spanish idealism, neglect, and preoccupation with affairs in other parts of the world, together contrived to relegate Trinidad to the position of a colonial slum in the Spanish empire. No serious or sustained attempt was ever made to develop its resources and, as time went by, a grandiose and visionary foreign policy ill-suited to Spain's resources of manpower and wealth rendered such an attempt more and more remote. All through the sixteenth and seventeenth centuries, while the Spanish Crown dallied in Europe involving itself in a series of wars and alliances, its vast New World empire lay virtually abandoned. A tortuous and complex machinery of government manipulated in the exclusive interest of the Crown, and indeed Spanish colonial theory itself, discouraged the development of initiative and independence in the colonies.

The Spanish Crown had nearly always been the hub of Spanish colonial enterprise. Except for the few decades of the late fifteenth and early sixteenth centuries, during which the great deeds of Spanish colonialism were accomplished by discoverers like Columbus, or by *conquistadores* like Cortes and Pizarro, the role of the Spanish Crown was unceasing and preponderant. As early as 1550 the Crown had achieved its first major objective. By that date, a little more than a half century after the discovery, and with Mexico and Peru barely pacified, Spanish authority in tropical America had already passed by design into the hands of royal governors and other royal officials.[1] Indeed, by the first decade of the sixteenth century, the Spanish Crown, by its treatment of Columbus had already indicated what was to be its constant attitude to private endeavour in the colonies right up to the end of the Seven Years' War in 1763. Not even the successful example of others could sway the Spanish Crown from its fixed determination. The proprietary system,[2] which Spain's great rivals, England and France, had successfully

1. J.H. Parry, *Europe and a Wider World, 1415-1715.* (Third edition. Hutchinson University Library. 1955), pp. 63-4.
2. For the British islands, see J.A. Williamson, *The Caribbee Islands Under the Proprietary Patents* (London, 1926); V.T. Harlow. *A History of Barbados, 1625-1685* (Oxford, 1926). Also of use is H. L. Osgood, *The American Colonies in the Seventeenth Century.* Three volumes. (First published by Columbia University Press, 1904; re-published at Gloucester, Mass., 1957).
    On the French side see, Nellis M. Crouse, *French Pioneers in the West Indies, 1624-1664* (New York, 1940): also his *French Struggle for the West Indies* (Columbia University Press, 1943).
    See, too, S.L. Mims, *Colbert's West India Policy* (New Haven, 1912).

used as a means of harnessing private effort for the very speculative business of colonial exploitation, was never pressed into the service of Spanish colonialism. Even in its most effete days, following the death of Charles V and later of Philip II, the Spanish Crown continued to cling to a private and personal supervision of colonial development. Spain's colonies existed for the sole benefit of the Crown. Their role was the production of wealth, narrowly interpreted by Spain as consisting of gold and silver and little else. Personal and exclusive preoccupations with a vast empire, disproportionate to the Crown's means and interpreted in the narrowest sense, were the chief causes of the defects of Spanish colonialism.

The corollaries of a system of exploitation thus interpreted were two in number. Firstly, given Spain's weakness from the seventeenth century onwards, effective development was highly selective, both as regards territories and, in the large mainland provinces, between different areas within the colonies themselves. In an empire stretching from well beyond Labrador to Tierra del Fuego only Mexico, Peru, the Greater Antilles, the Caribbean, some strategic parts of Central America, the northern tip of South America and the offshore islands like Trinidad and Margarita were "firmly" in Spanish hands. And even in the most important of these the Spaniards were "little more than the drivers of the slaves . . . destined to dig the pretious (sic) metals for the use of the manufacturing and trading nations."[3] Thus Trinidad, with no known sources of gold and silver, was abandoned and neglected, held, it would seem, for the day when such minerals might be discovered.

Secondly, exclusive intercourse between mother country and colony, under the closest possible control, became the one essential principle of colonialism, as the *flota* system, the *asiento* and the *casa de contratación* testify.[4] Unable, even unwilling, to develop its colonies, the Spanish Crown ruled out the possibility of their development by private Spanish enterprise, not to speak of the enterprise of foreigners. The result was inevitable. Dire want and unrivalled opportunity existed side by side in the Spanish colonies. Unfortunately, the analogy was susceptible of an even wider interpretation. At a time when, towards the close of the eighteenth century, with the notable exception of St. Domingue, the colonies of other European nations were beginning to suffer from the effects of long and systematic exploitation,

3. David Macpherson, *Annals of Commerce, Manufactures, Fisheries and Navigation with Brief Notices of the Arts and Sciences connected with them.* Four volumes. (London, 1805.) Vol. IV, p. 166, note.
4. For descriptions and analyses of the Spanish colonial system see, Wilhelm Georg Friedrich Roscher, *The Spanish Colonial System,* translated from the German by E.G. Bourne, (New York, 1904); Salvador de Madariaga, *The Rise of the Spanish American Empire,* (London, 1947), and his *The Fall of the Spanish American Empire.* (London, 1947); C.H. Haring, *The Spanish Empire in America* (Oxford University Press, 1947, reprinted by Harbinger Books, 1963); Jose M. Piernas Hurtado, *La Casa de Contratcion de Las Indias,* (Madrid, 1907).
    Also, Bernard Moses, "The Casa de Contratación of Seville", *American Historical Association,* Annual Report, 1894. (Washington, 1895); and his *Spain's Declining Power in South America, 1730-1806,* (New York, 1965).

Spain's colonies, underdeveloped and sparsely populated, presented a constant invitation to foreign attention.

For two centuries following the discovery of the New World and Spain's claim, except for the bulging eastern tip of South America, to the whole of it, Spain was, as S. de Madariaga has pointed out, the international enemy.[5] The very vastness of her colonial empire made it fair game for all. With so much to do and so few resources with which to do it, Spain could only fitfully contest the ambitions of other nations for their share, as Francis I of France had put it, in Adam's will. By the eighteenth century the savage depredations which had earlier marked these encroachments were a thing of the past, but the struggle between the nations for a share in the exploitation of Spain's ill-developed empire was still an international theme.

At the end of the eighteenth century this struggle was essentially a struggle between Britain and France, the two rival imperialisms which had already, since the end of the seventeenth century, replaced Holland, Portugal, and Spain herself, as the main contenders for colonial spoils. Disillusioned by the loss of the Thirteen Colonies, Britain was content, for the moment, to make her incursions by way of trade. The free port system in the West Indies, and the increase of direct trading with the South and Central American mainland colonies, particularly in the South Seas, furnished unwelcome signs of British aggressiveness and audacity.[6] In the interests of trade Britain showed herself willing, if necessary, to manipulate local disaffection against Spain in the South American colonies. British consuls in South America were, in the 1770's, instructed to report on how best difficult local situations might be exploited to promote British trading interests.[7] As this policy gained strength, the conquest of Trinidad in 1797 and its retention at the Peace of Amiens in 1802, was to become an important aspect of the British commercial design.

France for her part was determined to garner a larger share of the Spanish trade by relying upon her special relationship with Spain, the ties of which had been strengthened by the conclusion of the "Family Compact" in 1761. Thus, the years 1763-1770, the "golden period of French influence in

5. *Spain.* (London, 1931. Second edition) p. 45.
6. Allan Christelow, "Great Britain and the Trades from Cadiz and Lisbon to Spanish America and Brazil, 1759-1783", *Hispanic American Historical Review,* Vol. XXVII, 1947, No. 1, pp. 24-26.
   See also, Allan S. Brown, "The Expedition to the St. John's River and the Lake of Nicaragua, 1779-80", *Caribbean Historical Review,* No. II, December 1951.
   For the wider issues see, W.L. Dorn, *Competition for Empire, 1740-63.* (New York, 1940), pp. 251 ff.
   Cambridge History of the British Empire, Vol. I, (1929), Chaps. X, XVI, XXIII.
   J.D. Seeley, *The Expansion of England,* (London, 1909; first published London, 1883), p. 20 ff.
   For the free port system in the West Indies see, Frances Armytage, *The Free Port System in the British West Indies: A Study in Commercial Policy, 1766-1822.* (London, 1953).
7. Allan Christelow, *ibid., loc. cit.*
   See also, V.T. Harlow, *The Founding of the Second British Empire, 1763-1793.* Two volumes, (London, 1964), Vol. II, pp. 615 ff. in which Harlow discusses the 'liberation' of Spanish American markets against the background of Britain's historical preoccupation with the 'fantasy' of breaching the walls of Spanish monopoly in South America.

3

Spain", saw France intent on a plan to make her Spanish ally stronger by affecting a thorough reform of the Spanish apparatus for colonial trade and commerce under French direction and along French lines.[8]   The French interest was by no means altruistic. In the first place it was intended that Spain, made strong by France, should help the latter in her military ventures against Britain.   Secondly, France hoped to use her privileged position to reap the benefits of an extensive trade with the Spanish empire.

The direction of this policy of reorganization was for a long time a major French concern and became in the process the task of the highest French officials.   The French Prime Minister, Choiseul, was himself the guide and inspiration of the programme of reform.[9] With much effort French officials, by 1765, had managed to bring about a relaxation of many of the restrictions on trade between Spain and her colonies. In that year, a plan worked out under the personal direction of Choiseul made its appearance; and, in addition, one of the most important officials selected for the implementation of this policy in the New World, José de Galvez, owed his appointment as Inspector General of New Spain to direct French influence. Later, he repaid his debt by securing for the French West Indian islands limited trading privileges to ports in Venezuela, Cumaná and Guayana; and, through his influence, France also obtained the right to navigate the Mississippi as far as New Orleans, the right to trade in New Orleans and in Cuba, and permission to establish two French commissioners at Louisiana to regulate trade.[10]

These then were the two major challenges to the integrity of her empire that Spain faced in the latter half of the eighteenth century. One was openly hostile, the other was an embrace that Spain hoped to shrug off as soon as she dared. The opportunity to deal with at least a part of the challenge came in 1783. In this year Spain stumbled upon a specific solution to her problem of ineffective colonisation in Trinidad which profoundly affected the course of the Island's development over the next decade and a half and stimulated the growth of the more important aspects of the society over which Britain was to rule from 1797. As fate would have it, this solution, as we shall see, involved French participation. French participation and the coming of the French Revolution were to give Trinidad's society a particular flavour and content which was destined to make the Island a thorn in Britain's side and to force its conquest by that Power in 1797.

8.   A. S. Aiton, "Spanish Colonial Reorganization under the Family Compact", *Hispanic American Historical Review,* Vol. XII, 1932, p. 269.
      Also, R. D. Hussey, *The Caracas Company, 1728-84,* (Cambridge, Mass., 1934), p.. 226 ff, 229.
      And Allan Christelow, "French Interest in the Spanish American Empire during the Ministry of the Duc de Choiseul, 1759-1771", *H.A.H.R.,* XXI, 1941, *passim.*

9.   Aiton, *op. cit.,* pp. 273-4.

10.   Aiton, *op. cit.,* pp. 275-6.

In 1783, Trinidad displayed in miniature all the defects of the Spanish colonial system.[11] Agriculture was virtually non-existent. Manufactures were barely obtainable. Poverty and want existed on every side. The penury-stricken inhabitants were fractious, unruly and constantly bordering on rebellion. Hardship and disease made their discomfort acute. The first half of the eighteenth century had been witness to a series of sickening disasters. A disastrous hurricane in 1727 had been followed by an equally disastrous epidemic in 1737.[12] All in all, life had been, and was, generally and unrelivedly "nasty, brutish and short". Since 1757, when the Governor and the *Cabildo* had complained of the poor state of the economy, little or no recorded change had taken place. In that year, a memorandum to the Governor pointed out the dire lack of cattle, provisions, tools and paper, in a word, the scarcity of the necessities of life in an undeveloped frontier community. And the picture of squalor and neglect which the *Cabildo* painted in explaining its failure to keep the municipal buildings and roads in good repair, clear refuse, and keep its books in order,[13] had not improved by 1783.

In their misery and degradation the few inhabitants can easily be envisaged carrying on their interminable squabbles among themselves. The *Cabildo*, no doubt, still found reason enough to quarrel with the Governor, and with the Vicar General of the Catholic Church, as it had done in the years immediately succeeding 1757;[14] but matters never quite came to the pass that they had in 1745, when the *Cabildo* had imprisoned the Island's Governor for nominating a successor in the governorship, on going on leave, contrary to its own interpretation of the law of succession.[15]   This incident, and its sequel of imprisonment and banishment of several *Cabildo* members, had not yet been forgotten by either side, and severely strained relations between the people and the administration.

The Governor in his turn must have still found it possible to complain as one of his predecessors had done in 1759 of the "licentious behaviour and

11. Beyond a little agreed general information not much has so far been brought to light about Trinidad's history prior to 1783. Recent useful contributions include the following :-
   Josefina Perez Aparicio, *Perdida de la Isla de Trinidad.* (Seville, 1966).
   Jesse Noel, *Spanish Colonial Administration and the Socio-Economic Foundations of Trinidad, 1777-97.* (Cambridge University Ph.D. thesis, 1966).
   Francisco Morales Padron, "Descumbrimiento y Papel de Trinidad en la Penetracion Continental." *Anuario de Estudios Americanos,* Vol. XIV, 1957, pp. 93-159.
   Also his "Trinidad en el Siglo XVII" *Anuario de Estudios Americanos,* Vol. XVII.
12. Aparicio, *op. cit.,* p. 29.
13. L. M. Fraser, *History of Trinidad, 1781-1939.* Two volumes. (Trinidad, 1891), Vol I, pp. 7-8.
14. Sir Claud Hollis, *A Brief History of Trinidad Under the Spanish Crown,* (Trinidad, 1941), p. 75.
   Pierre-Gustave-Louis Borde, *Histoire de L'Isle de La Trinidad Sous le Gouvernement Espagnol.* Two volumes, (Paris, 1882). Vol. II, p. 128.
15. Hollis, op. *cit.,* pp. 73-4. The law in question is in the *Recopilación de leyes de los reynos de las Indias.* (Madrid, 1791). Reproduced in three volumes by the Consejo de la Hispanidad, Madrid, 1943. Lib. 5, Tit. 2, Ley 51.
   The *Cabildo,* in putting forward the claims of the *alcaldes ordinarios* to govern in the Governor's absence, would seem, according to this law, to have been in the right.

drunkenness" of the members of the *Cabildo*, of their disloyalty and total responsibility for the sad state of the Colony.[16]   While he lived in Port-of-Spain, then a small town of three or four hundred Spaniards, Frenchmen, Corsicans and free coloureds, all ekeing out a meagre livelihood trading, fishing, cultivating a few crops, and distilling an inferior rum,[17]   the *Cabildo*, in lofty disdain, presided at St. Joseph the better to emphasize the traditional differences between itself and the Island's Governors. St. Joseph, falling apart from lack of attention, was to suffer the ultimate calamity in 1784 when the Illustrious *Cabildo* finally condescended to remove itself to Port-of-Spain.[18]

Apart from these two towns, organized living was confined to the scattered Indian reserves and missions where Catholic priests attempted to fulfil Spain's religious obligations to the Indians. In the absence of good roads, the colonists confined themselves to scattered peripheral regions of the northwest, western and southern lowlands close to the sea[19]   which was, besides being the main means of heavy transportation, an important source of sustenance.

Society was hardly intimate; the closest bond between the inhabitants was the awareness of their common plight. Beyond that was their common Catholic faith and each individual's acute dependence on himself and his own resources. Spanish imperialism could have pretended what it liked but its pretentions hardly touched the daily life of these colonial subjects. The only law they knew was the law of necessity. Material need had forced so many breaches in the wall of legalisms with which they were hedged that law had lost nearly all meaning. The difference between the enactment and enforcement of law remained wide. The report of a seventeenth century Governor conducting a *residencia* on his predecessor was that everyone, even young children of ten or thereabouts, was guilty of the most flagrant violations of the law. [20]   The pattern thus early set had been sedulously maintained. Frequent involvement in illegal trade and other irregularities bred an indifference to authority. Trading with the foreigner, and Spanish neglect, undermined the Island's loyalty to the metropolis. The coming and going of many of the inhabitants in search of a better life was a constant theme.

16. Hollis, *op. cit.*, p. 75.   17 *Ibid.*, p. 74.

18. *Ibid.*, p. 81. Also, p. 77. E. L. Joseph, *History of Trinidad*, (Trinidad, 1837), p. 161 where the date is given as 21.8.1783, as K. S. Wise, *Sketches of Trinidad and Tobago*. Four volumes. (Trinidad, 1934-38), Vol. IV, p. 48. But, Borde, *op. cit.*, Vol. II, p. 182, gives 21.8.1784.

19. No single reliable authority can be quoted for this judgement. It is a deduction from later reports on the distribution of agricultural settlements throughout the Island. See, for example, *BM. Add. Mss.* 38356, pp. 5-6, "Memorandum on Trinidad", no date, no name; *B.M. Add. Mss.* 36499, pp. 93-106, *passim;* Capt. F. Mallet, *Descriptive Account of the Island of Trinidad*, (London, 1797). Also, D.R Harvey, *Economic Aspects of the Historical Geography of Trinidad since 1802*. (London University unpublished M.Sc thesis, 1955), p. 14.

20. Hollis, *op..cit.*, p. 7; Wise, Vol. II, p. 24 ff; *B.M. Add. Mss.* 36320, pp. 290-99.

THE POLITICS OF REVOLUTION

In 1783, the commerce of the Colony was entirely dependent on the visit of a 150 ton Dutch vessel two or three times a year.[21]   The colonists supported themselves "by raising a little Indian corn, by the almost spontaneous production of a large species of plantanes (i.e. plantains), keeping a few meagre cattle, killing wild cattle, and catching fish".[22]   Money was scarce; cocoa, maize, vanilla, indigo and cotton were bartered for the goods and wares bought by the Dutch.[23]   And while relatively large tracts of arable land were to be found in the interior, they lay unused and unwanted, more than enough for the simple needs of the small population totalling, in 1782, 2813 of whom 2082 were Indians, 310 were slaves, 295 were coloured and 126 were white.[24]   Sugar, the great West Indian staple, was produced, but in small and insignificant quantities. The first sugar factory, destined to be built in 1787,[25]   was still four years from being established. The profitable cocoa industry, destroyed by hurricane in 1727, had been reintroduced, but not on a large scale. In fact, for a variety of reasons, after nearly three hundred years of Spanish possession, Trinidad was not much better off than it had been at its discovery, little better, if at all, since 1765.

The presumed benefits of the aforementioned 1765 reforms in Spanish colonial trade had completely by-passed the Island. Some of the more restrictive aspects of Spanish colonial policy were eliminated by these reforms, which, among other things, opened the island ports of Cuba, Santo Domingo, Puerto Rico, Margarita and Trinidad to the direct trade with Spain. Similar changes in Spain increased the number of ports open to trade with the colonies. To Cádiz and Seville were added Alicante, Cartagena, Malaga, Barcelona, Santander, La Coruña and Gijón.[26]   Reforms like these, however, of wide and general application, could and did help only those areas of the New World enjoying at the time of the decree some reputation as sources of wealth, and a perceptible if not adequate volume of trade and commerce. Cuba, occupied by the British during the Seven Years' War, developing a taste for more and more "Manchester goods", and riding on a wave of prosperity since then, benefitted tremendously.[27]   So, too, did Puerto Rico for a brief period after 1768 when the entrepôt for supplying slaves to Havana, Cartagena, Panama and other principal markets was established there.[28]   But these were additional circumstances which, together with the

21. Bryan Edwards, *The History, Civil and Commercial, of the West Indies.* Five volumes. (London, 1819. edition), Vol. IV, p. 299.
      R. Montgomery Martin, *History of the British Colonies.* Five Volumes (London,1835), Vol. II, p. 242.
22. Macpherson, *op. cit.,* Vol. IV, p. 403.   23. Bryan Edwards, *op. cit.,* Vol. IV, p. 299.
24. Hollis. *op. cit.,* p. 81; Montgomery Martin, *op. cit.,* Vol II, p. 246; Fraser, *op. cit.,* Vol. I, p. 289.
25. Bryan Edwards, *op. cit.,* Vol. IV, pp. 302–3; Montgomery Martin, *op. cit.,* Vol. II, p. 242.
26. J. Lynch, *Spanish Colonial Administration, 1782-1810.* (London, 1958), pp. 18-19; A.S. Aiton, *op. cit.,* p. 271 ff; Hussey, *op. cit.,* p. 230; Christelow, *H.A.H.R.,* XXVII, *op. cit.,* p. 15.
27. J. F. King. "The Evolution of the Free Slave Trade Principle in Spanish Colonial Administration", *H.A.H.R.,* Vol. XXII, 1942, p. 43 and *passim.*
      H.H.S. Aimes, *A History of Slavery in Cuba, 1511-1868.* (New York and London, 1907), p. 32 ff.
28. King, *op. cit.,* pp. 40-1.

opening of the ports, gave an extra turn to the economies of these islands. In the absence of additional stimuli Trinidad remained as depressed an area as it ever had been.

The eighteen years between 1765 and 1783 were as dreary as all the years since the discovery. It was not that a plan consciously evolved for the Island's development had failed. The Spanish government well knew that merely opening the island ports to the *directo* with Spain would have little effect in changing the patterns of trade in small neglected colonies like Trinidad. But the manoeuvre was an essential experiment the result of which helped determine the extent of future modifications of trade in the richer mainland colonies.[29] In these circumstances the failure of the reforms of 1765 to benefit Trinidad in any way was a contingency that the Spanish government had half anticipated. It induced Spain to look more closely at future plans which might be applied to the mainland, but hardly evoked any particular concern over Trinidad. The very limited success of 1765 did, however, suggest that further measures of economic rehabilitation should be attempted, and in these Trinidad was included.

In December 1776, a *cédula* was published conceding to Spaniards and foreigners alike the privilege of settling in Spanish colonies on very generous terms. A new Governor, Don Manuel Falquez, was appointed for Trinidad and charged with executing the *cédula* in the Island.[30] A further administrative measure of September 1777 placed Guayana, Cumaná, Maracaibo, Margarita and Trinidad, formerly part of the vice-royalty of New Granada, under the captaincy-general of Venezuela,[31] and the new Intendant at Caracas, Don José de Abalos, was instructed to maintain a close supervision over the Island.[32] Success in developing Trinidad's resources continued, however, to elude Spain. As a result, the provisions of the *cédula* and of the administrative reorganization of 1777 were translated into English and French and circulated throughout the West Indian islands in an attempt to publicise the new programme.[33]

29. Christelow, *H.A.H.R.*, XXVII, *op. cit.*, p. 15, note 57.
   The point emerges quite clearly too in J.F. King's article. The restrictions on the supply of slaves to the mainland remained more stringent for much longer than the restrictions on trade to the islands. A *cédula* of 29.2.1789 regularising the free trade in slaves between Cuba, Santo Domingo, Puerto Rico and Caracas was the beginning, says King, of the territorial extension of the free slave trade principle to the South American mainland. *Op. cit.*, p. 50.

30. Hollis, *op. cit.*, p. 79; Borde, *op. cit.*, Vol II, p. 140. A summary of the *cédula* is in Hector Garcia Chuecos, *La Capitanía General de Venezuela: Apuntes para una Exposicion del Derecho Politico Colonial Venezolano.* (Caracas, 1945), pp. 54-5. Documento No. 15.

31. Chuecos, *op. cit.*, p. 20 ff; Chuecos, *Hacienda Colonial Venezolano.*, (Caracas, 1946), p. 14; Guillermo Morón, *A History of Venezuela*, (London, 1964), edited and translated by John Street, pp. 63-68.
   For a copy of the decree, dated 8.9.1777 see *La Capitanía General . . .*, Documento No. 16, pp. 55-6; also *T.T.H.S.*, No 533.

32. Borde, *op. cit.*, Vol. II, p. 140; Hollis, *op. cit.*, pp. 79 80.

33. *Ibid.*, p. 80.

Almost immediately, and undoubtedly as a result of this device, one Roume de St. Laurent came to Trinidad from Grenada with a proposal for the Island's development based on the immigration of French settlers from the French islands, and in particular from Grenada.[34]   St. Laurent was destined to duplicate in Trinidad the efforts that metropolitan France had expended in directing the course of Spanish colonial development on a wider canvas.   Perhaps the main reason for his success was the fact that he was prepared to confine his attentions to Trinidad. Special attention for Trinidad, given the size of the Spanish imperial problem, was perhaps too much to ask of Spain.   But if Trinidad's problems had a solution, special attention was needed to find it.

Roume de St. Laurent visited Trinidad for the first time in 1777. By that time the problems of Grenada which had stimulated his coming were a decade and a half in existence. Grenada had been one of the few West Indian islands actually to change hands at the end of the Seven Years' War. French at the outbreak of hostilities, it had been captured by Britain during the course of the struggle and was formally ceded to that Power at the Peace of Paris. From the moment of the cession right up to St. Laurent's advent to Trinidad, the French community in Grenada had been the victim of the most severe social, political and religious prejudices.[35]   Following on the conquest and the cession, the British flag had brought along in its wake a large contingent of British citizens determined to avail themselves of the opportunities created for them by the success of British arms.[36]   Britain tacitly approved this claim by heavily weighting the political scale in their favour. This was achieved by the simple expedient of issuing the usual Instructions to the new Governor, General Melville, to call an Assembly taking care to ensure that each prospective member subscribed to a declaration against transub-

34.   For the story of St. Laurent's efforts, see F.P. Renault, *"L'Odysée d'un Colonial sous L'Ancien Regime: Phillippe-Rose Roume de St. Laurent"*. *Revue   de L'Histoire des Colonies Francaises.* Vol. 9, *Huitième Année,* 1920, pp. 327-48.

Roume de St. Laurent gives his own account in his Memorial to the Spanish government, *"Reclamation du Citoyen Roume sur le rembursement que lui doit le Gouvernement Espagnol"*, dated 18.1.1796, *T.T.H.S.,* No. 739.

Of some indirect interest is the story of St. Laurent's career as an administrator in Tobago. See J.C. Nardin, *"Tabago, Antille Francaise, 1781-93".* *Annales   des Antilles,* No. 14, 1966, pp. 35-41, and bibliography pp. 100-102.

35.   See *Cambridge History of the British Empire.* Eight volumes. (Cambridge, 1929-59). Vol II,   pp. 150-2. Also, H.T. Manning, *British Colonial Government after the American Revolution, 1782-1820.* (Yale University Press, 1933), p. 64.

36·   L. J. Ragatz, *The Fall of the Planter Class in the British Caribbean, 1763-1833.* (Washington, 1928). Chapter IV, p. 115 ff.

Ragatz tells of the difficulties of British settlers in the Caribbean attempting to get new lands for cultivation and sees this as one of the reasons for their migration to Grenada. By 1772, he says, there were 166 new British settlers in the island,. They had begun to arrive even before the formal cession was complete.

stantiation.[37]   Thus the French, numerically superior but Catholic almost to a man, were denied the most important privilege the Crown was empowered to offer. In spite of their continued protestations against this injustice, the prohibition against their membership of the Assembly remained effective, though they were admitted to the franchise in 1766.

The situation was untenable. The Grenada proprietors resident in London, concerned with the potential dangers to their economic interests rather than with the petty vagaries of the West Indian social complex, prevailed upon Lord Hillsborough in 1768 to secure Privy Council approval for an Order admitting the French to both Council and Assembly in the Island.[38]   Thus did the French gain their political due; but political rights by themselves rarely redress social inequalities, and the French remained restive under the British rule. In 1779, they helped France to capture Grenada from the British, thus surrendering, in the eyes of the British citizens, any claim to favourable consideration when the Island was returned to Britain in 1783. The situation steadily deteriorated culminating, finally, in the complete extinction of French political rights and the bloody struggle of 1795.[39]

37.   *Cambridge History of the British Empire,* Vol. II, pp. 150-2. This is the main reference for the whole of this paragraph in so far as it deals with the French political plight in Grenada.
See R.P. Devas, *The History of the Island of Grenada,* (Grenada, 1964), p. 117. Devas underscores the strength of religious animosities existing in the Island by pointing out that in the insurrection of 1795 only one free coloured of note remained loyal to the British. Even so he had first of all to subscribe to the oath against transubstantiation before being given a commission in the militia of St. George's.
See also, Raymond Devas, *Conception Island or the Troubled Story of the Catholic Church in Grenada, BWI.* (London, 1932). Chapter V.

38.   *C.H.B.E.,* Vol. II, p. 152.
See also, Betty Russell, *The Influence of the French Revolution upon Grenada, St. Vincent and Jamaica.* University of the West Indies M.A. thesis in preparation. Mrs. Russell points out that the concessions of 1768 in Grenada were limited to the right to hold two seats in the King's Council and three in the Assembly. The French were at the same time also given the right to hold other positions of trust such as, for example, commissions in the militia and in the keeping of the peace.

39.   See R. P. Devas, *History of Grenada, passim.*
Also, John Hay, *A Narrative of the Insurrection in the Island of Grenada which took place in 1795,* (London, 1823).
(G. Turnbull); *A Narrative of the Revolt and Insurrection of the French Inhabitants in the Island of Grenada.* (Edinburgh, 1795). Analysing what he called "the more remote causes of the revolt" Turnbull declared that the "principal source was more indubitably in the great number of French inhabitants of every description, who were admitted, first as *capitulants,* or afterwards on various other pretences, to settle in Grenada. That ill-fated island may be said to have cherished a viper in her bosom that has at length stung her to the heart. But, though in general the French inhabitants entertained sentiments and principles inimical to the government, it were unjust and uncharitable to impute an equal degree of guilt or treason to all. Suspicion, however, will in future be attached to almost every Frenchman; and none but those who have given proofs of their loyalty, ought ever to be permitted to reside under the British Flag, either in Britain, or in any of her colonies."
The conquest of Trinidad was destined to bring about just such a development with such effects as we shall see.
Turnbull estimated the loss of property in Grenada as a result of the rebellion to be £2½ million sterling. See p. 163.

These were the circumstances which brought St. Laurent to Trinidad for the first time in 1777,[40] and these were the problems which time and again were to direct his steps to the Island, in the period 1777-83, as the fervent sponsor of French emigration from Grenada to Trinidad. To all appearances Roume came as the acknowledged leader and spokesman of a group of intending emigrants from Grenada - *"la plus voisine et la plus maltraitée des îles cedées à l'Angleterre".*[41] His immediate task was to discover exactly what the prospects really were, and how favourable would the terms of entry new settlers could hope to secure. Accordingly, he made several proposals and, in a closely reasoned argument convinced Don Manuel Falquez, the Governor, of the flexibility of his plan, and enlisted his aid in approaching the Spanish Crown.

It was St. Laurent's view that the French population of Grenada was convinced of the necessity to flee forever their present inhospitable home.[42] The question of where to go, he said, resolved itself into a choice between the United States of America and Trinidad. In America, the States of Georgia, Carolina and Florida seemed especially attractive because sugar, one of the crops cultivated by the French in Grenada, was grown in these States. Besides, such places were already populous and civilised; Trinidad St. Laurent could only describe as *"deserte et sauvage".* But, he continued, it would be foolish to decide the question in this way. The abstract reckoning of one territory against another should give way to considerations of policy and politics. And, in the end, such considerations were to prove decisive.

It was St. Laurent's belief too, that the seeming inequality of attractions between the United States and Trinidad could be altered in favour of the latter by the grant of substantial social, political and economic privileges to the new settlers. Such compensations, reinforced by the wish of the French colonists of Grenada to evade the complications of the American War of Independence would, he thought, be enough to tilt the scales in Trinidad's favour. In addition, he argued that the Spanish imperial problem in the Caribbean could best be solved by the prompt and decisive colonisation of its "desert" islands. If this were accepted, Trinidad for obvious military and commercial reasons connected with the defence and integrity of the Spanish mainland colonies ought to be speedily and effectively settled.

Finally, he suggested that the success of the experiment in respect of Grenada would undoubtedly induce the French nationals of Martinique and Dominica to avail themselves of the opportunities offered to them to emigrate to Trinidad. After all, the extent of their annoyances in their

40. F. P. Renault, *op. cit.,* p. 333; Borde, *op. cit.,* Vol II, p. 141.
41. Borde, *op. cit.,* vol. II, pp. 141 and 141-2.
42. For the substance of this argument see Borde, *op. cit.,* Vol. II, p. 144 ff.

respective islands, albeit from different causes — among which were numbered ants and hurricanes — differed only in degree from those of their compatriots in Grenada. If the inducements were favourable enough, one could reckon on a stream of immigrants drawn from about 383 families and their 33,322 slaves from all three islands. Reckoned at about four persons per family, this meant a potential addition of over 1,500 white colonists to Trinidad's population. Estimating possible emigration from Tobago, St. Vincent, St. Lucia and Guadeloupe at half this total one had a possible overall immigration of 2,300 whites and 50,000 slaves, exclusive of coloured families and their slaves.[43]

St. Laurent had argued very skilfully. He had no doubt overstated his case; within limits he was expected to. But he exceeded those limits when he suggested that the economic position in the French islands was so bad as to make his scheme credible to most of the French inhabitants. His view that Trinidad, because it was a new colony, would attract the French inhabitants of the old islands, might possibly have been proved wrong were it not for the very special factor of discontent that guaranteed the success of his scheme. Grenada, to take one example, was not an old sugar island at the time. Its production had been increasing steadily since 1763, and if by 1775 its export figures to Great Britain had declined[44] this was far from being a sign of stagnation.[45] St. Laurent, in his enthusiasm over his scheme, elected to conduct his argument on the broadest possible basis, and unhesitatingly suggested that almost every Frenchman then resident in the French West Indies eagerly awaited the day when a liberal immigration policy would enable him to move lock, stock, and barrel, to the undeveloped Spanish islands.

As a matter of fact, what St. Laurent proposed, but did not press, was the emigration of Frenchmen from Grenada, Guadeloupe, St Lucia and St. Vincent to the depopulated Spanish islands of St. Domingo, Puerto Rico, Margarita and Trinidad. The former islands he described repeatedly as *"les îles fourmillées"* — the pestered isles, pestered by ants, pestered by hurricanes and, he almost seemed to suggest, worn out by the inexorable logic of the plantation system. In those islands too many people were already competing for too few resources, swiftly diminishing. The Spanish islands on the other hand needed settlers, and in St. Laurent's view, the sophisticated population of the French islands with its skills and its wealth, was precisely what they needed.[46]

43. Borde, *op. cit.*, Vol. II, pp. 146-7.   44. Ragatz, *op. cit.*, p. 119.

45. *Ibid.*, p. 115. Ragatz's discussion of the usage of land in Grenada and the amount of land not yet opened up, together with the figures of sugar and cocoa production on p. 119 which were lower than the immediately preceding years but much higher than those of the 1760's, show that Grenada was still in the full flower of development.   46. Borde, *op. cit.*, Vol II, pp. 148-9.

The difficulties encountered by St. Laurent before the Spanish government implemented his scheme have been well told by Renault.[47] Nor were these difficulties minimised by an apparent need to dissimulate about his intention to emigrate to Trinidad.[48] Suffice it to say, however, that after a trip to Caracas in November 1781[49] and to Europe in the summer of 1782, St. Laurent, with the assistance of the Marquis del Campo, finally obtained the coveted cédula.[50]

The cédula of 1783 which ultimately resulted from St. Laurent's visit was a practical document called forth by the existence of specific problems. To understand this is to see Trinidad's development between 1783 and 1797 in its proper perspective. One of the problems centered in Grenada; the other was the problem of the singular lack of achievement of Spanish colonialism in Trinidad during the period since the discovery. It was St. Laurent's achievement to suggest the means whereby the particular dilemma of the French in Grenada, and the problem of Spanish imperialism with respect to Trinidad, might be solved by the implementation of a liberal and generous scheme of emigration from the French islands, and particularly from Grenada.

Published on November 24, 1783, the main provisions of the cédula for the colonization of Trinidad constituted a direct attempt to solve the two problems St. Laurent had helped to pose.[51] A policy of exclusion had precluded the introduction of labour and capital in sufficient quantities to make any impression on the abundance of fertile soil in Trinidad. Now, the accumulated lore of the past two decades acquired under the influence of a new school of Spanish economists, no less than the galling successes of the British free port system in further breaching the Spanish colonial monopoly, created a climate favourable to fundamental change.[52] Under St. Laurent's patient urging, and against a background of the increasing liberalization of trade and commerce which was the signal success of his reign, Charles III decreed a policy of trade and immigration to Trinidad more progressive than anything yet known to Spanish colonialism.

47. *Op. cit.,* pp. 336-42.
48. Cf. C. O. 101/21, Macartney : Lord George Germain, 24.10.1777, No. 40, enclosing, St. Laurent : Macartney, no date. This letter of St. Laurent's was written on his return from Trinidad where, in 1777, he had spent eighteen days, from March 16 to April 3. This letter is a report on Trinidad, and is a strictly factual account in which St. Laurent manages to disguise his enthusiasm so well that Macartney's covering letter to Germain describes St. Laurent as "not approving either of the people or the Government" in Trinidad. But in 1779 St. Laurent not only returned to Trinidad but accepted nomination to the Island's *Cabildo.* Cf. Hollis, *op. cit.,* p. 80.
49. Renault, *op. cit.,* p. 338.   50. *Ibid.,* pp. 340-43.
51. C. O. 295/1, "Extract of Rules for the Population and Trade of the Windward Island of Trinidad, abridged from the Spanish Ordinance published at Madrid, 1783." A printed copy of the *cédula,* in English, is to be found in Gertrude Carmichael's *History of the West Indian Islands of Trinidad and Tobago,* (London, 1961), pp. 363-69.   52. Lynch, *op. cit.,* pp. 15-19.

Even so there were definite limits to Spain's liberalism. These limits are discovered by reference to the trading privileges accorded France under the *cédula*. St. Laurent had suggested that, in compensation for permitting Frenchmen to emigrate to Trinidad, Spain should grant France the freedom of Spanish ports for a period of twenty years.[53] Spain of course did not grant this privilege. And though, as far as trade with Trinidad was concerned, France was accorded the status of most favoured nation, her trading relations with the Island were carefully controlled by a number of clauses in the *cédula*.

Bullion, for example, could not be exported to France.[54] Nor could trade be carried on between Trinidad and such ports of France where Spanish consuls did not reside. Where the trade was permitted, it was strictly controlled. In the authorised ports the consuls were to ensure the proper registration, marking and manifesting of all goods exported to Trinidad. The ships' captains were responsible for the proper and safe carriage of their cargoes to the Island, where the royal officials were instructed, in their turn, to check scrupulously all cargoes against the manifests in order to levy the five per cent duty to which this trade was subject. A similar duty of five per cent was to be levied on all produce taken away in French vessels. Such exports were to be taken directly to France or to other foreign ports, never to Spanish ports authorized to take part in the Spanish American trade. [55] The benefits of an official trade with France were to be limited, for the time being, to Trinidad. The general intention seems to have been that French participation in the trade to Trinidad was not to be used as a means of trading with the rest of Spanish America.

In cases of necessity, the seriousness of which was to be decided by the Governor, trading with French ports not having resident consuls was permitted. This trade was, as far as possible, to be confined to Spanish ships. Moreover, it was not to be exempted from the five per cent duty customarily imposed on French produce.[56] Beneath it all could be discerned a desire to promote Spanish shipping and interests as much as possible, to discourage, if not wholly to exclude the French. On the other hand, given France's favoured position, and Spain's inability to supply the Island with manufactures and foodstuffs, French interests were bound to prosper.

53. Borde, *op. cit.*, Vol II, p. 149. This request is not quite as strange as it sounds. It is a fact that at the same time Tobago, then a French island, was trying to persuade France that immigration should be sponsored to itself and not to Trinidad a Spanish possession. So that it could have been argued and probably was, that France was favouring a Spanish Colony and should get something substantial in return.

Cf. Eric Williams, *History of the People of Trinidad and Tobago* (Trinidad, 1962), p.58.

54. *Cédula*, Article 19   55. *Ibid.*   56. *Cédula*, Article 20.

One of the prime beneficiaries of the new policy, however, was Great Britain, a country the *cédula* was not intended to benefit, and against whose commercial predominance it was indirectly aimed. Trinidad needed slaves; but France and Spain were competitors for the purchase, not providers, of slaves: Britain was the chief purveyor of this important article of trade. [57] Between 1783 and 1787 over 20,000 slaves were re-exported from the British West Indies mainly to French and Spanish America.[58] To ensure and control the supply of slaves to her own territories, Spain was constrained in 1784 to grant an *asiento* to the Liverpool firm of Baker and Dawson for the supply of 4,000 slaves a year to Trinidad, La Guaira and Havana.[59] In addition, as reported in 1788, there was a flourishing trade in provisions, hardware and dry goods between Grenada, then British, and Trinidad. In return for these commodities Trinidad exported cotton to the value of 300,000 pieces of eight to Grenada.[60]

The central theme of the *cédula* was, however, the introduction of large numbers of new settlers into the Island. As such it laid the basis for the creation of a society entirely different from that which had existed before. The immediate result of the new policy was a dramatic increase in the Island's population and development. The population, as we have seen, numbered 2813 in 1782. By 1789, six years after the promulgation of the *cédula* it had leapt to 18,918. Of these, 2151 were whites, 4467 were free coloureds, 2200 were Indians, and 10,100 were slaves.[61] Port of Spain, in 1783 a miserable village of mud huts inhabited by a motley collection of equally miserable inhabitants, was by 1788 a small town of six hundred well-built houses of wood and shingle, with well-laid streets and some 3000 souls. [62] St. Joseph, about seven miles east of Port of Spain, was already a pale shadow of the new capital. The reforms of 1783 enhanced the superior attractions of Port of Spain as a seaport and administrative centre, and brought about the final eclipse of St. Joseph as the Island's chief town.

57. Macpherson, *op. cit.*, Vol. IV, p. 165. It is also noteworthy that imports of slaves into Trinidad from any source were exempt from all duties for ten years. In 1786 this exemption was made perpetual. See, C. O. 295/5 Gloster : Commissioners Picton and Hood, 28.3.1803, Appendix C.
58. Macpherson, *op. cit.*, Vol. IV, p. 155. Also, G. R. Mellor, *British Imperial Trusteeship, 1783-1850*, (London, 1951). Appendix 1, pp. 434-7.
59. W. O. 1/93, "Memorial of Edward Barry to Governor Picton", no date, enclosed in Picton : Dundas 13.7.1799. Also, Eduardo Arcila Farias, *Economia Colonial de Venezuela*, (Mexico, 1946), p. 398; Macpherson, *op. cit.*, Vol. IV, p. 166; J.F. King, *op. cit.*, p. 46; Mellor, *op. cit.*, p. 436.
60. Adm. 1/315, Report of Captain Ricketts on Trinidad entitled "Trinidada March 1788" and enclosed in Parker : Stephen, 13.9.1788. A piece of eight was a Spanish coin at that time worth about eight *reals* or 3s. 6d. sterling. The phrase was also used interchangeably for a dollar or *peso*.
See, too, F. Pridmore, *The Coins of the British Commonwealth of Nations*, (Spink & Son Ltd., London 1965). Part III, pp. 220-226.
61. L. M. Fraser, *op. cit.*, Vol. I, p. 289.   62.   Adm. 1/315, "Trinidada March 1788."

In the light of the dictates of the *cédula* the nature of the development of Trinidad's population was foreseeable. When one discounts the sections dealing with trade and commerce, five brief clauses exhaust the stipulations regulating the conditions under which immigration was permitted, and can quickly be summarised. Foreigners wishing to immigrate must be Roman Catholics and subjects of nations in friendly relations with Spain.[63] An oath of fidelity to Spain must be taken[64] Every white settler was entitled to four and two-sevenths *fanegas* of land, roughly thirty acres, for each member of his family and half as much for each of his slaves.[65] Blacks and people of colour, being free men and proprietors, received half of the proportion allotted to whites, the allotment to be increased if they brought slaves with them.[66] Lastly, after five years' residence, all settlers and their dependants undertaking to remain permanently in the Island assumed the rights and privileges of Spanish citizens, and could be admitted to civil and military offices according to their talents and circumstances.[67]

The cumulative effect of these provisions can be noted at once. In the first place, the *cédula* by its emphasis on the profession of the Roman Catholic faith encouraged the growth of a large French population in the Island, the French being then the largest non-Spanish group in the West Indies capable of fulfilling the requirement.[68] It has been suggested that the "religious test was .... loosely applied";[69] and it is difficult to see a colonial administration that indemnified new settlers against prosecution for debts contracted elsewhere[70] in an inquisitorial light. But the fact remains that the official policy was that the profession of Roman Catholicism should be an essential criterion of acceptance. Non-Catholics coming to the Island did so on trust and nothing else. The unfavourable application of the religious test, even once, if known, would have discouraged a substantial number of would-be immigrants. The odds, therefore, remained always in favour of Catholics. It was no accident that the first influx of settlers after the *cédula* reflected a high proportion of Frenchmen, "a fair proportion of Irish and (only) some English".[71] Together with the state of Franco-Spanish relations and the historical evolution of the *cédula* the scale of French participation in the scheme was not surprising.

Secondly, by establishing a relation between immigrants and the size of land grants while at the same time stating known conditions on which free

63. Article 1.   64. Article 2.   65. Article 3.   66. Article 4.   67. Article 5.
68. E. L. Joseph, *History of Trinidad*. (Trinidad, 1837), p. 165.   69. Hollis, *op. cit.*, p. 82.
70. Cf. Hollis *op. cit.*, p. 81, note 2. This fact has been noted by several commentators and recurs again and again in subsequent discussions below. But there was no stipulation whatever in the *cédula* for it. It was the personal policy of Governor Chacon. See, also Joseph, *op. cit.*, pp. 164-65; and Edward, *op. cit.*, Vol. IV, p.299.
71. Hollis, *op. cit.*, p. 82.

blacks and coloureds would immigrate, legal sanction was given to non-white planters as a property owning class. The basis was thus laid for the emergence of a large and settled coloured element in Trinidad society. Then, too, the clause[72] dealing with the accession to civil rights of new settlers, though susceptible to wide and varying interpretations in a slave society, at least recognized the possibility of a fuller participation in civil life than was accorded to free Negroes elsewhere in the West Indies. The security and scope which Trinidad offered to non-white property owners was unrivalled.

Thirdly, since the family unit is in its accepted sense relatively small, the ownership of land came to be directly related to the ownership of slaves. To take full advantage of the *cédula* one had to be a rather considerable slave owner. The growth of the slave population after 1783 was a reflection, on the one hand, of the size of the labour problem; but it was also a reflection of the fact that the acquisition of slaves facilitated the quick acquisition of land. Both factors, the size of the labour problem and the thirst for land, continually interacted upon each other. In 1783, Trinidad was, after all, a land almost completely untouched by human enterprise. To develop and cultivate it thousands of slaves were needed. As we have seen, a contract for the supply of slaves was awarded to an English firm in 1784. For various reasons, however, demand continued to outstrip supply and by 1792 the *Cabildo* was negotiating with a London house for slaves, independently of the contract held by Baker and Dawson.[73] In 1796, Governor Chacon estimated that the Island then needed about four to five thousand slaves annually, and warned that a significant increase in demand should soon be expected.[74] In the first six years after the conquest, from 1797 to 1803, in spite of the agitation against the slave trade in general, and the importation of African slaves into Trinidad in particular, 4 500 slaves were imported annually into the Colony.[75]

There was an ever-growing hunger and thirst for slaves. Dealing in slaves was extremely good business; so, too, was stealing. Raids on the neighbouring islands for the purpose of stealing slaves had been known in the past; [76] they were now increased. And, as Joseph has pointed out, since skin colour was the most certain badge of servitude, many free Negroes and mulattoes were kidnapped and brought to Trinidad, where, to their horror, they heard themselves declared slaves. A substantial traffic in stolen slaves and kidnapped freemen developed between Grenada and Trinidad, and was only

---

72. *Cédula*, Article 5.
73. Joseph, *op. cit.*, p. 177.
74. *T.T.H.S.*, No. 56. Chacon : de la Paz, 16.5.1796.
75. Sir William Young, *The West India Common-Place Book. . .* (London, 1807), pp. 21-22.
76. Cf. C. O. 101/21, Macartney : Germain, 24.10.1777. Concerning a raid on Tobago by Bonavita Pascal. Forty slaves were carried off to Trinidad.

halted by a law of the Grenada legislature declaring all persons arriving from Trinidad to be vagabonds, and thus liable to jail unless a bond was posted for good behaviour.[77]   The ownership of many slaves was, therefore, not only a question of labour; it was also a question of good business. The two aspects were of course intertwined, but with land being granted on a *per capita* basis the planter had every interest in acquiring as many slaves as he could. Slaves and slaves alone permitted a planter to acquire a large tract of land. But he had to work it. As the pressure for land increased the criterion of ownership was publicly stated to be the ability of the landowner to work such land as he possessed.   Effective occupation became the guiding principle of ownership, and those who held uncultivated land soon lost their right to it.[78]

The question of status must also be mentioned. Status is at the centre of the mores of a slave society. In the hierarchy of the slave society, to be a planter was not only to engage in one of the few fields of employment open to a gentleman; it was, besides being Governor, the proudest profession to which a man could aspire. It marked him out as a solid citizen, as a man of property in land and slaves invested not only with an economic stake in the community, but also with the purest interest in its continuation as a slave society.   He was, in the fullest sense of that quaint contemporary word, "respectable".   Men in other professions might fall under the suspicion of subversion, but never the planter.   Between himself and the community organized as a slave society there were the closest ties of self-interest.   The *cédula* of 1783 reinforced this relationship by its insistence that the ownership of land be determined by the ownership of slaves.

The result of all this for the free black and coloured community, visibly akin to the slaves, and themselves caught up in the system, can be imagined. It was nothing less than the undermining of the benefits that Trinidad seemed to hold out to them so abundantly. Under Chacon, the last Spanish Governor and a man of liberal intent, their position was secure; some of them were even admitted to commissions in the militia .[79]   British occupation of the Island from 1797 onwards was to reveal to them the full implications of their position.

As with the Island's population so with its production and trade. Figures of production began to rise and continued rising. Trinidad was completely transformed from the backwater it had been in 1783. Under the

77.   Joseph, *op. cit.*, pp. 166-67.

78.   *Parliamentary Papers.* House of Commons. 1826-27 (478). XXIII. Also, *T.T.H.S.* No 470. Additional Instructions from Governor Chacon to the Commissaries of Population, 12.3.1787.

79.   Cf. (John Baptista Phillip), *Address to the Right Hon. Earl Bathurst. . . relative to the Claims which the Coloured Population of Trinidad have to the Same Civil and Political Privileges with their white Fellowsubjects.* By a Free Mulatto. (London, 1824), p.11, and Appendix, Note A, p. 221.

stimulus of the *cédula* of 1783, further liberalized in 1786,[80] Trinidad stepped into line as a major producer of West Indian staples. In 1796, 159 sugar plantations produced 7800 hogsheads of sugar. One hundred and thirty coffee estates yielded 330,000 lbs. of coffee; 103 cotton estates accounted for 224,000 lbs. of cotton; and the revivified cocoa industry boasted 60 estates with an average yield of 1,600 lbs. of cocoa each.[81] Even so, the area of land actually in use was only 36,000 acres, one-twentieth of the acreage reckoned to be available for agriculture.[82]

In 1797, ten years after the first sugar works had been introduced, the British took over the Island as a going concern with a valuable and increasing trade and a barely tapped agricultural capability. Easy comparisons began to be made between Trinidad and French St. Domingue. At least one French writer is reported to have said that Trinidad's potential was greater than that of pre-revolutionary St. Domingue.[83] At the Island's conquest, the official British estimate of its potential was that 1293 plantations of sugar cane, 945 of coffee, 158 of cotton, and 304 of cocoa, each comprising 320 acres could be accommodated on Crown land not yet alienated.[84] In December of 1797 the Governor estimated that the year's sugar crop should yield 10,000 hogsheads each of 1,000 lbs. weight.[85]

The Island's trade had also shown a remarkable increase. Shipping, almost non-existent in 1783, averaged between 7500 and 8000 tons, inclusive of contraband, between 1784 and 1797.[86] Between March 25, 1799 and March 25, 1800 two ships carried off to London 762 casks of sugar, 1 cask rum, 138 casks coffee, and 132 bags of cotton; and this was a year when foreign demand for sugar and coffee was falling. The following year four ships took roughly twice as much produce to London. And between 1801 and 1802, ten ships sailed for London with 3773 casks of sugar, 109 casks of rum, 345 casks of coffee and 590 bags of cotton. Shipment from Trinidad to London had already outstripped that of Barbados in every respect though it was still less than that of some of the other West Indian islands.[87]

80. See C. O. 295/5, Gloster : Picton and Hood, 28.3.1803, Appendix C. The main provisions of the *cédula*, dated 30.1.1786, reduced the duty of 5% on foreign trade to three per cent, halved the tithes, and made the exemption of import duties on slaves perpetual. The trade with Spain, and such trade as was permitted between Trinidad and the other Spanish colonies continued, as before, to be free of all duties for ten years commencing from 1.1.1785.

81. J. J. Dauxion Lavaysse, *A Statistical, Commercial and Political description of Venezuela, Trinidad, Magarita and Tobago. . .* (London, 1820), p 332.

82. Fraser, *op. cit.*, Vol. I, p. 149.   83. Edwards, *op. cit.*, Vol. IV, p. 293.

84. C. O. 296/1, Picton : Dundas, 11.11.1797.   85. C. O. 296/1, Picton : Dundas, 17.12.1797.

86. Lavaysse, *op. cit.*, p. 333.

87. *Minutes of the West India Committee (Merchants)*, March 1794-1802.
See Minute of 24.9.1799 for an examination of the causes leading to the stagnation of foreign demand for sugar and coffee.

Throughout the years 1797 to 1801, a period of marked restiveness in the Island's history, it was found possible to collect only 1½% of the 3½% duty on imports and exports stipulated by the Crown for revenue purposes. Yet, there was a cash balance in the colonial chest of £20,235. 10s. sterling after expenditure. In 1799, the excess of receipts over expenditure was as high as 33,000 dollars; in no year between 1797 and 1801 did receipts exceed expenditure by less than 10,000 dollars.[88] The economic horizons seemed limitless, and the British were determined to keep it that way. June 6, 1797 witnessed the passing of an Act of Parliament making Port-of-Spain a free port.[89] Soon, the Governor was gleefully estimating that the Island could do a trade of £1,000,000 annually with the Spanish provinces. The imperial government was urged not to judge the volume of the Island's trade by its direct trade with Great Britain, since an important *entrepôt* trade had developed in that manufactures from various other West Indian islands, Martinique, Tobago, Barbados, St. Vincent and Grenada, found their way to the Island and eventually to the Spanish Main.[90]

In letter after letter Governor Picton suggested to the Secretary of State that the subversion of Spanish authority on the mainland, even to the point of active military intervention,[91] was the logical next step to the full realization of Trinidad's commercial potential. Enthused by such information, the Secretary of State though discouraging Picton's hostile designs on the continent, exhorted him to do all in his power to facilitate the Island's trade with the neighbouring Spanish provinces. He specifically ordered that passports guaranteeing free passage between Trinidad and the mainland should be given to the Spanish boats operating the trade, and undertook himself to ensure that British cruisers honoured these passports at all times.[92] Trinidad's *el dorado* seemed at last to have been realized.

Following on the conquest the Island maintained, and it seems, even increased its trading links with the mainland. With local production of foodstuffs small and inadequate, Trinidad was, and for a long time remained, dependent on the mainland for provisions. This supply was supplemented, at times supplanted, by imports from the American states and, to a smaller

88. C. O. 296/1, Picton : Hobart, 5.5.1802.
89. 37 Geo. 3. Cap. 77.   90. C. O. 296/1, Picton : Dundas, 21.4.1799.
91. Cf. C. O. 296/1, Picton : Dundas (Secret), 25.9.1801; C. O. 296/1, Picton : Dundas, 20.7.1797; and 16.10.1797. There is abundant evidence that the idea of invading the Spanish provinces from Trinidad long persisted in British thought ; but the invasion never materialised.One can only speculate as to the meaning of the following from Lavaysse. *"C'est à La Trinidad que Lord Melville établit, il y a quinze ans, le foyer d'une insurrection qui commença à Caracas, et devait boulverser le Perou et Mexique." Voyage Aux Iles de Trinidad, de Tabago, de la Marguerite et Dans Diverses Parties de Venezuela dans l'Amerique Meridionale.* Two volumes. (Paris, 1813). Vol. I, Foreword, p.xvii.
92. C. O. 296/4, Hobart : Picton, 29.6.1801. An earlier despatch on the exploitation of the trade with the mainland is in C.O. 153/31, Dundas : Picton, 8.4.1797.

degree from the British North American colonies, but it was never unimportant. The trade consisted mainly of the importation of livestock such as cattle, lambs, mules, horses, sheep, goats and poultry, beef and salted fish, and silver currency with which the Spanish traders purchased manufactures of British origin, particularly warm clothing, woollens and other apparel. [93] At times some foodstuffs were re-exported to the neighbouring islands, and, more regularly, mules and horses.[94]   Trinidad became, in fact, a very valuable *entrepôt* for trade with the Spanish mainland and with the other West Indian islands. Its trade with the mainland was especially valued, not only because it provided an outlet for British manufactures, very often at very inflated prices, but because it also attracted a good deal of Spanish currency of all kinds.[95]   In 1803, it was even the pious hope of the Under-Secretary of State that excess specie deriving from Trinidad's trade with the mainland would be regularly employed in defraying some of the expenses of the military establishment in the Leewards.[96]

Another contemporary view was to confirm the importance of the Spanish trade, and also to draw attention to the fact that the economic problems of Trinidad were no longer those of stagnation but those of inflation.   Thus, Fullarton, one of the three commissioners appointed to govern the Island in 1802, described Port-of-Spain as being "chiefly supplied with provisions from the Spanish Main." But he went on to lament the high level of prices prevailing in the town: " ...The doctrine that prices find their level", he moaned, "has not been verified here. For although near One Hundred Launches and Pirogas have arrived from the Continent within the Last Month, Besides quantities of flour and Indian corn from North America, still the price of living and lodging is so Exorbitant, that a Blacksmith asks three Dollars for shoeing a Horse, and a Merchant frequently pays Five or Six Hundred Pounds a Year, for the Rent of a House and Stores." [97]

The spectacular increases in trade and population and in plantation development had brought Trinidad squarely into the centre of the West Indian plantation system and in touch with the feverish enterprise that surrounded it. Long neglected though it had been, the Island had ultimately and very profitably benefitted from the attempts made since 1783 to launch it on the path of successful economic development. From that time onwards it was the cynosure of envious eyes and the focus of the hopes of those who still cherished aspirations of advancing themselves beyond their own wildest

93.   See W. O. 1/94, pp. 567-8 "Remarks on the Island of Trinidad"; also, C. O. 296/1, Picton : Hobart, 20.11.1801.
94.   W. O. 1/94. *Ibid.*   95. *Ibid.*   96.   C. O. 295/4 Sullivan : Commissioners, 6.1.1803 (Draft).
97.   C. O. 295/4, Fullarton : Sullivan, 12.1.1803.
       See also, *B.M. Add. Mss. 36499, Cumberland Papers*, Vol. IX, pp. 101 ff, and, Baron de Montlezum, *Souvenir des Antilles: Voyage en 1815, et 1816, aux Etats-Unis, et dans l'Archipel Caribe.* Two volumes, (Paris, 1818).

dreams. In the years immediately after 1783, however, the most significant outcome of the new development lay not so much in the aggregates in which trade and population were to be measured but in the quality of the changes then taking place. For this reason, Trinidad was fated to play a major role in the great drama of ideological upheaval then convulsing the Old and the New World alike.

*   *   *

Few events have so insistently highlighted the connection between European and West Indian affairs in the age of colonialism as has the French Revolution. From its outbreak in 1789, and all through its successive stages culminating in the Napoleonic hegemony and eventually in the Napoleonic defeat in 1815, the French Revolution exercised a constant and important influence over the course of events in the West Indies. Apart from the European scene itself there is no other that can rival the West Indies as a theatre for some of the grandest deeds associated with that first and greatest of the many ideological conflicts which have since dotted the pages of modern history. For Trinidad in particular, the Revolution in the West Indies was to be a decisive watershed ushering the Island on to a future that was in many ways markedly and irrevocably different from the past that preceded it.

The French Revolution, however, was first and foremost a European event, and it involved all the European countries in a conflict the scale and meaning of which they had not previously known. For the two virile imperialisms, Britain and France, it heralded the last great, insensate struggle for the spoils of this earth. On the British side, there was at stake Britain's worldwide empire, and at times, it seemed, the survival of Britain herself. For France, the French Revolutionary wars were, in the first place, wars of survival, then of ideology, and finally in their last degenerate phase a succession of aggressions perpetrated in the selfish interest of imperial expansion. In the event, the ultimate result was to be an outstanding British victory with monarchy and conservatism restored to Europe and with French power virtually expunged from India, the Mediterranean and the New World.[98] In the early years of the struggle, however, none but the most unrepentant optimist on the British side could have foretold such a conclusion.

In the West Indies, following on the outbreak of revolution in St. Domingue and on the triumph of the Jacobins in France, the struggle became quite as bitter as it was in Europe. Indeed, because of the obsession of both the principal belligerents with a West Indian strategy, the whole West Indian area was in the greatest turmoil. In addition, liberty, equality and fraternity, the radical objectives of the French Revolution, were sentiments that appealed powerfully to the subject slave and free coloured populations

98. See C.H.B.E., Vol. II, Chaps. III, IV, VII, XIV.

scattered throughout the West Indies. If, as Bryan Edwards has claimed, the outstanding British fault in the West Indian phase of the struggle was the failure to make war on a "great scale", the predilection for "an unmeaning succession of petty efforts",[99] the reason lay in part in the fact that the dichotomy between the interests of governors and the governed was nowhere so sharp. War was scattered and wide-ranging because geography and the prevailing social system dictated that it should be so. To conduct total war, in an era of sailing ships, on a group of islands restive with hope and caught up in the frenzy of international ideology, was a matter of the greatest difficulty.

In the first few years of the War, while the conflict of ideology was at its sharpest and British sea-power had not yet established a clear superiority over the French, West Indian islands changed hands with the utmost frequency. Guadeloupe, captured by the British in 1794, was lost to Victor Hugues later the same year. St. Lucia, taken by the British in 1794, was lost to "insurgent slaves and democratical whites"[100] in 1795. Dominica, Grenada and St. Vincent in incessant upheaval, wrested by the republicans in 1795, retaken by the British in 1796. Martinique taken and held by the British; but a few hundred of its citizens are sent into banishment for their republican principles. St. Domingue, in revolt against the French in 1791, is invaded by the British in 1793 and abandoned by them in 1798.

It was, as Dickens has said, an epoch of belief and of incredulity. Slaves were dying at the hands of their masters while others murdered theirs. Still others defended and offered succour to those who had kept them in bondage all their lives. Toussaint of St. Domingue was one of these. A middle-aged and privileged slave at the outbreak of the rebellion, he first packed his mistress off to a place of safety and then went forth to lead the revolt. All conventions were blurred. Planters alone were constant: "French today, British tomorrow, royalists, republicans, utterly without principles except in so far as these helped to preserve their plantations."[101] It was constancy after a fashion.

In Trinidad, as elsewhere in the West Indies, it was the fate of the Revolution to introduce a new element of instability into a fundamentally unstable society. The ideas of freedom and democracy, no longer the monopoly of abstract philosophers, constituted in the West Indies as in Europe the severest attack on established positions and institutions. As ideologies of progress and liberation they gave rise to new theories of social organization based on the exciting premise that liberty, equality and fraternity were the rights of all men. Spokesmen like Ogé, Sonthonax, Polverell and Victor Hugues brought the message to the West Indies. Toussaint, Dessalines,

99.   *Op. cit.*, Vol. IV, p. 119.   100.   Bryan Edwards, *op. cit.*, *Vol. IV, p. 3.*
101.   C. L. R. James, *The Black Jacobins*, (1st published 1938; second edition, New York, 1963).

Christophe, the masses of oppressed slaves, and even planters like the coloured man, Fédon, repudiated slavery and all its works. However imperfectly the new ideas were appreciated, the examples of resistance and revolt were powerful precepts for action everywhere in the West Indies.

Institutional inconoclasm, at once the hallmark and the insurance of the new revolt, threatened everything. Slavery as an institution seemed doomed; and West Indian society, the ethics, politics and economics of which were based on slavery, seemed doomed with it. Gradual collapse if not violent overthrow of a diseased Caribbean society seemed imminent. In St. Domingue, violent overthrow had already occurred and the threat was spreading southwards. The rapidity of its spread provided Britain, for the second time in half a century, with an *annus mirabilis;* but how different from the intoxicating victories of 1759 were the West Indian defeats of 1795. Tropical fever and ill-organized and poorly equipped bands of Negro slaves ravaged the British army as it had never been ravaged before. By 1796, three years after the outbreak of war with France, the British had already suffered enormous losses in the Caribbean: 40,000 soldiers were dead, 40,000 more rendered unfit for service.[102] Pitt and Dundas, intent on preserving the West Indian slave system and on destroying the power of France by striking at her Caribbean colonies, discovered when it was too late that they had nearly destroyed the British army.[103]

In Trinidad, the French Revolution, the first of the great "battles for men's minds", revealed the always present but until then largely suppressed differences between the aspirations of the Spanish government and those of the majority of its French citizens in Trinidad. The complete metamorphosis of Trinidad's society had been yet another result of the *cédula* of 1783. Trinidad, a Spanish colony, had become predominantly occupied by Frenchmen. It was not only that Frenchmen soon formed by far the major part of the population, or that they outnumbered the Spaniards, but that they soon dominated the mind and heart of the society. As early as 1784, after the first wave of new settlers had arrived from Grenada, Guadeloupe, Martinique, St. Lucia and Cayenne, Trinidad was, as E.L. Joseph has been at pains to

102. J. Steven Watson, *The Reign of George 111, 1760-1815.* (Readers Union edition, London, 1964), p. 370.
   The cost of the West Indian campaign can be determined by a comparison of the losses in Europe and the West Indies. In the Peninsular War, says Steven Watson, Wellington lost 40,000 men from all causes.

103. See, J. W. Fortescue, *A History of the British Army,* (London, 1899-1930). Thirteen volumes. Vol. IV, part 2, p. 385; also, Vol. IV, part 1.
   Also, Fortescue, *The British Army 1783-1802,* (London, 1905,) Lecture II . And, C. L. R. James, *op. cit.,* Chapter IX. This work, first published in 1938, tells the story of Toussaint's revolution. It would have been of value in any event since it deals with the revolt through the eyes of the slave; but it also happens to be a sound work of scholarship.

point out, "a French colony in all but name."[104]   The ratio between French and Spanish citizens was twenty to one.[105]   Mere numbers apart, it is not too much to say that the style and tone of the society was, and remained, predominantly French. Spanish was the official language, but French was the most widely spoken even after the conquest.[106]   French wines were drunk, French food eaten, French dress worn. At public balls French waltzes, minuets and country dances were all the rage.[107]   The French, disdaining "spleen and dullness", the sombre products of Spanish and English sobriety, imparted life and gaiety to the community.

In 1786, three short years after the *cédula,* the Island's most important Spanish institution, the *Cabildo,* was already dominated by Frenchmen. Of its ten members, one was Irish, two were Spaniards, and seven were French.[108] Even before the end of the five year period which was supposed to elapse before foreigners were admitted to full Spanish citizenship and the privileges of office, control of the *Cabildo* had passed into French hands. If, as a recent observer has truthfully remarked, Spain reigned but France governed,[109] there is no need to read an ominous interpretation into this development, at least not yet. As long as a sympathy of aims existed between France and Spain, there could be little harm in permitting in the organs of government an accurate reflection of the preponderance of French persons and interests in the Island.[110]   The fact was that the patterns of immigration had undoubtedly at first seemed more beneficial than menacing. Among the first wave of French immigrants there had been numbers of fraudulent debtors and doubtful characters, but there had also been quite a few respectable representatives of high-born French colonial and metropolitan families.[111]   These were the people who found places in the *Cabildo*. Some of them were of noble blood and, if anything, imparted a more erudite and conservative atmosphere to the society. It was understandably difficult for a colonial Governor to deny the perquisites of office to men of this group.

104.   *Op. cit.,* p; 165.   105.   *Ibid.,* p. 172.
106.   *Ibid.,* pp. 165-66. *Add. Mss.* 36499, pp. 97-9. Letter to G. Cumberland; writer indecipherable, 23.5.1802.
107.   *Ibid.,* pp. 97-9 and *passim.*
108.   Borde, *op. cit.,* Vol. II, p. 188, note. In 1785, the *Cabildo* had four Frenchmen, three Spaniards, and two Irish or English.
109.   Eric Williams, *op. cit.,* Chapter V.
110.   Borde, *op. cit.,* Vol II, p. 188, note. Joseph, *op. cit.* p. 169 ff., cites and discusses a proclamation by Chacon of 27.7.1785, regularising the procedure by which title to land was to be proved, and shows that the proclamation, which favoured the new as against the old (mainly Spanish) settlers was a triumph of the French interest in the Island. A copy of this document is in *Parliamentary Papers,* House of Commons, 1826-7, (478), XXIII. pp. 132-4. The same can be said of the Instructions of 1787 referred to in note 77, above.
111.   Lavaysse, *Statistical Descripiton . . . . . . ,* p. 190; Fraser, *op. cit.,* Vol. I, pp. 10-11.
See also, E. Hayot, *"Noblesse des Iles: Les Anoblis a la Martinique avant 1789" Annales des Antilles.* No. 12, 1965, pp. 9-40.

The danger, when it did come, came not from the respectable Frenchmen who controlled the *Cabildo* but from the increasingly large numbers of French revolutionaries, stirred by the ideas of nascent French republicanism who found their way to the Island. Indeed, Chacon never hesitated to turn to the *Cabildo* in his attempts to curb the influx of Frenchmen of this class after the outbreak of the French Revolutionary Wars. In 1794, he requested the *Cabildo* to appoint a committee to examine the circumstances attendant upon the arrival of all strangers in the Island, and informed them that he himself had deported some unsavoury arrivals.[112]   In March 1796, the *Cabildo* itself successfully remonstrated against the proposed landing of black auxiliary troops under the Haitian coloured leader Jean Francois.[113]   The Governor and the *Cabildo* were at one in opposing the growth of a revolutionary element in Trinidad. But the spirit of the age was much too strong for both.

Between the outbreak of revolution in St Domingue in 1791 and the conquest of the Island in 1797, there was an ominous and rapid growth in republican strength and sentiment within the Island. By 1795 there were already "over 2,000 French people" in Trinidad, and at least one attempt had been made to seize the Colony for republican France.[114]   Sponsored by a group of Frenchmen within the colony this plot was thwarted only by the fortunate arrival of a Spanish fleet. In October 1797, some months after the conquest, a similar attempt was defeated with fatal consequences for its leader, one M. Richard.[115]

112.   Fraser, *op. cit.*, Vol, I, p. 12.   113.   *Ibid.*, pp. 12-13.

114.   Hollis, *op. cit.*, p. 88. Hollis's "2,000 French people" must be interpreted as meaning male adults ; and most probably, both white and coloured Frenchmen. Hollis is obviously attempting an assessment of republican strength. There were certainly more than 2,000 French nationals in the Island as a whole, but just about that number of French *men*.

Generally speaking, population statistics are unsatisfactory. For the period before the conquest I have seen only the printed sources. It is doubtful whether manuscript sources exist even in Spanish. The loss of the *Cabildo* papers by fire in Trinidad in 1903 must have destroyed much of this evidence.

For the period 1787-1797, the two years for which population statistics are most accessible are 1789 and 1797, an occurrence fairly easily explained by the fact that almost all the writers so far quoted have conned from one another. Bryan Edwards is the outstanding exception and his figures, quoted by Borde, differ so widely from the rest as to make them suspect.

In spite of the unreliability of the population figures, certain trends can be noted. Slaves are not included.

1. Among whites, the French population tended to equal that of all other grown-ups together.
2. Among free coloured, the French existed in a ratio of about one and a half times the aggregate of all other nationals together.
3. In the whole population, white and coloured, male and female, children as well as adults, coloureds were twice as numerous as whites. While white men predominated among the white group, coloured women outnumbered coloured men. Since all the offspring of coloured women were coloured though many of them had white fathers, there was a high proportion of coloured children.

115.   Hollis, *op. cit.*, p. 88. Heaton Robinson, *Memoirs of Lieutenant General Sir Thomas Picton etc.* Two volumes. (London, 1836), Vol. I, p. 67.

As the Napoleonic Wars progressed and the revolutionary spirit grew, Trinidad began to look more and more like a French colony. Though Spain was neutral till October 1796, Trinidad had, in temper at least, ceased to be neutral long before Spain became allied with France. The local administration was powerless to prevent regular intercourse between Trinidad, Martinique and Grenada, and immigration to the Island reflected the fortunes of war in these Islands and in St. Domingue. Royalists from St. Domingue and Guadeloupe were followed by republicans from Martinique, Grenada, St. Lucia and St. Domingue, to be followed still later by a predominantly coloured republican group contingent on the defeat of the coloured Rigaud by the ex-slave Toussaint. Trinidad was the haven of the defeated. Royalists and republicans rubbed shoulders in their common refuge; but the republican element, in numbers and in sentiment, predominated. Even Julien Fédon, the Grenada revolutionary leader, was supposed to have been in the Island at the conquest.[116] Like him, there were doubtless many others who had fled before the successful British counter-attack of 1796. These were the "turbulent, intriguing men who (acted) as though the Island belonged to France rather than Spain."[117] There were also a large number of plain brigands, men of no particular conviction, determined to profit from the general confusion. From Trinidad, French privateers went forth to prey on shipping in the Caribbean,[118] or made a profitable living ferrying revolutionaries between the Islands.

Different origins gave rise to widely differing attitudes, and the clash of loyalties among the populace, Spanish, Italian, English, Corsican, Irish, and French of different persuasions, occasioned at least one important incident. Early in May 1796 two British frigates visited Trinidad, a Spanish island and ostensibly neutral. The republican French in Port of Spain were incensed by the visit and, feeling themselves provoked, attacked some British officers and men returning to their ship after having visited friends ashore. One of the British captains, Vaughan, retaliated by advancing on the town with a party of one hundred men. Rioting and bloodshed were avoided only by the interposition of the entire Spanish force, eighty strong, between the French republicans and the British, and by a declaration by Governor Chacon

116.   Fédon's presence in the Island at this time is entirely problematical. His fate after the Grenada insurrection of 1795 is still an unsolved mystery.

117.   Fraser, *op. cit.,* Vol. I, pp. 10-11.

118.   Adm. 1/4170, Dundas : Lords of the Admiralty, 31.10.1796; enclosing an Extract of Dundas : Abercromby (Secret), 28.10.1796. Also, Fortescue, *History of the British Army*, Vol. IV, part 1, p. 537. Heaton Robinson, *op. cit., Vol,* 1, pp. 46-7. Instructions to Abercromby, quoted. For the effect of the French Revolution on the Venezuelan mainland see, William Callahan, Jr., *"La Propaganda, la Sedición y la Revolución Francesa en la Capitania General de Venezuela (1789-1796)"* in *Boletin Historico* published by Fundacion John Boulton, Caracas, Venezuela, No. 14, May 1967.

at its head, that he was prepared to die rather than permit the violation of Spanish neutrality in this way. Later, Captain Vaughan atoned for his part in the affair (which Spain used as a pretext for declaring war on Britain) by committing suicide.[119]   And Chacon wrote to the Prince de la Paz complaining about the inadequacy of the Island's forces and the difficulty of keeping the peace in circumstances which made him "dependent on the goodwill of a public composed of people of other nations with but few of our own."[120]   The prerequisites of orderly government, sympathy between government and the governed, had vanished.

The overall development of Trinidad's society between 1783 and 1797 thus provides a sufficient explanation of its eventual conquest by the British. Trinidad's new prosperity attracted and held the British gaze. But so did the Island's increasing identification with revolutionary activity in the West Indies. A prosperous Trinidad in the hands of Spain was one thing; Trinidad toppling into the hands of revolutionary France, prosperous or not, was a much more serious matter. For French republicans throughout the West Indies, Trinidad provided all the attractions of a French revolutionary colony, with the added attraction, as long as Spain remained officially neutral, of protection from the British scourge. Because of the strength of republican feeling in the Island, Trinidad was, in British eyes, and in the language of modern power politics, a major threat to the security of the hemisphere, and a violent British reaction was not long in coming.

Ever since the outbreak of revolution in France and in St. Domingue Britain had found herself very deeply involved. In part this development grew out of the logic of traditional Anglo-French rivalry in the major spheres of international activity, but in part it also developed out of the sharp ideological conflicts which the French Revolution introduced into relations between Britain and France. Even prior to the outbreak of hostilities between the two nations, the traditional instinct for seeking advantage at the expense of France, and the inducements of groups and individuals, had provided very powerful arguments for British intervention.

In the West Indies refugees from St. Domingue had quickly made their way to Jamaica there to appeal for help from the British to put down the slave uprising in the French colony. Itself hard pressed and watchful for any outbreak, the Jamaican government could spare no soldiers, but had sent some arms.[121]   The French colonists, eager for more assistance, had thereupon dispatched two representatives, Baron Pierre Victor Malouet and M. Char-

119.   A full documentary account of this affair is to be found in *T.T.H.S.*, No. 153 See also, Adm. 1/4169, Canning : Nepean, 23.8.1796, enclosing a translation of a protest from the Prince de la Paz, no date. Also, Canning : Nepean, 6.12.1796.
See too, Aparicio, *op. cit.*, pp. 87, 91.

120.   Chacon : Prince de la Paz, 16.5.1796. *T.T.H.S.*, No. 56, p. 2.   121.   *C.H.B.E.*, II, p. 43.

milly, to London with an official offer to place St. Domingue under the protection of George III.[122]   Strong though the temptation had been, Britain had refrained from outright involvement in the early stages of the conflict, but Dundas, Secretary for War, had succintly declared that if, as seemed "highly probable", hostilities did ensue, the British government would favourably consider taking the whole of the French West Indies into its protection "so as to prevent the whole group from utter subversion." [123]

In addition to the overtures emanating from St. Domingue, others in a similar vein were put forward by royalist delegates from Martinique and Guadeloupe.[124]   Like St. Domingue, these two islands were troubled by the severest conflicts deriving from a multiplicity of causes including slave unrest, tension between the white and free coloured groups and between the white merchant and planter classes, plus all the added stress occasioned by the close and continuing effects which events in France exercised on the course of political, social, economic and ideological conflict in the islands.[125]   If, before the outbreak of hostilities with France, Britain had shown a reluctance to be involved on the side of the royalists, once war had been declared she had quickly and unhesitatingly adopted the mantle of protector of conservatism and royalism in the West Indies as well as in Europe. In the West Indies British involvement was spurred by the possibilities of suppressing rebellion in the French islands, and thereby of indirectly minimising the risk of similar outbreaks in the British islands while. At the same time, it was hoped that the vastly superior commercial potential of the French islands could be exploited to Britain's own benefit and to the disadvantage of France. Once embarked on this course, Britain had collaborated with French royalists and renegades to such an extent that an Act of Parliament was passed in 1795 [126]   permitting French subjects to be commissioned as officers in the British army and, according to their means and influence, to raise regiments to help fight the revolutionary menace in Europe and in the West Indies.

122.   *C.H.B.E.*, II, p. 43. See also, Bryan Edwards, *An Historical Survey of the Island of Saint Domingo, An Account of the Revolt of Negroes in 1791 and a Detail of the Military Transactions of the British Army in that Island in 1793 and 1794.* (London, 1796). *Passim.*

123.   *C.H.B.E.*, II, p. 43. Quoted from C. O. 137/91, Dundas : Williamson, 12.1.1793.

124.   *C.H.B.E.* , II, p. 43.

125.   See, Moreau de Saint Mery, *Description Topographique, Psysique, Civile, Politique et Historique de La Partie Francaise de l'isle de Saint Domingue.* Three volumes. (Philadelphia, 1797, new edition, Paris, 1958); C.L.R. James, *op. cit ;* James Leyburn, *The Haitian People,* (Yale University Press, 1941); Henri Bangou, *La Guadeloupe, 1492-1848; ou l'histoire de la colonisation de l'île liée à l'esclavage noir de ses débuts à sa disposition.* (No date, Editions du Centre); H. Salandre et R. Cheyssac, *Les Antilles Francaises : Histoire et Civilisation.* (Fernand Nathan, 1962); H. Lemery, *La Revolution Française à la Martinique,* (Paris, 1936).

126.   35 Geo. 3. Cap. 120. £ 427,259. 1s. 6d. was voted for the raising and supplying of emigrant regiments in 1795.
Also, Fraser, *op. cit.,* Vol. I, p. 15, note.

29

CHAPTER 1

Against this background of British action against republican France it was not surprising that the British should have regarded Trinidad, Spanish in name but increasingly French republican in sentiment, as a threat to the success of British attempts to pacify the Caribbean. Victor Hugues, that polished and ruthless practitioner of revolutionary *realpolitik,* had quickly grasped the significance of this fact. Schooled in the arts of "total war", the tactic of comprehensive involvement of all the people in the military struggle by which the French Republic had first saved itself and thereafter set out to subvert the sovereignty of its enemies, Hugues recognised the value of Trinidad in the conflict against Britain. Even before Spain and Britain were officially at war, he appreciated, too, that the logic of military strategy might force Britain, in defiance of Spain's neutrality, to attempt to capture the Island.[127] Accordingly, he offered Chacon military assistance in order to strengthen the Island's resistance. Chacon's reply is an interesting comment on the then existing situation. "We have," he wrote, "too many lawless republicans here already. Should the King sends (sic) me aid, I will do my duty to preserve his crown to this colony; if not, it must fall into the hands of the English, who I believe to be generous enemies, and are more to be trusted than treacherous friends."[128] The limit of Chacon's patience had been reached; the will to resist, when resistance became necessary, had been sapped.

As soon as war was declared between Spain and Great Britain in October 1796, the capture of Trinidad became pivotal to British strategy in the Caribbean. Trinidad, because of the "Principles and Persons which have lately been introduced there", had become "a cause of just alarm and real Danger to several of our most valuable Islands".[129] The Island must be taken. If it could not be held, then it must be destroyed.[130] Like Cuba in 1962, Trinidad in 1797 was the "imprisoned isle" of the Caribbean, and it

127. As did Captain Vaughan who believed that: "If the Republicans continue holding possession of the Island, it certainly cannot be considered a neutral post". *T.T.H.S.*, No. 153. Vaughan Christian, 9.5.1796.

128. Joseph, *op. cit.,* p. 187. Quoted. Also, Borde, *op. cit.,* Vol. II, p. 256. This passage is also a comment on Chacon's attitude to French republicanism as a whole. His thoughts on the Spanish connection with France would undoubtedly have been very interesting. He probably disapproved of it. At the conquest, the Return of Troops made prisoners showed seven French royalist officers in the Spanish force. W.O.1/86, pp. 105-6.
Devas, *op. cit.,* p. 123 recounts an episode in which a successful approach was made by the Grenada government to Chacon for help at the time of the 1795 rebellion. Chacon, says Devas, responded "with commendable rapidity" and sent forty soldiers, two armed brigs and a two masted schooner which, arriving off Grenville on March 5, were in St. George's on March 6. See also, M. Lozac'h, *"Aux Antilles, sous la Revolution. Marins français au service de l'Espagne".* *Annales des Antilles*, 1965. No. 12, especially pp. 83-90.

129. Adm. 1/4170, Dundas : Lords Commissioners of the Admiralty, 31.10.1796; enclosing, Extract of Dundas : Abercromby (Secret), 28.10.1796.

130. *Ibid.* Also, Adm. 1/4170, Dundas : Abercromby, 13.11.1796.

evoked a recognizable response. When on February 16, 1797, a large British force came to exact the penalty of Trinidad's "impolitic connexion" with France, resistance was not even nominal. The lack of Spanish resistance, extending even to the destruction of their own ships where they lay at anchor in Chaguaramas, was to be explained not only by the disparity between the British and Spanish forces,[131] which was real enough, but by the conviction of Governor Chacon and Admiral Apodaca that it was much better to rely on the "generosity" of their enemies than on the "treachery" of their friends.

        *   *   *

This, then, was Trinidad in the year of British conquest. Its population was reasonably large and was as varied as the sources from which it had sprung. The polyglot nature of the society had been firmly laid and awaited only the East Indian, Portuguese and Chinese immigrations of the nineteenth century to complete its present composition. The origins of the Island's inhabitants, slave as well as free, reflected more or less exactly the economic, social and political upheavals of the late eighteenth century.

At the very top, there was an old nobility from France enticed to Trinidad by St. Laurent's glowing description of the Island's prospects and determined to recover as much of their fortunes as they had lost in pursuit of the civilised attractions of Paris and Versailles. Such a one was the Duc de Grillon who was reputed to have petitioned for an extensive area of land on the eastern, or alternatively, on the southern coast of the Island.[132]. There were others who had adorned the *salons* of high society in St Domingue or some other of France's American colonies. To these had been joined, at a later stage, on the outbreak of the Revolution in France, relatives and friends who preferred the hazards of life in a new country to the near certainty of the guillotine in France. Still later there were those who had found in flight the surest refuge from the slave revolts that the Revolution had inspired in St. Domingue and other West Indian islands.[133]

There were also the French subjects who had been empowered by the British Act of 1795 to serve as soldiers in the British army.[134] Under this Act eight regiments of French renegades had been raised, some of whose officers looked forward to comfortable retirement in Trinidad as one form of reward from a grateful government. In future years two French soldiers of high rank, Baron de Montalembert and Colonel de Soter, the former of

131.   Gertrude Carmichael, *op. cit.*, pp. 370-73, contains a list of the British and Spanish sea and land forces. Also, W. O. 1/86, p. 101, "Return of Troops employed in the expedition against the Island of Trinidad." And, *Ibid.*, pp. 105-6, 109, "A Return of the Spanish Garrison of the Island of Trinidad made prisoners of war on the 17th February 1797". See also, Aparicio, *op. cit.*, pp. 119-21.

132.   Borde, *op. cit.*, Vol. II, p. 188.

133.   Fraser, *op. cit.*, Vol. I, pp. 65-7.

134.   See note 125 above.

whom had raised a force to fight in St. Domingue in 1795,[135] were to become substantial and highly respected planters in the Island. By 1802, men of this stamp, with their British counterparts, had become valuable and welcome recruits to the small ruling clique. Among this clique there were also a few Spaniards from Spain and Spanish America, men of approved manners and respectability who had no sympathy with the new republicanism. There were, in 1797, only a few British in this select group but they were destined to grow in influence with the change of government.

Lower in the social scale was the mass of the whites, Frenchmen, Spaniards, Englishmen, Scots, Irish Catholics and an indeterminate but small number of Italians and Corsicans. These were the small planters, merchants, artisans and tradesmen of the community. Their motives in coming to the Island were, for the most part, economic. Some of them, the French, had come from Grenada to escape a toilsome existence under British rule subsequent to the cession of 1763. These were some of the men on whose behalf St. Laurent had earlier argued the feasibility of the immigration scheme. Others, as he had predicted, had followed from the widely dispersed French West Indian territories stretching from Martinique and Guadeloupe in the north to Cayenne in the south. Among this lower group too were to be found those French whites who had espoused the republican cause elsewhere in the West Indies and, like Gaudetat the republican ringleader in the Vaughan [136] affair, had escaped to Trinidad.

Not a few English, and many more were to follow, had come to Trinidad to elude their creditors in the other islands. After a visit in 1803, a British writer was to claim that he knew one English planter, formerly of Antigua and then resident in Trinidad, who owed a Lime Street merchant £50,000. The same commentator questioned the value of Trinidad to Britain on the ground that the majority of English merchants and planters in the Island had elsewhere contracted so many debts to their British principals that their trade was unavoidably diverted into American channels in order to avoid the seizure of their goods in England. [137] Among this debtor class there certainly were some Frenchmen too, many of them from Grenada whence they had fled with their heavily mortgaged slaves before the Grenada Assembly had passed an Act for the better regulation of arrivals and departures from the Island.[138]

135.   W. O. 1/837, pp. 39, 41. De Soter, then a Lieutenant Colonel, accompanied the British expeditionary force to Trinidad, and was very highly regarded by Abercromby the British commander in chief. W. O. 1/86, pp. 127-8, Abercromby : Dundas, 20.1.1797, pp. 129-34; Abercromby : Ramkey, 28.2.1797.

136.   See, Chacon : de la Paz, 16.5.1796. *T.T.H.S.*, No. 56, p. 3.

137.   Pierre M'Callum: *Travels in Trinidad*. (Liverpool, 1805), p. 56.

138.   This was the same Act to which Joseph referred (see above, note 76). A copy of the Act, minus the insidious reference to Trinidad, is in George Smith's *Laws of Grenada*. (London, 1808), No. 73, pp. 275-80.

The free coloured and black element was large and important, if not in social status, certainly economically and politically. Since 1783, the scale of coloured immigration had been significantly large. The first coloured immigrants after 1783 had been relatively few in number and, in point of wealth and respectability, as eminent as their white counterparts, though not ennobled. They brought all their belongings with them, like the whites did, their families, jewels, furniture, and slaves.[139] But there was a difference. Trinidad was home. Luxuriating in the freer atmosphere of Spanish Trinidad, there they were and there they meant to stay. As legal immigrants encouraged to come to the Island by the *cédula* of 1783, they had rights and they meant to assert them. There were disabilities too, but everyone knew what they were, and the coloureds were most vigilant in ensuring that if these were not eliminated neither should they be increased. They had a legally defined status that made their social position better by comparison than that of any other coloured community in the West Indies. And it was from this eminence they were to take their stand on the constitutional question in future years.

What was, in 1783, a trickle, had become by 1789 a veritable flood of coloured immigrants. There were then 4467 free coloureds and blacks as against 2151 whites. The disproportion between white and coloured reflected the tendency for the free coloured, as an oppressed class, to be more prone to emigrate from other parts of the West Indies. Attracted by economic opportunity, a relatively liberal Spanish code and Chacon's even more liberal administration of it, they flocked to the Island in their hundreds. And when after 1790 there was a further wave of coloured migrants, mainly from St. Domingue, the fact that they flocked to Trinidad merely reflected the limited opportunities existing for coloured persons elsewhere in the West Indies.

As the coloured population grew in strength, events contrived to throw them all under a cloud of suspicion, distrust and open hostility. The West Indian counterpart of the French Revolution had begun with the aspirations of St. Domingue's *gens de couleur* for a position of equality with their white fellow citizens. It had ended in a slave revolt and the complete collapse of the St. Domingue plantocracy. Yet, it was not the slaves who had ultimately wrested the initiative, but the free coloureds, precariously poised between the whites at the top and the slaves below, who continued to bear the brunt of white hostility for the ensuing three decades. The slave's position was fixed. It was the free coloured, thought to be constantly rocking the boat by his "absurd" pretensions, who was regarded as the real threat to established society. For years after the St. Domingue uprising

---

139.   Borde, *op. cit.,* Vol. II, p. 188.

white patriots continued to see, or said they saw, the spectre of slave revolt behind every attempt by the free coloured to extend the area of his freedom.

In Trinidad, once the flame of republicanism had touched the Island, the whole dialectic of resentment was unquestioningly applied to the free coloured community. It was completely forgotten that of all West Indian free coloured communities the Trinidad community had least reason to be revolutionary. The free coloureds were prosperous and they were, by current standards, privileged. But they were coloured and many of them were French. The arrival of free coloured republicans fleeing from the British was all that was needed to set the face of society firmly against the whole free coloured class. The combination of colour, nationality and suspected political faith became death marks for Trinidad's free coloureds. All free coloureds were regarded as French, and, by association, as republicans. As the conflict sharpened not even Chacon remained proof against the prevailing sentiment. The amalgam of French republicanism and people of colour made "the danger of a rising more imminent every day", and Chacon lamented the absence of an adequate Spanish force for dealing with such emergencies as might arise.[140]

To the insensate fear of French republicanism, and more particularly French coloured republicanism, must be attributed the surrender of the Island in 1797. British conquest no doubt did hurt, but, like a lover's pinch, it was desired. Faced with a choice between French republicanism and and British conquest Chacon chose the British. This last despairing act resulted in the final and, as it turned out, irrevocable dissolution of the Island's ties with Spain. The unrest and disorder which had preceded the conquest meant that the restoration of order became the first preoccupation of the conquering forces. The advancement of the Island's security became the first and only criterion of good government. In restoring and maintaining order the brunt of British displeasure fell most heavily on the free coloureds and the French; and since it was easier to identify a man as coloured than as French it was a displeasure inevitably visited on the whole free coloured community. Yet it was this class that was in one way or another to determine the pace of constitutional progress in future years. Having provoked British conquest in 1797, the free coloureds dropped quietly from view. They were to make a decisive re-entry into the Island's politics in 1810.

140.　　Chacon : de la Paz, 16.5.1796. *T.T.H.S.*, No. 56, p. 7.

CHAPTER 2

THE POLITICS OF SECURITY

The articles of capitulation [1] concluded at Port-of-Spain on February 18, 1797 terminated Spanish sovereignty over the Island of Trinidad. In its place was established a British sovereignty which, in the first four years after the conquest, took the form of simple military occupation. The beginnings of constitutional government were to be made in 1801; for the time being the politics of security demanded only that the Island be rendered unable to contribute to the further success of republican ideology and activity in the Caribbean, and for this purpose simple military rule was quite sufficient. Above all else, the security of British possession of this easily won but highly prized conquest had to be assured. Thus, the immediate problems facing the conquerors had to do with the maintenance of law and order and the administration of justice, and not at all with the establishment of a constitution. In any case, the political problems associated with the establishment of constitutional government could only properly be faced after it had been decided whether Trinidad was going to be retained by Britain or handed back to Spain at the time of the eventual peace. It was clear, however, that for as long as the war continued, and barring an unforseen reversal in diplomatic alliances, it was Britain's intention to hold on to the Island as best she could.

The means first chosen by the conquerors for preserving the Island's security were those of conciliation. With the deliberate intention of offering as few causes of discontent as possible the decision was taken to continue the operation of Spanish laws in the Island. [2] Fully appreciating that the establishment of new laws might itself provoke disorder, General Sir Ralph Abercromby and Rear Admiral Harvey, commanders of the land and sea forces respectively, jointly proclaimed their determination to maintain the former laws of the Colony. [3] Later, Abercromby, as commander-in-chief of the expedition, communicated his intentions to the commandants of the various quarters and other responsible officials. [4] And in his subsequent Instructions to Lieutenant Colonel Picton on leaving him as military commandant of the Island, and in his letters to John Nihell, dated March 1,

1. A copy of the capitulation is in C.O. 296/1; and in W.O. 1/86, p. 83ff., enclosed in Abercromby: Dundas, *20.2.1797*. For a printed copy, see, Gertrude Carmichael, *op. cit.*, pp. 373-5.
2. W.O. 1/86, pp. 93-4. Circular dated 22.2.1797. Printed copy in *T.T.H.S.* No. 157.
3. W.O. 1/86, p. 95. See also, C.O. 295/16, Hislop : Castlereagh, 4.8.1807; enclosing Gloster : Hislop, 26.7.1807 and enclosures. A printed copy of this proclamation is in Fraser, *op. cit.*, Vol. 1, p. 297 ff.
4. W.O. 1/86, pp. 93-4, circular of 22.2.1797.

CHAPTER 2

1797,[5] appointing him Chief Justice and explaining in some detail the scope
of his duties, Abercromby made it clear that he intended Spanish law to be,
as far as possible, maintained. In addition, with the same end in view, all the
subordinate civil and judicial officers were confirmed in their posts.[6] So
that if, immediately after the conquest, security was perceived to be the
main objective, conciliation was the means chosen to obtain that end. Later,
however, the policy of conciliation gave way to one of terror and brutality
which effectively undid not only the work of the capitulation but also of the
years of construction which had preceded it.

The decision to continue Spanish law was, in several ways, central to
the subsequent history of the Island. While the decision was a convenient
one, taken on the ground of immediate expediency, its implementation was
complicated by the severest difficulties. Their own ignorance of the law was
only one of the problems with which the conquerors had to contend. Three
hundred years of neglect had done little to establish a widely diffused
knowledge of Spanish law throughout the community. Effective settlement
of the Island was of fairly recent date. Development was still in its infancy.[7]
The complex codes of law[8] with which Spain regulated a commercial and
planting community, such as Trinidad had become in the fourteen years
previous to 1797, were only imperfectly understood. Administrative
organization, almost entirely the work of Chacon, was still fairly rudimentary,
and a proper system of legal administration was still evolving at the conquest.

Not only was there a general ignorance of Spanish law. Such knowledge as existed was literally confined to one or two highly placed Spanish
officials. Among these were the Governor himself who though not trained
in the law was familiar with its provisions, and the *Asesor*,[9] judicial adviser
to the Governor and the only trained lawyer in the Island at the conquest.

5. See T.B. and T.J. Howell, *State Trials*, Vol. XXX, pp. 495-7. Quoted. For the two letters to Nihell
see *State Trials*, pp. 444-6; p. 495. Both letters were dated March 1. See also C.O. 295/12, in which
are found the enclosures for C.O. 295/11, Hislop : Castlereagh, 13.12.1805.

6. See, for example, Abercromby's letters to Nihell mentioned above.

7. In 1797 only 36,000 acres of Land, 1/20 of the amount estimated to be available for agriculture, was
in actual cultivation. Almost all the land then in cultivation had been brought into use since the
cédula of 1783.

8. The chief colonial code was the *Recopilación* to which reference has already been made. Other legal
codes known to Spanish judges in Trinidad and frequently consulted by them included: Juan de
Solórzano y Pereyra, *Politica Indiana* (Madrid, 1647). Reproduced in five volumes. Compañía Ibero-
Americana de Publicaciones, (1930). José Febrero, *Libreria de Escribanos, Abogados y Jueces*. Six
volumes, (circa 1797). Edited, revised and published in two volumes, (Madrid, 1825). Alonso de
Villadiego Vascuñana y Montaya, *Instruccion Politica y Practica Judicial* (Madrid, 1766). A discussion of the use made of these and some lesser known works is in Sanderson's *An Appeal. . . .*, pp.
18-9; and Howell, *op. cit.*, p. 540 ff.

9. For more on the *Asesor* see below, pp. 48-49

Apart from these two officials the majority, if not all, of the other persons concerned with the Island's administration shared a profound ignorance of Spanish law.

Thus, when after the conquest the Governor and *Asesor* departed from the Island they left behind them a void in the legal machinery which could only be filled by Spaniards who had no first hand knowledge of the law, or by foreigners whose acquaintance with Spanish law was as recent as their immigration to the Island sometime after 1783. Perhaps the sole exceptions were Don Christobal de Robles, an old Spaniard who had held various offices under the Spanish government, and St. Hilaire Begorrat, a Frenchman and member of the *Cabildo* who had immigrated in 1784. But these were only the most eminent and able of a group of officials and ex-officials who were, as a whole, sadly deficient in their knowledge of Spanish law.

Ignorance of the law and the lack of personnel qualified to administer it were not the only problems. Since 1777, Trinidad was part of the Captaincy-general of Venezuela. As such it had had access to the *Audiencia* at Caracas.[10] Cases could be appealed to the *Audiencia*, and all sentences of capital punishment had to be confirmed by it before they could be executed. As long as this link existed, the *Audiencia*, staffed by a complement of highly trained judges, ensured the observance of Spanish law in the Island. That link had been broken by the conquest. And where the defect of the suspended connection with the *Audiencia* might have been modified by the existence of a strong legal establishment in the Island, the absence of such an establishment contributed to undermine the fundamental basis of Spanish law.

An even more immediate source of difficulty derived from the parlous condition of the Island's *Cabildo*. In normal circumstances the burden of the administration of law and justice would have devolved onto the *Cabildo*. The most ancient, characteristic and enduring of Spanish colonial institutions, the *Cabildo* was for centuries at the core of the Spanish legal system.[11] A

10. At the creation of the Captaincy-general in 1777, Trinidad and all the other constituent territories of the new administrative division were removed from the jurisdiction of the *Audencia* of Santa Fe, to which they had previously belonged, and put under that of the *Audencia* of Santo Domingo. On July 13, 1786, however, an *Audencia* was created at Caracas with jurisdiction over all the provinces of the Captaincy-general of Venezuela. See, Chuecos, *La Capitanía General de Venezuela . . .* , pp. 23-4. Also pp. (56-9. Documentos Nos. 17,18, 19 pertaining to the creation and organization of the *Audencia*. See also, Chuecos, *Hacienda Colonial Venezolana*, p. 13 ff.

11. See, C.H. Haring, *The Spanish Empire in America*, (New York, 1947), Chapter IX. William Whately Pierson, Jr., "Some Reflections on the *Cabildo* as an Institution", *H.A.H.R.*, Vol. V, 1922, No. 4, pp. 573-96. The ensuing discussion draws heavily on both these publications. See, also, R.B. Merriman, *The Rise of the Spanish American Empire in the Old World and in the New*. Four volumes. (New York, 1918-34) Vol. 1, pp. 183-197, 221 ff, 473, 488-97; Vol. II pp. 144-52, 186. Merriman treats the early development of the Castilian *Ayuntamiento*, and regards the *Cabildo* as a colonial outgrowth of the institution.

CHAPTER 2

product of pre-Renaissance Spain, the *Cabildo* was a municipal institution whose original purpose had been the preservation of the rights of the townspeople against royal encroachment. As far as it had fulfilled this function, it had been democratic, representative, semi-independent, dedicated to the promotion of local and particular interests wherever it existed, and, in the opinion of some, had been the greatest guarantor of individual security and honest administration. By the end of the sixteenth century, however, it had become a casualty of the centralizing tendencies of the Crown, and had entered on its final stage of decadence when its offices, formerly elective, began to be put up for sale by Spanish monarchs as a means of raising revenue.[12]

    Transmitted to the New World in the Age of Discovery, the *Cabildo* had quickly taken root, and, in the performance of a multitude of functions in diverse places had earned for itself a variety of description. Some have written of it favourably, regarding it as "an institution of power, as a training school for future democracy."[13] Others have written disparagingly representing it as essentially an oligarchical institution which did much to retard the development of democracy in Spanish America.[14] Still others, eschewing either of these two theories have seen the *Cabildo* primarily as a sociological institution whose importance derived more from the social functions it performed and institutionalized and less from the political objectives it was thought to serve.[15] Stated in this way these three theories seem to mark the successive stages of development (or decadence) of the *Cabildo* in the New World. For it can be fairly stated that, as in Spain, the *Cabildo* in the New World eventually lost its original character becoming exclusive and oligarchical instead of democratic and representative, passing finally, in the era of Latin American independence, into an oblivion from which its sociological heritage alone rescues it.[16]

    The tendency to oligarchy had always been inherent in the composition of the *Cabildo* in the colonies. Native Spaniards tended to monopolize it, and were, in many colonies, alone admitted to its offices. Elsewhere, the colonial descendants of native Spaniards were sometimes admitted; and less frequently, as in Trinidad, non-Spaniards of approved birth and station. Noblemen, planters, scholars and the like generally gained easy admittance to the *Cabildo*; retailers of goods, shopkeepers and artisans could be admitted only by permission of the Crown.[17] Since the *Cabildo* had important fiscal

12. For the sale of public office in the New World see, J.H. Parry, "The Sale of Public Office in the Spanish Indies under the Hapsburgs". *Ibero Americana*, No. 37, (Berkeley and Los Angeles, 1953).
13. Pierson, *op. cit.*, pp. 575-6.   14. *Ibid.*, pp. 576-7.   15. *Ibid.*, p. 577.
16. The first *Cabildo* instituted in Trinidad was elected. By 1797 its offices were being bought from the Crown or distributed by the Governor or by the *regidores* themselves. Cf. Wise, *op. cit.*, Vol. III, pp. 39-50.
17. Pierson. *op. cit.*, pp. 584-5. Also Wise, *op. cit.*, Vol. III, p. 45.

38

duties relating to price fixing and the regulation of business activity in shops, inns and other commercial establishments, there were undoubtedly good reasons for this discrimination; in practice, however, the basis of exclusion was primarily social.

In Trinidad at the conquest the *Cabildo* was oligarchic. As was to be expected in a slave society, unimpeachable whiteness was an indispensable condition of membership. [18] But even among the whites, membership was restricted to a small group of colonists at the very top of society. This group consisted mainly of the most eminent planters who had either purchased their offices from the Crown, or had been elected to the *Cabildo* by their social *confrères* where elections were provided for. [19] Nationality among this little group was of no account; Englishmen, Spaniards and Frenchmen served alike. But social background mattered. Even the appointment of a relatively minor officer of the *Cabildo* could be attended by an embarrassing display of displeasure if he did not measure up to conventional standards of respectability, as Governor Chacon discovered when he appointed M. Francisco de Castro *escribano* to the *Cabildo*. [20] Political considerations also operated. Suspicion of republicanism was, of course, damning. Later, agitation for British laws, and subscription to any of the more liberal attitudes towards slavery effectively excluded even the most opulent from membership of the *Cabildo*.

Membership of the *Cabildo* was attended by the enjoyment of various privileges that gave its members, or *regidores* as they were called, a vested and continuing interest in its exclusiveness. A member of the *Cabildo* expected, and duly received, preference in the markets and other public places. Whether purchasing a leg of pork or a ticket for an evening's entertainment he expected and received the choice of what was best. He could wear a sword at times and in places where others were forbidden to do so. He was exempt from militia duty. He could not be imprisoned in the public jail. If incarceration was absolutely necessary, the *regidor* was to be imprisoned in a room in the town hall. If he was required to give evidence in a judicial matter, the *escribano* took the evidence at the house of the *regidor* and at the latter's

18. Cf. C.O. 295/10, Fullarton : Hobart, 27.3.1804. In 1803, Fullarton who wished to take de Castro to England as a witness in his intended prosecution of ex-Governor Picton was prevented from doing so on the ground that de Castro's deputy could not hold the office of *escribano*. It was alleged that this gentleman though he looked white was suspected of being a mulatto. This reason might well have been spurious. The fact that it was seriously advanced makes the point. One not only had to look white; one had to be known to be white.

19. As will be seen the Governor could also make appointments to the *Cabildo*. But the appointment was permanent only after it had been purchased. In 1804, de Castro spoke of having applied to the Crown for the office of *escribano*, the intention being to gain a permanent hold on it by purchase. Howell, *State Trials*, XXX, p. 253.

20. Begorrat later said that this appointment provoked the disgust of the entire community since de Castro had once been a common soldier and had served as barber to one Captain Litemondi. Howell, *State Trials*, XXX. p. 292.

convenience. At ceremonies of all kinds he was an honoured, distinguished and much-sought-after guest. [21] There was, too, the question of precedence. On public occasions members of the *Cabildo* deferred only to the Governor. Thus, the honour and prestige of the *regidor* were secure; none more so than the honour and prestige of the *alférez real* or standard bearer, whose office, duly purchased from the Crown, entitled him to precedence over all others in processions in which the *Cabildo* took part. [22]

In Trinidad, as in all the Spanish colonies, the *Cabildo* performed a variety of political, economic, social and religious duties. It was an integral part of the process of government and was normally though not always presided over by the Governor. It collected a number of specified taxes, usually in the form of rents, on city dwellings and on buildings owned by the *Cabildo* such as markets. It collected licence fees on certain articles of trade and commerce. Sometimes it was granted a warrant to collect on an *ad hoc* basis a tax for a particular purpose. At the request of the *Cabildo* the Spanish Crown had, in 1786, permitted an addition of one quarter of one percent to the three percent duty on imports and exports, for the purpose of building a wharf and constructing roads within the country. From this source revenue normally yielded between 2,500 and 3,000 dollars annually. From all sources 14,000 dollars were collected in 1804. [23]

Revenue thus collected was defrayed in the construction and upkeep of roads and buildings and other public amenities, and in the payment of public officers attached to the *Cabildo* such as the *escribano* or notary, the *alguaçil mayor,* several *alguaçiles* and one or more interpreters. [24] By 1809 revenue had risen to $21,656. 6 *reals* and expenditure to $6517 leaving a balance of $15,139. 6 *reals*. [25] Though the *Cabildo* often neglected its duties on pleas of impecuniousity, and often paid its officers and contractors very badly and sometimes not at all, [26] its total assets in 1809 amounted to $20,539. 6 *reals*. [27]

21. For the substance of this section see, C.O. 295/8, Hislop : Camden, 9.7.1804. Enclosed in this despatch are two papers from Messrs. Black, Begorrat, Langton and Nihell answering questions put to them on the *Cabildo* and other Spanish institutions. This despatch is an invaluable and unique source for an understanding of the *Cabildo* in Trinidad after 1783. See also, John Sanderson *An Appeal.,p..8 ff.*

22. For a discussion of the Spanish attitude to precedence and the prestige attached to the office of the *alférez real,* see Parry, *The Sale of Public Office in the Spanish Indies under the Hapsburgs,* p. 46.

23. C.O. 295/8, Hislop : Camden, 9.7.1804. See Messrs. Black's, Begorrat's and Langton's answers to the questions posed by Lieut. Governor Hislop. See also Nihell's report, same reference.

24. *Ibid.* Under the heading "Expenditure".

25. There were eight *reals* to the dollar or *peso.*

26. Cf. C.O. 295/25, G. Adderley : Jenkinson, 6.7.1810; enclosing Newman: Adderley, 15.4.1810. Newman who was deputy provost marshal in 1809 wrote to Adderley who held the patent to the office explaining why the office had returned so little of late. The main reason was that the prison, burnt down in the fire of 1808, had not yet been repaired by the *Cabildo;* prisoners could not be housed in it and the provost marshal, whose office required him among other things to take care

The maintenance of an equitable system of weights and measures, of coinage, and of decent standards of public health in the Island, but particularly within the town limits, also fell within its jurisdiction. It regulated the admittance of surgeons and physicians to practice. And on festive occasions, such as an official welcome to a high-ranking royal official, or the first entry of a bishop to the diocese, and on ceremonial feast days of the Church, the *Cabildo* played a prominent role, and was, as a body, accorded a high place of honour.[28]

Were these the only functions of the *Cabildo*, its exclusiveness and its decidedly oligarchic character would have been of comparative insignificance. But there was an additional function of the first importance performed by the *Cabildo*, namely, the administration of justice. And for this task oligarchy and exclusiveness ill prepared it.

Quite apart from the *regidores,* whose numbers varied according to the size of the town, there were two officials in whom the judicial functions of the *Cabildo* were almost exclusively vested. These were the *alcaldes ordinarios* who could not normally be chosen from amongst the *regidores* themselves.[29] Barring the Governor the *alcaldes* were the most senior officials of the *Cabildo* and they were judges. They were distinguished by the titles of *alcalde de primer voto,* or *alcalde* of the first election, and *alcalde de segundo voto,* or *alcalde* of the second election. The *alcalde* of the first election was senior to his colleague by reason of his having been elected one year before him. But apart from the fact that the presidency of the *Cabildo* devolved upon the former in the absence of the Governor, or of the *Asesor,* the Governor's deputy, there was no practical difference in their powers. Though they were not *regidores* they took an active part in all the proceedings of the *Cabildo* and had a vote[30]

Each *alcalde* had an equal and independent judicial authority, and under normal circumstances served for two years.[31] At the end of his second

---

of the prisoners, had little to do. The fault said Newman lay entirely with the *Cabildo*. Trifling repairs which had been made since the fire had not yet been paid for, and "not a single Tradesman will execute any work, whatsoever, for that board their Credit is so *bad.*"

27. C.O. 295/25, Smith : Liverpool, 1.7.1810; enclosure.
28. C.O. 295/8, Hislop : Camden, 9.7.1804; enclosures. Also, Sanderson, *An Appeal . . . .*, p. 8 ff.
29. Haring, *Spanish Empire in America*, p. 168.
30. *Recopilación*, Lib. 5, Tit. 3, Ley. 15.

31. Nor could they be re-elected until the expiration of two years. *(Recopilación*, Lib. 5, Tit. 3, Ley. 9). Nihell in his report to Hislop in 1804 says that they could only be re-elected after three years and this may have been the practice in Trinidad. In any case there had been relaxations of the rule in the past, but a general Instruction issued to Intendants in 1786 had reaffirmed the rule. After the conquest, in 1804, Messrs. Black and St. Pé were re-elected for an additional year.

year, the *alcalde* of the first election went out of office and his colleague, elected a year after him, succeeded to his title. Then, at an election held usually on the first of January the members of the *Cabildo* who were entitled to vote elected an *alcalde* of the second election. In theory, any citizen of substance and good character could be elected to office [32] and was under obligation to accept the appointment; in practice *alcaldes* were generally "planters, or persons living in society" [33] and needed no prodding to accept the honour. What had been conceived as a duty had become a coveted privilege.

Apart from the alcaldes there were three other judicial officers in the *Cabildo*. There was a *síndico* or *procurador general* whose function it was to guard the interests of the community at large and to seek to promote and encourage everything by which the community stood to gain. He was in fact, or was supposed to be, the watchdog of the people's rights. But since, though he could speak in the *Cabildo*, he had no vote and, like the *alcaldes*, was not necessarily a qualified lawyer, his powers to protect were severely limited.

There were also two *alcaldes del monte* who were partly responsible for the administration of justice in the country districts, their jurisdiction being shared with the commandants of quarters who had an original jurisdiction over offences of minor importance. Occasionally the *alcaldes del monte* sat in the *Cabildo*. But, like the *síndico*, they had no vote and took an even smaller part in the proceedings of the *Cabildo*.

These five offices, the two *alcaldes ordinarios*, the two *alcaldes del monte* and the *síndico*, were the only elective ones in the *Cabildo* and they were all concerned with the administration of justice. The other offices, almost all purchased from the Crown, were the aforementioned *alférez real;* the *alguaçil mayor*, or provost marshal or chief constable as he was later known; the *fiel ejecutor*, entrusted with the maintenance of a proper system of weights and measures in the markets and shops; the *depositario general* into whose keeping were entrusted the property, goods and possessions of minors, absentees and those who had died intestate; and the *alcalde provincial* or *alcalde de la Santa Hermandad* who had responsibility for bringing malefactors to justice for all crimes committed in any part of the country. These were called *regidores dobles*, to distinguish them from the *regidores llanos* or simple *regidores*, and to indicate that by virtue of the special offices they held they performed a function additional to that of a mere *regidor*.

32. *Recopilación*, Lib. 5, Tit. 3 deals with the functions, privileges, duties and qualifications of the *alcaldes ordinarios*. For this regulation, see Lib. 5, Tit. 3, Ley. 4.

33. Howell, *State Trials*, XXX. Evidence of de Castro, p. 258. Also, evidence of St. Hilaire Begorrat, p. 286.

There were in fact few *regidores llanos.* Between 1797 and 1802 the strength of the *Cabildo* inclusive of the *alcaldes ordinarios* varied between eight in the former year to twelve in the latter.[34] Of these there were, in December 1801, three *regidores llanos* out of a total membership of ten, including the *escribano.*[35] · While two months later, in February 1802, out of a complement of twelve, including the *escribano,* there were still three *regidores llanos* of whom one, Francisco de Castro, enjoyed the intermediate dignity of *regidor decano,* senior member of the *Cabildo,* a sort of Father of the House of Commons. The *regidores dobles* were the two *alcaldes ordinarios,* the *alférez real,* the *alcalde mayor provincial,* two *alcaldes de Hermandad,* the *alguaçil mayor,* and the *síndico or procurador general.*[36]

All these offices, of course, impinged upon the field of judicial administration; but the most important judicial functions of the *Cabildo* were exclusively invested in the *alcaldes ordinarios.* Once elected, the *alcaldes* performed their duties free from *Cabildo* interference. The *Cabildo* itself had, as a body, little or no judicial or executive powers. Power resided in its officers. The *Cabildo* existed as a self-perpetuating corporation to facilitate the exercise of power by those who had it and to permit the recruitment of the chosen few who did not.[37] In judicial matters, its authority was limited to the exercise of a little used right to hear appeals in civil matters involving sums not in excess of 70,000 *maravedis.*[38]

34. Spanish law, as has been already observed, provided a quota of *regidores* depending on the size of the town. Haring, *Spanish Empire in America,* p. 162, says that in small towns the number of *regidores* varied from four to six; in larger ones, it was eight, in metropolises, twelve. Pierson, *Some Reflectións on the Cabildo* . . . . , p. 583 says that no rule was "rigidly adhered to". Referring to *Recopilacion,* Lib. 4, Tit. 10, Leyes 1 and 2, he puts the alternatives at six and twelve. In C.O. 295/8, *op. cit.,* Nihell also says six or twelve. Trinidad at the conquest had six, later raised to ten by Governor Picton. Cf. Wise, *op. cit.,* Vol. III, p. 42. Sanderson, *Political Account of Trinidad,* (London, 1807), p. 24 ff refers to this increase.

It was, he says, a device of Picton's to gain greater control of the *Cabildo* by packing it with his favourites. These were, according to Sanderson, Messrs. Begorrat, Robles, Farfan, Bontur, and later, in the absence of one of the *regidores*, Mr. Shaw, Picton added Mr. Handley. One result of the Governor's increased control over the *Cabildo* was that the *alcaldes ordinarios* began to be elected from amongst the *regidores* themselves.

35. C.O. 295/2, Picton : Hobart, 27.4.1802; enclosure, *Address to His Majesty from the Cabildo of Trinidad,* dated 14.12.1801.

36. *Ibid.* An Address to the Governor, dated 1.2.1802, enclosing a representation made to the *Cabildo* by the Island's inhabitants. Copies were provided in French and Spanish.

37. Cf. Sanderson, *Political Account* . . . . , p. 24. Alluding to the members of the *Cabildo,* he comments that while formerly elected by the King of Spain, "now they elect each other: filling up a vacancy as it occurs. . ."

38. About $300.00. Cf. C.O. 295/4, Fullarton : Sullivan, 8.3.1803; enclosure, answer to Query No. 2. See Nihell's account, C.O. 295/8, *op. cit.* Also, *Recopilación* . . . . , Lib. 5, Tit. 12, Ley. 17.

As has been said earlier, the two *alcaldes* constituted two separate courts of equal rank and of an original jurisdiction. The Governor constituted a third.[39] Together these three courts dispensed justice in all civil and criminal cases. But whereas the Governor was expected to act as often as possible with the advice of his *Asesor,* the *alcaldes* usually acted without the benefit of legal advice. As a result it would seem that although all civil and criminal cases could theoretically be tried before any of the three courts "at the free Option of the Plaintiffs in civil causes and of the prosecutor in Criminal", the Governor's court enjoyed a pre-eminence over the other two. Thus, actions brought by and against planters were usually tried in the Governor's court; so, too, were all the important cases which originated in the country except in the town of St. Joseph.[40] It seems, too, that though the *alcaldes* were competent to try criminal cases, such cases were in fact usually tried by the Governor.[41] In addition, the Governor as Intendant, constituted a court of Intendant before which crimes against the Crown were recognizable.[42] And there were, too, the minor provincial courts administered by the commandants of quarters and the *alcaldes del monte.* But among the multiplicity of courts those of the *alcaldes ordinarios* held pride of place, mainly because they tried by far the majority of cases arising within the community. Common practice reserved for them all but the most important civil cases involving residents of St. Joseph and Port-of-Spain; and these were considerable in number. The complexity of Spanish law particularly in a land-holding community, spawned litigation, and the fact that Trinidad was a new developing community with property rights very informally drawn provided abundant opportunity for legal disputation.

Besides, there were no appeal courts in the Island, a fact that enhanced the jurisdiction of the *alcaldes.* All appeals, except for those very minor ones allowable to the *Cabildo,* were to the *Audiencia* at Caracas. In capital cases the right of appeal to the *Audiencia* seems to have been possessed by slaves as well as free men.[43] But appeal was not only expensive, it involved a long

39. C.O. 295/8, *op. cit.,* Nihell's account. Also, *Recopilación . . . .* , Lib. 5, Tit. 2, Ley. 7.

40. C.O. 295/8. *op. cit.* Nihell's account.

41. *State Trials,* XXX. John Nihell's evidence, pp. 310-11. See also, Pierson, *op. cit.,* pp. 593-4. "As to judicial administration, Solórzano has stated that *corregidores* (a *corregidor* was a high administrative and judicial authority, not always, but often a Governor) rarely permitted the *alcaldes ordinarios* to settle a criminal case." Cf. *Recopilación . . . .* , Lib. 5, Tit. 2, Ley. 1, which allows them to.

42. Charles Reis, *A History of the Constitution of Trinidad.* Two volumes. (Trinidad 1929), Vol. I, p. 154; *Parliamentary Papers.* House of Commons, 1826-7. (551), XXIII.

period of waiting during which the harm likely to ensue from a decision of an *alcalde* might become permanent or irreversible. Thus the *alcaldes* were a most important source of decisions.

It is difficult to assess the *alcalde* system as a legal system. If, as Salvador de Madariaga has brilliantly argued, the psychological orientation of the Spaniard is towards *el honor*, [44] then the system, executed by Spaniards in normal circumstances, must have been a good one. But circumstances were not normal in Trinidad at, or just prior to, the conquest; nor was the system operated solely by Spaniards. There was illimitable opportunity for misdealing and chicanery, and the evidence suggests that public duty was often converted into private profit. Even if, as seems plausible, the *alcaldes* were somewhat analagous to English justices of the peace, they disposed of so much more authority that the analogy soon founders.

Had evidence of corruption not made itself manifest there were still several questions relating to the competence of the *alcaldes* to administer law and justice which might yet have provoked comment at the conquest. The manner in which the leading planters and social figures took turns at dispensing justice on matters in which they were themselves often interested, was an obvious invitation to corruption, and to the objective observer, a source of structural weakness. That the judges were not qualified lawyers was perhaps of little account in a society where there were no lawyers to take advantage of the fact. But some of them were not even literate. Ability to read and write was, according to Spanish law, a criterion indispensable to the position of a judge. [45] But it was one that, for obvious reasons, was ignored in Trinidad as in most Spanish colonies. [46] St. Hilaire Begorrat's statement that "to undertake the office of *alcalde* in ordinary it is not necessary to ... know to write or read", [47] hints at how much the exception had become the law. Begorrat was one of the pillars of Trinidad society. He filled the office of *alcalde* several times in a public career that spanned four full decades. He was a stout and dogged defender of the rights and privileges of the *Cabildo*. Yet he, who objected to de Castro's membership of the *Cabildo* because he had been a common soldier, saw nothing wrong in admitting that, in Trinidad, illiteracy was not a necessary disqualification from judicial office. But reading and writing were necessary adjuncts of the

43. *State Trials,* XXX, pp. 606 ff., where the case of Francisco the slave of Dom Manuel Sorsano on trial for murder of another slave on 15.8.1790, is discussed. Francisco made his escape while his sentence was being considered in Caracas.
44. *Englishmen, Frenchmen, Spaniards: An Essay in Comparative Psychology.* (London, 1931, 3rd edition), *passim,* and especially Introduction, pp. 3-13.
45. *Recopilación. . . . ,* Lib, 5, Tit. 3, Ley. 4.
46. Pierson, *op. cit.,* p. 584 for an observation on the Spanish colonies.
47. Howell, *op. cit.,* Begorrat's evidence, p. 286.

administration of justice: thus, the notetakers and scribes whose business was the business of reading and writing were able, in some cases, "to govern the decisions of these judges."[48]

*   *   *

Such was the structure of judicial administration in the Island at the conquest. Considerations of structural weakness did not suggest the urgent reform of the system. In any case, once the decision to maintain Spanish laws had been proclaimed, such considerations could hardly have been represented as potent arguments for fundamental change. The opportunity for tampering with the administration of justice in the Island was presented when some of the inhabitants, immediately after the conquest, came forward with charges of corruption against the legal officers. Abercromby's references to these charges, thrice repeated in subsequent letters to Lieutenant Colonel Picton, and to John Nihell[49] whom he appointed Chief Justice on March 1, 1797, furnish the only direct evidence that such charges had in fact been made. But an Address from some of the inhabitants to Picton two months later, dated April 5, 1797, provides strong corroboration of the complaints which Abercromby claimed to have received.

In this Address, the subscribers complained bitterly of the operation of the Island's courts. They spoke at length of grave acts of injustice, and urged that, even then, two months after the conquest, extraordinary measures were necessary to curb the activities of "that assemblage of men of justice, the majority of whom no doubt presented instances of corruption of which no other could furnish examples..." In short, the *alcaldes* were charged with violating the laws, perverting the ends of justice and dishonestly administering the duties of their office. Even after Abercromby's intervention, the maladministration seems to have continued unchanged. For the Address went on to state that relief would be ineffectual as long as Picton, in reforming the system, continued to have recourse to several of the men complained of, whose interest it was to support each other and to bury in darkness what the petitioners were desirous of making known to the world.[50] This was, if ever there had been, a *cri de coeur*. The petitioners suggested a plan for reforming the tribunals and invited the Governor to use it or to use any other device that appealed to him.[51] What they were interested in was change. Any

48. Sanderson, *Political Account* . . . , p. 19.

49. See his letters of March 1, 1797 to Nihell, and his Instructions of the same date to Picton. *State Trials*, XXX, op. cit., pp. 444-6, 495.

50. Heaton Robinson, *Memoirs. . .* , Vol. I, pp. 148-53. Copy of an Address to Lt. Col. Picton From some of the inhabitants of the Island.

51. Joseph, *op. cit.*, p. 207, note, says that Picton appointed a committee of five to investigate these grievances. The recommendations of the committee and the Governor's actions have not been recorded.

reform that helped to curb the rapacity of the judges and to protect the inhabitants' property would be welcome. One suspects, however, that they aimed at a change of personnel rather than a change of institutions, for in a few respects the institutions had already undergone significant change.

Trinidad, as we have seen, was surrendered to the British on February 18. Within two weeks, and before Abercromby departed from the Island a new court was created largely superseding the existing Spanish courts. In part, this change was necessary if British sovereignty over the Island were to be properly asserted. But it was also compelled by the scale of corruption prevalent in the Island at the time of conquest. As difficult as it is to set precise limits to the corruption that existed, the worst can fairly be assumed.

Spanish colonial law abounded with difficulties and delays, was expensive,and, because of the notorious abundance of office holders connected with its administration, was particularly prone to corruptive influences. This was no fault of the code itself; Spanish attempts to resolve the ever present conflict between law and justice were painstaking and detailed. Nevertheless, because of the lack of high moral, judicial and administrative standards of the men who mattered, corruption in Spanish judicial practices was often present on a high scale. So much so that it has been suggested that corruption at all levels, but particularly at the highest, throughout the Spanish colonial empire, "was one of the fundamental causes for the administrative reforms that were introduced in the last quarter of the eighteenth century." [52] Even Chacon's critics, however, would hesitate to level charges of corruption at him. But his vacillation and weakness at a time of marked social instability, contributed to what seems to have been a high degree of organized corruption in the Island's courts. Not that the courts were the only institutions so affected. But in a society in which politics and the judiciary were so closely intertwined, malpractices in politics and administration were disproportionately reflected in the affairs of the courts.

It is equally difficult to identify the precise sources of corruption and double-dealing. John Nihell whom Abercromby later appointed Chief Justice was *alcalde* of the first election in the year of conquest. Nihell claimed to have been entirely ignorant of even the smallest suggestion of corruption; [53] any other claim by an office holder would have been chivalrous in the extreme. But that Abercromby also appointed Nihell to the chief justiceship, is either an indication of the absence of specific charges against him, or of Abercromby's refusal to believe them if they were made. On the other hand the *Asesor*, whose departure at the conquest has already been noted,

52. C.E. Castañeda, "The Corregidor in Spanish Colonial Administration", *H.A.H.R.*, Vol. IX, (1929), p. 447.
53. *State Trials*, XXX, p. 310.

was dismissed and sent off the Island on the ground that he was clearly implicated in fraud and peculation. The charges against him were that he inspired and participated in embezzlement in the office of the *depositario general.*[54]

Perhaps the most accurate guess would be that such corruption as existed occured at the level of the execution of judicial decrees. Offices like the *depositario general* and the *fiel ejecutor,* though not themselves judicial, were sufficiently closely connected to the judiciary to clothe their incumbents with the majesty of power. Such officials were moreover the agents of the courts, as the *alguaçiles* were, and the ordinary citizen in conflict with them suffered from the prejudice of suspected guilt. Where, as in the office of the *depositario general,* large sums and valuable properties were often in dispute, the temptation to embezzle must have been fortified not only by the helplessness of the average citizen but also by the fellow-feeling existing between corrupt officials and equally corrupt judges.

If, as the petition of April 5 reveals, there was a certain vehemence against the existing judges, then the reorganization of the system was necessary in order to minimise the sources of friction and discontent in the Island. But, having dismissed the *Asesor* in the interest of security and good government, Abercromby created a void in the Island's legal administration. For the *Asesor,* or *Auditor* as he was sometimes called, was the officer accredited to the Governor with responsibility for advising him on all matters pertaining to law and justice. He assisted the Governor in drawing up decrees and advised him in the exercise of his judicial powers. The *Asesor* was, in fact, legally responsible for the Governor's pronouncements on law when the latter acted on his advice. If, for some reason, the Governor wished to override his *Asesor* or follow contrary advice, he could do so, but he then became responsible for the results of his action. In some ways the judicial power of the *Asesor* even exceeded that of the Governor. For example, no sentence of court martial could be executed without his positive approval; in this respect he acted like the *Audiencia* in capital cases. In addition, he was considered the Governor's deputy and succeeded to his civil powers in case of death; the military powers of the Governor devolved upon the senior military officer. And he also presided in the Governor's absence at *Cabildo* meetings and other functions.[55]

There is little doubt that the absence of the *Asesor* vitiated the practice of Spanish law. Corrupt as he was alleged to be, the *Asesor* was,

54. C.O. 295/8, Hislop : Camden, 9.7.1804. In his summary of the Island's administration which prefaces the main body of the Report, Lt. Governor Hislop alludes to the dismissal of the *Asesor* under "Estates of Absentees and Minors"
55. See C.O. 295/8, Hislop : Camden, 9.7.1804 and enclosures.

because of his legal training, the hub of the wheel of Spanish judicial practice. Always available for consultation by the *alcaldes,* continually advising the Governor, he was the man whose task it was to maintain the fabric and temper of Spanish law. His removal displaced not only the one trained lawyer on the Island, but the only official specially charged with the maintenance of the integrity of the Spanish legal system.

Faced with the problem of reorganization, General Abercromby created the entirely new office of Chief Justice and appointed John Nihell to it. Abercromby's awareness of the extent to which he had departed from Spanish practice is evident from his letters to Nihell, but he regarded the existence of corruption and other questionable legal practices as a sufficient justification for his reforms. In his first letter to Nihell, Abercromby directed that the Chief Justice was not in future to be guided by the strictest dictates of Spanish law, but by "the instructions ... you shall receive from me through the Lieutenant Colonel Picton..." Any attempt to adhere too strictly to Spanish law would, he said, under an English government, lead to confusion and would retard the administration of justice. [56]

What detailed instructions Nihell did receive are not clear. [57] It is certain, however, that Picton, like Abercromby, left Nihell with the clear impression that the maintenance of law and order was not to be jeopardised by a too scrupulous adherence to Spanish law. The tone of judicial administration in the ensuing years owes much to Abercromby's final exhortation and assurance to Picton whom he left behind as military commandant of the Island.

> "I have placed you in a trying and delicate situation, nor, to give you any chance of overcoming the difficulties opposed to you, can I leave you a strong garrison; but I shall give you ample powers: execute Spanish law as well as you can; do justice according to your conscience, and that is all that can be expected from you. His Majesty's government will be minutely informed of your situation, and, no doubt, will make due allowance." [58]

In these circumstances, the formal recognition of Spanish law could only provide a canopy under which government, freed alike from Spanish and English law, could become arbitrary.

Apart from the instruction passed on by Lt. Col. Picton and his Commission from Abercromby, Nihell's conscience was his only guide.

56.   *State Trials,* XXX, pp. 444-6.
57.   See above pp. 35-36.
58.   Heaton Robinson, *op.cit.,* Vol. I, pp. 36-7.

Nihell who seems to have been overawed by the responsibility thus thrust upon him, wrote to Abercromby after he had received his first letter of appointment asking for some further clarification of his duties and powers. He seems to have been particularly sceptical about Abercromby's assurance that all his judicial decisions made in good faith would be regarded as valid "although (they) may be contrary to the form and spirit of the Spanish laws."[59] Accordingly, Abercromby's second letter proposed the creation of a substitute *Asesor*. In all civil cases Nihell should consult with three of the "most intelligent and upright men" in the Island; or consult an able lawyer! Having by one way or the other received an opinion upon such points as he wished, he was then to give judgement. Thus, not only was Nihell given absolute freedom in choosing his advisers; he was even permitted to direct their attention only to such points as he wished. The *Asesor*, it is hardly worth saying, would himself have decided what points were worthy of his consideration. Functionally, the substitute for the *Asesor* started with two severe handicaps.[60]

The precise position of the newly appointed Chief Justice in the hierarchy of judicial authorities is easily determined. Next to the Governor he was the most important judicial officer with wide judicial and administrative powers. His court almost completely superseded those of the *alcaldes ordinarios*. His jurisdiction was not, like theirs, limited to the municipalities of Port-of-Spain and St. Joseph, but extended over the whole Island. He was legally invested with all the authority necessary to eliminate the "great extortions, and unnecessary accumulations of law proceedings" to which *escribanos, procurados* and other officers had resorted in order to increase their fees. He was expected to institute new rules of procedure aimed at simplifying legal practice, no matter how contrary these might be to the Spanish forms. He had powers of dismissal too, and was expected to invoke them to "deprive of their employment any *escrivano* (sic), *procurador*, or other officer of your tribunal, whenever you find them, or any of them, guilty of extortion, malpractices in their offices, or disobedience of your orders."[61]

59. See Abercromby's first letter of March 1 to Nihell. *State Trials*, XXX, pp. 444-6.

60. The argument of this and the preceding paragraph is deduced from a study of Abercromby's two letters to Nihell, the references to which have already been given. Nihell's letter to Abercromby has not been seen. That it was written is deduced from the opening paragraph of Abercromby's second letter. He wrote; "Lt. Col. Maitland having laid before me your letter and paper containing notes, relative to the office of chief magistrate, which is continued in you, in consequence of the proclamation issued for the maintenance of the former laws of the colony, until his majesty's pleasure is known: I have the honour to return such answers as the occasion calls for, directing you, at the same time, to consider this letter as your sufficient authority for acting according to the directions contained in it." The remainder of the letter was taken up with the proposal about the replacement of the *Asesor*, a point to which Nihell had undoubtedly drawn his attention. See *State Trials*, XXX, p. 495.

61. Abercromby's first letter.

The Chief Justice also differed from the *alcaldes* [62] in that, as we have seen, they traditionally dealt with civil cases only, criminal cases being reserved for the Governor; and while he was not strictly bound by Spanish law, the *alcaldes,* who derived their power from the *Cabildo,* were bound to observe this law in so far as they understood it. Nihell was competent to try both civil and criminal cases subject only to an appeal to the King-in-Council in civil matters involving sums in excess of £500 sterling, and to the Governor in criminal cases, without whose approval no sentence in a criminal case could be executed. Thus, in the reform of the judicial machinery, Spanish precedents and practices ceased to be the only rule of judicial conduct; they were merely a guide to be dispensed with when necessary. While Picton groped his way towards a realization of his own strength the reality of the change was only dimly appreciated; in fact the tenor of legal administration had been fundamentally changed by the time Abercromby had left the Island sometime in March. The conquest had witnessed the abrogation of Spanish sovereignty; Nihell's appointment marked the demise of Spanish law. In British eyes law had to be efficient and accessible, its execution swift and certain. The leisurely scrupulousness and the intolerable lethargy of the Spanish code were gone forever.

*   *   *

The making of a constitution, as has already been observed, was not the object of the conquerors in 1797. Nevertheless, the constitutional problems which were to dominate the Island's history after its cession to Britain in 1802 were immanent in the settlement of 1797. Between 1797 and 1801 the most significant development was the establishment of a full-fledged system of arbitrary government which underwent no significant change in the years prior to the grant of a Legislative Council in 1831. Stripped of its pretence, its humbug and its self-seeking, the agitation for British laws after 1802 was a justified reaction against the consequences of 1797.

Under Spanish law two institutions checked the prevailing tendency to arbitrary rule by royal Governors, Captains-general and Viceroys in the colonies. One of these was the *Cabildo* whose role has already been discussed, and which, to the extent that it existed independently of the Governor and

---

62. Strictly speaking this judgement must date from the beginning of 1798. Nihell himself was an *alcalde.* In 1797, he was *alcalde* of the first election. It was because he was, and because Abercromby's policy was to permit all officers, except those he had dismissed or who had left of their own accord, to continue at their posts, that he was appointed Chief Justice. His elevation was completely due to the fact that he was, at the conquest, the senior *alcalde.*

exercised duties and privileges of its own, restricted the exercise of arbitrary government. The other institution was the *Audiencia*.

The *Audiencia* was a most effective instrument of colonial government. Its genesis lay in the desire of the Crown to curb the power of the royal officials in the colonies and to make them subservient to the authority of the metropolis. Its members were trained lawyers and, almost invariably, peninsular Spaniards appointed directly by the crown. Its chief function was that of surveillance. In the judicial sphere it functioned as a court of appeal. In the political sphere it functioned as a council of advice to viceroys and governors in administrative matters, and had the power of censuring their conduct. It possessed, too, the right to review and pass judgment on their administration on the conclusion of their term of office. "It was", in the words of C. H. Haring, "the center, the core, of the administrative system, and the principal curb upon oppression and illegality by the viceroys and other governors."[63]

The conquest of 1797 necessarily suspended the operation of the *Audiencia* in the Island, and, in transferring its powers to the Governor, Sir Ralph Abercromby completely lost sight of its essential principle. Conceived as a limitation on the Governor's powers, the *Audiencia* in Trinidad was ironically made to enhance and extend the exercise of that power. The Governor not only possessed all civil and military power, and an original jurisdiction in civil and criminal cases inherited from his Spanish predecessor; he possessed also, as an appeal court, the high judicial authority previously residing in the *Audiencia*. In criminal matters he was the highest court of appeal; in civil matters in respect of sums exceeding £500 sterling, an appeal was allowed to the King-in-Council. On all other matters the Governor had the final word. What this appellate power meant was that the Governor had a complete discretionary interpretation of the Island's laws. He was ignorant of these laws, and possessed neither the legal background,[64] nor, like Nihell,

---

63. *Spanish Empire in America*, p. 136. For an extended treatment of the *Audiencia*, see J.H. Parry, *The Audiencia of New Galicia in the Sixteenth Century: A Study in Spanish Colonial Government.* (Cambridge, 1948).

64. An inconvenience of which Picton only complained after his excesses had brought about his arrest and trial in England. C.O. 295/10, Picton: Privy Council, 8.10.1804. On this occasion he wrote, "The Colony of Trinidad was committed to my Military Command as a Soldier: I am no Lawyer and it would not be reasonable to expect of me, or of any other Officer placed, as a matter of Duty, in such a Situation, the Sudden knowledge of an intricate Science, which in all Countries, requires years of laborious Assiduous Study to administer with any degree of Precision. The first Object, in such a Situation, is self-Preservation, to which every other Consideration, of whatever Importance, must yield. The Officer must be at ease respecting the Safety of his Garrison, and of the Post confided to his Charge, before he can enquire into the Laws of the Country, which has unwillingly submitted to his Arms: he must secure their Subjection, before he can with Safety enter into the Subtilities (sic) of their Jurisprudence." A passage that says much more about Picton's attitude towards government than it does about his deficiencies as a lawyer!

the saving grace of long residence in the Island, to aid him in their interpretation. Thus, from this moment on, as Sanderson complained in 1812, "the judicial system of Trinidad became irremediably defective, according to Spanish law, in its most valuable jurisdiction."[65]

By degrees, all effective power, judicial, civil and military, was combined in the Governor's hands. If anyone succeeded the *Asesor* in the exercise of his authority it was the Governor, not Nihell nor the three wise men he was expected to summon on difficult occasions. Indeed, the Governor and the Chief Justice were soon at outs and the latter was not only shorn off most of his duties but dismissed for a brief period.[66] In the Calderon case,[67] which was destined to focus metropolitan attention on the Island's administration during this period, it emerged quite clearly that all the important judicial decisions, in this case the committal to torture, were taken by Picton.[68]

Under the former system, Spanish government had been authoritative but not arbitrary; after the conquest, it was nothing if not arbitrary. Don

---

65. *An Appeal* .., p. 17.

66. Picton explains in a letter to Frederick, Duke of York, Commander in Chief of the Army. Trinidad's population he said was fractious and disorderly, and " . . . the weak Character on whom the Appointment of Chief Justice had casually fallen by the pusilanimity of his Conduct, Contributed to increase the Relaxation and Spread the disorder. I was under the necessity of taking everything upon myself." P.C. 1/3557, Unbound Papers, Picton: Duke of York, 10.11.1803. Also, C.O. 295/13, Fullarton: Castlereagh, 18.11.1805; enclosing Nihell: Fullarton, 7.2.1803. Also, M'Callum: *op. cit.*, pp. 177-9.

67. The Calderon case was a *cause célèbre* of early nineteenth century British criminal history. The facts are simple enough. Louisa Calderon, a young mulatto woman of Port of Spain living in a state of concubinage with a white Spaniard, Pedro Ruiz, successfully conspired to rob him of 2,000 dollars with the aid of her lover Carlos Gonzales. On discovering his loss Ruiz made a report to Lieutenant Colonel Picton who straightaway committed Calderon to prison. Two days later, on December 9, Picton instructed St. Hilaire Begorrat, *alcalde* of the first election, to proceed with the investigation of the complaint, which he did until December 31. After Calderon had been in prison for about two weeks Begorrat, not satisfied with the replies she had so far made to his interrogations, applied to Picton for permission to use torture. This was on the 22nd, and permission was given on the 23rd, whereupon torture was immediately applied. Still the young woman held out with the result that she was tortured again on the 24th. In all she spent 74 to 76 minutes on the picket, 52-53 minutes on the first occasion, and 22-23 minutes on the second, after which Begorrat pronounced himself satisfied with the replies she had then made. This was the offence for which Picton was later tried in England. Only one thing remains to be said; it has already been said by Salvador de Madariaga. As offensive as this incident was there were much more serious ones for which Picton could have been tried and wasn't. For a record of the trial see, *State Trials*, XXX, pp. 231-450. Also, Fraser, *op. cit.*, Vol. I. pp. 214-22. For a lurid and much dramatized description of the picketting see, (Anonymous), *The Trial of Governor Thomas Picton for Inflicting the Torture on Louisa Calderon, a free Mulatto.... in the Island of Trinidad.* (London, 1807). A contemporary report of the first trial is in, George Theodore Wilkinson, *The Newgate Calendar*. Two volumes. (Panther Books, 1962), Vol. II, pp. 91-98. Madariaga's comments are in his *The Rise of the Spanish American Empire*, (London, 1947), pp. 320-323.

68. See Begorrat's testimony, *State Trials*, XXX, pp. 286-7.

Christobal de Robles even went so far as to advise the Governor that there
were no legal restraints on his power.

> "The circumstances of the conquest have virtually com-
> bined in you the whole power of the government. You are
> supreme political, criminal, civil, and military judge. You
> unite in your own person the separate powers of the governor,
> tribunals, and royal audience of Caracas; our laws enable
> you to judge summarily, without recusation or appeal.
> Circumstances like the present have been foreseen by our
> lawyers, who have provided remedies equal to the occasion.
> You are not shackled by forms or modes of prosecution. If
> you do substantial justice, you are only answerable to God
> and your conscience." [69]

What de Robles wrote might well have been true. Spanish lawyers undoubtedly had foreseen and catered for firm government in extraordinary circumstances. But "substantial justice" was expected to be done. It is not at all
clear that "substantial justice" was done. What was plausible in the turbulent
period immediately after the conquest became less so as time passed. But
the severities then visited on offenders in the name of security became the
rule of conduct in the immediately ensuing years. [70]

At the conquest all Abercromby's efforts had been directed towards
the establishment of a "Mild & Equal Government, well knowing that if I
were to act otherwise, the disaffected could give us much useless trouble in a
Country so little cultivated and of so great extent." [71] Hence, the generous
capitulation; hence, the continuation of Spanish law; hence, the confirmation of all the subordinate civil and judicial officers. But Picton, left to his
own devices, created as odious and obscene a tyranny as any country has
ever known. The agitation for British laws, itself impelled by a yearning for
a despotism of its own, gained much momentum in later years by ascribing
to itself the quality of a protest movement against the wilful oppression
first established by Lieutenant Colonel Picton. [72]

69. Heaton Robinson, *op. cit.,* Vol. I, pp. 54-7. Quoted.

70. S. de Madariaga, *The Rise of the Spanish American Empire,* p. 322.

71. W.O. 1/86, pp. 129-34, Abercromby: Ramkey (Private), 28.2.1797.

72. See Sanderson, *An Appeal. . . . ,* pp. 26-31. Writing for a British audience in 1812, when Picton after
his two trials in 1806 and 1808 had been restored to public favour, Sanderson refrained from directly
attacking the national hero, as Picton then was. Besides, because of his hard usage at the hands of
Judge Smith, who was appointed in 1808 to execute Spanish law in the Island, Sanderson was
primarily concerned with establishing the defects of that law. Yet a perusal of the following passage,
combined with a knowledge of the Island's government from 1797 to 1802, leaves little doubt as to
the real culprit. After referring to the ignorance of the judges, Sanderson wrote: "The consequences
of such ignorance were marked by its usual concomitant, an irremediable, a fatal temerity, which

Untrammelled by Spanish law the Island's government was further impaired by a complete absence of British imperial scrutiny. The first despatch from Secretary of State Dundas foreshadowed the *laissez-faire* attitude which predominated in British circles during the first years of British occupation. It also revealed the mainsprings of imperial concern with the new acquisition. Written on April 8, 1797, this document which ran into several pages dismissed the problems of government rather off handedly in the first few paragraphs. Thus Dundas wrote that since "Sir Ralph Abercromby ..... will have given you such directions as appeared to him most proper for the government of the Island, for the preservation of its internal tranquillity, and for its defence against any attempt of the Enemy to recover this valuable Possession .... I think it unnecessary to say any thing more on this subject." [73] Trade, however, unlike war and government, was much too important a subject to be left to generals, and Dundas expounded at length on what measures should be taken to realize the trading prospects of that " valuable possession". Until September 1801 when he was appointed civil Governor with a Commission and Instructions to appoint a Council of Advice, Picton , as military commandant, was sole arbiter of the Island's fortunes.

To his credit it must be said that the Island's administration owed much to his energy and initiative in this period. Administrative efficiency supplanted administrative chaos and served the cause of economic prosperity as well as of internal vigilance. In Port-of-Spain, the police, which had been greatly relaxed in the last days of Spanish rule, was reorganized and increased in strength. Street patrols became a regular feature of town supervision. Curfews were imposed, and the movement of persons in and out of the Island was strictly regulated. [74] In the Island as a whole strong contin-

plunged them deeper and deeper at every sanguinary step. Tortures to extort confession of sorcery, witchcraft, and obeism (sic), public mutilations in the marketplace for such chimerical crimes; and even the burning of the living and dead together in the streets of Trinidad, have stained the character of that unfortunate colony with the blood and ashes of the devoted victims of superstitious cruelty, practised under the authority of ignorant judges." *An Appeal. . .* , p. 27. In 1807, Sanderson was much less guarded in his references to Picton and lashed him mercilessly, heaping scorn on his "energy, firmness and imposing character" which had in Sanderson's opinion, retarded and not advanced the immigration of whites to the Island. *Political Account. . . .*, p. 102. See also, pp. 47-8; 108-9.

73. C.O. 153/31, Dundas: Picton, 8.4.1797. Compare Dundas's confidence with Abercromby's anxiety. Writing after the conquest the latter expressed a desire to return to Europe as soon as possible. He was not sick, he said, but "The complex nature of the Civil & Military duties of a Commander in Chief (are) too much for me, and I cannot discharge both. . .to my own satisfaction." W.O. 1/86, pp. 129-34, Abercromby: Ramkey (Private), 28.2. 1797.

74. C.O. 295/2, Picton: Hobart, 18.2.1802; enclosure entitled, *Reglement pour servir d'Instruction aux Commandants des Differens Quartiers de la Colonie,* dated 20.8.1800, *passim.* Also, Gertrude Carmichael, *op. cit.,* pp. 44-7.

gents of militia were raised, organized and trained in the arts of war.[75] The commandants of quarters, numbering twenty-four at the conquest, were increased to twenty-eight. First instituted by Chacon in 1784,[76] they were made to perform, as they had done since, a wide range of judicial and administrative functions.[77] Their duties included the superintendence of the country police and the examination of the passports of those wishing to travel in the coasting vessels plying between Port-of-Spain and the country districts. They were expected to ensure that no strangers settled in their districts without the express permission of the Governor. They could hear and decide cases involving sums not in excess of one hundred dollars, roughly the equivalent of £23. 6. 8d sterling. Where the amount was more they were expected to collect evidence and statements and transmit them to the Governor for decision by one of the higher courts. They had no jurisdiction in criminal cases, but they had powers of arrest and detention. They also served as sub-commissaries of population and provided most of the statistics from which the annual reports of population and produce were compiled. They witnessed contracts; supervised the surveying and distribution of land; enforced decrees of sequestration against plantations; supervised the appraisal of disputed or sequestered property; inventoried the property of intestates, and supervised that of absentees and minors.

The supervision of the slave system must be numbered amongst the most important of their duties. A new slave code was proclaimed on June 30, 1800, the implementation of which was largely the work of the commandants.[78] They were to investigate cases of illegal or undue punishment of slaves.[79] They were to order and superintend the punishment of slaves whose acts warranted a heavier punishment than owners, managers and overseers were permitted to give.[80] And they had a general responsibility for ensuring that the provisions of the ordinance were obeyed. Infringements of the several clauses pertaining to the clothing, lodging and sustenance of

75. Gertrude Carmichael, *op. cit.*, pp. 46-7.

76. C.O. 295/24, Smith: Jenkinson. (Private. 2.3.1810; Appendix No. 1. For documents on the development of the office see, *T.T.H.S.* No. 470. For comment, Reis, *op. cit.*, Vol. I, pp. 40-1; Joseph, *op. cit.*, p. 174.

77. The best contemporary summary of the work of the commandants is given by Sanderson, *Political Account* . . . , pp. 32-48: *An Appeal* . . . pp. 11-12. The present account relies heavily on both.

78. C.O. 295/2, Picton: Hobart, 18.2.1802; enclosure. A printed copy of the ordinance is in C.O. 295/ 14. Also, Gertrude Carmichael, *op. cit.*, pp. 379-383.

79. Ordinance, Article 6.

80. *Ibid.*, Article 5. Owners were limited to the infliction of thirty-nine lashes.

the slave [81] were to be investigated by the commandant and fines were to be levied according to the nature of the offence. [82] They were expected, too, to act as coroners: a duty, according to Sanderson, that was "shamefully neglected" thereby resulting in many uninvestigated deaths and casualties among the slaves. [83]

In their superintendence of the slave system as in their other duties they were assisted by squads of *alguaçiles,* said by Sanderson to be "generally of the lowest class of Spaniards; and, often, coloured men, or negroes, capable of every degree of chicane, and ready tools of tyranny and rapine." [84] Abuse of the slaves was a common feature of the system. Commandant as well as *alguaçil* often inflicted unwarranted and unauthorised punishment, even in defiance of the owner: in North Naparima, says Sanderson, a slave was placed naked on a nest of stinging ants. [85] Relations between *alguaçil* and slave were, however, sometimes more idyllic. The movement of slaves was regulated by a system of passes operated by the plantation owners and managers. Often a slave was arrested and detained even when in possession of a pass. But sometimes conspiracies were hatched between the commandant, the *alguaçil* and the slave. "The Slave proposes to the *Alguazil* (sic), or the latter entices the former, to meet him, and submit to be carried before the Commandant, even at the risk of the whip, to share in the reward which the owner is obliged to pay, to the Commandant, on his Negro being restored to him; whereby loss of money is added to loss of labour." [86]

While the office of commandant was being refurbished new administrative offices were being created and old ones made to serve new needs. Abercromby himself had begun the process of innovation and re-creation by appointing Josiah Collin to the many-faceted position of superintendent of imports and exports, receiver of duties and regulator of the ports of the Colony. [87] Collin had also been invested with the duties of colonial treasurer, collector of customs, harbour-master and receiver of wrecks. He was charged with the supervision of all aspects of the Island's trade and authorized to collect a 3½% duty on all but a few of the Island's imports and exports, [88] a duty which became from henceforth the sole source of colonial revenue.

---

81. *Ibid.,* Articles 1, 2, 3, 4, 7, 8, 9, 10, 13, 14.

82. *Ibid.,* Article 15.

83. Sanderson, *An Appeal . . . ,* p. 12.

84. Sanderson, *Political Account,* p.32.

85. Sanderson, *Political Account,* p. 48. See also, pp. 42-48.

86. *Ibid.,* p. 36.

87. W.O. 1/86, pp. 207-210. Instructions to Collin, 15.3.1797.

88. W.O. 1/86, Article 6. For exemptions, mainly on stores and provisions for the garrison, see Article 10.

In future years Picton continued to add to, and modify, the administrative structure existing at the conquest. Collin himself was shorn of some of his duties. In 1801, John Henry Jacobs was, by commission from the Governor, appointed to the harbour-mastership; and, in 1803, a collector of customs was established by warrant from the Commissioners of Customs in London. From June 1801, Collin's principal duties became those of colonial treasurer.[89]

After his appointment as Governor in September 1801 and the institution of a Council of Advice, Picton made several new appointments. A clerk of the Council was appointed, as was an Attorney General [90] in the person of Archibald Gloster, and a Governor's secretary. An Anglican chaplain, whose salary of £200 sterling, paid by the Island's treasury, almost equalled the stipend paid to four Catholic curates and two sacristans, had been appointed in May. In November 1802, the chaplain, the Reverend John Henry Chapman, was given the new post of rector and an additional salary of £600 sterling which, with fees, made him far and away the highest paid clergyman in the Island.[91] The cession, and the Commission of government which followed, witnessed the further increase in administrative appointments. The office of *alguaçil mayor* was amalgamated with its English near-equivalent of provost marshal and a new incumbent was appointed to it. A naval officer, a commissary of population and a surveyor general were also appointed.[92] One feature of some of the new appointments was that they were filled by deputies who acted on behalf of patentees in London, or more precisely, of patentees in the office of the Secretary of State for War and the Colonies.[93]

In the judicial sphere, the re-establishment of a *consulado* or com-

89. C.O. 295/22, Hislop: Castlereagh, 4.10.1809. Return of Offices. C.O. 295/23, Hislop : Liverpool: 14.4.1810, No. 11, for Return of collector of customs.

90. The Attorney General is the only one of these whose appointment can be exactly traced. See, C.O. 295/2, C.O. 296/1, Picton: Hobart, 6.2.1802. The other appointments were surely made but dating them is difficult.

91. C.O. 295/22, Hislop: Castlereagh, 4.10.1809. Fees averaged, between 1.1.1806 and 31.12.1808, £ 239. 14. 7¾d. sterling annually.

92. *Ibid.* A commissariat of population had been established by Chacon in 1787, with a first commissary and two sub-commissaries. (*T.T.H.S.* No. 470). The department was reorganized in 1803 under the Commission of government, and discontinued in 1807. The surveyor's department, established in 1803, was abolished in 1808. See, C.O. 295/20, Rutherford: Castlereagh, 13.1.1808; C.O. 295/17, Williamson: Cooke, 5.4.1807.

93. The offices concerned were those of naval officer, provost marshal, and clerk of the Council. George Adderley, who was not of the Secretary of State's office, was the only patentee to fill his office in person, if only briefly. Adam Gordon, patentee of the naval office, and James Chapman, patentee of the clerkship of the Council, were both clerks in the Secretary's department. See, C.O. 295/22, Hislop: Castlereagh, 4.10.1809. Also, D.M. Young, *The Colonial Office in the early nineteenth century.* (London, 1961), Appendix III, p. 266.

mercial court emphasized the departure from purely Spanish forms of jurisprudence. First established by Chacon in 1794, the court had been operated
as a department of the main *consulado* at Caracas.[94] It had adjudicated in
disputes between merchants and had taken cognisance of all matters of trade,
shipping, purchases, contracts, insurance and the like that were in any way
connected with maritime commercial activity. In this respect, it bore a close
resemblance to the instance court in the English vice-admiralty.[95] Between
1794 and 1797, few cases of consequence had actually been brought before
this court, but they had been determined according to Spanish law.[96] The
conquest had naturally broken the connection with Caracas, and the court,
re-introduced by Picton after the conquest, emphasized summary and
expeditious judgment instead of the scrupulous observation of Spanish law
and procedure. Neither English nor Spanish law was observed. Cases were
determined according to equity, without any set principles of conduct.
Lawyers were excluded from participation and there were few facilities for
appeal against the court's judgments.[97]

The results of this administrative and judicial reorganization must
now be noted. In the first place, the tightening of the machinery of internal
control was the prime objective of administrative and judicial reform and
carried a high social cost. The life of the community was subject to the
sole will of the Governor. His overall control was enhanced, not modified,
by the creation of new offices and the reorganization of old ones. Most of
the new officials, particularly the commandants, owed their appointments
solely to him, could be dismissed by him and were susceptible to the crudest
pressures of coercion. As we shall see, after the agitation for British laws
in 1802, several officers were relieved of their commissions in the militia
for having subscribed to the Address requesting constitutional change.[98]
Also, the process of reorganization was accompanied by the introduction of
various devices intended solely to coerce. One of these, the picket, was introduced by Picton[99] under sanction of an old Spanish law[100] in order to

94. C.O. 295/8, Hislop: Camden, 9.7.1804; Nihell's report, enclosed.
95. See, Carl Ubbelohde, *The Vice Admiralty Courts and the American Revolution.* (Chapel Hill, 1960),
     pp. 12-13; 18-19.
96. C.O. 295/8, Hislop: Camden, 9.7.1804; Nihell's report, enclosed.
97. Sanderson, *Political Account . . .* , pp. 114-20.

98. See Chapter 4,   pp. 104-5.
99. It was successfully established at Picton's first trial that he had first introduced the picket into the
     Island. State Trials, XXX, pp. 260, 264-5,467.
100. For the legal sanction of torture under Spanish law see, *State Trials*, XXX, pp. 540 ff, 594 ff. Several
     laws are therein quoted to support the use of torture in judicial examination.

extort confessions from recalcitrant witnesses. Subsequently the use of this instrument on the mulatto girl, Louisa Calderon, in 1801, resulted in his arraignment for the crime of torture before the high court in England in 1806. [101] Another creation was a Commission of 1801 before which slaves suspected of practicing sorcery, obeah and administering poison were investigated and, on conviction, mutilated, hanged, drawn, quartered and burnt alive. [102]

Of great importance, too, was the rapid extinction of Spanish legal and administrative practices. Nor was Spanish law replaced by English law. A stage was arrived at where Spanish and English precedents were both pressed into the service of expediency and convenience. In elucidating the duties of some offices, for example, the provost marshal's and the court registrar's, established practices were imported wholesale into the Island from the other British colonies. When a new office was created and, as invariably happened, an Englishman was appointed to it, the administration of the office owed more to English than to Spanish precedent. The official was instructed to collect fees in the same manner as they were collected in the old British islands, [103] often for duties that did not exist under Spanish law. [104] So much so that it has been pointed out that administrative practices were often introduced in order that officials might collect their fees. [105] Still, Spanish law lurked in the background. If the Island had any law at all it was, officially, Spanish. Property disputes, so far as they were decided by law (sometimes they were not), could only be decided according to Spanish law. So far as it is possible to make a clear distinction, it might be said that civil law, except for the *consulado,* was administered according to the Spanish code, and criminal law, according to whatever prescription of convenience currently prevailed.

101. *State Trials,* XXX, p. 225 ff.

102. For the personnel of this Commission see, C.O. 295/12, in which are contained the enclosures of Hislop: Castlereagh, 13.12.1805, which is in C.O. 295/11. See also, C.O. 295/15, Fullarton : Windham, 29.7.1806, for arguments against the legality of the Commission. *B.M.Add.Mss.* 36,499, pp. 104-105 gives an estimate of the numbers of persons punished and the manner of their punishment. The estimate of "several hundred" punished is much too high; but the descriptions of the punishments are graphic and accurate. See also, M'Callum, *op. cit.,* p. 187 ff. Sanderson's assertion that the imputation of sorcery was a favourite excuse of commandants for the ill-treatment of slaves is worthy of note; as is his contention that the widespread apprehension of obeah must have increased the manifestations of the "evidence" of obeah. *Political Account. . . ,* p. 46.

103. W.O. 1/86, pp. 207-210. Instructions to Josiah Collin, Article 12.

104. See C.O. 295/22, Hislop: Castlereagh, 21.11.1809, No. 78; enclosing Smith: Hislop, 20.11.1809, on the conflict between the office of *alguaçil mayor* and that of provost marshal.

105. D.J. Murray, *The West Indies and the Development of Colonial Government, 1801-34* (Oxford, Clarendon Press, 1965), p. 195.

The fusion of Spanish law, English law and caprice was manifestly unworkable. "It was impossible", as Sanderson said, "that any thing short of a complete Spanish system, or some other complete system in lieu of it, could operate otherwise than incompletely." [106] In the twilight period of transition from Spanish to British sovereignty it was perhaps to be expected that an indeterminate something would be the result of the clash of the two systems. The point is that the product was never regarded as hybrid. In British ministerial circles the assumption that Spanish law prevailed in Trinidad continued unchallenged until 1808. In 1825, a Colonial Office clerk writing a summary on the government of Trinidad, even suggested that "all the modifications in the law & judicature of the Colony have been made subsequent to the appointment of a new Chief Justice in 1809..." [107]

This was not at all so. To argue the point as to whether and to what extent Spanish law can, even in the best of circumstances, be administered under an English government, is to indulge in the wildest speculation. The fact was that in Trinidad the attempt to administer a pure Spanish system was, until 1808, never made. Both by accident and design the post-conquest period witnessed the continuing modification of Spanish law in the Island. And while the Island's inhabitants were acutely aware of the change, the British government took the orthodox view that, until a British constitution was granted to the Island enabling it to make its own laws, Spanish law continued regardless of the modifications it was made to undergo. But this was not a sufficient theory when applied to Trinidad. If there was any coherence in Spanish colonial policy that coherence was derived from Spanish law alone. Between Spain and her colonies there was nothing of the constitutional relationship that existed between Britain and hers. Between the British colonies and the metropolis the main relationship was constitutional. Thus law could and did differ from metropolis to colony and even between colonies themselves[108] without altering the fundamental

---

106. Sanderson, *An Appeal. . .* , p. 21.

107. C.O. 296/3, Introduction to a precis of the Island's Correspondence, dated 1.7.1825.

108. The main body of law of relevance here would be the slave law. Lord Mansfield's judgement in the Somerset case emphasized the difference between British metropolitan and colonial law respecting slavery. See, *State Trials*, XX, pp. 2-82. Also, *State Trials*, XXX, p. 934ff for its application to the Picton trial. A perusal of John Henry Howard's *The Laws of the British Colonies and other parts of America. ...* Two volumes, (London, 1827), reveals the differences between the colonies. Another difference between mother country and colonies is to be seen in the laws of mortgage. The rates of interest on mortgage loans were generally higher in the colonies. Cf. C.O. 295/24. Smith: Jenkinson, 13.5.1810. Also, Richard Pares, *Merchants and Planters,* (Cambridge, 1960), p.44. In this connection however, the mortgage laws are of much less importance. They represent the minutiae of the prob-

connection with the mother country. Not so with the Spanish colonies where the strongest, indeed the only, link between themselves and Spain was legal not constitutional. One has only to look at the indivisibility [109] and, to some extent, the immutability of Spanish colonial law to assess the strength of the legal connection. Law was indivisible because it emanated from the same source, the metropolis, and with slight exceptions, [110] was the same for all colonies. It was immutable because the inspiration was invariably the same, the continuing moral dilemma of Catholic Spain as a world Power with materialist ambitions and aspirations.

Salvador de Madariaga asserts that "The main orientation of the Spanish Empire is . . . not economic nor political, but spiritual." [111] And this assertion at once makes intelligible the particular place of law in the Spanish system. It is of course true that law had an intrinsic value in Spanish metropolitan development. If constitutionalism was the result of political development in England in the sixteenth and seventeenth centuries, legalism was the peculiar result of Spanish political development during the same period. [112] Thus, legalism institutionalised the notary in old Spain [113] as it was to institutionalise the practices of the *requirimiento* in the New World. [114] But law also served a very practical end. In the colonies it was made to assist the subject in treading the very narrow path between salvation

---

lem and can be paralleled by similar differences between Spain and the Spanish colonies. See, however, Jerome Nadelhaft, "the Somersett Case and Slavery: Myth, Reality and Repercussions", *The Journal of Negro History*, Vol. LI, No. 3, 1966, pp. 193-208. The author challenges the orthodox view of the importance of the Mansfield decision in the Somersett case and asserts that what Mansfield really decided, on June 22, 1792, was that "a slave could not be shipped from England against his will." Mansfield's decision did not free the 14,000 Negroes then in England, he argues, and quotes Mansfield himself as interpreting what he had done as simply amounting to a prohibition on the master of a slave taking his servant out of the kingdom against his will.

109. Cf. the main Spanish colonial codes, e.g. *Recopilación de las Indias. . .* and *Las Siete Partidas.*

110. The main exceptions were of two kinds. There were first of all the special provisions made by the Crown itself for the government of special and, for the most part, important areas such as the principal cities in South and Central America. The *Recopilación* contains several instances of such legislation; and we have seen that special provision was made for the administrative succession in Trinidad. The second main body of exceptions was provided by the administrative regulations made locally by Viceroys and other royal officials for good government in their districts. There were also, of course, the laws pertaining to economic development which were frequently different in different areas: we have also noted this with regard to the gradual extension of the free slave trade principle in the Spanish colonies. All basic laws of wider import, the regulation of judicial procedure, the treatment of slaves, were promulgated by Spain and were the same throughout the colonial empire.

111. *Englishmen, Frenchmen, Spaniards*, p. 170.

112. Lewis Hanke, *Bartolomé de Las Casas: An Interpretation of his Life and writings*, (The Hague, 1951). Chapter 1, *passim*.

113. J.H. Parry, *The Sale of Public Office in the Spanish Indies under the Hapsburgs, op.cit.*, p. 6.

114. Hanke, *op. cit.*, p. 7.

on the one hand and damnation on the other; between the altruism and humanity of Las Casas and Montesinos, and the greed and lust of the *conquistadores,* the ideal being the calculation of Bernal Diaz who hoped "to serve God and the King and also to get rich."[115]   Thus, as keeper and guide of the nation's conscience, the Spanish Crown saw "the notion of jurisdiction as the essential function of authority. Though he legislated continually, the king was . . . regarded primarily as a judge, the chief of judges."[116]   Thus, too, the highest organs of colonial control were legal bodies, as were the Council of the Indies and the *Audiencias;* and the most reliable servants of the Crown in the colonies were highly trained lawyers, as were the *oidores.*

In Trinidad, the conquest destroyed the legal orientation of the society. Local practices, notwithstanding, the possibility of appeal to properly constituted legal bodies before 1797 had exercised some restraint on the grossest forms of corruption: a man's property might be stolen but his life could not be casually sworn away. After the conquest, the Governor was the highest tribunal of appeal in criminal cases, and the King-in-Council the highest in civil cases, an arrangement that was itself an astonishing and significant departure from Spanish custom. The economic orientation of British colonialism turned Spanish law on its head and made the preservation of property a higher aim than the preservation of human life.

The slave system reflected the change Spanish law had undergone. Picton's slave code of 1800 has been described as generous and humane. The lack of any provision for manumitting the slave population was nevertheless a very significant omission. The Francisco case, already referred to,[117] revealed a picture of slavery completely unknown to post-conquest Trinidad society. It depicted the slave as part of a society that recognised his possession of a moral and social status. Francisco committed murder at a "wake" held for a dead slave and attended by slaves.[118] The murder, committed at three a.m. when, after the conquest, slaves could have been abroad only at their peril, arose out of a dispute over religious observance.[119] Francisco had a fiancée to whom he was shortly to have been married; banns

---

115. Hanke, *op. cit.,* p. 9. Quoted from Bernal Diaz del Castillo, *Historia verdadera de la conquista de la Nueva España* (Two volumes). (Mexico, 1943). Vol. II, p. 394. Hanke's *The Spanish Struggle for Justice in the Conquest of America,*(Philadelphia, 1949), and *Aristotle and the Indians* (London, 1959) are very useful on this theme.

116. J.H. Parry, *The Audiencia of New Galicia . . .* p. 3.

117. See above, p. 45. note 43.

118. *State Trials,* XXX, p. 611.   119. *Ibid.,* p. 619.

CHAPTER 2

were to have been published in church in anticipation of this event.[120]   And
Francisco, as we have seen, escaped from jail while awaiting confirmation of
the sentence of death passed upon him.[121] Such details confirm the picture
of a slave system in which the misfortune of servitude did not deprive the
slave of his essential human rights.[122]

Picton's code, "generous and humane" as it was, observed one criterion
only, that of efficiency.   Thus Saturdays, which formerly belonged to the
slave for working on his own account, were taken away because they encouraged idleness.[123]   And though slaves were manumitted after the
conquest, manumission occurred in an atmosphere at best increasingly

120. *Ibid.*, p. 618.

121. See above, p. 45 note 43.

122.   The difference in harshness of the systems, if any, and the implications of such differences between the Anglo-American and the Latin American forms of slavery have, of course, blossomed into
one of the major areas of concern for scholars preoccupied with the slave systems of the New World
and their legacies. Several interesting contributions have been made to the subject. Among these are:
Frank Tannenbaum, *Slave and Citizen* (first published by Alfred A. Knopf, 1946; reissued, Vintage
Books, no date); Stanley Elkins, *Slavery: A Problem in American Institutional and Intellectual Life*,
(Chicago, 1959); David Brian Davis, *The Problem of Slavery in Western Culture*, (Cornell Univer-
sity Press, 1966); Kenneth M. Stampp, *The Peculiar Institution: Slavery in the Ante-Bellum South*,
(New York, 1956); Eugene D. Genovese, *The Political Economy of Slavery*, (Vintage Books, 1967;
first published 1961); Orlando Patterson, *The Sociology of Slavery*, (McGibbon and Kee, 1967);
Elsa V. Goveia, "The West Indian Slave Laws of the Eighteenth Century", *Revista de Ciencias Sociales*,
Vol. IV, No. I, March 1960, pp. 75-106; Arnold A. Sio, "Interpretations of Slavery: The Slave
Status in the Americas", *Comparative Studies in Society and History*, April 1965, pp. 289-308, and
S. Mintz's review of Elkins's book in *American Anthropologist*, LXIII (June, 1961), 579-87.
    It is now generally agreed that the Tannenbaum thesis presents a slightly romantic view of the
differences between the slave systems of Anglo-America and Latin America. In fact the latest conclusions support Professor Goveia's very able early (1960) contention that,
"The rule of force inherent in slavery produced comparable results in the Spanish, British and French
colonies of the West Indies though variations were introduced by the degree of their dependence on
slavery and by differences in their political traditions. . . Both in their content and in their enforcement, the West Indian slave laws follow a remarkably consistent pattern, imposed by the function of
the law in maintaining the stability of these forms of social organization on which rested the whole
life of the West India colonies during the eighteenth century." *Ciencias Sociales, loc. cit.,* pp. 103,
105.
    Another aspect of this view is that which explains the seeming difference in harshness between the
systems in terms of the maturity of the economic systems of the slave societies under examination.
By this token Cuba and Saint Dominique at their zenith were slave societies in which the treatment
meted out to the slaves were basically no different from that experienced by slaves in the British West
Indian colonies and in the Southern United States of America. Tannenbaum ignores this possibility
altogether. Elkins, elaborating on Tannenbaum, takes the view, it seems, that the economic systems
of the British and North American slave colonies were intrinsically maturer than those of the French
and Spanish colonies - and so, as well as for other reasons, their systems were harsher. But this is
obviously insufficient when applied to Cuba and Saint Dominique, admittedly the exceptions. Trinidad seems to be an exception of yet another kind, and the author hopes one day to elaborate upon it.

123. C.O. 295/2, Picton: Hobart, 18.2.1802; enclosure. Article 9.

indifferent, often openly hostile, to manumission.[124]   Prosperity and the
vast returns accruing to capital in the first five years following the conquest
were the economic conditions that bolstered the prevailing attitude to slavery
and manumission.   Even the slaves themselves seem to have been affected by
the general prejudice against manumission by which the British slave system
was chiefly distinguished from the Spanish.   The story has been told of a
slave who, having enough money to purchase his own manumission, went out
and bought himself a slave instead. [125]   Whether he did it because it was
easier to purchase another slave than to procure his own manumission is not
recorded; but it is certain that Trinidad during 1797 to 1810 was far from
being the slave paradise described by Baron de Montlezum in 1818.[126]
    The prospect of a slave buying a slave introduces the right note of
gentle irony with which to make a wider judgment on the Island's subsequent
history.   Deprived of a coherent system of Spanish law by the conquest,
Trinidad, at the mercy of expediency and convenience, floundered from crisis
to crisis.   In time the Island became a by-word for capricious government,
an object of unbounded amusement in erudite and vulgar circles alike.[127]
Arbitrary government by Picton was to be followed by a period of confused
government under a Commission, to be followed by further periods of
arbitrary government.   Spanish law was to be modified, abandoned, imposed
and finally abandoned.   The succession of experiments was to lead an
anonymous writer in the *Trinidad Gazette* to complain in 1825 that, "since
this Island became a British dependency, its inhabitants have been subjected
to a constant series of experiments until, as the cook said of the eels she was
skinning, we are pretty well 'used to it.' Government, laws, Judges, Tenures,
Securities and Courts of Justice, have been constantly involved in the rapid

124. *B.M. Add. Mss.* 36,499, p. 103.   125. *Ibid.*

126. *Souvenirs des Antilles: Voyage en 1815 et 1816, aux Etats-Unis, et dans l'Archipel Caraibe.* Two
    volumes. (Paris, 1818). Vol. I, pp. 282-3, wherein slavery is described in Trinidad as existing in
    name only.

127. The most diverting of these comments was perhaps Peel's injunction to Goulburn in 1812. The
    source is obviously erudite. "You will", he wrote, "immortalise yourself if you will frame a con-
    stitution for Trinidad - it has baffled all your predecessors who have uniformly left it as they found it
    governed by Spanish law and petitioning for English. Trinidad is like a subject in an anatomy school
    or rather a poor patient in a country hospital and on whom all sorts of surgical experiments are tried
    to be given up if they fail and to be practised on others if they succeed. Stephen is the operator and
    there are occasional consultations with Doctor Wilberforce and Zachary Macaulay on the state of the
    patients health and the progress of the experiment. The poor patient has to go through some very
    severe operations, she is now actually bound down for a most painful one, a registration of slaves with
    penalties upon penalties on those who fail to observe the regulations of an Order in Council prescribed
    by Dr. Stephen. . . " Peel: Goulburn, 12.8.1812. Quoted. D.J. Murray, *The West Indies and the De-
    velopment of Colonial Government, 1801-34,* (Oxford, Clarendon Press, 1965) pp. 81-2.

whirl of innovation, until it has become a matter of dispute what Tribunals are in existence, and what system of law their decisions are regulated by." [128]

As it was in 1825, so it was, in lesser degree, in the years immediately succeeding the conquest. Trinidad's laws were, from the inception of British rule, neither fish nor fowl; and thus, for a long time, they remained. Spanish law remained by concession of the conquerors, and it was the interests of the conquerors not those of the inhabitants that prevailed. Thus, while Spanish law had at first been retained as a conciliatory measure intended to allay discontent, it became at a later date one of the important means whereby the interests of security were promoted. What there was in Spanish law that was hostile to the promotion of these interests was anathema, and was dispensed with; what there was in Spanish law that was favourable to the promotion of those interests, was retained. The mixture of Spanish and English law that thereby resulted was an important means of effecting security as well as social change. It permitted the introduction of torture as easily as it facilitated the substantial modification of the rights of the free coloured population. By retaining something of Spanish law the domination of the merchant by the planter class was, as we shall see, [129] made possible. At the same time the introduction of some English law was used to blunt the demand for a more thoroughgoing reform of the existing constitutional and legal structure.

Above all, however, the admixture of Spanish and English law permitted the exercise of caprice and convenience in the administration of the Island's affairs. It was partly because of this that the British government was fated to find itself, to its great embarrassment, forced to resist the arguments of those who urged the alternative "simplification" of the adoption of British laws and a British constitution. Meanwhile, the idea of experimentation, to the dismay of many, but to the ultimate advantage of the humblest and most defenceless sections of the West Indian society then in being, was to continue to prevail.

128. Fraser, *op. cit.*, Vol. II, pp. 186-8. Quoted.

129. See below,   pp. 122 ff.

PART TWO

THE YEARS OF EXPERIMENT

CHAPTER 3

THE VANGUARD SOCIETY I

The notion of Trinidad as an Island of experiment was always closely linked with the question of constitutional change, and so developed imperceptibly out of events which at first seemed to have nothing to do with experimentation. Neither the establishment of constitutional government in June 1801 nor the Island's cession to Britain in March of the following year seemed likely to give rise to developments other than those which were closely associated with the conventions of the past. Thus, it was the confident expectation of many of the persons interested in the Island's affairs, that, if not immediately, certainly in due course, the Island would be established as another British colony enjoying, as they would have said, the blessings of British laws and a British constitution. This was the conventional view which, in the absence of other indications, could not be regarded as unreasonable; but it was also the view which, in the long run, was destined to by unrealized. By the early months of 1802 the notion of experimentation was beginning to flourish. Thereafter, by accident as well as by design, it was to be the dominating theme in the Island's history up to and well beyond the year 1810.

The establishment of constitutional government in Trinidad was itself a mild event. On February 16, 1801, Secretary of State Dundas wrote to the Lords Commissioners of the Privy Council concerned with trade informing them that the appointment of Lieutenant Colonel Picton to the civil governorship of the Island was being considered, and requesting their consideration of the matter.[1] On April 20, their Lordships having obliged, the appointment was approved by the King-in-Council.[2] Thereafter, some delay ensued arising out of a change of ministry by which Pitt was replaced as Prime Minister by Henry Addington, latterly Speaker of the House of Commons and later first Viscount Sidmouth, and Dundas was, in his turn, replaced by Lord Hobart as Secretary of State at the War Office.[3] As a result of these changes the despatch containing Picton's Commission and Instructions never went out until some eight weeks had elapsed. It was finally despatched on June 29, and was received by Picton in early September.[4] From this time onwards the Island's government was on a constitutional footing.

Hitherto, in so far as the government of the Island had had a constitutional basis this was to be found in the articles of capitulation, in the proclamation

1. P.C. 1/3557, Unbound Papers, Bundle I.
2. *Ibid.*
3. J. Steven Watson, *The Reign of George III. 1760-1815*, (Readers Union edition, London 1964), *passim.*
4. C.O. 296/1; C.O. 295/2, Picton : Hobart, 8.9.1801.

of the conquerors, and in the Instructions issued to Picton by Sir Ralph Abercromby on his departure from the Island.[5] The Commission and Instructions now issued to the Governor superseded these as the main instruments of government. Few changes were, however, made; the principal effect of the articles of appointment was to confirm the *ad hoc* arrangements which Abercromby had made for the Island's government. Lieutenant Colonel Picton, now Governor, was instructed to continue to be guided in his administration "as nearly as circumstances will permit (by) the terms of the Capitulation . . . the ancient Laws and Institutions that subsisted . . . previous to the Surrender . . . subject only to such directions as you shall now or hereafter receive from Us . . . or by Our Order in Our Privy Council or to such sudden and unforseen Emergencies as may render a departure therefrom absolutely necessary and unavoidable . . ."[6] He was informed that all executive powers of government were entrusted to him and that "all such Powers as were heretofore exercised by any Person or Persons separately or in conjunction with the Governor of the said Island,"[7] now belonged to himself alone.

He was to ensure that the courts continued to operate according to the laws by which the Island had been governed before its capture, and he himself was confirmed in the exercise of such judicial powers as belonged to the Spanish Governor before him. The Roman Catholic Religion was to be maintained according to "its former legal Establishment"; and "the exercise of such mode of Evangelic worship" as others may have adopted or brought with them was to be protected.[8] Those laws of trade which had not been altered or modified by the Order-in-Council making Port-of-Spain a free port were to be "strictly observed and maintained".[9]

One innovation stood out from this chronicle of confirmatory provisions. The Governor was instructed to choose from amongst the Island's proprietors a Council of Advice, consisting of not less than three nor more than five members [10] to assist with the administration of government. He was free to refuse any advice proffered by the Council if he thought such refusal to be in the Island's best interests, provided always that on all such occasions he transmitted to the Secretary of State the details of the differences of opinion between himself and the Council and his reasons for acting contrary to their advice. In fact, the constitutional settlement of 1801 bore all the marks of a temporary expedient. It had been conceived at a time when, to the Pitt government, the prospects for peace had seemed somewhat remote. The Island's future was yet to be determined, and Spain was very likely to press for its return at the end of the war. The whole notion then had been to pro-

5. See Chapter II, pp. 35-36.
6. C.O. 296/4, Hobart : Picton, 29.6.1801, Instructions, Article 5.
7. *Ibid.*
8. *Ibid.*, Article 15.
9. *Ibid.*, Article 6.
10. *Ibid.*, Article 2.

duce a rough and ready compromise primarily intended to put an end to five years of military rule, but to leave open the possibility of future constitutional advance along familiar lines if the Island were retained by Britain. To this end Picton was instructed to furnish a report on the Island so that appropriate constitutional alterations might in future be made. [11] In the event, with the triumph of the idea of experimentation, and of its corollary, continued imperial supervision of the closest kind, the constitution of 1801 was to become, with minor alterations, the basis of government for the next thirty years. It endured while successive British governments evinced varying degrees of interest in the Island's constitutional problems and it was only substantially modified by the introduction of a Legislative Council in 1831 which itself remained virtually unchanged for nearly a hundred years thereafter. [12]

Though the idea of experimentation was dominated, both in the minds of British ministers and of the Island's inhabitants, by thoughts relating to constitutional change, it would be a grievous error to suppose that the constitution, and that alone, were at issue. Indeed, there is a good deal of evidence in favour of the proposition that while ministers continued to hold conventional views on the subject of constitutional development in Trinidad, and believed that it would be necessary only to delay the grant of a representative Assembly for some unspecified time, other considerations were at the same time urging the growing necessity of withholding such a grant for as long as possible, probably of never making it at all. What seemed to be pre-eminently a constitutional question was really a much wider problem of social construction. What seemed to be purely a matter of constitutional contrivance in Trinidad in 1801 was to become, in reality, the problem of all the British West Indian islands, and, in some of its aspects, the problem of very many more of the colonies which Britain already possessed or was later to acquire.

The real question was: what sort of political accommodation was possible between white, planter-dominated West Indian governments and the masses of a population composed of free coloureds, slaves, and later, ex-slaves? In Trinidad, the large foreign white element pushed the dilemma still further. What sort of government was best suited to a West Indian colony the majority of whose citizens were foreign and coloured, and the majority of whose inhabitants were, taken in the aggregate, slaves? These were the questions - one general, the other particular - which were to be answered if the problems of the society then being formed were to be properly resolved.

11.   Instructions, Article 17. The report was to be under the following heads: Legislature; Executive Government; Courts of Justice; Number and different Orders of the Island's Inhabitants; Revenue; Commerce; Religion and Religious Establishments; Military; Estates of Absentees and Minors. Picton's Report is an enclosure in Picton : Hobart, 18.2.1802, C.O. 296/1; C.O. 295/2.

      See Hewan Craig: *The Legislative Council of Trinidad and Tobago* (London 1952), Chapter II.

12.   Documents relative to the introduction of the Legislative Council in 1831 are in C.O. 296/10 and C.O. 380/134.

In part the answers were political and constitutional, in part they were social, and in part, too, because of the age in which they were posed, they were exceedingly ideological.

It cannot really be said, however, that the British government acted consistently as if the problems of organization in Trinidad in 1801 were of the complexity alluded to above. To British ministers it seemed, quite incorrectly, that these were the conventional problems associated with the settlement of the government of a conquered island. True, the Island was a slave colony, but so were all Britain's previous conquests in the Caribbean; and if the slave question complicated the issue, it was not thought at first to do so unduly. Nevertheless, almost despite itself, ministerial opinion slowly became adjusted to the view that the settlement of the Island's government was a very serious matter indeed, not to be settled by quickly deciding to introduce an Assembly or by hastily conceding to either one or the other of the factions that began to dispute the form the settlement should take. The evolution of this view is itself very interesting. It had to do with problems of general and particular significance which shall later be discussed. For the moment it is sufficient to make the point merely by indicating the evolutionary nature of the thinking about the problems of Trinidad.

In the long run, there were three despatches which indicated the gradual development of British ministerial thinking about the constitutional problem in Trinidad. The first was Lord Hobart's letter to the Commissioners of government appointed in October 1802 to administer and report on the Island. [13] This letter stressed the disproportion between British and foreign whites in the Island, and argued that it was this disproportion which provided the chief reason for not immediately granting a representative form of government. The second despatch was Lord Liverpool's letter of November 27, 1810. [14] This despatch pointed to the large numbers of free coloured citizens in the Island whom it was not proposed to enfranchise (and indeed whom, Lord Liverpool said, it might be inadvisable to enfranchise), and argued that this was the chief ground for refusing representative institutions. The third despatch was Goderich's of January 30, 1832. [15] Representative institutions were refused on the ground that such a measure could only be introduced at the cost of entirely abandoning the interests of the slaves. There was, in fact, a progressive upgrading on the part of the British government of the cost of representative institutions. Much of the reason lay in the fact that, as has already been said, the reality and seriousness of the problems were for a long time incorrectly appreciated. But it also lay in the fact that, as soon as one criterion for constitutional advance was laid down, the structural complexities of the society forced other and more serious considerations to the fore. Much of the complexity of the constitutional issue derived from the fact that the British government found itself continually

13.   C.O. 296/4, Hobart : Commissioners, 16.10.1802.
14.   C.O. 296/4, Liverpool : Hislop, 27.11.1810.
15.   C.O. 296/10, Goderich : Grant, 30.1.1832.

forced to avoid taking decisions which, though once feasible, had been rendered imprudent by the progress of events. The main arguments in support of this contention will be advanced in other placed throughout this book and in particular in Chapter Four. For the time being it is intended to limit the discussion to those factors of wider significance which can be seen to have played a part in the development of the idea of experimentation.

The first problem to be resolved is that of determining the extent to which, structural complexity apart, the idea of experimentation was the product of good, old, British 'fumble' or of conscious deliberation. The temptation to give pride of place to British 'fumble' is strong; but the evidence overwhelmingly suggests that attitudes to constitutional development in Trinidad, and by extension, the attitudes to experimentation, had a more conscious origin. This is not to say that British ministers unfailingly laboured to establish the roots of what was later to become known as the Crown Colony system. They did not, and even if they did, their success owed a great deal to acts of chance and good fortune the occurrences of which could not have been foretold or reckoned upon. Nevertheless the accumulative experience of the old colonial system, the disappointments and the conflicts to which it had given rise in recent times, and, most importantly, the exigencies of the military struggle with France, highlighted again and again the great advantages to be derived from the maintenance, contrary to custom, of a greater degree of direct supervision over colonial territories than had so far obtained. It was this sentiment - at first no more than that - which gradually hardened into something near approaching a resolution as the years progressed, gave a decisive consistency to ministerial attitudes to constitutional change in Trinidad in the period 1801 to 1810, and helped to create the cornerstone of the Crown Colony system that was later to come into being.

In appreciation of this argument it is well to remember the message of Lord Hobart's letter of October 16', 1802.[16] This letter clearly indicated that the one complication steadfastly and consciously recognized by British ministers, at the time of writing, as a factor making for caution in the settlement of the Island's government, was the Island's large foreign white population. Embarrassing as this population was, however, its presence did not really constitute a novelty. If there were no reliable precedents for dealing with such a population, there were precedents nonetheless. It may have been difficult to interpret the lesson of these precedents, but the concensus might well have been that, after a period of time allowed for adjustments between the British and foreign whites, representative institutions could, with some measure of success, be granted.

Grenada in 1763 was a case in point. There, as we have seen, Britain gained a colony predominantly settled by French whites. But this had not prevented the grant of a legislative Assembly, though, as we have also seen, subsequent events were to cast grave doubts on the wisdom of the measure. [17]

16.   See note 13.   17.   *Cambridge History of the British Empire*, Vol. II, p. 151 ff.

Canada was another example. In 1760 British arms wrested from France a large expanse of territory to the north of the Thirteen Colonies peopled almost entirely by Frenchmen. Between the cession in 1763 and the Quebec Act of 1774, Canada had very much the same sort of government as that introduced in Trinidad in 1801, namely a Governor and a Council of Advice. In 1774, the Quebec Act had introduced a legislative Council, and in 1791 the Constitutional Act created two provinces, Upper and Lower Canada, and granted a legislative Assembly to each. [18] In Upper Canada this was fated to be another unhappy experience [19] and it is more than likely that the unhappy consequences of introducing the Assembly system into Grenada and Canada, the two outstanding examples in the second half of the eighteenth century of foreign populated territories passing under British rule, ultimately pre-disposed against a repetition of the experiment.

Nevertheless, Grenada and Canada, though outstanding because of their misfortunes, were not the only examples of foreign populated territories under British rule. Tobago, St. Vincent and Dominica, all ceded by France in 1763, also had large French populations. Yet, like Grenada in 1763, and like Canada in 1791, they were granted representative institutions. Thus, if anything, an important new principle of colonial government seemed to have been established. As has been pointed out, representative institutions which had formerly been regarded as *jus sanguinis,* a right of Englishmen as Englishmen, came to be acknowledged as *jus soli,* a system inherent in the territories under British sovereignty and direction".[20] By 1794, however, British military activity in the Caribbean had helped to multiply other examples of foreign populated islands under British rule. In that year, Sir Charles Grey, then commander-in-chief in the West Indies, requested that Martinique and French St. Dominigue, both in British hands, should be put on a civil and constitutional basis as soon as possible.[21] The result was a constitution that drew heavily on the experience of Canada between 1763 and 1791 and which became in time the "nucleus . . . of government in half a dozen British colonies for more than a quarter of a century".[22] Between 1801 and 1831 Trinidad was one of these colonies.

The constitution of 1794 was a careful blend of firmness and conciliation. It derived not only out of the experience of war and the prevailing wartime

18. See G.S. Graham, *British Policy and Canada, 1774-1791.* (Imperial Studies No. 4, 1930), Chapter II. Martin Wight, *The Development of the Legislative Council, 1606-1945.* (London, 1946), pp. 36-7. Also, H.B. Egerton, *A Short History of British Colonial Policy, 1606-1909.* (ed. A.P. Newton, 12th edition, London, 1950), p. 215 ff.
19. See H.T. Manning, *The Revolt of French Canada, 1800-1835,* (London, 1962), p. 64 ff.
20. Martin Wight, *op. cit.,* p. 45. Quoted.
21. *Cambridge History of the British Empire,* Vol. II, p. 151 ff.
22. H.T. Manning, *British Colonial Government after the American Revolution, 1782-1820.* (Yale University Press, 1933), p. 342.

conditions which explain its firmness, but also from the experience of Grenada and Canada and the need to treat the French in Martinique and St. Domingue as the British sympathizers which in fact they were. Thus, as in Canada between 1763 and 1774, the constitution vested all power in the hands of a Governor who was to be assisted by an advisory Council whose advice he was not compelled to accept. But whereas, in Canada, French law had, in 1763, been replaced by English law, the new constitution stipulated that the ancient laws of the two Islands should be maintained. Freedom of worship was granted to Roman Catholics and Protestant forms of worship were also allowed. Religion was no bar to civil employment; an oath patterned on that prescribed in the Quebec Act was to be taken by Roman Catholics. The old fiscal system was to be continued under the superintendence of the British Treasury, and no new taxes were to be imposed. [23] In so far as a legislative Council was not granted, it is clear that the system supplanted in Canada by the Quebec Act of 1774 was being applied to the French West Indian islands of Martinique and St. Domingue in 1794, and became the pattern for Trinidad's constitution of 1801.

In an assessment of the merit of the constitutional experience in the colonies the constitution of 1794 constitutes a clear watershed. In so far as British colonies had been invariably granted representative institutions, the new constitution was a departure from custom. That a constitution of a similar, though not identical, type had been implemented in Canada between 1763 and 1774 does little to affect this judgement: Canada had been promised an Assembly "so soon as the State and Circumstances of the said (Colony) will admit thereof ...." [24] The grant of an Assembly had been long delayed, but there had been good reasons for this. The population of Canada was wholly French at the conquest. Apart from being recent enemies in uncomfortable proximity to the North American colonies, Canada's Frenchmen were Roman Catholics, and there were many who felt, as Lord North did in 1774, that it was unsafe "for this country . . . to put the principal power into the hands of an Assembly of Roman Catholic new

23. C.H.B.E., Vol. II, pp. 154-5. For the Canadian experience see G.S. Graham, British Policy and Canada, p. 19 ff. The strength of the Canadian example was an important factor in the arrangements. It extended even to the institution of the advisory Council. The predecessor of that Council was to be found in Canada in 1764. One commentator has argued that the Canadian Council furnished "the earliest example of an institution that was to be the predominant form of the colonial council in the ensuing transition from the old representative system to the crown colony". Wight, op. cit., p. 36. Martin Wight, however, (op. cit., p. 48 ff) also speaks of the 1794 constitution as being modelled on the Quebec Act. In my opinion this constitution owes much more to the Canadian settlement of 1763 to 1774 than it does to the Quebec Act. There is, however, no question of its indebtedness to both. The omission of all references to a Council and an Assembly, and the formulation of an oath to be taken by Roman Catholics are amongst the most important provisions of the Quebec Act to be widely used in Governors' Commissions in future years. For a copy of the Quebec Act, see A.B. Keith, Speeches and Documents on Colonial Policy, 1763-1917, (World's Classics, Reprint in one volume, Oxford, 1948), pp. 53-65.

24. Keith, op. cit., p. 5.

subjects" [25] Besides, the French population of Canada had had no experience in the theory and practice of self-government. To grant an Assembly was either to render government ineffective, or to entrust the machinery of government to the tiny minority of British settlers who knew how to use it. [26] But the grant though long delayed had finally been made in 1791. The West Indian constitution of 1794, on the other hand, particularly by its extension to the other British colonies acquired during the French Revolutionary wars, marked the end of the grant of the Assembly system to British colonial territories.

That the West Indian constitutions of 1794 marked the end of an era was not of course realized by British ministers at the time. Engaged in the day to day business of imperial management, handling problems as they arose, ministers saw 1794 as only one more constitutional experience to be pressed into future service when needed. Besides, the era of the French Revolutionary and Napoleonic Wars was a transitional era and though there were many opportunities for implementing the new system a commitment to the past still persisted. Britain was after all fighting a war to preserve the past, to restore monarchy in Europe, and to reimpose slavery in the West Indies. No matter how large the extension of imperial autocracy in the new colonies, the possibility of the eventual accession of these colonies to the constitutional status of the old British possessions was not definitely ruled out until at least late as 1810.

In Trinidad, as will be seen, the British government, despite its avowals to the contrary, continued to flirt with the idea of an Assembly until 1808, only deciding against its introduction in 1810. The years between 1801 and 1810 were years of indecision, when the balance often seemed to be about to be tilted irrevocably in one direction or the other; when the notions of inherent right to representative government in the colonies that led the Whigs to castigate the Quebec Act of 1774 as incorporating the very "language of despotism" [27] seemed likely to triumph over the new notions of trusteeship and imperial responsibility for humane government in the colonies.

The difficulty of making the new policy, if policy it was, intelligible to Parliament was another problem. Parliamentary supremacy in colonial affairs had been enshrined in the Canada Constitutional Act of 1791 which had furnished the first example of the constitutional settlement of a colony by Act of Parliament.[28] Henceforth, neither Canada nor any other British

25. R. Coupland, *The Quebec Act, A Study in Statesmanship*, (Oxford, 1925), p. 99.
Egerton, *op. cit.*, pp. 206-7 puts the Protestant population of Canada in 1764 at 400. This population was mainly British. The Catholic population, mainly French, was 80,000. On p. 208 Egerton quotes from a report of 1766 in which the French population was estimated at 80,000 out of 100,000.

26. Familiarity with the Assembly system was to be the objective of French Canadians of a later age. See, Manning, *The Revolt of French Canada*, p. 64 ff.

27. Coupland, *The Quebec Act*, p. 96. Quoted.

28. Bernard Holland, *Imperium et Libertas*, (London, 1901), p. 98.

colony could easily sustain the argument that their legislature derived from the Crown, was independent of Parliament and in some ways analogous to it. [29] This was a gain for British ministerial authority. On the other hand Parliament began to take an increasing interest in colonial affairs just when the exigencies of imperial policy were forcing ministers to take decisions relating to the colonies that might be unpopular with Parliament. Being thus liable to a stricter accounting for colonial government, ministers were extremely reluctant to discuss colonial affairs in Parliament. Thus, as late as 1810 the West India Committee in London could throw the Secretary of State into a fright by merely promising to raise the Trinidad question in Parliament. [30]

As long as sentiment and parliamentary strategy continued to militate against the overt adoption of a new policy of direct control and supervision in the colonies, ministers continued to vacillate between a policy of conciliation and one of coercion. The loss of the American Colonies stimulated indecision. There were those who felt that the Thirteen Colonies could have been saved by the implementation of a more generous and flexible policy by Britain [31] and there were those who felt that a spirit of firmness and the stern exercise of imperial authority alone could save the remnants of the empire.[32] The same ministers belonged at times to both camps. Dundas for example has been depicted as the too-willing tool of the West Indian interest. [33] Yet it was Dundas who, as we shall see, went ahead with the plan to form Black Regiments in the West Indies in the face of bitter West Indian opposition. In fact, there was much to be said for both conciliation and coercion, but viewed in the perspective of history it is plain that coercion or, if one prefers, imperial reorganization, was the more dynamic idea and was destined, in the circumstances, to win out in the end. Rebellion in Ireland,[34] anarchy in India,[35] revolution in the West Indies, the need to demolish the slave trade and slavery, were all to invalidate the theory of conciliation and turn the imperial system into a full-blooded apparatus of centralized supervision.

The zenith of this system lies outside the limits of the present period. Except for the abolition of the slave trade, the major acts associated with

29. This was of course the great constitutional debate of the American Colonies prior to the Revolution. See, for example, C.H. McIlwain, *The American Revolution: A Constitutional Interpretation.* (First published 1923; reissued by Cornell University Press, 1958), *passim.* The amelioration of slavery in the West Indies was to make the supremacy of Parliament a live issue in Jamaica in 1827. Cf. Accounts *and Papers.* House of Commons. 1827-8. XXVII. No. 4, 4.12.1827. See also, R.L. Schuyler, *Parliament and the British Empire,* (New York, 1929), Chapter IV.
30. C.O. 295/24, Inglis, Marryat, Manning and Lushington to Liverpool, 4.5.1810.
31. *Cambridge History of the British Empire,* Vol II, pp. 148-9.
32. K.E. Knorr, *British Colonial Theories, 1570-1850,* (First published 1944. London, 1963), pp.212-3.
33. Fortescue, *History of the British Army,* Vol. IV, Part I, pp. 376-8; 432.
34. *Cambridge History of the British Empire,* Vol. II, pp. 130-6; 154-9.
35. *Ibid.,* pp. 139-43; 154-9.

imperial supervision of West Indian government were to come after 1812. The slave registration and amelioration programmes, the **abolition of slavery**, the institution of apprenticeship and the reorganization of post-emancipation West Indian society occurred between 1812 and 1865, if one takes the Jamaica rebellion at Morant Bay as marking the close of an epoch. [36] Yet it is possible to perceive in the Trinidad constitutional question the inception of a general movement towards the assertion of a wide-ranging imperial authority over colonial affairs.

Three of the substantial questions which help to indicate quite clearly the development of this movement towards the assertion of authority in colonial affairs, and which had a lot to do with the development of authority in Trinidad, arose out of the legal and constitutional issue of *Campbell vs Hall* in 1774, the attack on the slave trade prior to its abolition in 1807, and the conduct of the wars of the French Revolution in the West Indies.

Campbell vs Hall was important because it helped to dramatise the obstructive power of the West Indian Assembly and had helped to form an attitude of caution and watchfulness on the part of the imperial government. After granting an Assembly to Grenada in 1764, the Crown attempted to continue the imposition of the 4½% duty on exports which had been imposed by prerogative at the cession of 1763, but which had not been specifically reimposed at the moment of granting the Assembly. A planter named Campbell challenged the impost on the ground that once an Assembly had been granted legislation on such matters was the privilege of the Assembly, not of the King's prerogative, and sought a ruling in the English courts. In a celebrated decision Lord Mansfield ruled against the Crown, but drew attention to the fact that the Crown had only erred in that the Commission issued to the Governor of Grenada empowering him to summon the Assembly had not reserved any legislative rights to the King or to the Governor but had vested these in the Assembly. Hence the Crown could not now use its prerogative power to tax in Grenada. The clear implication remained, however, that if it wished the Crown could have reserved such a right. [37] Thus though the decision was a triumph for colonial intrepidity, it also gave birth to a pronounced reluctance on the part of British ministers to divest the Crown too quickly of its rights in colonies subsequently ceded to Britain.

The limitations imposed on the prerogative by grant of an Assembly were again highlighted in Grenada after 1783. The refusal of the British

---

36. See, R.L. Schuyler, *Parliament and the British Empire,* Chapter IV; F. J. Klingberg, *The Anti-Slavery Movement in England,* (Oxford University Press, 1926); W.L. Burn, *Emancipation and Apprenticeship in the British West Indies,* (London, 1937); W.L. Mathieson, *British Slavery and Its Abolition, 1823-1838,* (London, 1926); *British Slave Emancipation 1838-1849,* (London, 1932); Douglas Hall, *Free Jamaica, 1838-1865,* (Yale University Press, 1959); Philip D. Curtin, *Two Jamaicas,* (Cambridge, Mass., 1955); Roy Augier, "Before and After 1865: The Consequences of Morant Bay", *New World Quarterly,* Vol. II, No. 2, pp. 21-42.

37. A.B. Keith, *op. cit.,* pp. 35-52. Also, A. Shortt and A.G. Doughty (eds.), *Documents relating to the Constitutional History of Canada, 1759-91,* (2nd edition, Ottawa, 1918), pp. 522-31.

citizens to admit Frenchmen to the Grenada Assembly has already been dealt with as one of the causes contributing to the emigration to Trinidad in 1783 to 1797.[38] The constitutional aspect of the case was discussed by British law officers in England, and in 1790, the contention of the British inhabitants was upheld, on the ground "that when the Crown had established a constitution in 1763 it thereafter possessed no prerogative power of amendment",[39] and so could not force the admission of Frenchmen to the Assembly. The effect of this legal opinion, like Lord Mansfield's decision of 1774, was to establish that by granting representative government to a conquered colony the Crown had divested itself of further legislative power over that colony with the result that the desired legislation either had to be passed with the cooperation of the colonial legislature or by recourse to Parliament - both of which were fast becoming increasingly unpalatable alternatives.

What doubts the British government might have had about the extent of the King's prerogative power in Trinidad were resolved in 1802. In answer to a query respecting the legality of imposing the 4½% duty on exports in Trinidad, the British Attorney General submitted that no restraint existed by reason of the capitulation or any other document on the King's legislative authority in the Island.[40] The 4½% duty was not however imposed, but the 3½% duty on imports and exports which had been imposed at the conquest caused just as much discontent. Nevertheless, despite constant attack British ministers refused to countenance any argument against its legality or to recognize the need for its abolition.

The second issue was even more serious. Its relevance was much more immediate than *Campbell vs Hall* had been. It made Trinidad a key factor in one of the great debates of the time, perhaps of all time, and brought together in the most direct manner the two different but connected topics of constitutional change and experimentation. In fact, the cession of Trinidad to Britain in 1802 proved to be the forerunner to one of the high points in the conflict over the abolition of the slave trade.

The cession occurred at a time when the abolitionist movement was in the doldrums. Since 1800 the movement had gone into a prolonged period of inactivity. Outside Parliament, the circumstances were no longer receptive to agitation. The public indignation which Wilberforce and his band had successfully whipped up against the Trade by a programme of public meetings, pamphleteering, petitioning, and the organization of corresponding societies,[41] had succumbed to the reaction that followed on the news of the

38. See Chapter I.
39. *Cambridge History of the British Empire,* Vol. II, p. 152. Quoted. Wight, *op. cit.,* p. 37.
40. C.O. 295/2, Law : (Hobart), 22.3.1802. Two letters, same date.
41. See E.M. Howse, *Saints in Politics,* (Second edition, London, 1960). Also, Bryan Edwards, *op. cit., Vol. IV, pp. 307-490.*

excesses of the French Revolution across the Channel.[42] In Parliament, the strategy was, according to Clarkson, "not to press the abolition as a mere annual measure, but to allow members time to digest the eloquence, which had been bestowed upon it for the last five years, and to wait till some new circumstances should favour its introduction".[43]   Accordingly, the years 1800 to 1803 were to pass by without the customary annual notion.   In 1802, however, Trinidad became the incarnation of those "new circumstances" which were to call forth a new burst of energy directed against the slave trade.

The cession could hardly have occurred at a more propitious moment for the abolitionist cause.   The change of government in Britain had clearly indicated that the prospects for abolition had become even worse: as Wilberforce himself confessed, there now seemed to be little prospect of "affecting much through the medium of Parliament".[44]   But even before the change the abolitionists had been forced to give up all hope of securing the quick destruction of the Trade.   Their strategy had become one of badgering and harrassing it out of existence.   It was true that Wilberforce hoped to obtain government assistance in effecting abolition of the Trade by international agreement between the signatories to the Peace of Amiens.   Nevertheless, anticipating failure, he was willing to try once again to "lay this great subject before parliament . . . (and) if defeated in the main question . . . would try the subordinate ones";[45]   thus, the supply of slaves to foreigners, the exemption of certain districts around Sierra Leone, from the slave trade the occupation of Carib lands in St. Vincent, and "above all, prohibiting the Trade in slaves for clearing and opening new lands . . . which the acquisition of Trinidad renders peculiarly necessary",[46] were strategic milestones on the road to the complete extinction of the Trade.

Abolitionist strategy, therefore, turned upon the concentration on the "subordinate" questions, and among these, in 1802, Trinidad was the main objective.   Already, in 1798, Wilberforce had had to exert himself to prevent

42. P.A. Brown, *The French Revolution in English History*, (1st published 1918)*passim*; G.D.H. Cole and Raymond Postgate, *The Common People, 1746-1946*, (4th edition, 1949), Chapter XIII; Howse, *op. cit.*, pp. 39 ff, pp. 51 ff; G.S. Veitch, *The Genesis of Parliamentary Reform*, (1st published 1913; reprinted London, 1965), pp. 108 ff; S. Maccoby, *English Radicalism, 1786-1832. From Paine to Cobbett*, (London, 1955), *passim*.

43. Thomas Clarkson, *The History of the Rise, Progress and Accomplishment of the Abolition of the African Slave Trade by the British Parliament*. Two volumes. (London, 1808), Vol. I. p. 489; Howse, *op. cit.*, pp. 42-5.

44. Robert Isaac and Samuel Wilberforce, *The Life of Wilberforce*. Five volumes. (London, 1838), Vol. III, p. 30.

45. Wilberforce, *op. cit.*, p. 30.

46. *Ibid.* This was an expedience with which the abolitionists were very unhappy. Writing to Lord Muncaster on April 14, Wilberforce expressed himself as being "sick, as well as you, of half-measures, and am filled with indignation whenever I think of what is going forward all the while we are trifling and trimming between our consciences and our purses". *Life of Wilberforce*, III, p. 46.

the covert extension of the slave trade to which Pitt had almost agreed. It had been proposed that slaves be brought from the old islands to Trinidad, and to St. Vincent after the Caribs had been removed to the South American mainland. But this would have meant the extension of the slave trade to the old islands; Wilberforce thereupon prevailed on Pitt to disallow the project.[47]

Similarly, rumours that Prime Minister Addington proposed to issue commissions for the sale of lands in Trinidad and St. Vincent stimulated abolitionist anxiety, and later abolitionist action. Pitt's own reluctance to permit such sales was recalled; and comfort was taken from a recent conversation Wilberforce had had with Addington.[48] Pitt himself, aware of the general anxiety, wrote to Wilberforce on February 4, 1802 assuring him that, after a long conversation with Addington, there was every reason to believe that the latter had "in no way committed himself on any point that can lead to an increased importation of Negroes".[49] In spite of Pitt's assurances, however, Wilberforce was unconvinced, and Addington remained an unknown factor in the abolitionists' calculations.[50]

The new abolitionist assault on the Trade was initiated by George Canning in the House of Commons, on April 2,[51] in a speech which for several months made the settlement of Trinidad the central issue of the abolition controversy. It was immediately obvious that the motion was preliminary to a still more important one relative to the cultivation of the Island of which Canning had already given notice, and which was eventually debated on May 27.[52] For the moment, however, Canning was to content himself with a few requests for information about the state of agricultural enterprise in the Island.

The official position with respect to the slave trade provided the starting point for the debate of April 2. In 1792 it had been agreed in Parliament that the Trade should be gradually abolished;[53] and in 1797, an Address sponsored by the friends of the Trade, though admittedly not with the best intentions, had prayed George III to "take such measures as would lead to to the dimunition and ultimate abolition of this Trade".[54] The Address had

47.   R. Coupland, *Wilberforce*, (Oxford, 1923), pp. 273-4. Also, Howse, *op. cit.*, p. 54.
48.   Wilberforce, *op. cit.*, Vol. III, p. 36.   49.   *Ibid.*, pp. 37-8.
50.   The responsibilities of office probably had something to do with Addington's indecision. In 1799, Pitt had also earned the abolitionists' distrust. James Stephen had then written to Wilberforce, "Mr. Pitt unhappily for himself his country and mankind, is not zealous enough in the cause of the negroes, to contend for them as decisively as he ought, in the Cabinet any more than in parliament". Quoted from *Life of Wilberforce*, by Klingberg, *op. cit.*, p. 114. Addington's affliction remained with him however; as his biographer has pointed out, he consistently voted against abolition in future years. Cf. Hon. George Pellew, *The Life and Correspondence of the Right Honourable Henry Addington, First Viscount Sidmouth*. Three volumes. (London, 1847), Vol. II, pp. 445-7.
51.   *Parliamentary Register*, Lords and Commons. 3rd Series, Vol. 17, 1802, pp. 403-7.
52.   *Parliamentary Register.* Lords and Commons. Vol. 18, 1802. The full debate is on pp. 535-65.
53.   *Parliamentary Register.* Lords and Commons. 3rd Series. Vol. 17, 1802, p. 403; See, too *Ibid.*, Vol. 18, p. 540. See also, Coupland, *The British Anti-Slavery Movement, p. 99.*
54.   *Parliamentary Register.* Vol. 17, 1802, p. 403.

been, in fact, an attempt by the West India interest to allay by deception any more effective means for the suppression of the Trade. It was not in the interest of the abolitionists, however, to affect to see anything but un-animous agreement on the issue of ultimate abolition, and Canning did not. Both his motions of April and May merely dealt with the implications for ministerial action of an agreement which he took to be beyond dispute.

Given the understanding reached in the House on ultimate abolition, there was, in Canning's opinion, an obvious need for the rationalization of the relationship between the alienation of agricultural land in Trinidad and the capability of the existing slave population to farm that land. In other words, only so much land should be released for cultivation by the govern-ment as could reasonably be cultivated by slaves already resident in the Island. If it was intended, on the other hand, to promote the cultivation of Trinidad by increased importations of slaves then the slave trade would, quite obviously, be enormously extended. Not only should care be taken to prevent the extension of the slave trade as the consequence of the economic development of Trinidad, but the wider question of the use to which new acquisitions should be put seemed also to be raised. Current opinion was that the slave trade and slavery were indispensable to the material develop-ment of the colonial empire. But conquests and acquisitions, the results of war, should not be allowed adversely to affect the gradual abolition of the Trade to which Parliament was already committed. Restricting the argument to a simple syllogistic formula, he reminded the House that it had given an undertaking to affect the gradual abolition of the Trade; to extend slavery to Trinidad as the principal if not the exclusive means of cultivating the Is-land's new lands would be to encourage the extension of the Trade; hence, the alienation of new lands in Trinidad should be kept in strict proportion to the means then existing to cultivate them.

The experience of Jamaica, in 1795, had been that 250,000 slaves were needed to cultivate the one million acres of agricultural then estimated to be in Jamaica; a ratio of one slave to every four acres of land. Trinidad, with its estimated 800,000 acres [55] of which at the conquest only one-eighteenth was in a state of cultivation, employing some 10,000 slaves, had a ratio of about one slave per acre. Proportionately then, whatever the final figure, such a large number of additional slaves would be needed as to make the slave trade a very profitable business indeed. [56] As for the anti-abolitionist

55. This figure was an underestimate. But contemporary figures fluctuated widely. One estimate gave 1,287,680 acres, another 1,536,000. (Cf. W.H. Burnley, Observations on the Present condition of ... Trinidad ... (London, 1842), p. 107. A modern assessment gives the total area as 1,192,845 acres with about 339,000 acres fit for cultivation. An Economic Survey of the Colonial Territories, 1951 (London, H.M.S.O., 1953), Vol. IV.

56. Sir William Young as we have seen averaged imports between 1797 and 1802 at 4,500 annually in spite of the strictures on the trade. The trade became more not less profitable even after its abolition in 1807. See, Eric Williams, "The Intercolonial Slave Trade after its Abolition in 1807." Journal of Negro History, Vol. 27, 1942, pp. 175-92.

argument that abolition would irreparably harm the interests of West Indian proprietors, Canning mentioned it only to obliterate it at once. He was, he said, very mindful of those interests, so much so that it was precisely because there was, at that time, so little British property invested in the Island that he thought it to be eminently fair to prospective investors to have government enunciate at once a policy which would save them from taking untoward financial risks. [57]

Another point to be considered was the existence in Trinidad of Spanish laws facilitating the resumption of lands which had not been put in a proper state of cultivation. He wished to know what were the criteria by which resumption was determined. If, as he suspected, the criteria centered on the amount of labourers employed on the land in question, and if the land was liable to resumption if inadequately cultivated, then the question to be decided was what was the optimum relationship between land and labour if the land were to be properly cultivated. The Jamaica example had suggested one slave for every four acres; accurate figures should be acquired with respect to Trinidad, so that a proper policy pertaining to land use could be devised and implemented. [58]

The abolitionists' demand, as voiced by Canning, was that the government should supply a full account of all information transmitted by the Governor since the conquest with respect to the population and cultivation of the Island; of the relationship between the labouring population and agricultural land; of the plans for proposed allottment and distribution of land that had been or were to be transmitted to the Governor. In addition a detailed record of all grants, sales, settlements or resumptions of land that occurred since the conquest, and the criteria and authority by which they were made, should be supplied. [59]

This the government professed itself unable to do. The information, said Prime Minister Addington, just did not exist. And, though he realised the necessity of such data as an aid to forming "a correct opinion of the value of that important acquisition", [60] he could not but say that the most diligent enquiry had produced no information of the sort for which Canning had asked. No information was available, nor could then be made available on resumptions, sales, grants or anything else; but the Secretary of State would be directed to do everything "that could be reasonably expected". [61] Apart from this, however, he had no objection to the motion!

Even so, the anti-abolitionists were determined to extract their pound of flesh. Canning had said in the course of his speech that among the great variety of opinions about abolition "he had never heard anyone attempt to maintain that, if the Slave Trade did not now exist, it ought to be commenced" [62] General Gascoyne, Member for Liverpool, said that Canning was

57. *Parliamentary Register.* Vol. 17, p. 404; also, Vol. 18, pp. 539, 541, 546.
58. *Ibid.,* Vol. 17, pp. 404-5; Vol. 18, pp. 543-5. 59. *Ibid.,* Vol. 17, pp. 404-5.
60. *Ibid.,* Vol. 17, p. 406. 61. *Ibid., loc. cit.* 62. *Ibid.,* Vol. 17, p. 403.

CHAPTER 3

wrong. He, Gascoyne, would have maintained precisely that. He was always mystified why anyone should want to hinder or abolish a trade that was obviously so beneficial to Britain. In any case, it was his opinion that unilateral abolition by Britain would serve little purpose; at that very instant, he said, other countries were making every effort to extend the Trade. As for restricting its application to one island, he thought it most injurious for Parliament to embark on piecemeal interference with the Trade. He proposed instead to lay before the House an account of the produce of the West Indian islands in coffee, rum, sugar, cotton, etc., to show how prodigiously these had increased of late and to call the attention of Members to a proper appreciation of their interest. [63]

Despite this defiant advocacy of the anti-abolitionist cause Canning's motion was passed, largely because Addington had shown it to be so harmless. The abolitionists were in despair. The indifference of the government, the still implacable hostility of the slave traders, the weakness of the abolitionist position, all had been revealed. No wonder that Wilberforce continued to be apprehensive, and to lament the possibility that the character of Parliament should further be sullied "if, after having resolved by an immense majority that the Slave Trade should be gradually abolished, we should enter on the cultivation of a new settlement, the complete peopling of which, with negro slaves, reckoning the number always lost in opening uncleared lands, would take over a million beings." [64]

The certainty of the debate on Canning's motion seeking to prevent the cultivation of Trinidad, except under the most rigorous conditions, itself seemed to be in doubt. The debate was twice deferred, then fixed for May 13, and again postponed. When it was finally taken on May 27, 1802, [65] Canning's contribution was as incisive, brilliant and well reasoned, as Addington's was evasive, fumbling and obtuse. Perhaps, after all, Addington's statement was the high point of the debate; few British Prime Ministers could ever have delivered themselves of a sorrier pronouncement. Canning's case, simply stated, clearly put, revolved around the new factor which the conquests of the recent wars had injected into the consideration of the slave question, and was really only an erudite extension of his April debate. But, following the abolitionist strategy of tilting only at the subordinate questions, he took care to point out that his motion had nothing to do with the abolition of the slave trade; he was concerned only to prevent its extension. Thus he proclaimed:

63. *Ibid.,* Vol. 17 p. 407
   Gascoyne's point about the injudiciousness of piecemeal interference with the slave trade was to gain powerful support later. A legal opinion of 1806 pointed out that Trinidad could only be excluded from the operation of the slave trade by Act of Parliament, not by the use of the King's prerogative. C.O. 295/15, Piggott : Windham, 25.6.1806; Piggott : Privy Council, 3.6.1806.
64. Wilberforce, *op. cit.,* Vol. III, p. 37.
65. *Parliamentary Register.* Vol. 18, pp. 535-65.

"I have nothing to do with the slave trade ... carried on for the supply of our already existing establishments in the West Indies; I have no thought of invading or endangering the vested interests of West India proprietors .... Whatever may be the fate of the existing slave trade, the question of creating a new slave trade for the cultivation of new land in a new colony is fit matter for separate discussion; and the question of, whether this be the only, or the best mode of turning the Island of Trinidad to good account? (sic) is one which it becomes us seriously to investigate, and to investigate *now*". [66]

This was a statement of abolitionist tactics no less than of abolitionist belief.

Addington for his part lamented the unfortunate timing of the motion; found it difficult to "see how this question could be fairly discussed without entering upon the general question at large"; [67] thought it in bad taste that such a proposition should be brought forward so soon after the cession of Trinidad to Britain, "although the general question upon the trade to which the proposition referred had been allowed to sleep for five or six years"; [68] swore that when he had given instructions for the proceeds of the sale of uncleared lands in the colonies to be used for the "relief of the pressure ... arising from the present charges on this country ... the Island of Trinidad was not then in his contemplation"; [69] and finally wondered aloud as to what the motion really did mean. It was not a call for immediate abolition; it did not hasten the object of gradual abolition, and even if it did, the circumstances in which the House had given that pledge had changed. Parliament had been prevented by the recent War from fulfilling its pledge. [70] By now confining a vote to Trinidad he could not see how that pledge could even be partly redeemed and therefore could see no reason for assenting to it. [71]

Addington had of course deliberately evaded the issue. The object was not the abolition of the slave trade, gradual or otherwise, but to secure the pledges of the House from violation by preventing the extension of the trade. While it was therefore arguable that any attempt at piecemeal abolition had the ultimate extinction of the trade in view, Addington could only rebut the abolitionist argument by repudiating the pledges already made by Parliament. This he came very near doing. Canning, he said, was entitled to know what was being done about those pledges; was even entitled to ask why they were not yet carried out; but this motion only convinced him that any attempt to prohibit the extension of the slave trade to Trinidad would injure it in other quarters. It was not wise to adopt this motion now; now that St. Domingue was at the ebb of its productive powers, it was unthinkable that Parliament should sanction "this premature check upon the cultivation of the island of Trinidad". [72]

66. *Ibid.*, p. 539.   67. *Ibid.*, p. 556.
68. *Ibid., loc. cit.*   69. *Ibid.*, p. 557.
70. *Ibid., loc. cit.*   71. *Ibid., loc. cit.*   72. *Ibid.*, p. 558.

CHAPTER 3

Besides, there were many difficulties. Even if the importation of African slaves were stopped, Parliament could not intervene to prevent importations from the other West Indian islands; to do this would be to prejudice at once the wider question. And as he had claimed to have made an exception of Trinidad from his scheme for raising money from the sales of uncleared lands, so now he exempted Trinidad from the customary laws of slave agriculture. He had it on the best authority that Trinidad was a different island from all the rest. Less than half the number of Negroes used in any other West Indian island would yield twice the volume of produce when set to work in Trinidad; "the labour of forty negroes would be more than equal to that of one hundred in any other island, except Jamaica".[73] Trinidad's soil was good, the quality of its canes excellent; crop culture was hardly needed.

After all this, to the amazement of the House, and to the discomfiture of General Gascoyne, Addington agreed to the motion. Gascoyne, consistent to the end, went on record as saying that "it was necessary, for the support of our West India Colonies, that the slave trade should be increased instead of being abolished."[74] And Wilberforce remembering the previous conduct "of the Right Honourable Gentleman himself" and the manner in which the fairest prospects held out by Addington were wont to end in disillusion, despaired aloud amidst vociferous calls to order by General Gascoyne.[75] Thus the motion was passed and the House was pledged not to permit the alienation of lands in Trinidad except on stated terms.

The enunciation of these terms had been the climax of Canning's opening speech. He had called for a totally new conception of West Indian society. He had urged the abandonment of the slave trade as a first step towards the construction of a society based not on coercion and cruelty, but on freedom and liberty. In this he was at one with James Stephen the elder who, in a series of four letters, addressed to Prime Minister Addington in early 1802,[76] had urged a similar programme of reconstruction. If the Haitian revolt had done nothing else, said Stephen, it had destroyed forever the whole psychological paraphernalia of inferiority which, as much as anything else, had kept the slave in subjection to his master. No longer would the slave cow in dread of those "nameless dreadful consequences" which careful indoctrination had taught him to expect as the fruit of revolt against his master. He had been taught that white slavemasters could be confronted in arms with success, and without the dire consequences "at which the soul was formerly appalled".[77] As Canning too had said, security and self-interest, and the need to eliminate as quickly as possible those internal weaknesses by which a population was created which had to be defended on

---

73. *Ibid.*, p. 560.   74. *Ibid.*, p. 564.
75. *Ibid.*, pp. 564-5.
76. James Stephen, *The Crisis of the Sugar Colonies.* . . . . . (London, 1808).
77. Stephen, *op. cit.*, p. 72.

the one hand and suppressed on the other, [78] had made it imperative that a new basis of social organization be found at once in the West Indies.

The urgency of this argument was one which Canning, Stephen and the whole abolitionist host hoped would recommend itself to all those who would, perhaps, have opposed the limitation of the slave trade on every other ground. Napoleon's expeditionary force was even then busily engaged trying to reimpose slavery in St. Dominigue. [79] If it succeeded, Napoleon's attention would turn to the British West Indies, and the creaking Peace of Amiens would collapse in a new and expensive war; a society of free men would be the surest guarantee against the success of such an assault. [80] And if it failed, West Indian slavery was bound to become insupportable. [81]

Canning had also urged the encouragement of new classes of settlers to cultivate Trinidad; *peons* from the South American mainland and free blacks and creoles from the other islands. The labour and industry of Trinidad's native Indians should be encouraged. Similarly, soldiers of regiments stationed in the West Indies should be urged to become cultivators in the Island, irrespective of whether they were British or foreign; it mattered only that they were free. [82] These, and not "capitalists" [83] battening on the labour of vast organized gangs of slaves should be granted land. [84] At the same time, earnest attempts should be made to diversify West Indian agriculture beginning in Trinidad. Cattle raising, the cultivation of crops other than sugar, all these were worthy objects of West Indian endeavour possessing the great merit of dispensing with the continuing need for slave labour. [85] "But no; set the Britisher before a commercial dictionary," he perorated, "and there finding, under the head West-India island, the word *sugar*, and under sugar the word *slave*, you will look no further; sugar cultivation and slave trade will comprise the whole of your boasted policy, and Trinidad will be cleared and cultivated by labour from Africa, like all your other settlements, and brought, as quickly as possible, to the same state of wealth and weakness that belongs to them." [86] Here through one of its noblest representatives, speaks the voice of nineteenth century British liberalism urging a policy of experimentation which was ultimately to result in the abandonment of the Assembly system in the interests of the unrepresented majority of Trinidad's citizens. [87]

From the government Canning demanded an assurance that grants or sales of land in Trinidad would be authorized only on the expressed condition that "no negro to be thenceforth imported from Africa shall be employed

78. *Parliamentary Register.* Vol. 18, p. 548.
79. See, for example, C.L.R. James, *The Black Jacobins,* Chapters XII and XIII.
80. *Parliamentary Register.* Vol. 18, p. 548.
81. Stephen, *op. cit.*, pp. 77-111; *passim.*   82. *Parliamentary Register.* Vol. 18, pp. 550-1.
83. Canning's word, not mine; in the circumstances used with disdain. *Ibid.*, p. 550.
84. *Ibid.*, p. 550.   85. *Ibid., loc. cit.*   86. *Ibid.*, p. 549.
87. Canning's effort on this occasion was one of his noblest, sullied only by his known contempt for Addington. Sir Charles Petrie, in his *Life of George Canning,* (London, 1932), p. 37, has pointed out that his motives might well have been as much political as they were philanthropic.

on those lands,"[88] and on the understanding that if the condition were violated, the land would be resumed; that no grants or sales should be made until Parliament could make proper provision for the "prohibition, limitation, or regulation" of slave imports into the Island from Africa ; and that a plan of regulations for the cultivation and improvement of Trinidad in a manner least likely to interfere with the pledges of the House on the slave trade, and conducive to the stability and security of the colonies and their interests, be laid before the House.[89] Addington in his turn pledged that no grants would be made that would discourage the influx of free settlers into the Island, and eliminate the possibility of laying a new basis for the formation of a new society.[90] And he announced that it was the government's intention to send out a Commission for the purpose of acquiring all the information which would be needed to make a decision about the Island's political future.[91] A geographical survey which was already made would help the government determine what should be done about the other demands Canning had made.[92]

As will be seen, the scheme never got off the ground. The Commission was sent out, but soon disintegrated; the ambitious plans for settlement and redevelopment which were associated with it were abandoned or scrapped. As for land grants, none were made during the period 1801 to 1810. Land was given on a temporary basis, with no real title to it. Even so the purpose of Canning's demand, that grants and sales should be rigorously controlled, was not kept in view. After 1805, planters began to get additions to their holdings on the ground that improvements, or the extension of slave provision grounds, were necessary; no one stopped to question the increase in the slave population which necessitated such improvements or extensions.[93]

88. *Parliamentary Register.* Vol. 18, p. 554
89. *Ibid., loc. cit.*   90. *Ibid.,* p. 562.   91. *Ibid.,* pp. 560-1.
92. A possible reference to Mallet's survey. See also, C.O. 296/1, Picton : Hobart, 11.11.1797.
93. The first planter to get an addition to his holding under the new terms was Samuel Span, a Bristol merchant with large holdings in the quarter of Tacarigua. Two conditions were attached to the grant: first, that it was used only for the upkeep of his existing slave population, not for new imports: secondly, that he entered security of £3,000 not to import new slaves, and used the land only for extending provision-grounds, erecting new buildings and improving new ones. C.O. 295/11: C.O. 296/4, Camden : Hislop, 25.2.1805. The Span grant let loose a flood of similar applications, many from prominent officials in the Island, as for example, Attorney General Gloster. Sir·Alexander Cochrane, later naval commander-in-chief in the West Indies, and some of the larger commercial firms also put in claims. Cf. C.O. 295/17. Gloster : Castlereagh, 13.6.1807; C.O. 295/20, Cochrane : Castlereagh, 30.1.1808: C.O. 295/17, Petition of Eccles & Co., dated 12.5.1807. In 1809 a report by the Governor showed that 147,437¾ acres of land had been granted by the Spanish Government. Since the conquest, 41,609 acres had been held in occupancy for use as provision-grounds, and 28,017 acres petitioned for were not yet occupied. In addition the Governor claimed that the policy of permitting land to be held in occupancy for use as provision-grounds had begun paying dividends: during the American embargo the Island had been almost self-supporting in foodstuffs derived from these lands. C.O. 295/21. Hislop : Castlereagh, 1.7.1809, No. 66: Also, C.O. 295/20, Hislop : Castlereagh, 22.2.1809, No. 50; C.O. 295/23, Tolley : Liverpool, 7.3.1810, No. 5.

The confusion prevailing in land tenureship later led to the appointment of a commissioner to investigate the problem. See *Parliamentary Papers.* House of Commons. 1826-7. (478) XXIII. "Report of the Commissioner of Enquiry on the Subject of Titles to Lands in the Island of Trinidad."

Yet the government was committed to a particular task of reassessment an innovation in Trinidad. For this it was necessary to retain effective political power in the hands of the Crown. And though the objectives of Canning's two speeches were ignored, their general effect was to prolong the period of direct imperial supervision and to temper the slave system in the Island. The fact that land grants were only temporary and could be revoked mollified the behaviour of the most ruthless slavemaster. The tone of Canning's speeches set the pattern for future years. Trinidad came to be regarded as a hothouse for the germination of ideas associated with the liquidation of slavery; hence, for instance, the attempt at Chinese immigration in 1806, [94] and Isaac Hartman's proposal for the establishment of a manorial system in the Caroni district to be developed by both slave and free labour. [95] An indirect but important effect of the Canning plan lay in the fact that the failure of the Commission sent out to implement it resulted in the development of strong local interests in favour of a nominated legislature, and this at a time when a united demand for representative institutions might just possibly have succeeded.

The third formative influence making for experimentation, the influence of the French Revolution, was narrowly limited to the constitutional sphere. What seemed to be at stake in Britain's relations with her West Indian colonies in wartime was the extent of control at the disposal of the mother country in pursuing the objects of the war. Because of this the French Revolution was important for two reasons. First of all, during the war years, in the conquered colonies, the severity of the conflict sanctioned a form of superintendence over West Indian affairs which the imperial power was loathe to relinquish thereafter. Secondly, it unfavourably highlighted the obstructionist tendencies of the West Indian Assemblies which came to be regarded in wartime as sources of grave embarrassment, if not of positive risk. In Trinidad, because of the large foreign population and the suspicion of republicanism under which the population laboured, security became the criterion of good government. Firm, even despotic rule was the first priority. And, in contrast with the strict control possible in Trinidad, the wayward self-seeking of the Assemblies was to draw much unfavourable comment and to help create a climate in favour of much firmer government in the colonies.

From the inception of the war against France Britain became obsessed with the need for a vigorous campaign in the West Indies. It was the acceptance of the over-riding importance of such a campaign which set the stage for West Indian interference in the course of the war. Popular and official sentiment in England were at one in conceding the paramountcy of a West Indian strategy; but popular and official sentiment seem to have been wrong. [96] Even Bryan Edwards who, as we have seen, criticised the manner

94. See below, Chapter 7, pp. 215 - 6.   95. C.O. 295/25, Hartman : Perceval, 1.8.1810.
96. Holden Furber, *Henry Dundas, First Viscount Melville 1742-1811*, (London, 1931), pp. 98-9. See also, *Cambridge History of the British Empire*, Vol. II, p. 42 ff; 62-3.

in which the battle was waged, never doubted the premises on which that struggle was founded. Edwards accepted the validity of the West Indian strategy and criticised it within the framework of that belief. Others have since, however, attacked the belief itself.

Dundas's biographer has attacked him for his "conservative trend of mind . . . (his) thraldom (to) the old ideas of the importance of the French West Indies, ideas which dated back to the Seven Years' War and before",[97] and for his conviction that decisive victories in the West Indies could cripple French republicanism in Europe, and has castigated "that most fatal tenacity"[98] with which he held to his faith. J.W. Fortescue, historian of the British Army, uttered criticisms of a similar sort though he chose, because of his low estimate of Dundas, to criticise Pitt instead.[99] On Pitt he cried abundant shame, and taunted his determination to strike at France in the West Indies - to strike on the "tip of the tail, when what was needed was a blow at the heart".

"Pitt", he said, "was fascinated by the idea of the West Indies, and would think of nothing else. He knew, or might have known, that the commerce of the French West Indies was already half ruined, the plantations burned, and the slaves in revolt. He knew, or should have known, that in the West Indies he would have to contend, not with the troops of an effete monarchy, but with three hundred thousand negroes, fighting men of ferocious bravery, drunk with the blood of white men, maddened by the sense of freedom, and not likely to submit tamely to the soldiers of slave owners like the British. He knew, or should have known, that even if he mastered the French islands, he would need large garrisons to hold them; and that his soldiers would die like flies, while the black would thrive unharmed. He knew or thought of none of these things; he consulted no military men; and by his ignorance and thoughtlessness he paralysed the arm of England during six fateful years".[100]

Fortescue was, of course, only partly right. Misconceived as Pitt's strategy was, it had its logic; and if Pitt was wrong, so too were the French. Pitt's object was no less than the destruction of the trading power of France and the consolidation of British commercial strength at the expense of an

---

97   Furber, *op. cit.*, p. 98.

98.   Furber, *op. cit.*, p. 99.

99.   *The British Army, 1783-1802*, p. 37. Dundas, says Fortescue, was "a hard drinker and a hardened jobber, with a genial manner, incredible conceit, and convenient absence of principle. He knew no more of war than a monthly nurse, but had not the wisdom even to be conscious of his ignorance. Yet Pitt believed in him implicitly then and to the last. . . ." A more favourable view of Dundas is given by another of his biographers who says of him, that he never wished the War Office, and remained "only at the express wish of his colleagues and the King". Cyril Mathieson, *The Life of Henry Dundas First Viscount Melville*. (London, 1933) p. vii, Preface. Also, pp. 222-3, and Chapter XII on the war objectives and the W.I. campaigns.

100. *The British Army 1783-1802*, pp. 37-8.

old rival. [101]   And French efforts were largely directed towards the attainment of a similar objective., This apart, however, the constitutional significance of Pitt's plan is to be found in the fact that war in the West Indies, in the circumstances of the French Revolution, meant not only the assumption of a conciliatory posture to West Indian governments, but also the participation of the West Indian Assemblies in some aspects of that war.

The stress of war produced several occasions of conflict.   There was the difficulty of correctly assessing the military priorities, a difficulty made all the more critical by the feeling in each island that its own defence should be the prime object of the war.   There was the inevitable bickering over expenditure between the metropolitan and colonial governments.   There was, too, the questionable military authority of the islands' Governors who, as commanders-in-chief under their Commissions, interfered with the conduct of operations whenever they could. [102]   And the legislatures never hesitated to obstruct the enforcement of unpopular measures.   In Grenada in 1795, the legislature refused to permit the proclamation of martial law, agreeing finally only when General Irving threatened to withdraw the troops from the Island. [103]   But none of these collisions was quite as crucial as those provoked by the attempts to raise West Indian regiments of Negro troops, and to settle in the British colonies some of Britain's allies from St. Domingue.

Almost as soon as the West Indian campaign began Britain conceived the idea of raising some regiments of Negro troops to aid in the defence of the islands. [104]   The fatal liability of European soldiers to tropical diseases was only one of the reasons for the new policy. Campaigns in other parts of the world stretched British military reserves to the breaking point.   The usual sources of supply were drying up. Irish troops were less in numbers than before, and were poorer in quality. [105]   Military commitments in Europe meant that no troops could be dispatched to the West Indies, and even if they could be, raw recruits unused to the West Indian climate stocked the hospitals and nothing else. [106]   By 1799, the composition of the majority of the troops in

101. J. Steven Watson, *op. cit.,* p. 370. The cost of the West Indian campaign can be determined by a comparison of the losses in Europe and the West Indies. In the Peninsular War, says Steven Watson, Wellington lost less than 40,000 men from all causes. In the West Indies by 1796 there were 40,000 dead, and 40,000 unfit for service.
102. Perhaps the Fort George issue in Trinidad is as good an example as any of the conflicts likely to arise on this score. It is a story on its own. See: C.O. 318/25, p. 321, Myers: Camden, 30.7.1804, p. 5; C.O. 318/27, p. 13, Meyers : Camden, 12.3.1805, No. 53; C.O. 295/9, Hislop : Camden, 10.12.1804; C.O. 295/9, Hislop : Camden, 18.12.1804; C.O. 318/27, Camden : Myers (Draft), 18.4.1805. See also, H.O. 30/1, pp. 157-9, Brownrigg : Huskisson, 14.11.1795, for an early ruling on the subject.
103. Fortescue, *History of the British Army.* Vol. IV, Part I, pp. 455-6.
104. H.O. 30/1, Dundas : Williamson, 17.4.1795; Balcarres : Dundas, 29.11.1795.
105. H.O. 30/1, pp. 208-15. Extracts from Private and Confidential Letters from the Lord Lieutenant, of Ireland, January 1795. H.O. 30/2, Huskisson : King (Private & Secret), 13.11.1799.
106. H.O. 30/1, p. 88, Abercromby: Huskisson, 20.2.1797.

the West Indies provided an accurate index of the prevailing crisis: they were in the main *"blacks, foreigners* and *Irish Rebels"*. [107]

In 1795, soundings were made of West Indian opinion in England, and a paper was submitted by the Secretary of State for War and the Colonies on the subject. [108] The West Indian proprietors living in England, and the West Indian agents, were confident that 3,000 Negro troops could be easily raised with the cooperation of the island legislatures. It was not the first, nor was it to be the last time that West Indian opinion in London and the other British cities completely misjudged the reaction of the West Indian Assemblies.

Details of the new policy were outlined by Dundas in 1796, [109] and in January 1797 Abercromby circularised the West Indian Assemblies on the matter. [110] It was intended to raise five regiments of black troops each of a strength of five hundred men. For the purposes of recruitment, each island was to be allotted a quota to be filled in part by enlistment of free people of colour, the rest of the quota to be made up by outright purchase of slaves from the various islands at a price not exceeding £70 each. [111] The costs of purchase were to be borne by the British treasury; the costs of supply and upkeep were to be a charge on both the British and West Indian governments.

In Barbados the reaction to these proposals was swift and ominous. The Council promised its assistance. In the Assembly, however, the Speaker himself, Sir John Gay Alleyne, led the opposition to the scheme. A series of resolutions were passed *nem. con.* by the Assembly deprecating the measure. It was argued that raising regiments of Negro troops was more likely to prove the means of the Island's destruction than of its defence; that able bodied Negroes were the "worst of characters", and that since they were "the objects of the message" the result of the scheme could only be murder, destruction and ruin; and that even if these evils did not ensue, "yet the lesser evil of negro-men raised to a condition so superior to their fellow slaves, will be severely felt, as loosening the Bonds of that present subordination which so happily subsists throughout the Island, not less to the ease and comfortable support of the Negro Slaves themselves, than to the Profit and Satisfaction of their various Proprietors. . ." [112] Thus Barbados had to be excluded from the scheme.

107. H.O. 30/2, Huskisson : King (Private and Secret), 13.11.1799. Huskisson's emphasis.
108. H.O. 30/1, Dundas : Portland, 26.8.1795.
109. The despatches contain no direct reference to the new policy but Abercromby who left England for the West Indies in November 1796 seems to have had oral instructions from Dundas to carry out such a plan.   110. W.O. 1/86, p. 47. Circular letter from Abercromby.
111. W.O. 1/86, pp. 59-60; 63; 67-8 containing instructions for the purchase of the Negroes.
112. W.O. 1/86, pp. 51-7, Ricketts : Abercromby, 18.1.1797: Resolutions of the Assembly enclosed, dated 17.1.1797. See also, W.O. 40/9. p. 1. And, Bryan Edwards, *op. cit.*, Vol. IV, pp. 91-102.

Details of the proposals were then issued to the Army Officers [113] who were expected to aid in the recruitment, and a contract was given to James Bontein, Esq., to raise 2,500 black or coloured troops. [114] And on January 23, the Governors and Presidents of the Islands, Barbados excluded, were again circularised. [115] The response to this initiative was no more encouraging. The Islands objected to the form of the proposals, the cost of the slaves, and indicated a general unwillingness to comply; the plan had failed. [116] Abercromby wrote again merely recommending the measure and leaving the method of enlistment to the Islands themselves. [117] He was determined that the plan should not be abandoned because of differences over procedure: "the Islands shall be indulged in any ways they please, provided we get the Men at Seventy Pounds Ster'g each; which is a Sum that might not be exceeded". [118] Still the Assemblies held out, and what could not be done by design eventually had to be done by deception. The government imported Negroes direct from Africa taking every possible precaution to conceal the fact, and by July 1798, Black troops were formed and quartered in Dominica. [119]

Jamaica was Barbados and the other Islands writ large. In 1795, the Earl of Balcarres, then Governor, had written of the general hostility to the idea of raising Negro troops, [120] and the plan had not then been pressed. However, in January 1797, the British government intimated its anxiety about the measure. [121] The central contention was the increasing difficulty of supplementing the West Indian forces by recruitment from Europe. It was feared that in cases of emergency it would no longer be possible to augment the West Indian soldiery with "promptitude and effect". And it was particularly necessary that reinforcements should be speedily available for any Island under attack since the spread of republican ideology had brought Britain face to face with "a new and certainly more powerful enemy, than any we have ever yet had to encounter". On every consideration of policy the recruitment of Negro troops was viewed as absolutely imperative. Portland's call was repeated by the commander-in-chief, Frederick Duke of York, who recommended the raising of black troops on grounds of the most urgent military necessity. [122]

113. W.O. 1/86, pp. 59-60; 63; 67-8; 71-3.
114. W.O. 1/86, pp. 67-8. Agreement between Abercromby and James Bontein Esq.
115. W.O. 1/86, p. 75.   116. *Ibid.,* pp. 211-2, Abercromby : Dundas, 19.3.1797.
117. *Ibid.,* pp. 215-6, Abercromby : (No name), 20.3.1797.
118. *Ibid.,* pp. 211-2, Abercromby : Dundas, 19.3.1797.   119. Fortescue, *op. cit.,* Vol. IV, Part I, p. 543.
120. H.O. 30/1, Balcarres : Dundas, 29.11.1795.
121. C.O. 140/78, *Journals of the Assembly of Jamaica,* Vol. IX, p. 645, Portland : Balcarres, January, 1797, See, also Helen Taft Manning, *British Colonial Government after the American Revolution,* p. 240 ff.
122. C.O. 140/78, p. 645, Brownrigg (for Duke of York) : Balcarres, 9.1.1797.

CHAPTER 3

Balcarres found the Assembly unmoved by the messages of Portland and the Duke of York. At a meeting on Friday July 28, 1797, the Assembly condemned the proposal on three grounds. It was contrary to the Island's laws which specifically prohibited the arming of slaves. It was contrary to the Island's policy of maintaining "the distinction and subordination of ranks, by which the peace, good order, and safety of this island, have hitherto . . . been preserved" and which would be subverted by the ambitions to which serving in the regular army would give rise. In any case it was bound to affect the coloured people who "whilst they remain enrolled in the militia, preserve the ideas of colonial subordination . . . whereas, if they should be embodied as regulars, they would entertain notions of equality, and acquire habits pernicious to the welfare of the country". [123]

This uncompromising refusal by the Jamaica Assembly dismayed official opinion in England. Portland contented himself with an expression of shock at the Island's stand. [124] The Duke of York, unfettered by political responsibility, observed with characteristic military bluntness that he could not see how a measure, recommended by every officer of rank and experience of the West Indies, could "be relinquished to gratify the ungrounded apprehensions of a few". [125] For his part all the relevant considerations had already been examined. It was certain that Britain could no longer undertake the manning of West Indian forces with European troops. Levies of Negro troops just had to be made. [126]

In the late months of 1797 there was every indication of a growing crisis. In November Portland informed Balcarres that he had recently received a legal opinion on the only objection of substance the Assembly had made, that was, that an Act passed by the colonial legislature in December 1796 had made it illegal for Negroes to bear arms. Legal opinion was that the Act could not be construed as in any limiting the Crown's prerogative to provide for the defence of the Island as it saw fit. [127] This opinion, and the timing of the despatch are of some importance, for Portland wrote after and not before a conciliatory gesture had been made in England.

The representatives of the Jamaican interest in London had acted once more. They had approached Portland with the request that Jamaica should be allowed to raise and supply a defence force of white soldiers as an alternative to the proposed scheme of Negro recruitment. [128] Portland was de-

123. C.O. 140/78, *Assembly Journal,* Vol. IX, pp. 647-8.
124. C.O. 138/42, Portland : Balcarres, 9.8.1797.
125. C.O. 140/89, p. 5. Duke of York : Balcarres, 1.8.1797.
126. Contemporary evidence suggests that this was a correct judgement. An anonymous report on Jamaica written at about the same time pointed out that the question was not whether Negro troops were desirable; it was whether they were necessary. And to that question the answer must be "yes". See C.O. 137/122. Report at the back of the volume.
127. The Act was passed on 21.12.1796. See, C.O. 138/42, Portland : Balcarres, 4.11.1797.
128. C.O. 138/42, Portland : Balcarres, 12.9.1797.

lighted with the offer; in the coming months he was to display an eagerness for compromise that was not entirely matched by the Jamaican Assembly. Just as evident was his delight in the possibility of shifting on to Jamaica not simply "a considerable share of the expence" [129] of the Island's defence, as he had once hoped, but all of it. He wrote to Balcarres instructing him to use all his powers of persuasion to extract a formal offer of 4,000 troops. This the British government would be prepared to regard as a "full and ample compensation for the description of corps, of which you had been instructed to recommend the establishment". [130]

Presented with this demand, the Jamaican Assembly dithered and demurred and immediately cut the number by half. [131] It did not relish the prospect of meeting the whole cost of the Island's defence, and said so. It did not want an army of its own; it would be content merely to meet the additional expenses involved in having a number of British regiments permanently quartered in the Island. Finally, however, after an extremely rough passage, a series of resolutions were discussed and approved by a Committee of the whole House on November 28, 1797, and the Assembly undertook to provide for a force of two thousand white men. [132]

It was hoped by the Assembly that the majority of the troops would be obtained from Great Britain, Ireland, and the British North American colonies, the rest to consist of foreign European Protestants. Enlistment would be for periods varying from five to nine years, at the end of which the the ex-regulars would be settled on plots in the Jamaican hinterland. The Jamaican Agent in Britain was accordingly instructed to make arrangements to have non-commissioned officers accompanied by their families. Thus it was hoped to provide a permanent force, reliable and inured to the climate, while at the same time increasing the white population and advancing the Island's cultivation. [133]

This was not what the British government had envisaged. It was impossible to raise new troops in Britain, Ireland or Europe; [134] the scheme was to be implemented by simply re-deploying the troops already in the West Indies. Jamaica would be thus deprived of the privilege of selecting its own troops. And worst of all, from the Jamaican point of view, the British government took pains to point out that though the regiments would be appropriated to the "exclusive Service of Jamaica" His Majesty must retain the

129. C.O. 140/78, *Assembly Journal*, p. 645, Portland : Balcarres, January 1797.
130. C.O. 138/42, Portland : Balcarres, 12.9.1797.
131. C.O. 140/89, pp. 36-7, *Assembly Journal.* Meeting of 28.11.1797. Resolution 8, and amendment.
132. C.O. 140/89, pp. 36-7, *Assembly Journal.* Meeting of 28.11.1797.
133. C.O. 140/89, pp. 36-7, *Assembly Journal.* Meeting of 28.11.1797.
134. C.O. 140/89, p. 133 (Extract) Balcarres : Portland, 10.5.1798.

right to change troops when, and as often as, he should think proper, provided that on all occasions replacements of an equal number were made. In spite of spirited protests, the Jamaica Assembly, lest the original scheme be reverted to, accepted the decision. [135]

The mechanics of colonial politics soon exposed the brittleness of the compromise. The time was late 1799. The uneasy truce with Toussaint, signed on June 13, 1799, [136] was beginning to cause some concern in Jamaica. Britain was being urged to keep Toussaint occupied and Jamaica safe by lending aid to Rigaud. [137] Balcarres was suggesting that Toussaint be regarded in "no other light but as an Enemy". [138] French spies were being caught in the Island; [139] there were rumours of insurrections and invasions. In the midst of the confusion, Balcarres wrote a curious despatch suggesting that the Island's internal security would be very much improved if the military establishment were placed "in the hands of the British government". [140] He described himself as being "most improperly tied up, as is always the case when the Military Establishment is paid locally, and not by the Parent State." [141]

Portland of course was nonplussed. He could not bring himself to believe that control of Jamaica's military forces did not reside "in the hands of the British government"; nor could he be persuaded that Jamaica's troops, irrespective of the manner in which they were raised and paid could be subject to any control other than that of the duly appointed Governor and commander-in-chief. The Governor's control of the armed forces, as he, Portland, understood it was subject to no "control or check of the Council or Assembly, separately or jointly", and he reminded the Governor that he was responsible "in His military character" to His Majesty alone. Finally, he requested a "clear and distinct exposition of the difficulties, if any such exist, that stand in the way of your free and uncontrolled disposal of the Military force under your command in the Island of Jamaica". [142]

In reply, [143] Balcarres painted a lurid picture of Assembly interference in the defence of the Island, and all because the control of military expenditure had been conceded when Britain had agreed that Jamaica should bear the cost of her own defence. It was, indeed, said Balcarres, "a Question

135. *Ibid.,* pp. 278 ff. Meeting of 7.3.1799. Also, C.O. 137/101, Balcarres : Portland (Secret), 9.2.1799; Balcarres : Portland (Private), 3.3.1799; Balcarres : Portland, 11.4.1799 and enclosures.
136. C.L.R. James, *op. cit.,* p. 229.
137. C.O. 137/103, Balcarres : Portland, 19.12.1799.
138. C.O. 137/103, Balcarres : Portland, No. 1, 28.10.1799.
139. C.O. 137/103, Balcarres : Portland, 7.12.1799.
140. C.O. 137/103, Balcarres : Portland, No. 1, 28.10.1799.
141. C.O. 137/103, Balcarres ; Portland, No. 2., 28.10.1799.
142. C.O. 138/42, Portland: Balcarres, 11.2.1800.
143. C.O. 137/104, Balcarres : Portland, 24.5.1800.

deserving of being examined, whether from the strange and uncertain State of Saint Domingo, Jamaica can be managed under the same Constitution as formerly, and by her antient (sic) system. Great Britain has surely granted to Jamaica the management of her own Military Establishment . . . and the Constitution of the island is entirely overthrown". [144]

The point was that the Jamaicans, having paid for the defence of the Island, were determined to spend their money to their own satisfaction. The management of the Island's defence had been taken out of the Governor's hands. The Board of Forts and Fortifications, over which the Governor had immemorially presided, had been replaced by a new Board of Works set up by the Assembly with its own establishment of officers presided over by a new chairman. Some of the members of the new Board were not even members of the Assembly; they were merchants of Kingston, with the result that the Board met alternately at Spanish Town and Kingston, never at King's House as before. The Governor was never consulted nor informed of its activities. Its business methods were shoddy and corrupt, its manner tardy and negligent. It invariably accepted the lowest tender for its contracts, with the result that the job was often badly done, sometimes not done at all. Requests and directions made by the Governor went unheeded , often undiscussed. The Governor was nothing but a "Cypher". In his opinion, the Board must be dissolved, and Britain must "employ Troops of any description she pleases". It was his opinion that Jamaica could not be adequately defended "without the assistance of Negro Force".

And so indeed it was. The same anonymous observer, probably a spy, corroborated Balcarres's assessment. [145] These were perilous times, he said, and it was surely astonishing that while Britain was busy strengthening the hands of executive government in other parts of the world, (and extending the area of punitive and reactionary legislation at home) that the Jamaican juggernaut should be allowed to run riot. No effort should be spared to correct the situation. It might be that the British government would find it necessary to take "upon itself at least for a year or two great part of the military expense at present paid by the Island of Jamaica . . . but of this I am sure, that any expense we might incur ought to weigh little in the scale when compared to the necessity of strengthening the hands of the Executive at the present moment and relieving it from the state of degradation and nonentity into which it has sunk".

Thus it was that in early 1800 Secretary for War Dundas informed the Jamaica Agent that, as a result of the reorganization of the defence of the West Indies attendant on the evacuation of St. Domingue, it was necessary

144. *Ibid.*
145. C.O. 137/122. Report at the back of the volume.

to station more troops in Jamaica, some of them, unavoidably, Negro. [146]
He was well aware of the Island's views on the subject, but in the interests
of the Empire he could no longer continue "to compromise with the
opinions which exist in Jamaica, against this description of Force." [147]
When one considers the still vehement protests of the Island's white inhabit-
itants it is obvious that no single act could have so dramatically signified
Britain's increasing exasperation. [148]

Balcarres, who had complained that for the past thirty years there had
been in the Island a "uniform and systematic plan to reduce the influence &
Power of the Crown", [149] was himself superseded. [150] The pretext was his
contravention of the navigation laws; [151] more likely was the government's
belief that the usurpation of the executive power was largely due to
Balcarres's inability or unwillingness to assert himself. [152] Nor did the disappearance at sea of his first replacement, Major General Knox, [153] long delay Balcarres's removal. Major General Nugent was immediately sent out. [154]
Firm and determined government was called for, and Balcarres could not
provide it. If reform of the Jamaica governmental structure were needed,
the exigencies of war offered greater opportunities for success than could be
hoped for in times of peace. The chosen issue was the enlistment of Negro
troops; the chosen instrument was a new Governor.

All the signs were, however, that when the question of the reorganization
of the Assembly system became critical, British ministers would retreat.
Even while urging a policy of firmness, Portland was warning that the
Governor should exercise every discretion. The Assembly must be pushed,
but no so far that they should "carry their resistance to the last extremity,
so as to have recourse to the alternative of refusing all Supplies, not only
for black, but for His Majesty's European Troops in Jamaica, and for such
other publick Services both Civil and Military, as are now provided for by the
Island. Should this prove to be the case, highly advantageous as experience
has shown the employment of black Troops to be . . . suspend any endeavour
to bring it about, until you shall receive further Orders from hence". [155]

146. C.O. 138/39, Dundas : Sewell, 14.3.1800. Also, C.O. 138/42, Portland : Balcarres, 18.3.1800.
147. C.O. 137/103, Portland : Balcarres, 18.3.1800.
148. C.O. 138/42, Portland : Balcarres, 19.3.1801. See also, C.O. 137/104 which contains a record of a protest meeting held on May 6, 1800 by the Jamaica planters in London. They now agreed too that Negro troops would be a bad thing.
149. C.O. 137/104, Balcarres : Portland, 24.5.1800.
150. C.O. 138/42, Portland : Balcarres, 20.8.1800.
151. C.O. 138/42, Portland : Balcarres, 29.5.1800.
152. This was the opinion of the anonymous informer who, on this showing, must surely have been a spy. C.O. 137/122.
153. C.O. 138/42, Portland : Balcarres 19.3.1801.
154. C.O. 138/42, Portland : Balcarres, 12.5.1801.
155. C.O. 138/42, Portland : Balcarres, 19.3.1801.

The Addington ministry was to experience similar difficulties and to retreat with as little grace. In September 1802, Secretary of State Hobart, clearly distressed, wrote to Prime Minister Addington about a threatening development in Jamaica. Jamaica was not paying as much as she should for defence, and seemed likely not to consent to pay more. Governor Nugent was in a quandary: should pressure be exerted or not? Hobart recommended that "we must tread back as fast as we can, & not quarrel with the Island of Jamaica, unless they should be determined to drive us to Extremities; which I trust cannot be the case". [156] Addington accepted the proffered solution; the Assembly was excused, the Governor blamed. "The zeal of General Nugent has brought us into a Difficulty & I see no way out of it but that which you are disposed to pursue . . . Our Case is not such as could justify us in attempting to push the Point against the Assembly at present . . . if we were to create a Quarrel by Perseverance, it would appear that we did so because we were disappointed in our Hopes. . ." [157] Lord Melbourne's Bill for suspending the Jamaica constitution in 1839 was, in terms of attitudes, eons away.

Compared with Jamaica, Trinidad at times seemed to be doing penance for the other's sins. The Island agency was the issue chosen by the British government to underline Trinidad's inferior status. Agencies had been traditionally appointed by the Islands themselves. In Trinidad, although an Agent was appointed as early as 1801 on the Island's initiative, [158] the demands of patronage were too insistent for the office to be left at the undisputed disposition of the Colony. Almost as soon as the office was instituted a recurring battle was joined between various Secretaries of State and the Island over the right of nomination. Finally, the quarrel broke into the open whereupon Joseph Marryat, the Island's candidate, submitted a long "Case" on the subject, threatening in the last resort to air the matter in Parliament. [159] Marryat argued, with some justice, that the appointment of an Agent by the Secretary of State was demonstrably in conflict with the duties of the office since the Agent's main duty was, he maintained, to represent a point of view often at variance with those of British ministers.

When the Island pushed its defiance to the extent of actually nominating Marryat to the office of Agent, the Secretary of State thought it was time to act. Writing in support of Mr. Maling, an incorrigible incompetent who happened to be the government's candidate, the Secretary of State read Governor Hislop a very sharp lesson indeed. The Island's subordination to

156. *Hobart Papers.* (Bundle B), Hobart : Addington, 2.9.1802.

157. *Hobart Papers.* (Bundle B), Addington : Hobart, 4.9.1802.

158. C.O. 298/4, Minute of Council, 18.4.1810.

159. C.O. 295/20, A Statement of the issues involved in the dispute over the Agency in 1808. The triumph of ministerial control over the appointment of Agents for the new colonies is briefly discussed in L.M. Penson, *The Colonial Agents of the British West Indies,* (London, 1924), pp. 233-4.

the Crown was painstakingly and cruelty spelt out for the Governor's benefit and he was instructed to conduct himself as the King's representative, not as the Council's lackey.

"There is at present in Trinidad", wrote the Secretary of State, "no regular Colonial form of Government analogous to the old Governments of the other West India Islands, but the Island is governed by His Majesty's Prerogative in Consequence of the Capitulation as you have repeatedly been informed.

The Colonial Revenues therefore, and the Appointment to all offices in the Colony are entirely subject to His Majesty's Pleasure, and there is no Authority in the Colony, that is known or recognized here, which can order the Expenditure of any Sums of Money, except the Governor under His Majesty's Authority.

Neither is there Authority in the Island which can create a new office, or appoint a new Officer, or remove an Officer appointed except the Governor under the Authority of His Majesty and you are restricted to the Power of suspending Officers, who misconduct themselves 'till His Majesty's Pleasure is known.

It is therefore wished that you would not on any Account permit His Majesty's Authority and Prerogative, which are entrusted to your Care, to be intrenched upon by any other Body, and that you would guard them from any Intrusion whatever." [160]

*　　　　　*　　　　　*

The reasons embodied in the refusal of the West Indian Assemblies to cooperate in the enlistment of Negro troops also illustrate the impulse and prejudices of contemporary West Indian society. At the lowest level there was the belief that the £70 sterling offered by the British government for each slave was too small. [161]   There was, too, the jealousy of various interested persons in the Islands that they had not shared in the contract. [162]   There was also the fact that in Barbados and Jamaica where a greater degree of relative security prevailed throughout the war, planters were unwilling, as Fortescue has said, to see their slaves "distracted from the task of making money for their owners to so trivial an employment as defence of the country". [163]

The main reason though lay elsewhere. Assemblies just could not believe that Negroes, many of them ex-slaves, could be anything but a threat to the

160. C.O. 295/19; C.O. 196/4, Castlereagh : Hislop (Private), 4.2.1808. In 1810, a strongly worded despatch from Lord Liverpool on the same subject read the Governor almost exactly the same lesson. See C.O. 295/23, Liverpool : Hislop (Private), 3.8.1810.
161. W.O. 1/86, Abercromby : Dundas, 13.3.1797.
162. *Ibid., loc.cit.*   163. *History of the British Army*, Vol. IV, Part I, p. 542.

country when bearing arms. They found it impossible to believe that "negro soldiers would act with sepoy fidelity".[164] If these Negroes so acted, the Assemblies might well have thought, the lesson to be drawn from their conduct would do the greatest harm to the planters' cause. · It would disprove at one stroke everything the slave apologists had been preaching for years.

One of the beliefs central to the slave system was the belief that the Negro's inheritance fitted him for nothing else but servitude. To have slaves strutting around in uniforms, displaying a discipline and self-respect quite unassociated with the degradation of serfdom could only make furious those whose system was founded on the inherent incapacity of their chattels. Slaves had been constantly used in the armed forces for fatigue duties, fetching and carrying, clearing sites and building fortifications. This was permissible. It was quite a different thing to put them, or the free coloureds for that matter, in uniforms and make them members of disciplined regiments on an equal footing with white regulars.[165] The whole social system was, in the view of the Assemblies, threatened.

The argument was simple. Habit, not force, is the most potent of social sanctions. Force is resorted to when habit fails, is least used because it is most disruptive. A slave society must of necessity be the most regimented of all societies. In a free society, order is the price of efficiency; in a slave society, order is the premium of existence. And the distinctions of social function which help to determine and indicate slave status are as vital as the coercion which is the ultimate resort of the slave owner. Thus, the Jamaica Assembly feared the prospect of a slave bearing arms as much as it feared a Maroon attack, and was probably unable to distinguish between the two. To put the slave, ex-slave and the free coloured in the regular army was the first step on the high road to chaos and revolt. For the free coloureds, it was certain that while they served in the militia they would "preserve their ideas of colonial subordination"; it was not so certain that they would not "entertain notions of equality" once they were enlisted as regulars.[166]

To the planter and his ilk, every advance of the depressed groups, every variation of the rules of social conduct was a threat not only to their emotional security, as with the rat in the experimental psychologist's cage, but to their very life. Imprisoned within his small, restricted, fear-ridden world, the slave owner not the slave deserves our pity.

*   *   *

Yet another sensitive issue was to underscore the difficulties inherent in dealing with the planter dominated West Indian Assemblies. In 1798, Tous-

164. Edwards, *op. cit.*, Vol. IV, p. 91.   165. Edwards, *op. cit., passim*, especially pp. 42-82.
166. C.O. 140/78, p. 647. Meeting of 28.7.1797.

saint expelled the British from St. Domingue. The French royalists and property owners who had encouraged the forlorn hope that British intervention would salvage for them the shreds of the way of life to which they were once accustomed, now saw that life doomed forever. It was certain that they could not stay in St. Domingue. They had to be resettled, and Britain their collaborator and protector had to resettle them.

It soon became painfully obvious that they could not be resettled in Jamaica where most of them would have liked to go. Members of the Jamaica Assembly did not, of course, object to royalist French planters; but they stoutly objected to their slaves. [167] And nothing that Lord Balcarres could do would budge them. It was reasonable to point out, as Balcarres did, that the slaves had, by their devotion to their masters, given irrefutable proof that they were not tainted by republicanism and thirsting for white blood as the Assembly alleged. It was all too plain said the Governor that these slaves preferred "slavery under the British government, to freedom under that of the rulers of St. Domingo". [168] Equally clear was the fact that many of the French would be destitute without their slaves. Whole families he pointed out existed "solely on the support of one Male Negro, who brings them commonly 1 dollar per Day". [169]

It was all in vain. The Assembly maintained that the military operation in St. Domingue had not been for Jamaica's benefit; any attempt to involve Jamaica in St. Domingue's affairs at this stage was unjustified and unwarranted. The Governor, on the other hand insisted that Jamaica's well-being had been the sole cause of the protracted involvement in St. Domingue, and Jamaica had a duty to assist. But the Governor had over-reached himself. The St. Domingue campaign had not been for Jamaica's sole benefit; and in any case a committee of the Assembly found that the Governor had actively encouraged the French royalists and their slaves to come to the Island. This the Assembly could not forgive; the scheme was irrevocably off.

Thus it was that master followed slave on the southward trek from Jamaica. Some of the refugees went to British occupied Martinique; others went to Trinidad to introduce another element into that Island's turbulent population. A letter of March 5, 1799, [170] peremptorily informed Lieu-

167. See Edwards, *op. cit.*, Vol. IV, pp. 96-102. 168. *Ibid.*, pp. 97-8.
169. C.O. 137/103, Balcarres : Portland, 2.1.1800.
170. C.O. 296/1, Dundas : Picton, 5.3.1799. Cf., also, C.O. 137/103, Balcarres : Picton, 20.1.1800. In part Dundas' letter read: "A considerable number of the inhabitants of St. Domingo having, in consequence of the evacuation of the British possession in that Island, fled with their negroes for refuge to Jamaica, but their continuance there appearing liable to many objections, Lord Balcarres has been instructed to remove them to some other Quarter; and as the same considerations are applicable in some degree to every British Settlement, it has been determined to convey the Negroes in particular to Martinique - but as some few of the proprietors of St. Domingo, from their unequivocal and uniform adherence to the British Interests, have been allowed to proceed with their Negroes to Trinidad, Colonel Picton is directed to receive any such who may arrive there, under the sanction of Lord Balcarres, in a proper and suitable manner. . ."
When Picton replied on May 14, 1799, it was merely to state that the emigrants who arrived with the proper certificates would be received. Trinidad, in this matter, was not even capable of the

tenant Colonel Picton that some of the refugees were on their way to the Island, and should be received on arrival. There was no discussion; there was nothing to discuss. Trinidad was a conquered colony under a military government. In Martinique the question was slightly more negotiable, but there were obvious limits to negotiation. The British government was unlikely to forget the boon of military rule in Trinidad and Crown Colony government in Martinique which facilitated the introduction of the French emigrants into those Islands.

In 1797, Abercromby wrote of the West Indian Assemblies: "They delight in opposition, and make speeches from the London Magazine". [171] It was a most outspoken denunciation of the West Indian system of government. It expressed not simply the view of a frustrated and disgusted commander, but the attitude of an age. The feeling that West Indian Assemblies were inherently irresponsible was widespread in ministerial circles. But the Assemblies were sheltered by the constitutional usages of centuries; they had rights and they had powerful defenders.

The new colonies on the other hand possessed no rights. They were all colonies of conquest, not of settlement. In the circumstances of war sanctions for firm government could easily be found if they were needed. Even as conquests, because of the disaffection of large sections of the population, the new colonies seemed an integral part of the French threat. Besides, the ruling classes were almost invariably in favour of British rule, and they were willing to surrender their political ambitions for security. Thus, the constitution of 1794 was devised to meet the needs of royalists in the French islands who were quite content with the meagre political role conceded them. Religion and the established laws were maintained as a concession to local sensitivity; but effective military and civil power remained in British hands. At the end of the war in 1815 those of the colonists who had welcomed authoritarian rule in the years of crisis chafed at its restrictions and impositions. But that was after more than twenty years of war had accustomed Britain to the habit of wielding power in the new colonies. Circumstances had provided Britain with a sanctioned authority she was later loathe to relax in the face of the problems arising out of the abolition movements. The principle of firmer government was destined with time to be extended from the new to the old colonies. Trinidad's constitutional experience was to play an important part in the fashioning of that principle.

---

resistance of which Martinique was. The former was then under military government; Martinique had the Constitution of 1794. On May 1, 1800 Picton was writing that all but 39 of 300 St. Domingo Negroes, refused at Martinique, had been allowed to land despite the protests of the *Cabildo* and some of the inhabitants. Cf. C.O. 296/1, Picton : Dundas. 1.5.1800.

171. W.O. 1/86, pp. 215-6, Abercromby : No name, 20.3.1797.

CHAPTER 4

THE VANGUARD SOCIETY II

The internal consequences for Trinidad of the developing dialogue over experimentation were very closely related to the formal cession of the Island in March 1802 and to the complex state of its population at the time of the cession. News of the signing of the preliminaries of peace in early October arrived in Trinidad about the middle of November. Thereafter it was not long before it was manifest that initial rejoicing attendant on the outbreak of peace would give way to a bitter and acrimonious conflict over the constitutional question.

In so far as experiment was an internal concern, its proponents were to be found among those who were, for one reason or the other, opposed to the development of the traditional forms of representative government in the Island. It must not be supposed, however, that at the time of the cession, there was a conscious espousal by this group of the idea of experimentation in constitutional matters. In the first place, the lines of conflict were not clearly drawn largely because, before the cession, the constitution was not an active issue; and secondly, it might well have been that it was already plain to the perceptive that the idea of experiment could hardly be piecemeal, and that notions of social organization were likely to arise to which they were sure to be hostile. Nevertheless, it was but a brief moment before those most anxious for constitutional change had by their actions brought into being the formation of interest groups around which the idea of experiment in constitutional matters was soon to be debated.

The immediate consequences of the receipt of the news of the cession were themselves the result of the actions of the British inhabitants who at once resolved to move an address of loyal congratulation to the King by way of celebration. At the same time, about fifty of the leading British merchants began to subscribe to a dinner scheduled for December 10, the day on which hostilities were to cease in the West Indies.[1] Public advertisements appeared in the press soliciting signatures for the Address and announcing the venue of the proposed dinner, the store of one Thomas Higham, an affluent Port-of-Spain merchant. Meanwhile, the Address itself was being prepared by the prime movers in the affair, John Sanderson an aspiring lawyer and alleged member of the London Corresponding Society, John Shaw, a major in the Island's militia, Steven Rutherford a lawyer, and Higham himself. When finally that document made its appearance, the efforts of this earnest quartet were seen to have produced something more than had at first been anticipated. For, apart from congratulating the King

1. M'Callum, *op. cit.,* p. 163.

on the close of a "long and expensive" war and thanking him for his gracious confirmation of the acquisition of "this most valuable conquest", the document asked him to extend to his "faithful and affectionate subjects in this colony the privileges and protection of the British constitution as experienced by a free representation in a House of Assembly, and in a Trial by Jury". [2]

To this request, Governor Picton's reaction was immediate and ominous. An angry edict banned the proposed dinner, and its promoters were officially warned that persistence in the undertaking would provoke the Governor's severest disapproval. Efforts to treat with Picton by sending a deputation to him to discuss the conditions on which the dinner might be held met with a stern rebuff, the two delegates being advised that any attempt to do so would be treated as an act of sedition and the diners dispersed by force. Thus, the dinner had to be abandoned. [3]

The ban imposed on the dinner seems to have discouraged but not to have unduly deterred the promoters of that event. The leaders conferred and affected to believe that Picton's displeasure was the result of a freakish repugnance to public dining; in any case, they saw, or pretended to see, no reason why the business of the Address could not be pursued. Indeed, they managed to convince themselves and the majority of their compatriots that the circumstance of a *"British* governor struggling to prevent the extension of *British* laws to a *British* colony" was so extraordinary and repugnant as never to be contemplated. [4] And in this conviction the next step was blithely taken.

On Thursday December 18, [5] about one hundred and twenty inhabitants attended a meeting at Wharton's Tavern, a Port-of-Spain grogshop, for the purpose of addressing the King. Picton, it seems, took no steps to prevent the meeting, no doubt feeling that his attitude to a petition for British laws at this time had been sufficiently indicated. And from the subsequent pussilanimous behaviour of some of the gathering it is only charitable to assume that few had anticipated that a second attempt would be made to address the King on a change in the system of government. Yet, this is precisely what happened.

The crowd having assembled, William Harrison, an unoffending and respectable well-to-do merchant, on terms of some intimacy with the Governor,

---

2. *Ibid.*, pp. 159-61. Sanderson, *An Appeal,* pp. 47-50.

3. Reports of these proceedings abound, but since no two reports agree they only add to the confusion. The essential events are agreed upon but the chronology is extremely variable. ·See, Fraser, *op. cit.,* Vol. I, pp. 136-40; M'Callum, *op. cit.,* pp. 156-168; Gertrude Carmichael, *op. cit.,* p. 52; Sanderson, *Political Account. . . ,* pp. 81-90.

4. M'Callum, *op. cit.,* p. 157.

5. This is the date most used by commentators. It is the one referred to in a series of depositions collected by Picton outlining the details of the affair and transmitted to London in C.O. 295/2, Picton: Hobart, 27.4.1802. However, in an Address from Thomas Higham and John Shaw to William Fullarton, first commissioner of the Commission of government appointed in 1802, the date of the meeting is given as December 5. See, C.O. 295/5. The following narrative is drawn mainly from the depositions enclosed in Picton's letter.

was quickly elected chairman by public acclamation. This done, the meeting turned to a discussion of the contents of the proposed Address, the radicals urging, as before, the insertion of a specific claim for a British constitution and British laws. A lively debate ensued, the proposal being finally accepted after some opposition. The Address, in duplicate, was circulated for signatures, and the meeting, noisily guided by Sanderson and his colleagues, then turned to a discussion of the method of transmitting the Address to England. The novel proposal that the Address should be sent to appointed agents in London, by-passing the Governor, petrified the more timid hearers. This suggestion had at least the merit of consistency; but it was one thing to have Picton reject an already proscribed form of Address, and quite another to attempt to avoid the issue by going around him.

On this issue two factions seem to have emerged. One was led by Sanderson urging direct transmission to England, and the other by William Lockheed, gentleman planter and reputed Fellow of the Royal Society of Edinburgh.[6] As these two champions wrangled the meeting grew more and more disorderly, the chairman himself finally joining the disaffected who had begun to leave. And as the meeting grew smaller, the rump, consisting mainly of the radicals, resolved itself into a committee and decided to collect more signatures for the Address and forward it to their London agents.

The events of the next few days were as stormy as the meeting at the Tavern had been. Some of the deserters, fully contrite and repenting their rashness, were among the first to advise Picton of the late proceedings at Wharton's. William Harrison, by his own admission, was prominent among the informers. Picton, of course, was furious. He sent for Thomas Higham, roundly abused him, and demanded the Address. Higham, at whose store the Address had been left for signing, truthfully replied that he did not know where it was. In fact, anticipating the Governor's summons, he had deliberately left it at his store some time past and wandered off, loudly voicing the hope that someone would remove it to a safe place. Someone had, but Higham found little comfort in the fact. Angered by what he conceived to be Higham's prevarication, Picton had him arrested and jailed, whereupon Highman's friends threw the Address on to Harrison's verandah whence it found its way to the Governor.

With this Higham was released, but Picton's anger died slowly. Higham and Shaw, both ranking officers in the militia were dismissed from their posts. Similarly treated were Messrs. Winterflood and Bostock, officials in the Customs,[7] and stern warnings were delivered to others whom, like Ephraim Painter, captain of the armed schooner run by the government, Picton found it inconvenient to dismiss.

---

6. C.O. 295/23, Hislop : Liverpool (Private) 20.5.1810; enclosing Hislop : Smith, 11.5.1810, for this information on Lockheed's background.

7. M'Callum, *op. cit.*, pp. 164-5. Sanderson, *Political Account...*, p. 89. Also, C.O. 295/5. Address of Higham and Shaw to Fullarton requesting reinstatement as militia officers.

During the next two months, while Picton remained strangely inactive, a copy of the Address, secretly transported to England, was being assiduously circulated in London. Rumours filtering back to the Island of attempts to use the circumstances surrounding the signing of the Address to depict Picton's government as harsh and tyrannical roused him to action. In February 1802, some sixty persons were examined before the *alcaldes* on the affairs of December 18. While this was being done, an Address from some of the British inhabitants, publicly stating their attachment to Picton's person and government, and repudiating the attempts made to discredit him, was sent to the Secretary of State, Lord Hobart.[8] Later the depositions of the witnesses followed[9] and Picton had the satisfaction of being able to remit yet another Address in his support signed by some of the original subscribers of the prayer for British laws.[10]

Such were the details of the events which, on the local scene ushered in the sharpest controversy over the future of the constitution and brought into being the emerging factions which were thereafter to contest the prospect of experiment and change in all its manifestations.

In 1802 Trinidad already was a very complex society with a very cosmopolitan population. Men of nearly all nations and as many creeds were to be found resident in the Island. But in its essence, as we have already seen, the society was not so much foreign as French, both with respect to its free coloured and white communities. In 1802, apart from the Indians and the slaves, numbering 1166 and 19,709 respectively, there were 5275 free coloured and 2261 whites. Of the free coloureds 599 were of British origin, 1751 were Spanish and 2925 were French. Of the whites 663 were British, 505 were Spanish and 1093 were French.[11] So that, in the whole of the free population, the British found themselves in a minority of about five thousand when compared with the foreigners who were mainly French. More important though, since the free coloured were generally regarded as a

8.   C.O. 295/2, Picton : Hobart, 18.2.1802.
9.   C.O. 295/2, Picton : Hobart, 27.4.1802.
10. C.O. 295/2. Extract from the *Trinidad Weekly Courant,* edition of Monday February 13, 1802; enclosed in Picton : Hobart, 18.2.1802.
11. C.O. 295/4, Commissioners : Hobart, 3.3.1803. The number of French whites is here given as 1,095 making a total of all whites as 2,263, not 2,261. The figure was adjusted by Fullarton to 1,093 in his pamphlet *Colonel Fullarton's answer to Colonel Picton's Address. No. LXXXIII, p.* 168. See, too, Fraser, *op. cit.,* Vol. I, p. 288; Sanderson, *Political Account,* pp. 96-102. In addition, Sanderson challenges the official figures, and puts forward a point of view worth noting. He suggests first of all that the British population was probably substantially more than shown in the census returns. During the first seven months of 1802, he says, the British community benefitted by an immigration of 592 newcomers, 535 men and 57 women. In addition there were 101 new foreign whites, and 189 free coloureds male and female. As for slaves, 10,643 were brought to the Island: 6,037 were kept, and 4,606 re-exported. Secondly, Sanderson argues that if the official returns are correct then a large number of Britishers must have emigrated by October when the census was usually taken; and argues further that the grant of British laws would alone have been able to stem this flow of emigrants. One must bear in mind, however, that the winning of a British constitution and British laws was precisely the point of Sanderson's literary effort.

homogeneous class of whom the French were only the most loathsome, was the fact that the British white population of 663 opposed a foreign white population of 1598, nearly three times its size. And in 1801, when the petition for British laws was made, this proportion was even less favourable to the British. Then, the total white population had been 2153, and since the increase of 108 in 1802 was, it seems, mainly British, they must have been in 1801 in a smaller, though not much smaller, minority. [12]

The characteristics of the growing conflict arose more or less completely from this fact of demographic complexity. In the face of this complexity Picton's attitude was not only the most important but also the most interesting. His hostility to the activities of the British party in late 1801 and the early months of 1802, and the reasons for this hostility, constitute an important event in the history of the struggle for British laws and a British constitution. It was important, too, that it was the free coloured section of the community which aroused in his mind the greatest misgivings about the turn events seemed to be taking. With security in mind, his first objection was founded on the conviction that the Island itself would inevitably be imperilled by the continued agitation of the constitutional question. In explaining his actions at the time of the Wharton's Tavern affair he was later to allege that the British agitation in support of the Address had nearly provoked serious consequences because of the opportunities for revolt it offered the free people of colour who, he said, "were at that time in considerable fermentation owing to the Events at Guadeloupe, where their Colour had gained an ascendancy in the Government". [13]

In 1804 however, maturer by two years, and sharpened by his life or death controversy with Colonel Fullarton, Picton offered a more reasoned and thoughtful explanation. [14] He was not averse, he said, to the British gaining in Trinidad the positions of influence and ascendancy which they sought by the attempted introduction of a British constitution. But he deplored the belief that power and influence could only be obtained by a reckless agitation for a change of government. The free people of colour, to take the largest section of the free population, could not be expected tamely to acquiesce in constitutional innovations in which they could not participate. The humiliating disqualifications which would render them ineligible to execute the functions of councillor, assemblyman, and judge, would at once convert a conventional disability into a legal one, as in the other West Indian islands. The old colonies, he continued, had at least been a *tabula rasa* on which a particular type of society had been slowly formed. Thus, in those colonies, the white colonists ruled not only in virtue of their own, but of everyone else's, belief in their right to rule. In Trinidad, however, the

12. See Fraser, *op. cit.*, Vol. I, p. 288.
13. C.O. 296/1; C.O. 295/2, Picton : Hobart, 18.2.1802 and 21.5.1802.
14. C.O. 295/10. *Report of the State and Affairs of Trinidad by Colonel Thomas Picton late Governor and Commissioner for the Affairs of that Island. . .* February, 1804. Cf. C.O. 296/1; C.O. 295/2, Picton : Hobart, 28.6.1802.

background of Spanish social and legal precedent had created an edifice, a social structure, a certain relationship between the white and coloured community which must be destroyed "before we can rear another to replace it." [15]

In Picton's view moreover, Trinidad's large and restless coloured population made the policy of public agitation for British laws a particularly senseless and fatuous one. More so when the desired ends, as he believed, could be obtained by merely passing over "this delicate subject" in silence. The same tokens of kinship and belonging that informed the demands of the British inhabitants for the forms of government established in the old British colonies, should assure them that the system of government in Trinidad, whatever it was - and Picton did not scruple over his preference for a strong arbitrary government - would ultimately operate to further their best. interests.

Picton's philosophy was as complete as it was insidious, and was as consistent an argument for arbitrary government as one could wish. Of the free coloureds he wrote that "The only mode of rendering these people useful without their becoming formidable to the Colony, is to leave them where they are; to establish no more Artificial distinctions; to humiliate them by no unnecessary Marks of Degradation or Incapacity. You need not promote them to any Offices of importance of honour, but it is not necessary to show them, that you have raised an insuperable Bar to their *Advancement* or *Ambition*". [16] Indeed, what angered Picton in 1801 was not the reasonable expectation among the British of the perquisites accruing from British conquest, but their recklessness in openly pursuing a course that was dangerous, and perhaps worse, unnecessary.

Nor was Picton alone in holding to this opinion. A contemporary of Picton's, a retired army captain, at that time lieutenant colonel and commandant of the Trinidad Rifle Corps of militia, voiced the same sentiments in almost the same words. He too favoured a strong government. He too saw the Island's varied population as an immoveable barrier to the immediate grant of popular institutions. To him, because of the differences in language, customs and heritage, representative government was unthinkable. The introduction of such a form of government could be admitted only on the dangerous "system of equality that proved so ruinous to St. Domingo, or else denying a large portion of the population and property the right of being represented". [17] For him too the answer was obvious, with the exception that, for him, not only the coloured population, but the whole mass of foreigners, made its adoption imperative. He urged a system of government "as may silently legislate for the general welfare not subject to the petty cavilings and trifling vexations a popular plan would be subject to . . . if it is thought advisable to permit juries to be formed . . . should His Majesty think

15.   C.O. 295/10. Picton's report of February 1804.
16.   C.O. 295/10. Picton's report. Also, C.O. 296/1; C.O. 295/2, Picton : Hobart, 28.6.1802.
17.   C.O. 295/9, J.P. Kingston : Sullivan, 17.1.1804.

it expedient to send out a Judge or Chief Justice . . . of high and respectable character, independent of the colony, a mode occurs to my mind of providing juries for the Courts with facility *if all questions of qualifications are permitted to lie dormant"*. [18]

This plan foreshadowed the appointment of an officer of the rank of high sheriff, to whom the Governor and Council would annually present a list of persons competent to serve on juries. This list, one may well suppose, would have contained no coloureds and few foreigners. From the names presented to him the officer concerned would then have chosen jurors for service in the courts, by a process of rotation as effective as it would have been discreet.

"Thus also", wrote Kingston, "the questions of whites and coloured people will be least noticed, they are much to be deprecated, and it is fortunate when they are passed over as silently as possible. I do conceive it is much to be lamented that the coloured people are not only so numerous, but that they are landholders to such an extent. To deprive them of their property is unjust . . . (but) every obstacle must be thrown in the way of increasing the numbers of black or coloured landholders. Their power arose in St. Domingo from neglect, carelessness and contempt of them in the *Government,* and *they* began the destruction of that country." [19]

Like Picton, Colonel Kingston believed that the processes of government in such a community must be efficient and efficacious; but they must also be hidden from sight. Here, in its secretive nutshell, is the essential nature of arbitrary, discriminative government. The embryonic Crown Colony government which was developing in Trinidad was conceived not through differences about ends but rather over the means to attain ends which were already generally agreed.

One cannot easily determine the spring and source of Colonel Kingston's philosophy, but it is remarkable that he, a "poor player" strutting and fretting his hour upon life's stage, should have so closely agreed with Governor Picton. Picton had had time to think, time to brood. And his analysis of Trinidad's constitutional problem was founded on an appreciation of what was the single most important fact in the Trinidad of his day, the complexity of its population.

Whatever Picton's reaction to this fact might have been it is also undoubtedly true that his judgements were coloured by the prejudices of his day, by his experiences as a soldier who had seen active service against the French in the West Indies, [20] and by the presuppositions which he as Governor chose to make regarding the security of the Island committed to his charge. As for this last consideration, Picton was convinced as we have seen,

18. *Ibid.* My emphasis.
19. C.O. 295/9, J.P. Kingston : Sullivan, 17.1.1804.
20. Picton came out to the West Indies in 1794 and took an active part in the revolutionary wars that preceded the capture of Trinidad. See, Heaton Robinson, *op. cit.,* Vol. I, p.21 *et seq.*

that the question of the Island's constitutional development should be decided in absolute secrecy, insulated, as it were, from those dangers likely to derive from public discussion and agitation. As a soldier he believed that Trinidad was at all times susceptible to an attack by hostile forces, or to insurrection fomented by foreigners within.[21] Such experience as he had had in the West Indies led him to regard the free people of colour as the most dangerous group by far. In 1799, he described them to Henry Dundas, Secretary for War, as "irreclaimable Republicans, whom nothing but the arm of authority, continually exercised without relaxation, can ever keep in order - formidable not only on account of their numbers and disposition but for their known communication with the Enemy, and ready to cooperate with any Invader".[22] But the French free coloureds were the worst: "a dangerous class which must gradually be got rid of . . . the adoption of proper measures will gradually decrease their Numbers".[23]

Governor Picton's venom was not, however, directed at the free coloureds alone. Time and again he showed himself to be severely critical of the conduct of the British and foreign whites; often indeed the British drew his severest censure. But a vital difference existed in that while the whites were usually depicted as respectable with but a few exceptions to the general rule,[24] Picton always found himself under the melancholy necessity of describing the free coloureds as on the whole dangerous and unruly, some only being more so than others.

In fact, between Picton and the free coloureds not only was there a complete absence of all sympathy, but an active antagonism that, to a large extent, explained Picton's aggressively stern administration. The Governor describing his position in 1797, when after the conquest he was left as military commandant of the Island, likened it to that of a "Camp surrounded with enemies, and the severities I applied were fully authorized by my station and circumstances".[25] Needless to say the brunt of these severities fell most heavily on the slaves and the free coloureds; the latter Picton most certainly numbered amongst his foes on the ground that the "2000 Men of Colour" in the Island were "all irreconcilable enemies of His Majesty's Government".[26] He never seemed to be aware that some of the free coloureds were British in origin and had resided in the Island before the conquest. For his own purposes he affected the belief that all the Island's free people of colour had come to Trinidad hotfoot from the revolutionary orgies

21. See for example: C.O. 295/2; C.O. 296/1; P.C. 1/3557, Picton : Hobart, 20.5.1802. Also, Picton's address to the Council in Trinidad on 14th April 1803, copied in *A Statement, Letters and Documents respecting the Affairs of Trinidad: including a Reply to Col. Picton's Address to the Council of that Island. . .* by Colonel Fullarton, (Lond. 1804), pp. 161-6.
22. C.O. 296/1; W.O. 1/93, Picton : Dundas, 1.1.1799.
23. C.O. 295/2; C.O. 296/1, Picton : Hobart, 18.2.1802.
24. See for example, C.O. 295/2, Picton : Hobart, 18.2.1802.
25. Picton's Address to the Council of Trinidad dated 14.4.1803, reproduced in *A Statement, Letters and Documents. . .* by Col. Fullarton, p. 162.
26. Picton's Address to the Council of Trinidad dated 14.4.1803, *op. cit.*, p. 162.

of the neighbouring islands. Depiciting them as such afforded him a seemingly unassailable justification for the callousness of his rule. Indeed how else could one deal with such a class, actuated by a spirit of turbulence and revolt, but by a vigorous application of "the arm of authority, continually exercised without relaxation"? [27] Against such a belief one can only offer that of Colonel Fullarton who, on quitting the Island in 1803, declared that he had found no evidence of such singleminded insubordination among the foreigners, free coloureds and slaves since the conquest of 1797. [28] One might say that this was largely the result of Picton's active and vigorous management. But then one would have to concede that Picton with a small, and, by his own assertions, inadequate and sometimes indisciplined force at his disposal performed the most successful suppression of incipient revolt in the West Indies of that era.

One does not deny that there was a keen sense of coloured resentment of Picton's rule; there was a good deal of resentment among some whites too. But it is a fair claim that the resentment of the free people of colour stemmed directly from the treatment they received at Picton's hands. Contrasted with the rule of Chacon, his Spanish predecessor, Picton's governorship marked the beginning of a steady erosion of the rights of the free people of colour that was not halted until Governor Woodford, on the instructions of Lord Bathurst, issued a proclamation on January 5, 1826, revoking certain sections of other proclamations discriminating against the free coloured. [29] Chacon, despite the stipulation of the Laws of the Indies had, for example, granted commissions to black and coloured men in the Island's militia. He had done so by reason of the 28th article of the *cédula* of 1783 [30] which had exempted Trinidad from the observance of customary colonial law where this might be repugnant to the intent of the *cédula;* and that *cédula,* as noted elsewhere, had provided for the participation of all new inhabitants in the civil life of the community. [31] Thus, a partial list provided by Dr. J.B. Philip the mulatto author writing in 1824, showed that by 1796 Chacon had commissioned twelve black and coloured officers holding ranks of ensigns, lieutenants and captains in the militia. No distinction was made between them and their white colleagues with whom they paraded on all occasions on terms of equality. [32] After the conquest, however, in violation of the 12th article of the capitulation, Picton downgraded them all, segrega-

27.   C.O. 296/1; W.O. 1/93, Picton : Dundas, 1.1.1799.
28.   Philip , *Address to the Right Hon. Earl Barthurst*. . . . . p. 31.
29.   C.O. 298/6, Minutes of meeting of 5.1.1826. C.O. 295/70, Woodford : Bathurst, 8.1.1826. No. 545; and enclosures. Also, Fortunatus Dwarris, *The West Indian Question Plainly Stated: and the Only Practical Remedy Briefly Considered* . . . (London, 1828), pp. 72-6.
30.   C.O. 295/1, from Extract of the *cédula*. For a printed translation see Gertrude Carmichael, *op. cit.* Appendix 1, pp. 363-9.
31.   See above, pp. 15-16.
32.   *Op. cit.,* p. 11 and Appendix, Note A, p. 221.

ted the troops and put the coloureds, ex-officers included, under the command of a white sergeant. [33]

This was a bitter pill for the free people of colour, who, whatever the Spanish code might have been, were accustomed in Trinidad to a manner of treatment far in advance of anything to which coloured colonists of other islands could aspire. With a cruel disregard for the feelings of this class, Picton consummated their public humiliation by the introduction of the most rigorous restrictions and enactments regulating their social life. Coloured people wishing to give a ball had to apply to the commandant of the quarter in which they lived for permission, and had to give an undertaking not to admit slaves under penalty of a fine. [34] Free people of colour were pressed into service as *alguaçiles* or petty constables, an occupation which they soon monopolized as a further mark of their degradation. As *alguaçiles* they were forced to do daily turns of guard duty at the homes of the commandants and other officials. Even coloured proprietors of some standing were not exempt from such duty; indeed these often found themselves the particular objects of malicious annoyances and insults offered them out of pique. [35] The harrassment of the free coloured by noisome regulations of this type became in fact a regular feature of the Island's administration under British rule.

In 1807, for instance, Governor Hislop had the Council impose a tax of sixteen dollars on balls given by free people of colour. [36] This followed an ordinance of November 1804 directing free coloureds and slaves to retire to their homes by 9.30 p.m. [37] A further order of December 12, 1804, called on all free coloureds to show that they had taken the oath of allegiance, and directed them to produce proofs of their manumission. [38] On September 12, 1810, following a petition by the free coloureds for proper consideration in any change of the Island's constitution, an ordinance was passed requiring them to walk with a lighted lamp when out at night, to refrain from playing musical instruments in the grogshops at any time of the night or day, and empowering any citizen to arrest any Negro, freeman or slave, seen carrying a cudgel in his hand. [39] The alacrity with which this last exhortation was obeyed forced the government eight days later, on the 20th, to issue a precise definition of a cudgel as meaning a large heavy stick "with knots, or ferrules

33. *Ibid.*, p. 11. This was a violation of the terms of the capitulation. See, E.L. Joseph, *op. cit.*, pp. 211-12. And Joseph was if anything an apologist for Picton. Also, Dwarris, *op. cit.*, pp. 72-4. For counter arguments see, Sanderson, *An Appeal. . . .* p. 128.

34. C.O. 295/2, Picton : Hobart, 18.2.1802. Enclosure entitled *"Reglement pour servir D'Instruction aux Commandants des Differends Quartiers de la Colonie"*, Trinidad 20.8.1800. Art. III, sub-section entitled *"De La Police Generale"*, p. 41. Also, Philip, *op. cit.*, pp. 29-30.

35. Philip, *op. cit.*, p. 33. C.O. 295/2, Picton : Hobart, 18.2.1802. *Reglement. . . .* Art. I, sub-section entitled *"Des Alguazils"*, p. 48 *Alguaçiles* were first to be recruited from propertyless free coloureds and artisans. But the article provided for the recruitment of planters too should it be necessary. Evidently it was often found necessary to do so.

36. Dwarris, *op. cit.*, pp. 75-6.

37. C.O. 298/1. Council meeting of 29.11.1804.

38. Philip, *op. cit.*, pp. 35-6.   39. *Ibid.*, pp. 36-7.

of brass, iron, etc." and not canes carried for fashion or convenienec. [40] From time to time regulations establishing discriminatory fees for public services were passed, not all of them wholly injurious to the free coloureds. For example, amputation of a black or coloured leg cost less by law than a similar service rendered to a white one; [41] but the proper order was kept by other stipulations such as Attorney General Gloster's suggested poll tax of thirty shillings per head on free coloureds as against twenty shillings on whites and five shillings on slaves, [42] and must in any case be balanced against a regulation such as that of the 3rd of August 1819 requiring suitors to describe their condition, whether white or coloured, when making application to the law courts. [43]

In 1801, however, the free people of colour though an important factor in the circumstances surrounding the British appeal for British laws did nothing to influence the outcome of that appeal one way or the other. Apart from their rumoured unrest, which loomed large in the Governor's calculations, their role was a passive one. They made no petitions, advanced no claims, claimed no rights. Indeed, for all the evidence of interest on their part they might well have been unaware of what was taking place.

In marked contrast to the free people of colour, the foreign whites, French, Spanish and a small sprinkling of other nationalities, took an active and continuing interest in the affair from its very inception. Many of them, like the British, welcomed the cession. Four years of British rule had accustomed them to the benefits of an aggressive commercial policy which, even during the war, had placed a high priority on keeping open the trade with the Venezuelan mainland. Besides, the foreign groups were strongly laced with French refugees from St. Domingue and the other insurgent islands who, whatever their misgivings about Picton's mode of government, did not hesitate to draw the obvious parallel between the calm and security of Trinidad and the confusion of her neighbours to the north. Opposed to them, however, were the French republicans of whom there were quite a few "ever intriguing", in the words of E.L. Joseph "to overturn the British Government". [44] But the sentiments of the republicans were more than counterbalanced by those of the Spaniards who were generally most amenable to British domination, and by the French royalists. Between the Spaniards and the royalists on one hand and the republicans on the other there was of course no comparison in influence. One group, the former, had the inestimable advantage of the Governor's ear and the privilege of being vocal. The other, naturally, had to disguise its true sentiments; certainly it could not advertise them. And these were emphatically not the authors of that "respectable" body of opinion which Picton represented as the consensus of the foreign inhabitants.

40. Philip , op. cit., pp. 36-7. Also, C.O. 318/76, Woodford : Bathurst, 12.6.1825. No. 633; enclosure No. 13.
41. C.O. 318/76. Ibid.
42. C.O. 295/16, Gloster : Hislop, 26.7.1807; enclosed in Hislop : Castlereagh, 4.8.1807.
43. Dwarris, op. cit., pp. 75-6.   44. Op. cit., pp. 205-6.

Economically the white foreigners were of greater importance than their British counterparts. In 1802, most of the landed proprietors were foreigners, among whom were to be found the Island's most opulent planters.[45] Contrasted with the British, who were with few exceptions mainly merchants, tradesmen, commission agents, and lesser professionals, the foreigners, as a class of agriculturists, were more in keeping with the traditional structure of West Indian economic enterprise. Not only did they have more and larger plantations than the British; they also grew a wider variety of agricultural produce. Even in 1801, when the British agricultural interest was much stronger than in 1802, the predominance of the foreigners was still evident.[46] But few foreigners in 1802, as in the succeeding years, were merchants of any standing. Scattered on estates throughout the Island they represented an interest notably different from that of the British merchants concentrated in Port-of-Spain - a point which the French belaboured in their memorial to the King in 1810 on the proposed introduction of British laws.[47]

The views of the foreigners on the constitutional question derived, therefore, partly from an appreciation that as planters they represented an interest that was in some opposition to that of the merchants who were in the forefront of the clamour for British laws. As planters, too, they were conservative and intensely distrustful of any public agitation that could possibly stir the imagination of the slaves on whom their prosperity depended. Needless to say, the refugees among them placed a particularly high premium on security and public calm remembering only too well that what had begun as a debate over privileges in St. Domingue had ended as a full-scale slave revolt. But perhaps their keenest suspicions were aroused by the behaviour of the British claimants whose boisterous conduct, posturings and overbearing manner could only be made worse by the introduction of a form of government peculiar to them, and doubtlessly operated in their interests.

In December 1801 the Cabildo, still very much the stronghold of the white foreigners, communicated with the Governor on the question of the Island's constitution.[48] It flatly repudiated the attempt to introduce British laws and a British constitution, and enclosed Addresses illustrative of the strength of feeling among the foreigners against the measure. In addition it requested the Governor to forward to the King what was in effect a counter petition which it had approved on December 12. The main arguments urged in these various documents must have given Governor Picton immeasurable comfort. Beginning with a denunciation of that liberty which had in recent times shown itself to be "the most absolute of despots", the *Cabildo* argued

45. W.O. 1/94, Picton : Hobart, 14.12.1801.

46. C.O. 295/24, Smith : Liverpool, 14.2.1810. Also, Sanderson's *Political Account*, p. 62.

47. C.O. 295/24, Hislop : Liverpool, (Private) 12.10.1810, containing an Address from *"Les Nouveaux Sujets de Votre Majesté. . ."* from Trinidad's French community.

48. C.O. 295/2, Picton : Hobart, 27.4.1802, enclosures.

that there was a special case for regarding Trinidad, because of its varied population, as an Island best served by "a greater degree of Authority to its executive Government than is commonly granted by the British Constitution". And closed by suggesting that representatives freely chosen by the Islands' twenty-three parishes, and eight *barrios* or districts of Port-of-Spain, should meet with two *Cabildo* members in a convention presided over by the Governor-in-Council to discuss future changes in the Island's government.

The French who had separately addressed the *Cabildo* advanced similar arguments in a characteristically philosophical tone. Precipitate change, they said, was always attended with very great danger. When such change involved a sudden departure from something as fundamental as a country's laws, from the usages, customs, even prejudices to which men have grown accustomed the result could be incalculably evil. Laws expressed the character of a people and must always accord with the sentiments and capabilities of the people for whose guidance they were intended. "The plant which in one region would produce the sweetest fruit, would, when transplanted without proper precautions, produce the bitterest weeds." The rights, contracts and conventions which hold together the fabric of a society cannot be prejudiced without the greatest harm. Moreover since law was nothing but the expression of the will of the majority, to introduce a system of law contrary to the interests of that majority was a violation of every principle of good government. The French whites, busily engaged counting heads, completely ignored the claims of the free coloured but remembered their Rousseau.

*　　　　　　*　　　　　　*

If the introduction of a British constitution and British laws was for the foreign whites a "leap in the dark", it was, for not a few British inhabitants, a necessary condition of their advancement. Between 1783 and 1802, the British settlers in Trinidad were transformed by a series of events from a small appendage to a larger community of Frenchmen and Spaniards under Spanish rule, into a still small but increasingly militant and domineering faction under British rule. As an explanation of this change, the substitution of British for Spanish dominion was of course fundamental. But other factors were equally important.

In 1783, Trinidad's attraction for British settlers, the bulk of whom came from the old British West Indian islands, was solely and exclusively economic. Financial misfortune, at all times the constant companion of West Indian economic enterprise, and the great and overwhelming "difficulty of getting forward in the old settled British islands"[49] provided the main incentives for British immigration to Trinidad. Thus, the immigrants who took advantage of the *cédula* of 1783 were very far from being of the class of the Beckfords of Jamaica who, in the eighteenth century, were West Indian plantation magnates in the grand manner, or of the Codringtons or

49. W.O. 1/94, Memorial from the English settlers enclosed in Picton : Dundas, 11.1.1800.

the Borryaus of the same period who owned and supported lavish establishments in several West Indian islands.[50]   And if Trinidad did come quite close to having its local magnate, it was, significantly, in the person of a domiciled English merchant.   Edward Barry, apparently the sole exception to the general proposition about British immigrants of this period, journeyed from London in 1783-84 and obtained by personal suit at Madrid an *asiento* to supply 4,000 slaves annually to Trinidad and the province of Caracas. Later, he settled in Trinidad as a merchant and planter. Meanwhile, unable to fulfil his contract for the supply of slaves, he subcontracted to the Liverpool firm of Baker and Dawson who eventually gained the whole contract. And Barry's grandiloquent schemes petered out in a squalid contest for debt brought by Baker and Dawson against him for sums well in excess of $100,000.[51]

Nor did British immigration to Trinidad in the years between 1783 and 1797 connote the vigorous extension of mature West Indian or British metropolitan capitalism to Spanish Trinidad. Trinidad's British population was from its inception composed mainly of casualties in the West Indian 'rat race', feverishly attempting to resuscitate and refurbish their long dead hopes of acquiring that increasingly elusive West India fortune. Washed-up attorneys, managers and overseers, self-professed lawyers and doctors, entangled merchants, heavily encumbered planters and plain hangers-on; these were the people who immigrated to Trinidad from the British islands in the late eighteenth century. Migration, the classicists would have us believe, nearly always conforms to a distinct and recognizable pattern: the hiving-off of the vigorous and enterprising individuals of a community in search of fuller self-expression and greater opportunity elsewhere. British emigration from the old West Indian islands to Trinidad after 1783 was certainly not that. The majority of the new immigrants were, as Pierre M'Callum, a noted apologist for Trinidad's British population, put it, "British runaways, or more properly speaking . . . *scape-hemps,* from the other West Indian islands",[52] financial failures, encouraged and protected by the new Spanish laws operative in Trinidad, hurriedly fleeing the environs of their economic humiliation.

A memorial of Thomas Worswick and Sons, bankers and merchants of Lancaster, requesting Governor Picton's aid in recovering a debt of L8,090. 19s.8d. from the estate of one O'Brien, a fugitive planter from St. Kitts, chronicles the story of one of these debtors.[53] And O'Brien, like Barry, was surely not the typical immigrant, since he possessed enough wealth to live in

50.   For an idea of the size of the holdings of the Beckfords and the others see, R. Pares, *Merchants and Planters* (Economic History Review Supplement, No. 4, 1960), p.25.

51.   W.O. 1/93, p. 371 *et seq.* For some of the ramifications of this contest see Carmichael, *op. cit.,* pp. 243-5, though there is a suggestion of confusion here in that the firm Baker and Dawson is referred to in the index as Barry and Dawson. Barry was partner to Baker and Dawson in so far as he sub-contracted to the Liverpool firm for the importation of slaves; but he had no other formal connection with it. See, also, Dr. E. Wise, *Sketches of Trinidad and Tobago, 4 vols.,* 1936, Vol. IV, p.60. And *Parliamentary Debates,* New Series, Vol. VII, p. 1814.

52.   *Op. cit.,* pp. 141-2. 53.   W.O. 1/93, p. 705.

brief opulence in Trinidad from his arrival in early 1790 until his death in 1791. Perhaps more typical were the executors of his estate, a Mr. Geagon of St. Kitts and Dr. Andrew Clarke of Trinidad who defied the death-bed wish of O'Brien and the best efforts of Worswick to liquidate the debt. In particular the determination of Geagon, whose son had a financial interest in O'Brien's estate, to keep the unliquidated assets of the estate for himself, exactly portrayed the greed, indiscipline and corruption which were the dominating ethos of the society.

Cupidity and sharp dealing were indeed the stock-in-trade of prevailing business enterprise and were the accoutrements of the well placed no less than of the totally dispossessed, a fact that heightened the pervading atmosphere of financial corruption. Ex-Governor Picton, whose attorney was presumably a man of some standing, described himself in 1804 and 1805 as being systematically despoiled of the proceeds of his estate, Aranguez, by the machinations of that individual.[54] In September 1805, Picton was constrained to transfer the attorneyship to Messrs. Gloster and Begorrat, and to demote McDonald the former attorney to overseer. In doing so he made it quite plain that one of the essential tasks of the new attorneys was to keep a sharp eye on the overseer. "For God's sake", he wrote, "take an Early opportunity of examining Mc Donald's Accts - he cannot be (trusted) in anything.[55]

Peculation and fraud were not of course the monopolies of the British population. Many foreigners were equally adroit practitioners of these arts. Judge Smith in 1810, adverted to the case of Don Antonio Portel, commandant of the quarter of Santa Cruz, who, as executor of the estate of the deceased Don Cristoval de Robles, had defrauded Robles's two daughters of "more than one half of their Inheritance".[56] In 1808, the Spanish revolt against the impositions of Napoleon made Spain Britain's ally in the long Napoleonic struggle. It also provided the opportunity for Don Jose Ramon de Muxica, Spanish treasurer in Trinidad before the conquest,[57] to make official representations, through Admiral Apodaca the Spanish Minister in London, for the payment of a large debt still outstanding on an estate he had sold to Valentina de Basanta a Spanish resident in the Island.[58] Like the British, the French and Spanish inhabitants of Trinidad seldom scrupled to advance their own cause by outright chicanery and misdealing.

Various devices were habitually enlisted in the cause of personal enrichment. For instance, the hazards of a journey abroad were not limited to the dangers likely to be encountered at sea on board ship; a man might survive these and return to find himself dispossessed. The exploitation of one's absence by one's rivals, competitors, or creditors real or fancied, was one

54. *B.M. Add. Mss.* 36870, pp. 46-7, Picton : (Begorrat), no date; and Picton : Begorrat, 18.9.1805.
55. *B.M. Add. Mss.* 36870, pp. 46-7, Picton : Begorrat, 18.9.1805
56. C.O. 295/25, Smith : Liverpool, 30.9.1810.
57. Wise, *Sketches . . .* , Vol. III, p. 69.
58. C.O. 295/22, Bayot : Robinson, 16.9.1809. C.O. 296/4, Castlereagh : Hislop, 10.10.1809.

contingency against which Spanish law did not adequately provide. True, there was a *depositario general* theoretically responsible for the property of absentees, intestates and minors, but the impartial administration of the duties of that office was a factor on which the colonists learned not to rely; nor perhaps would they have welcomed such impartiality. In 1807, Don Juan de Montes complained that his estate had been greatly reduced by the spoliation of some of his property during his absence from the Island, and petitioned the Secretary of State for a grant of land in remuneration, having proceeded to England, as he conceived, on government business as a witness in the Picton affair. [59] Similarly circumstanced was one James Cadett, whose house was, in his absence, the object of the unwelcome attentions of John Burnley Littlepage, with, it would seem, the active connivance of Judge Smith. [60] And Lieutenant Briarly, whom we shall certainly meet again, warmly thanked Governor Hislop in 1806 for having intervened to prevent his house being sold for an "imaginary debt" while he, Briarly, was off the Island. [61] Precipitate seizure and sale of an absentee's property had obvious advantages over the prolonged litigation normally ensuing under due process of Spanish law.

By 1797, the British community had by fair and foul means succeeded if lifting itself by its own economic bootstraps. Many of them had become successful planters, many more prosperous merchants and tradesmen. There were yet a few indifferent characters among them, chronic loungers devoid of industry if not of ambition, keeping a sharp lookout for the main chance. But by and large, prosperity and the mild liberalism of Chacon's government had induced in them a complacent and unprotesting acquiescence in their continued citizenship under Spanish rule. Some of them as we have seen even participated in the higher levels of the civil life of the community such as it was.

Docile acknowledgement of a situation they could not change, and which after all had been good to them, did not however blind them to the advantages to be derived from British conquest. They correctly judged that this conquest, when it occurred, marked the beginning of the last stage of their full economic rehabilitation. Two years after the conquest, in 1799, the British community was demonstrating all the anxiety of a propertied class anxious to conserve the amenities and privileges of property. Fearing that Trinidad might be returned to Spain at the peace which they then thought to be imminent, the British settlers sought to guard against the ruin they felt would follow from that event due to their enthusiastic welcome of the British forces and administration. They petitioned for the exaction of certain stipulations in their favour when the articles of peace should be signed. These included immunity from prosecution for offences thought to have been committed against Spain while the Island was under British rule,

59. C.O. 295/17, Fawkener : Shee, 7.2.1707, enclosure.
60. C.O. 295/26, Nihell : Marryat, 4.1.1811, enclosed in Marryat : Peel, 28.2.1811.
61. C.O. 295/21, Briarly : Hislop, 16.6.1806, enclosed in Hislop : (Cooke), 28.3. 1809.

the recognition of the validity of all transactions relating to commerce and property concluded under the British government, the concession of the right to leave the Island with full benefit of the property acquired there, and the appointment to Trinidad for at least five years of a British consul whose salary would be paid by the British inhabitants themselves. [62]   As long as British dominion continued they were, however, eager to extract the last ounce of economic advantage from the connection.   In August 1799, the Island's merchants memorialized the Colony's plight pointing out that though its commerce had, since the conquest, increased with "unexampled rapidity" there was still no direct communication with the United Kingdom. Trinidad's mail which at that time came via Grenada was described as often wandering around the West Indies for periods of about six weeks arriving finally by an uncertain, "circuitous and precarious rout". [63]

Of some significance in the development of an important British economic interest in the Island was the intrusion of organized British capital after the capitulation.   The orgiastic delight of the British government with Trinidad's commercial advantages has been already illustrated.   The eager acceptance by the British mercantile interest of the opportunities created by the Free Port Act of June 1797 must now be noted.   In November 1798, the firm Turnbull, Forbes and Company, on Huskisson's advice, decided to open an establishment in Trinidad, [64]   and by 1799 the mercantile interest with direct connections in England had grown so strong as to make effective representations to the Secretary of State against Governor Picton.   It alleged that Picton,   in contravention of the navigation laws, was permitting a disproportionate amount of the Island's produce to be exported in American ships to the detriment of the export trade to Britain. [65] By February of the same year a group of London merchants were so well established in the Island that they were already petitioning the Treasury against the 3½% duty on imports and exports which they represented to be an unjustified restriction on its trade. [66] Similar petitions against the duty by other British merchants, such as those of the Merchants and Manufacturers of Glasgow in 1804, [67] became a standard part of the armament of protest against the system of government administered in Trinidad, an agitation which in this respect perhaps attained its zenith in Gloster's proposal of 1810 to make Trinidad a free port in the fullest sence of the term, "like St. Eustatius before 1780". Urging the abandonment of "the old pertinacious adherence to our *Navigation* Acts" Gloster prophesied that Trinidad could thus become the "mart and Emporium of the

62.   W.O. 1/94, Memorial enclosed in Picton : Portland and Picton : Dundas, 11.1.1800.
63.   W.O. 1/93, Memorial of 15.8.1799, enclosed in Picton : Dundas, 15.8.1799.
64.   W.O. 1/93, Turnbull, Forbes & Co. : Huskisson, 13.11.1798.
65.   W.O. 1/94, Dundas : Picton, 7.4.1800. For Picton's replies see, W.O. 1/94, Picton : Dundas, 9.7. 1800. Also : W.O. 1/94; P.C. 1/3557, Bundle 1, Picton : Dundas, 20.7.1800.
66.   For Dundas's query to Picton see, W.O. 1/93, (Draft) of Dundas : Picton, 23.2.1799. The Memorial or a copy of it has, however, not been seen. For Picton's reply see C.O. 296/1, Picton : Dundas, 14.5.1799 in which he says that the duty has never been collected at a rate higher than 1¼%.
67.   C.O. 295/9, Boyd Alexander : Secretary of the Privy Council, 2.1.1804.

West Indies" This would doubtless provoke the "Jealous Spirit of Jamaica
. . . but", said Gloster, whose contempt of mutinous West Indian Assemblies
was boundless, "it would be indeed a good mode of punishing that refractory
settlement". After all, he continued with malicious humour, Trinidad had
for long been an Island of experiment. Then try "experimentally" the full
fledged free port system: "it would even astonish the heads that devised and
promoted the scheme". [68]

The merchants thus introduced into Trinidad had many qualifications for
the leadership of the struggle for a British system of government, with every
material interest in promoting that object. First of all, as merchants they
tended to converge on Port-of-Spain the Island's capital and only seaport.
Here, living and working together, they developed a community of outlook
and feeling and were able to coalesce their efforts in the pursuit of a common objective. More than any other group in a country riddled with faction
and divided by poor transport they possessed the facility of meeting and
discussing their plans and goals. Secondly, a merchant unlike a planter is a
gregarious being. His occupation forces him to look outside himself, to make
acquaintances, to explore contacts. Historically he was responsible in the
early Renaissance period, as much perhaps as anyone was, for the growth
and spread of lay education. In this connection the transition from an
itinerant to a sedentary form of commerce, and with it the necessary development of the skills of organization and correspondence, and the mastery of
the tools of financial management, were of supreme importance in the
merchants' development. [69] And now in Trinidad his occupation bequeathed
him the very skills needed for effective organization and agitation. Moreover he was an integral part of a community whose economic roots lay deep
in metropolitan Britain; thus he could and often did enlist the aid of powerful
voices in his cause. Committees of British merchants, committees of British
merchants and residents, committees of English settlers: call them what you
will, the dominating influence was mercantile. In 1805, there was a Commercial Committee officially acting as a sort of clearing house for grievances
affecting the mercantile community, and unofficially, almost surreptitiously,
doing duty as a standing committee for the agitation for British laws and a
British constitution, the absence of which was undoubtedly the chief
mercantile grievance. [70] And the ramifications of the Dickson case, in which
the Commercial Committee played a part, revealed the close connection
between local and British metropolitan mercantile interests. [71]

Thirdly, in his public position the merchant enjoyed a precise advantage
over the planter his natural rival. The chief dependant of a planter was, apart
from his family, the slave, a voiceless, rightless chattel. Particularly was this

68. C.O. 295/25, Gloster : Hislop, June 1810, enclosed in Smith : Jenkinson (Private), 8.7.1810.
69. See, for example, Wallace A. Ferguson, "The Church in a Changing World", *American Historical Re-
    view*, Vol. 59, 1953, pp. 1-19.
70. See, C.O. 295/11, Hislop : Castlereagh, 28.9.1805, and its enclosures in C.O. 295/12.
71. *Ibid.* The Dickson case is discussed in Chapter Seven, below.

so in Trinidad where most plantations were personally supervised by their owners. The dependants of a merchant, his clerk, his shop assistant, the lounger who maintained a precarious respectability through his gifts, perhaps even his errand boy, were often whites with recognized rights and privileges. A white person, regardless of his condition, could lend his name, he could sign a petition, he could swell a crowd; he had, in a manner of speaking, influence. Several of the individuals interviewed after the Wharton's Tavern affair were precisely of this type, under-aged petty clerks, unemployed persons, small artisans and tradesmen, all in some way dependent on the Port-of-Spain merchant for their livelihood. Of the sixty-odd depositions taken on Picton's orders, only two were taken from overseers, one of whom was unemployed.[72] They were the only representatives of the **planting** interest. There were probably others, doing double duty as merchants **or** planters or some permutation in between.[73] If so the failure to say **or** to indicate an occupation closely allied to the **normal** duties of a plantation was a significant omission. Similarly, of the 451 subscribers to the petition for British laws and a British constitution in 1810, Judge Smith put 256 firmly in the category of "either unknown . . . **or** . . . known to be not worth a dollar . . . **Merchant's clerks, apprentice boys, printers devils** and the offal of the Community".[74]

The merchant position on constitutional change was crystal clear; the British planter position was less so. The British planters,in a minority among the British inhabitants, to some extent acquiesced in the early demand for constitutional change, but their enthusiasm was, as we shall see, severely circumscribed by a recognition of the practical advantages offered the plantation class by the Spanish laws regulating the recovery of debt. The merchants on the other hand, once they were recognized as the leaders of the struggle for a British form of government, attracted the support of all the dissidents who thought they had something to gain from that measure. Chief among these were the new arrivals after 1797 with whom the merchants formed a natural alliance. In contrast to the pre-1797 settlers these newcomers were, like many of the merchants, a landless class forced to catch as catch can in an increasingly competitive and speculative society.

Governor Picton was not authorized to make grants of land and he made none.[75] Lands were granted in occupancy with no secure title to them, thus reducing their value to the holder. Landed property could of course be bought from those who held a grant from the Spanish government, but

72. C.O. 295/2; P.C. 1/3557, Bundle No. 2, Picton : Hobart, 27.4.1802, enclosures.
73. The division of planter and merchant does not mean that all planters were on one side and all merchants on the other. On the whole the planter community was less heterogeneous than the merchant community. Many merchants speculated in plantations and were themselves planters since investment in plantations remained the major form of investment available to people with money. Such merchants, however, clearly thought of themselves as merchants first and planters second.
74. C.O. 295/24, Smith ; Jenkinson; 13.5.1810.
75. W.O. 1/93, (Draft) Dundas : Picton, 5.3.1799. W.O. 1/94, Picton : Dundas, 1801

naturally went to the highest bidder. Some of the foreigners who wished to leave the Island after the conquest grew rich selling their estates at inflated prices[76] which few newcomers could pay. The chief buyers in most cases were the richer merchants who in turn speculated with their new acquisitions.[77]

For most of the newcomers, it was hard enough just living. With local production of foodstuffs small and inadequate,[78] the scarcity of provisions from the Venezuelan mainland owing to the vigilance of Spanish *guarda costas,* or even the indiscriminate activities of British cruisers,[79] sometimes threatened the Island with famine.[80] And the constant arrival of new settlers and slaves did much to worsen the situation.[81] Even if one did manage to get a small estate it was difficult to stock it adequately. Slaves of choice quality were sold to Governor Picton, and doubtless to some others, at £46 per head payable in bills at three months sight; on the open market inferior specimens fetched £85 with a hefty interest charged for credit.[82] Whether a small estate was at all desirable was a different question. In 1799, Picton estimated that a viable sugar estate should consist of not less than two hundred acres, incurring an outlay of £8,000 sterling.[83]

Thus in the years immediately following 1797 the wheel had again turned full circle. As in the period after 1783, there was again a British community embracing within it a largely dispossessed segment of population ready for any adventure. Such people were exploitable and they were exploited. The credits and the favours which they sought of the merchant not only put them in his financial debt, they also made them his political appendages. So that Picton was right when, with unconscious irony, he described the British community, one sixth of the Island's free population, as being in large measure "attached to commerce . . . (with) no fixed property".[84]

76. C.O. 295/2, Picton : Hobart, 18.2.1802. In fact Picton refers in this letter to a very mobile speculative class of foreign proprietors, mainly French and Italian, who realized substantial profits from the rise in property prices consequent on the cession and thereafter departed from the Island. They were distinct from those other foreign whites who had come to the Island to rebuild the fortunes which had been ruined or lost during the French Revolutionary struggles in the West Indies.
77. Sanderson, *Political Account,* pp. 73-6.
78. Trinidad was, and for a long time remained, dependent on the mainland for provisions. This was supplemented, at times supplanted, by imports from the American states and, to a smaller degree, from the British North American colonies. The trade with the mainland consisted mainly of the importation of livestock such as cattle, lambs, mules, horses, sheep, goats and poultry; beef and salted fish and silver currency with which the Spanish traders purchased manufactures of British origin particularly warm clothing, woollens etc. At times some foodstuffs were re-exported to the neighbouring islands and, more regularly, mules and horses. See, W.O. 1/94, pp. 567-8, "Remarks on the Island of Trinidad"; and C.O. 296/1, Picton : Hobart, 20.11.1801.
79. W.O. 1/94, Picton : Hobart, 18.9.1801.
80. See, for example, W.O. 1/94, Picton : Dundas, 20.10.1800.
81. *Ibid;* Enclosed proclamation, dated 7.10.1800.
82. C.O. 295/10, *Report on the State of Trinidad . . . ,* by Col. Thos. Picton etc.
83. C.O. 296/1, Picton : Dundas, 14.5.1799.
84. C.O. 296/1; W.O. 1/94, Picton : Hobart, 14.12.1801.

From this fact Picton drew an important political moral. The introduction of a new constitution, he pontificated, must await the arrival of a "large number of respectable English Settlers"; this regimen of "low English Merchants"[85] would not do. In the existing circumstances "the concession of a free legislature would be productive of serious consequences".[86] In the meantime a nominated Assembly should be introduced and Spanish law should be maintained while gradual changes were carefully made. The whole should be regarded as an experiment lasting roughly from three to five years, at the end of which time changes in the Island's population, and more particularly in the British section of it, should permit the introduction of the full fledged Assembly system. Determined to leave nothing to chance Picton recommended by name ten British residents, seven Frenchmen and four Spaniards, as prospective nominees to the proposed Assembly.[87] Of the English, only two, William Brown and J. Eccles, were merchants. Not surprisingly, they were complete nonentities as far as the movement for British laws and a British constitution was concerned.

Between this grasping, pushful and acquisitive British mercantile community and the staid planter class composed mainly of foreigners, there was a deep and abiding conflict of economic interest which was reflected to a large extent in the attitude of the two groups towards the question of constitutional change.

In its most acute form this conflict belonged to the period 1797-1802. Between the conquest and the cession, the introduction of organized British capital infused new life into the Island's commerce and agriculture. Speculation, as we have seen, ran riot. New lands were taken into cultivation, new estates were begun, old ones were bought and sold and slaves were purchased by their thousands. Under the stimulus of rising sugar prices, sugar production increased steadily and spectacularly. A total production of 5,908,457 lbs. in 1798 rose to 8,419,859 lbs. in 1799 and leapt to 15,461,912 lbs. in 1801, falling slightly in 1802 to 14,164,984 lbs.[88] Coffee, cocoa and cotton

---

85. C.O. 295/2, Picton : Hobart, 18.2.1802. The phrase is Picton's.

86. W.O. 1/94, Picton : Hobart, 14.12.1801.

87. *Ibid.*, Picton's nominees were:

English:			
Sir James Bontine (sic)	Wm. Lockhead	Wm Brown
John Lynch	Wm. Hall Esqrs.	J. Eccles Merchants
Chas. Farrel	Wm. Jarvis	
Ph. Langton	Chas. Odeon	

Even Picton's two favourite merchants did not, it seems, quite rate the appellation "esquire". Planters were "esquires"; merchants however respectable belonged to a different, and lesser breed.

French:			
Baron Montalembert	Mr. De L'Oppinott	Mr. Begorrat Snr.
Mr. Mondilbion	Mr. La Hante	Mr. Coulanges
Mr. Demarais		

The "Mr." is Picton's own aberration.

Spanish:			
Don Vincente Bonttur	Don H.F. Farfan	Don J. Moyan
Don J.V. Indave		

88. Sanderson, *Political Account.....*, p. 100.

also increased in production, but less steadily than sugar and often with great and disturbing fluctuations. [89]

Generally speaking, the economic prospects were good and remained good until the beginning of 1802. But in the eagerness for quick profits very unsafe economic practices had prevailed. [90] Planters borrowed too much at interest rates that were much too high. Merchants lent too much on too little security. Commission agents, concerned mainly with their commissions, goaded their London principals into advancing more and more goods to clients who were already heavily indebted. [91] Very few business transactions were made in cash. Estates were bought on credit, and operated under the stimulus of still more credit. With money scarce prices rose. High commodity prices were matched by falling sugar prices due to over-production, to the greater embarrassment of the sugar planter. The high level of production plus the accumulation of credit contributed to falling prices abroad. Produce shipped in part payment of debts depreciated alarmingly in price on arrival on the London market. London merchants grown wary of credit began to insist on cash and to call in outstanding debts. Merchant houses in Trinidad faced with such demands pressured local debtors for payment; and at this point, due to the incapacity of debtors to pay, the bubble burst. The boom had run its course. Credits ceased, merchant houses fell, and planters were ruined. [92]

Here the constitutional attitudes of the merchants on the one hand and of the planter on the other intrude; for the attitudes of both were conditioned to a large extent by sectional responses to the economic predicament. For the merchant, recovery of his debt depended on the realization of his hopes that, on the cession, the introduction of British laws would give him the same advantage over his debtors as that given to creditors in the other British West Indian islands. The over-committed planter, however, looked to the maintenance of the Spanish legal system to protect him from the exactions of the merchant.

As far as the recovery of debt from sugar estates was concerned, Spanish law rendered the process of recovery interminable, expensive and uncertain. In the first place, in contrast to the system then prevalent in the British West Indies which allowed seizure of a plantation by the first creditor presenting unredeemed demands against an estate, the Spanish system permitted legal process to be instituted only when the total debt amounted to at least two-

89. *Ibid.,* For example, coffee fell from 388,990 lbs in 1798 to 278,271 lbs in 1802; cocoa fell from 235,020 lbs in 1798 to 138,669 lbs in 1802; and cotton varied from 173,899 lbs in 1798 to 317,395 lbs in 1800, to 190,210 lbs in 1802.

90. Sanderson provides the best account of such practices. See *Political Account...,* p. 90 ff: and *An Appeal....,* p. 33 ff.

91. Sanderson, *Political Account. . . ,* p. 67.

92. See, *An Appeal. . . ,* p. 37; *Political Account,* pp. 65-6.

thirds of the appraised value of the property.[93]   When the debt was less than the value of the entire estate only the sugar could be taken in execution of it.[94]   Nor could slaves or implements be seized and sold in satisfaction of any debt as was common in the other British islands.[95]   Under the English system, too, the first creditor to levy on an estate took possession and kept possession of it until his debt was paid, or sold it to recover his loan; thus not only the interest of the proprietor but that of the other creditors suffered. Spanish law circumvented this ruthless procedure by the equally ruthless one of saddling the creditor not only with the costs of his own action, but with that of the debtor if he should fail to establish his whole claim.[96]   In addition the debtor could take refuge in a *concurso* of his creditors.

An indebted Spanish planter wishing to resort to a *concurso* had only to cede his property to the courts, inform his creditors that he had done so, and then leave it to them to establish their respective claims.[97]   Assuming that satisfactory claims could be established the court then addressed itself to determining the priority of the claims, itself a tortuous process carefully enunciated by Spanish law.[98]   Meanwhile the planter retained possession of his estate and received an allowance for tending it.[99]   He could even, if he wished, further complicate the process of recovery. He could, for example, induce a third party to intervene seeking to be paid in advance of the existing creditors. This would involve in most cases the production of evidence and the citation of a witness, a process the court was enjoined to facilitate by allowing sufficient time to the plaintiff to do so. If a witness lived in a distant part of the Island, the time to be allotted varied between eighty and one hundred and twenty days; if he lived in another island, six months; in Europe, eighteen months.[100]   If the evidence when produced was insufficient or inadmissible, more time was given for the provision of the additional evidence or for appeals to the *Audiencia* or to the King.

If after all this one or two creditors succeeded in establishing their claims and settling their priorities, then the sale of the estate in vindication of the debts could be a source of new difficulties. The usual method was sale by auction, but the property could not be sold for less than two-thirds of its

---

93. For a discussion of the differences between the Spanish and the English systems see C.O. 295/24, Smith : Liverpool, 14.2.1810. Also, *Parliamentary Debates.* New Series. Vol. VII, 1822; Marryat's speech in the House of Commons on July 25, p. 1806 ff, and particularly p. 1819 ff. Also, Fraser, *op. cit.,* Vol. II, p. 136 ff.
94. *Recopilación*, Lib. 5, Tit. 14, Leyes, 2, 3, 4 and 5.
95. Sanderson, *An Appeal.* . . . , p. 38.
96. *Parliamentary Papers.* House of Commons, 1826-7. (551) XXIII, p. 32.
97. *An Appeal.* . . . , pp. 41-2. Also, *Parliamentary Papers*, 1826-7. (551) XXIII, pp. 84-5 where in reply to queries put by the Commission of Legal Enquiry the Chief Justice and the Judge of Criminal Enquiry define the *concurso* and its manner of operation.
98. *An Appeal.* . . . , pp. 41-2. See also *Recopilación*, Lib. 5, Tit. 14.
99. *Parliamentary Debates*, Vol. VII, 1822, p. 1822.
100. Sanderson, *An Appeal.* . . . . p. 39.

appraised value, payable in cash at the time of the auction.[101] Since cash dealings were rare, a purchaser often could not be found.[102] If a purchaser was not found than the creditor had to buy the estate himself, often against his will, since his object was to recover his money not to put out further sums in the purchase of an estate that might well be grossly over-valued.[103]

Even after buying the property his difficulties were not at an end. If there were other creditors with claims against the estate, he had to pay them. And he had to give security to maintain the estate in good condition for a specified time pending a possible appeal by the former owner. Even so, at this stage, or at any of several stages prior to it, the plaintiff could be challenged by the planter's wife claiming restitution of such sums as she had allegedly spent in improving the estate. If the wife was dead, the children, who, under Spanish law were minors till the age of twenty-five, could come forward and demand the proceeds of the maternal share of the estate.[104] Or the new owner might find himself opposed, even at this late stage, by another creditor claiming to possess a more privileged lien on the estate.

It is hardly surprising if Trinidad's sugar planters were said to belong to a "privileged order".[105] Creditors grew so wary of the courts that proceedings were seldom instituted against any estate with any other object than that of establishing preference or priority over other creditors.[106] To do otherwise and to try to recover an outstanding mortgage or debt was to involve oneself in protracted and expensive litigation.

If the Spanish legal system favoured the planter it must not be supposed however that the merchants had suddenly found themselves, in late 1801 and early 1802, the sport of laws produced as if by magic to foil them. They and their principals had long known of the existence of those laws. British merchants had helped persuade Governor Chacon that a proclamation legalizing interest rates on mortgage debts would aid the Island's industry.[107] Their commerce had always been a calculated risk, though often more than rewarded by their profits. And after the conquest they worked diligently for the Island's cession confident that with the introduction of British laws they would easily recover their debts.[108] To these men, and to their principals in London, Bristol, Glasgow and the other British trading centres, the continuation of Spanish laws after the cession was a severe blow. It was construed as having no other effect but that of shielding debtors from the consequences of their debt. It was, they believed, a device intended to encompass the ruin of a loyal and enterprising merchant community. Conversely, the grant of the

101. *Ibid.*, p. 40.   102. Sanderson, *An Appeal. . . . ,*p. 40.
103. *Ibid.* Also, *Parliamentary Debates*, Vol. VII, 1822, p. 1819.
104. *Parliamentary Debates*, Vol. VII, 1822, p. 1823. Also, *Parliamentary Papers*, 1826-7. (551) XXIII, pp. 34-5, contain an exposition with references to Spanish law of the wife's right to *gancancias* on which this privilege was founded.
105. Sanderson, *Political Account*, p. 115.   106. Sanderson, *An Appeal. . . .* , p. 41.
107. *Parliamentary Debates*, Vol. VII, 1822, pp. 1819-20.   108. Fraser, *op. cit.*, Vol. II, p. 139.

Assembly system of government and British laws was represented to be the only means of rehabilitating the Island's economy by permitting the easy recovery of debt, freeing credit, and ultimately benefitting the planter himself.

The planters did not of course see matters in exactly the same light. Attorney General Gloster, himself a planter, undoubtedly spoke for most planters when he described the Trinidad merchantile population as "the rakings of England, Ireland, and Scotland; fellows without family, fortune or education; who as attorneys and managers, raise themselves upon the ruin of the planters, whom, when they oust from their estates, they succeed in the legislatures". [109] But this was abuse which, however true, did not gainsay the fact that the desire to hold on to his heavily encumbered estate was a compelling factor contributing to the planter's hostility to British laws. Gloster himself said as much in 1804. He admitted that the planters were heavily committed to the British merchants, dreaded the introduction of British laws, and were, to a large extent, "more privileged than they ought to be. . ." [110] The constitutional struggle of the next few years was to evoke again and again the economic conflicts of the period 1797-1802.

*   *   *

The importance of the Wharton's Tavern affair lies in the fact that it brought about for the first time the confrontation of the various groups whose attitudes to the constitutional question were to be of significance in the years ahead. The free coloureds alone had remained silent. Yet by their mere presence they exercised a profound influence on the positions taken by the more active contestants. Events were eventually to show that the free coloured position was stronger than anyone could at this time have foreseen.

The immediate result of the constitutional agitation of late 1801 and early 1802 was the appointment of a Commission to preside over the Island's government and to make recommendations on its constitution and future development. The Tavern affair coincided with the public discussion then taking place in England about the uses to which the new acquisition should be put. Discontent in Trinidad and abolitionist pressure in Parliament resulted in the British government's undertaking, at the end of Canning's debate in May 1802, [111] to send out a fact-finding Commission to report on the Island. But such a Commission need not have had administrative and political powers; the fact that it did was a major victory for the protagonists of a British constitution whose agitation had at least had the effect of supplanting Picton as sole Governor.

From Picton's point of view this was as unexpected a decision as any that could have been taken. In frequent despatches between Governor and

109. Sanderson, *Political Account. . . . , p* 93. Quoted from Gloster's *A Letter to the Earl of Buckinghamshire, Late Secretary of State, Respecting Affairs in Trinidad in 1803. . .* , (London, 1807).

110. C.O. 295/8, Gloster : Hislop, 4.7.1804; enclosed in Hislop : Camden, 9.7.1804.

111. See Chapter 3, pp. 85-6.

Secretary of State the constitutional problem had been thoroughly aired. Picton had done most of the talking, but he had had no reason to believe that his admonitions were unwelcome. His latest proposal for a nominated Assembly had not evoked much interest in London, but his opinion that the grant of representative government should be long deferred had met with the warmest approbation. Unfortunately in Picton's view, the same despatch that informed him that there was at present no intention of establishing an Assembly in the Island, also told him that his letters of April and May 1802 on the Tavern affair had been "the first official intimation . . . received of any dissatisfaction prevailing in the Island under your Government". [112] Accordingly, it had been decided to place the Island's government in the hands of a three-man Commission of which, he, Picton, would be a member. The first experiment designed to resolve the Island's constitutional future and the shape of its society had begun. The vanguard society was on its way.

112. C.O. 296/4, pp. 66-8, Hobart : Picton, 9.7.1802.

CHAPTER 5

"THE MOST TRAGIC EXPERIMENT OF ALL"

That the vanguard society did not immediately get very far is to be explained in terms of the failure of the Commission which had been appointed to create it. The Commission not only failed but failed disastrously. In fact the appointment of the Commission inaugurated one of the most unfortunate episodes in the Island's history, the effects of which, because of the failure of the Commission to achieve its important objectives, lingered on and influenced the course of events for many years.

The Commission of 1802 consisted of three persons, one of them being ex-Governor Lt. Col. Thomas Picton who had alone administered the Island since its conquest in 1797. The others were Mr. William Fullarton, civil commissioner and chairman of the Commission, and Commodore Samuel Hood of the Royal Navy. Fullarton, as first commissioner, was responsible for civil administration; Picton as second commissioner was responsible for military affairs; and Hood, the third commissioner, was responsible for naval matters.[1] Altogether the Commission comprised a team entrusted with the task of completely reorganizing Trinidad's society on new and hitherto unexplored lines, the purpose being to facilitate the introduction of a form of government less irksome to the Island's British and foreign subjects than the arbitrary system that had so far prevailed. This was an experiment of the first magnitude. And if, as successive commentators have woefully complained from this date onwards, Trinidad under the British rule came to be regarded primarily as an Island of experiment, then this was the first, the most ambitious, and incomparably the most tragic experiment of all.

The appointment of the Commission had no exact precedent in British colonial government. If the appointment were founded on precedent that precedent was Malta where, in 1801, a Commission had been appointed for the government of that island.[2] A year later, in Trinidad in 1802, what seems to have been a modification of the same idea was used by the British government in its first serious attempt to determine, among other things, the form and structure of the Island's future government. The conflict over the constitutional question, highlighted by the Wharton's Tavern affair, was complemented by the new urgencies of the political situation in Britain arising out of the slave question, and together propelled the British government into taking precipitate action to resolve them.

Yet, the questions raised by the debates of April and May 1802 in the House of Commons were nothing if not fundamental. Given the circum-

---

1. C.O. 296/4, Hobart : Picton, 9.7.1802.   2. See *Cambridge History of the British Empire*, Vol. II, pp. 172-82. Also, W. Hardman, *History of Malta, 1798-1815*. (London, 1909), passim.

stances of the day, the settlement of the government and the economic re-organization of a conquered slave colony in the West Indies in the early nine-teenth century were likely to test the mettle of the strongest and most talen-ted British administration. This the Addington government most certainly was not. Addington, Prime Minister since early 1801, ruled by grace of Pitt, and both he and Pitt knew it. Indeed, Addington's was the classic caretaker administration.[3] While Addington lumbered about on stage, Pitt, the dom-inating political personality of his age, at first unobtrusively and then boldly, stalked the wings. From his very accession to the supreme office the new Prime Minister was haunted by the spectre of his fall. Pitt, Prime Minister for eighteen years, could not, despite his best intentions, quite accommodate himself to the prolonged ascendancy of anyone but himself.[4]   Even Addington seems to have had difficulty adjusting to his unexpectedly high estate: he accepted the premiership only after being assured of Pitt's sup-port,[5] and seems even to have consulted Pitt on some of his ministerial ap-pointments.[6]   Nor would others permit Pitt to forget that he had been Prime Minister once, and could be again. The loyalty of party hacks clamour-ing for place and power,[7] and the support of talented persons like Canning who had, in a letter of unctuous irony, resigned his office of Paymaster-General on Addington's rise,[8] could only be gratified and kept by the con-tinuing imminence of their leader's return to office.[9] Thus, pressure on Pitt resulted in pressure on Addington and tended to undermine the authority and stability of the latter's government.

In the early months of 1802 Addington faced the first crisis of his premiership. The Peace of Amiens was the particular issue upon which the political future of the Addington government seemed to rest.   That

3.   For this very reason nearly every politician of talent avoided it like the plague. It was an adminis-tration in which, as one Tory peer put it with curious relish, there were "none of those confounded men of genius".   As another critic put it, however, in an unattributed parliamentary attack it was, more precisely, a truly "rickety administration, a thing of shreds and patches".
      Hon. George Pellew, *The Life and Correspondence of the Right Hon'ble Henry Addington, First Vis-count Sidmouth.* Three volumes, (London, 1847), Vol. I, p. 355.
4.   Pellew, *op. cit.,* Vol. I, pp. 330-4. As Pellew said (p. 334) it was certainly a "startling fact that, where-as Mr. Addington accepted the government in 1801 with the entire approbation and promised co-operation of Mr. Pitt, so he resigned it in 1804 in consequence of the latter's coalition with Mr. Fox, until at that time his decided political opponent".
      Also Richard Pares, *King George III and the Politicians,* (Oxford, 1953), pp. 136-8, 164.
5.   Pellew, *op. cit.,* Vol. I, pp. 330-4.
6.   One of these appointments being it would seem, Hobart's. See the *Hobart Papers,* Bundle B, (C. 328). These papers are lodged at the Aylesbury Record Office, Buckinghamshire, England. Bundle B, (C. 328) contains a summary of various communications and conversations between Hobart and Addington, Lord Auckland, Pitt, and the Marquis of Buckingham on 10.2.1801 and with Grenville, another "kingmaker", on 12.2.1801.   7.   Cf. Pellew, *op. cit.,* Vol. I, p. 332.
8.   *Ibid.,* p. 321. Paymaster General Canning : Addington, 15.3.1801. Other letters in a similar vein followed on March 16, 18.
9.   An expectation that did not prove well founded in Canning's case. On Pitt's return to office Canning was given the Treasurership of the Navy, a non-Cabinet post, much to his disappointment, and largely because of the virulence of his attacks on Addington which had the effect of discrediting him with Pitt. Sir Charles Petrie, *Life of George Canning,* (London, 1932), pp. 35, 39.

Addington survived the crisis was due in large measure to Pitt's avoidance of all embarrassing criticism, a strategy that emphasized Pitt's ascendancy as much as it drew attention to his generosity. But Addington's survival was also due to his somewhat successful presentation of Trinidad and Ceylon, the only two acquisitions retained from all Britain's conquests, as noteworthy additions to the Empire. By over-emphasizing the commercial potential of these two colonies Addington rallied much Parliamentary support for his pact with Napoleon, but only at the expense of converting Ceylon and Trinidad into priceless political assets. Ceylon, popularly linked with the defence of India, rewarded Addington's faith; but Trinidad, whose retention by Addington has been praised by his biographer as a certain proof of his "discriminative judgement", [10] was a different matter. Enmeshed in the snares of the slave question it could even prove, as the parliamentary debates of April and May 1802 fully demonstrated, to be a rather brittle asset.

Granted therefore the desirability of founding a decision about Trinidad's future on the most perfect knowledge of its condition and prospects, the determination to set up a commission to do so was in part a political decision. Battered by Canning and the other abolitionists in Parliament, Addington conceded nearly everything, though most ungraciously. And when, in reply to Canning's virtual motion of censure against his government for its policy of development in Trinidad, Addington announced the appointment of the Commission, he was more concerned with lifting Trinidad out of an acrimonious public debate than with the quick and efficient solution of the Island's problems. The Commission was in fact an ill-fashioned and hasty contrivance. It was intended to avoid decision by indefinitely delaying it, to court the comparative safety of inaction rather than risk the dubious effects of decision. Trinidad was a potential threat to the government's well-being and had to be decently shelved.

What was more, the imperfect precedent of a similar experiment in Malta in 1801 stood to hand. The attractions of this recent example and the promptings of political expediency proved irresistible. Lord Hobart, by no means the most industrious or indefatigable of ministers, regarded his Maltese brainchild as the proper subject for reincarnation in Trinidad, with very few modifications. The most obvious modification, that of the size of the Commission, was made: three in Trinidad were to perform the work of one in Malta. But the less obvious and more important safeguards necessary to ensure the proper functioning of a three-man Commission, most importantly

10. Pellew, *op. cit.*, Vol. II, p. 50.
   Pellew, in vindication of the Peace also claimed that Addington's negotiations fulfilled the main principle established by Pitt in 1800 for the conclusion of the war.
   ". . . we must insist", Pitt had written, "on retaining such part of our requisitions as are essential, not for their own intrinsic value, but for the security of our ancient possessions in the East and West . . ."
   Pitt : Addington, 8.10.1800. Quoted, Pellew, *op. cit.*, Vol. I, p. 263. On this reckoning, Ceylon was necessary for the protection of India, Trinidad for the protection of West Indian slave society.

the unequivocal definition of duty and responsibility, were ignored, and fell far short of the very precise arrangements prevailing in the case of Malta. [11] Thus perished in Trinidad the experiment of government by Commission which might well have been a real contribution to British colonial administration at the beginning of the nineteenth century: and with it also perished the first serious attempt to devise for a slave colony in transition a form of government appropriate to its particular needs. [11a]

The Civil Commission of 1802 was launched in an atmosphere of adventure, and its spirit was the spirit of ambition. The British political genius for making the best of indifferent circumstances was hardly ever displayed to greater advantage. Every nerve was strained to give the impression that the institution of the Commission was a project which the Addington Government had long and lovingly conceived. Every probable defect was viewed as a virtue. Even the plurality of commissioners, which was later to give rise to so much embarrassment, was for Lord Hobart a fact of supreme merit since he believed that "from the Union of Civil, Military and Naval Talents combined in the persons selected for this Service, advantages must arise which cannot be expected from the labours of any one individual." [12]

The same atmosphere of ambitious intent surrounded the enunciation of the Commission's terms of reference. As Lord Hobart wrote in his despatch of October 16, 1802, the consideration mainly prompting the appointment of the Commission "arose from the expedience of preparing for the consideration of His Majesty in Council a System of Government, applicable to the peculiar Circumstances of the Island, where the population, tho' at present very limited, is composed of various Nations, distinct in their Language Customs and prejudices, and where a very extensive Tract of Country remains to be settled under a Climate supposed not to be unfavourable to European Industry and with advantage of a Soil, known to be particularly fertile". [13]

11. See *C.H.B.E.*, II, pp. 172-82. Hardman, *op. cit.*, pp. 350-7, 358-9.
11a. See for contrast though, Sullivan : Picton (Private), 18.1.1802. The spirit of this letter was completely different. What was later entrusted to the Commission of 1802 was here being entrusted to Picton. But this was before the Wharton's Tavern Affair and the two House of Commons debates of April and May 1802 on the proposed cultivation of the Island. The relevant extract from Sullivan's letter reads as follows: "The opportunities which a residence of four years have given you of observing the character of the British and foreign Inhabitants of T'dad and of investigating the nature of their Commercial relations with the Continent of South America must have enabled you to collect much interesting information upon those subjects and as the attention of Govt will soon be directed to the consideration of them, I am instructed by Lord Hobart to desire that you will be pleased to send him for H₁M's Information a detailed Statement of such observations & suggestions as you shall judge may be made conducive to the substantial benefits of H.M.'s subjects in the Island of T'dad whether with a view to their commercial Intercourse to the Regulations of Police, or to the measures that may appear to you best calculated to operate as an encouragement for extending the cultivation and Improvement of the Island".
12. C.O. 296/4, Hobart : Picton, 9.7.1802.
13. C.O. 296/4, Hobart : Commissioners, 16.10.1802.

CHAPTER 5

But if the establishment of an acceptable form of civil government consistent with Trinidad's very heterogenous population and "peculiar circumstances" was the major task awaiting the Commission's attention, it was by no means the only one. Copies of the commissioners' Commission and Instructions which accompanied this despatch revealed that the new undertaking was to be a full-scale investigation of Trinidad, its condition and its prospects, from every imaginable point of view.[14]

First of all, the commissioners were to prepare a general report under nine separate heads.[15] ranging from the nature and scope of the Island's civil government, its economic and commercial organization, and the size and composition of its population, to the workings of the *depositario general,* the office provided under Spanish law for the administration of the estates of absentees and minors.[16]

Secondly, they were to provide an accurate account of all lands and property belonging to the Crown, the tenure under which they were held and the manner in which they were administered; the methods best suited to making future grants and leases; a report on the prospects of obtaining timber, flax and hemp for use in the Royal Navy; and an investigation into the mineral resources of the Island, the incidence of gold, silver, copper and other mineral deposits.[17]

Thirdly, the commissioners were to make annual reports on the state of the Island's trade, suggesting means by which it could be increased. Similar reports were to be made on its fisheries, agricultural produce, imports and exports, births, baptisms and deaths, immigration and emigration, the size and state of preparedness of the militia, shipping to and from the Island, the number of vessels employed and their tonnage. Surveys of rivers, landing-places and ports and harbours, if not already made, were to be prepared; fortifications and storehouses were to be erected, and all arms and ammunition in the possession of private persons were to be inventoried.[18] And , lest the

14. For a copy of the Commission, see C.O. 296/4, pp. 73-81. For a copy of the Instructions, see C.O. 296/4, pp. 81-110. Additional Instructions on trade, with specimen forms of the returns the Commissioners were expected to make, are in C.O. 296/4, pp. 110-20. A draft of the Commission is also in C.O. 380/134, Nos. 22 and 25.
15. These were, according to Article 25 of the Instructions, Legislature; Executive Government; Courts of Justice; Numbers and different classes of Inhabitants; Revenue; Commerce; Religion and Religious Establishments; Military; Estates of Absentees and Minors.
16. For a comment on the *depositario general* in Trinidad see C.O. 295/8, Hislop : Camden, 9.7.1804, enclosure from Black, Begorrat, Langton and Nihell.
17. Articles 26-28 of the Instructions. These three clauses seem to have formed part of an extract of an Order-in-Council of September 22 laid on the table of the House of Commons approving the Commissioners' Instructions and drawing particular attention to other subjects on which further reports were required.
    The Order-in-Council has not been seen. Evidence of its existence is provided by Arthur Mills, *Colonial Constitutions: an Outline,* (London, 1856), p. 266.
    On pp. 266-71 there is a list of Orders-in-Council and parliamentary papers relating to Trinidad. Lists for other West Indian islands are also contained in the volume.
18. Articles 27, 28, Instructions.

want of specific authority might have restrained the commissioners from doing anything which they might have thought to be necessary, an additional article gave them discretionary power to initiate any venture falling within the spirit and intention of their Commission and Instructions.[19]

In addition, numerous enclosures re-iterated and re-emphasized the objects to which the commissioners were to address themselves. and contained numberless remarks and suggestions for their guidance.[20] Detailed memoranda on the Island's cultivation and future population were included. In these Lord Hobart expatiated at length on the desirability of introducing new classes of settlers to Trinidad - a subject to which he had already alluded in a letter to Governor Picton in early February,[21] apparently before the decision to empanel the Commission had even been considered. On that occasion he had told Picton that current opinion in England against the importation of African slaves into Trinidad might make it necessary "to have recourse to other than the common modes for the Settlement and Improvement of that valuable acquisition" - a speculation that had drawn from Picton, himself a plantation owner, the retort that those who "declaim so violently against the Slave Trade (should) give themselves the trouble of examining it more nearly, and not wholly depend for their information upon the representation of Philanthropists, whose humanity too frequently resides upon the tongue without ever visiting the heart."[22]

This earlier despatch illuminates one of the more significant purposes of Lord Hobart's immigration scheme. The fact was that Trinidad, as Lord Hobart had then informed Picton, was to be a proving ground for the introduction of a white yeomanry farming and working on the more healthy slopes and producing crops which, like cocoa and coffee, were less dependent on the rigorous labour demands of plantation-produced sugar. As seen by Lord Hobart in February 1802, the new scheme of settlement was to be "a Groundwork of Colonization, which offers to my mind incalculable advantages to Trinidad in particular, and ultimately to all the West Indian Settlements."[23] So that, were a white yeomanry to be successfully established in Trinidad, attempts would have been made to extend the experiment to the other West Indian islands with the intention of making the West Indies less dependent on the slave trade. Alternatively, Hobart had suggested, the solu-

19. Article 29, Instructions.
20. Of twenty-nine enclosures only Nos. 20-29 are in C.O. 296/4. It may be assumed that these are the really important ones. The subjects of the other papers are listed and some of them, like No. 7, an "Extract of a Letter from a West Indian Merchant" of 30.1.1802, and No. 16, "Letter from Mr. President Ottley, of St. Vincent, January 1802" would probably have been of some interest. No. 2, the only other paper of seeming importance among the ones not reproduced, a "General State of the Population & Agriculture of Trinidad in July 1797 from Mr. Mallet's survey" doubtless contained information easily accessible elsewhere.
21. C.O. 296/4, Hobart : Picton (Private) 18.2.1802.
22. C.O. 296/1, Picton : Hobart, 12.4.1802.
23. C.O. 296/4, Hobart : Picton (Private), 18.2.1

tion might lie in the encouragement of Indians and Spanish *peons* from the continent to Trinidad there to be employed as wage labourers in the clearing of lands and the cultivation of the soil. The prospect of regular employment for wages, together with food treatment and the "advantages they would experience under a British Government" were all incentives which, he seemed to think, would powerfully appeal to the bucolic Indian and Spanish peasantry. But this was, even in Hobart's estimation, an inferior alternative and it tended to be neglected in future despatches.

Picton's implied criticism of the settler scheme did nothing to moderate Hobart's enthusiasm and in October he returned once more to the subject. This time the new factor of projected Chinese immigration to Trinidad was introduced in the shape of a long and wordy memorandum which had been submitted in July for Lord Hobart's consideration by Captain W. Layman of the Royal Navy. [24] Layman, a man of obvious liberal intent, quoting Adam Smith to demonstrate the iniquity and unprofitabilityof slavery, sought to substitute Chinese peonage for Negro thraldom and successfully prodded the government into an unfortunate venture which came to an unseemly end in August 1807. [25] Another enclosure, unsigned but by its tone unmistakably Hobart's [26] discussed the possibility of engaging industrious Protestant dissenters from Ireland and Scotland to go to Trinidad accompanied by their religious ministers. For such families a sort of indentureship was envisaged with immigrants entering into contracts to work for Island proprietors or on government projects for five years at stipulated wages and the grant of small plots of land. Ministers and members of the Established Church were also to be encouraged by the offering of similar, though more substantial, inducements. Another contemplated source of white settlers was the pension list of the Army and Navy. Pensioned soldiers and sailors were to be invited to emigrate to Trinidad in the hope that they would act as "useful counterpoise in the

---

24. C.O. 296/4, Hobart : Commissioners, 16.10.1802; enclosure No. 22, dated Clapton, 18.7.1802. Enclosures 23 and 25 are also of some interest. For a full statement of Layman's views on Chinese immigration to the West Indies see his *Outline of a Plan for the Better Cultivation, Security & Defence of the British West Indies,* (London, 1807).

25. Layman also provided a table - enclosure 24 in Hobart's letter-purporting to prove that whereas the cultivation of 640 acres by slave labour would involve an initial cost of Ł49,690 sterling, Chinese labour for a similar undertaking would involve an outlay of only Ł26,435 sterling. The recurrent annual expenditure he estimated at Ł568 sterling less by Chinese than by Negro slave labour.

    Chinese peonage was perhaps not Layman's intention; but it was a result which would have ensued from the importation of non-white agricultural labourers into white dominated Trinidad. For some of the consequences of Layman's proposals see, C.O. 295/16, Hislop : Castlereagh, 1.8.1807.

    Layman was, of course, not alone to be blamed for the failure of this early attempt to introduce a Chinese population into Trinidad. As he said in yet another memorandum of October 1806 warning of the possible miscarriage of the experiment, the principle of his plan had been admitted by being acted upon, but the means differed considerably from those which he had recommended. See, C.O. 295/15, Layman : Fawkener, 28.10.1806.

26. C.O. 296/4, Hobart : Commissioners, 16.10.1802, enclosure No. 20.

political sense to the Dissenters", and to help in the formation of a new colony which stood to benefit substantially by the "habits of Order and Discipline" inculcated in them by long years of active service. The recruitment of selected convicts was also contemplated, the idea being to provide them with the means of rehabilitation and an opportunity of making themselves useful citizens in a new environment.

With a view to improving methods of cultivation an extract of a letter from a Mr. Skerritt to Prime Minister Addington, dated May 1802, was also enclosed. This letter, specially recommended by Lord Hobart to the attention of the commissioners, urged the application of the steam engine to the grinding of canes in preference to the wind and cattle mills which were then in general use in Trinidad.[27] Skerritt, himself a planter in a Dutch colony, argued the greater economy and efficiency of steam as borne out by his own experience, and drew attention to the possibilities of humanising the work of the slave by lessening the planter's dependence on factors over which he had little or inadequate control. By regularising the hours of work through the use of steam, the necessity to work at night, sometimes all night, would be obviated. Similarly, the use of steam operated saw mills, which Skerritt suggested should by law be established in every district, would result in sub stantial economies to the proprietary class and benefits to the labour force, the latter deriving from the expectation that a reduction in the price of timber, theoretically at least, would have enabled the proprietor to provide better housing for his slaves.

All this was, even for a Commission of three, a very ambitious programme. The question of time would not have been a very important factor, since Lord Hobart seemed blithely to have contemplated the possibility of the Commission's proceeding with its business over a period of years. On the other hand, lack of money would have presented a more serious threat to the successful conclusion of the affair.

Lord Hobart's despatches hardly dealt with the question of finance. The general expectation seemed to have been that, apart from the migrants' passages which the British government was willing to provide and pay for, all expenses were to be charged against the Island's revenues. Housing, clothing, rations, and all the expenses attendant on the pursuance of the various schemes of settlement would have been, like the commissioners' salaries, charged to the Island's account.

The mass of correspondence with which William Fullarton bombarded successive Secretaries and Under-Secretaries of State for the colonies on his

---

27. C.O. 296/4, Hobart : Commissioners, 16.10.1802; enclosure No. 21. In 1801 there were 7 water mills, 2 windmills and 183 cattle mills in Trinidad; in 1802 the figures were 5, 2 and 224 respectively. There were also a large number of coffee and cotton "mills", few, if any, of which were steam operated. See, C.O. 295/6, Return of Population etc. presented by the Commissary of Population to the Commissioners in March 1803, and dated 1.10.1802.

return to England after the failure of the Commission contains some of the clearest indications of the Government's buoyant optimism in regard to the financing of the Commission's activities in Trinidad. From these it seems quite clear that, in a series of discussions in England, Lord Hobart had explained to Fullarton that the Island's revenues were expected to meet the major part of the costs of the enterprise. [28] Salaries represented a large part of these costs. The salaries of the three commissioners, £3,000 to Fullarton, and £2,000 each to Picton and Hood, plus the emoluments of the minor officials appointed to serve with the Commission amounted in all to about £10,000 sterling, payable from June 1802. [29] Thus, if Picton's salary is excluded on the grounds of its' being for a long time a normal colonial expenditure - it was even reduced from the £3,000 he formerly got - there was still a new recurring charge of some £8,000 sterling annually attached to the Island's revenues. This takes no account of the incidental expenses incurred on surveys, the purchase of implements, the clearing of lands, and the upkeep and rental of ships used in the surveys. Some of these expenses proved in the event to be quite high. For example, during the brief existence of the commission in Trinidad, £2,003 sterling were spent on the hire of a schooner for the accommodation of white settlers. [30] Afterwards, expenses resulting directly from the Commission's activities accounted for a further £8,544 sterling of which the surveyor general's department alone accounted for £7,572. [31] Such costs, set against the Island's average revenue of about £16,000 for the two years 1801 to 1802, provided a sufficient explanation, quite apart from the wastefulness of the actual expenditure incurred, of why the colonial chest with a reserve of about £21,000 at the end of 1802 [32] was completely dry at the end of 1803. Indeed, expenditure was for 1803 at £36,000, [33] nearly two and a half times the revenue received for that year or any of the two preceding years.

28. Fullarton's discussions with British officials on the financial aspects of the Commission's activities in Trinidad are scattered throughout the miscellaneous volumes of Trinidad correspondence, 1803-1808.
The following are of particular interest: C.O. 295/9, Fullarton: Sullivan, 21.1.1804. C.O. 295/10, Fullarton : Sullivan, 27.1.1804; Fullarton : Sullivan, 12.3.1804; Fullarton : Hobart, 27.3.1804; Fullarton : Camden, 10.7.1804. C.O. 295/13, Fullarton : Cooke, 23.7.1805; Fullarton : Castlereagh, 24.8.1805. C.O. 295/15, Fullarton: Shee, 16.8.1806, enclosing a copy of Castlereagh: Fullarton, 5.11 1805.
29. C.O. 295/9, Fullarton : Hobart, 27.3.1804.
30. C.O. 295/9, Hislop : Camden, 25.12.1804.
These amounts, rendered in £sterling, are converted from dollars which were common currency in Trinidad at this time. Conversion is approximate, since many factors affected the exchange rates from time to time and the monthly rates of exchange, which fluctuated greatly, are not always provided. On average $1.00 equalled 4s. 8d. The £ currency was in much more general use than the £ sterling and seems, despite fluctuations, to have averaged about one-half of a £ sterling.
31. C.O. 295/9, Hislop : Camden, 25.12.1804.
32. C.O. 295/10, Fullarton : Sullivan, 6.2.1804.
33. C.O. 295/8, Hislop : Hobart, 20.2.1804, enclosure.

"THE MOST TRAGIC EXPERIMENT OF ALL"

The conclusion can hardly be escaped that Treasury parsimony, an over-ambitious programme of investigation and development, and a good deal of honest misunderstanding about the strength of the Island's finances relative to the burdens imposed on it, combined to lay the foundations of Trinidad's future financial embarrassments. In the light of these embarrassments the pious hope expressed by John Sullivan, Under-Secretary of State, that excess specie from Trinidad's trade with the mainland would be used to defray some of the expenses of the military establishment in the Leewards [34] reads rather curiously; but it illustrates the cheerful faith with which the British government, conditioned by glowing reports of the Island's economy, regarded the financial aspects of the undertaking.

Financial mismanagement cannot be reckoned, however, among the major causes contributing to the failure of the Commission. The Commission failed for other reasons which we shall later explore. Appointed in October 1802, it was hopelessly split by the middle of the following March, and destroyed beyond repair by July. By the end of July the Island's government had already been put into the hands of Colonel Thomas Hislop, and the commissioners, relieved of their responsibilities, were returning to England by separate routes. In England Fullarton was to exhaust the last years of his life, until his death in 1808, in a long, bitter and much publicised prosecution of Picton on several charges of cruelty and, specifically, for the torture of Louisa Calderon. Picton himself was to test the resources of his mind and the money of his friends in his defence and, after a period of public obloquy, expire somewhat gloriously on the battlefield at Waterloo. Hood, though unwavering in Picton's support, was in many ways a bystander in the whole affair, and, after his brief interlude in Trinidad, returned to active service in the Royal Navy, becoming commander-in-chief of the Leeward Islands station and, like Picton, enjoying the satisfaction of being knighted before his death in 1814.

*   *   *

The Trinidad phase of the Commission's activities began with Fullarton's departure from Portsmouth on November 26, 1802, accompanied by his wife, her sister the Hon. Miss Mackay, and the subordinate officers attached to the Commission. Commodore Hood, who should have joined the party at Portsmouth, was unavoidably delayed by affairs connected with the worsening situation between Great Britain and France, and was eventually left behind [35] With a fair wind, the Ulysses, accompanied by two tenders intended to be used in surveys of the Island, made a swift crossing, and the small

34. C.O. 295/4, Sullivan : Commissioners, 6.1.1803.

35. C.O. 295/10, Fullarton : Hobart, 27.3.1804. Also, *A Statement, Letters and Documents respecting the Affairs of Trinidad, including a Reply to Col. Picton's Address to the Council of that Island; submitted to the Lords of His Majesty's Most Honourable Privy Council.* By Colonel Fullarton. (London, 1804), pp. 2-5

Also, *Hobart Papers,* (Bundle B.), Addington : Hobart (Secret), 13.10.1802.

137

flotilla arrived at Barbados on December 21 without serious mishap.[36] At Barbados Fullarton met Hood, who had meanwhile also sailed for the West Indies. Hood, necessarily detained at Barbados on one or two naval matters, invited Fullarton to linger with him while the rest of the group proceeded to Trinidad. Fullarton declined, and sailing on to Trinidad, arrived there on January 3, 1803, and landed on the 4th.

Picton, who since October had been handling only the necessary and urgent business of his government in anticipation of the Commission's arrival,[37] welcomed Fullarton with every mark of politeness and esteem but without noticeable enthusiasm. He introduced him to the officers of the civil and military establishments and to the prominent citizens assembled for the occasion. Fullarton for his part was equally civil and, after taking the prescribed oaths and claiming his seat ·in the Council and the *Cabildo,* addressed both bodies stressing the need for co-operation and his own desire to do as much as he could to further the objects of the Commission.

The spirit of optimism and co-operation that marked the opening of the Commission,[38] barely survived the ceremonies that had occasioned it. Almost at once the two commissioners, Fullarton and Picton, as if impelled by forces beyond their comprehension or control, embarked on a feud which, at first occasioned by honest misunderstanding, soon degenerated into a vicious and odious vendetta which reduced the process of administration to an absurdity, stultified the operation of the Commission, and resulted in the commissioners' eventual recall.

On the day following Fullarton's disembarkation one of the two local newspapers - the *Courant* edited by Matthew Gallagher, for some time printer to the government - carried a report of the previous day's proceedings. In it Mr. Fullarton was described as having not only reciprocated the politeness with which he had been welcomed but, as Fullarton was to say later, as having "bestowed unqualified praise and approbation on all the proceedings under General Picton's government, not only in my name but in the name of His Majesty's Ministers".[39] Fullarton was chagrined but was unwilling to

36. One event of importance seems nevertheless to have occurred. Whether it was the tedium of the voyage, or his natural garrulousness, Fullarton seems to have been very unguarded in his references to his future role in Trinidad and his intended relationship with his two colleagues, and in particular with Colonel Picton. In addition, he and Mr. Woodyear, the secretary to the Commission, conceived a mutual dislike for each other - a development that ensured the retelling of some of his less discreet utterances at very embarrassing moments in the future.
Cf. C.O. 298/1, Minute of Council, 13.7.1803. Also, p.   , below.

37. C.O. 296/1, Picton : Hobart, 18.10.1802.

38. C.O. 295/4, Minute of Council, 4.1.1803 for the official opening of the Commission.

39. C.O. 295/10, Fullarton : Hobart, 27.3.1804. This letter of Fullarton's, already referred to, shall be referred to with some frequency in future discussions of the Commission's activities. A sixty-three page effort, it is an attempt at self-vindication by Fullarton. It's particular merit lies in the fact that it gathers together all the different strands of a very tortuous and involved transaction, the details of which are scattered throughout several volumes of correspondence. It has the merit of not differing on points of fact from the known details of the story. The interpretation of the facts is of course

annoy Picton by an outright refutation. He therefore charged George Adderley, the patentee of the office of provost marshal who had been a witness to what he had said, and whom he might have already conceived as a substitute for Woodyear, to inform Lord Hobart that he had not so expressed himself, being "totally unacquainted" with the transactions he was supposed to have sanctioned.

This was on the 5th. On the following day, the 6th, Archibald Gloster the attorney general, and Woodyear the secretary to the Commission, now revelling in the appellation of public secretary, approached Fullarton with a proclamation obviously inspired by Picton asking him to concur in its publication. The proclamation purported to promote public tranquillity by allaying any apprehension of abrupt change in the laws or in the personnel of the public service by a commissioners' declaration "that all Laws, usages and employments should continue in full force". [40] On impulse, Fullarton agreed. Later, on reflection, and while the proclamation was still with the printer, he decided to retract or at least reconsider his agreement. Whether he suspected the motives that had inspired the proclamation or whether, as he said, he thought it improper to acquiesce in such a publication while Hood was still at Barbados is an open question; since Hood did not join the other commissioners till late February this was a line of reasoning that could, if logically pursued, have resulted in a long period of voluntary inactivity. But, having resolved that his consent should not be so lightly given, the first commissioner decided to act on his resolve. Accordingly he sent Mr. Burke, the assistant secretary to the Commission, to Gallagher, the printer, at six o'clock the following morning with instructions to procure a proof of the proclamation and to instruct Gallagher not to issue it until Fullarton had agreed to the proof. Gallagher replied that he would himself attend at Fullarton's office with the proof at 8:oo a.m. But he did not; instead, the proclamation was printed and distributed without any further reference to the first com-

---

Fullarton's. But the facts are fully corroborated, where they deal with Picton's activities, by Picton's own and other peoples' correspondence. C.O. 295/4 which contains most of the Minutes of Council for the six months of 1803, and C.O. 295/5 which contains most of the correspondence ofthe Commissioners, provide a wealth of corroborative evidence for the facts outlined by Fullarton in his letter.

See also, C.O. 295/10, Picton : Lords of the Privy Council, 12.9.1804. An important letter in that, unwittingly, it reveals the extent of Woodyear's responsibility for this first affair.

And, Fullarton, *A Statement* . . . . , pp. 2-5.

Other publications detailing the events of the Commission are:-

Archibald Gloster, *A Letter to the Right Honourable the Earl of Buckinghamshire, late Secretary of the Colonial Department, Respecting Affairs in Trinidad in 1803, and in Answer to William Fullarton Esq.,* (London, 1807).

William Fullarton, *A Refutation of the Pamphlet which Colonel Picton lately addressed to Lord Hobart,* (London, 1805).

Thomas Picton, *A Letter addressed to the Rt. Hon. Lord Hobart, His Majesty's Late Principal Secretary of State for the Colonial Department,* (London, 1804).

In this publication Picton challenges Fullarton's veracity on two points. See pp. 40-59 ff.

40.   C.O. 295/10, Fullarton : Hobart, 27.3.1804.
Fullarton, *A Statement* . . . . , p. 4. The phrase is quoted by Fullarton from the proclamation.

CHAPTER 5

missioner. Fullarton, by then thoroughly annoyed, severely reprimanded
Gallagher, and ordered him to pull down all the proclamations which he had
already posted. Gallagher did so, excusing his precipitation and apparent
insubordination on the ground that Woodyear had countermanded Fullarton's
order reminding him that he, Woodyear, was the public secretary and was
responsible for employing and paying Gallagher who should therefore do
what he was told. Whereupon Fullarton rounded on the offensive Woodyear
and reprimanded him in his turn.

This affair marked the beginning of the deterioration of the relationship
between Fullarton and Picton. Picton was of course mortified by Fullarton's
handling of the affair, not without cause. For it was quite obvious that,
irrespective of the motives of the first commissioner in having the proclamation pulled down, their removal could only have given rise to the most un-
bridled speculation. It was, even if Fullarton did not so intend it, construed
as a deliberate snub to Picton whose previous acts the proclamation was intended to confirm. On the other hand, the persistence and indelicacy with
which the attempt to induce Fullarton to underwrite Picton's government was
pursued would have awakened suspicions in the most naive soul. It did in
fact stimulate Fullarton to an investigation of the precise nature of Picton's
former government.

Picton's motives might however have been less sinister than Fullarton
seems to have supposed. He might only have wished, quite naturally, to
obtain such support from Fullarton as would have redeemed his somewhat
humbled state in the eyes of the Island's inhabitants. After all he had been
sole arbiter of the Island's affairs for six years. It was no easy thing, as he
himself said, to be given a "Subaltern Situation" in the government
he had alone administered for so long. [41] But the fact remains that his
clumsy attempts at personal rehabilitation provoked Fullarton's suspicions.
And once Fullarton's suspicions were aroused, Picton's previous administration could not bear examination. Picton's rule had been, by Picton's
admission, firm and unrelaxing, even though he never tired of pleading the
difficulties of his situation as a sufficient justification for his firmness. But
"firmness" in his construction and in the eyes of his apologists, could easily
be, and was construed by his antagonists, certainly by Fullarton, as unnecessary tyranny; and, as we shall see, not without cause. For, on investigation, Fullarton discovered that twenty-four persons had suffered death,
torture and mutilation at Picton's command, and various others had been
exiled from the Island to the detriment of t h e i r property and their
possessions. [42]

41. C.O. 295/10, Picton : Camden, 23. 6. 1804.
42. C.O. 295/5. A tabulated table of punishments meted out to offenders in Trinidad from 13.8.1801
to 3.4.1802 reads as follows:
1 person - burnt alive; 7 persons - hanged and burnt; 3 persons - heads cut off and put on poles on the
public roads; 2 persons - branded on both cheeks; 3 persons - ears cut off; 4 persons - feathered and

If honest error provided the chief clue to this first fracas, honest error does not explain the subsequent disturbances involving the commissioners. The postures most characteristic of the later acts of both individuals had already been taken. Picton, smarting under the removal of the proclamations, regarded Fullarton as the determined destroyer not only of his present position but also of his past reputation as administrator of the Island during the past six years. Fullarton, on the other hand, thought he detected the unmistakable stink of gross injustice and oppression, and interpreted every act of interposition by Picton as another crude attempt at disguising and hiding from him what in the end he felt he must know. This was unfortunate. Picton and Fullarton were, until their meeting in Trinidad, complete strangers to each other. And two days after their first encounter, before they had even had the opportunity of becoming properly acquainted, the seed of enduring distrust had been well and truly sown between them. Distrust, suspicion and antagonism were to colour all their future relations. From this time on acts performed by the two commissioners, in the eyes of the contestants themselves, lost all intrinsic significance; whatever importance was attached to them derived not from the nature of the acts themselves, but from the identity of their authors.

Fullarton's attitude to Picton was powerfully strengthened by a visit to the jail. West Indian jails during the slave era have justly merited an imperishable notoriety. But of all the vile, pestilential holes that disgraced the West Indies in the first half of the nineteenth century Trinidad's was probably the the vilest. In the other British West Indian islands, jails were regarded as institutions that temporarily obliterated the social and physical distinctions of race, class, colour and sex. Statistically, the probability of a white man's going to jail was appreciably less than for a black man. But jails were receptacles for all defaulters, Negro or white, slave or free, debtor or criminal, male or female. Indeed, the day may not be long in coming when some scholarly sociologist will descry in the West Indian prisons of the period the germ of West Indian confraternity. To this thesis, however, Trinidad will be a notable exception.

In Trinidad several categories of persons were, according to Spanish law, exempt from incarceration in the common jail. Chief among these were the *Cabildo* members. [43] But deriving from this legal privilege the right was extended to the classes of persons from among whom *Cabildo* members were usually drawn; thus members of Council, for whom the Spanish law did not provide, were similarly protected. If they were not protected as councillors, then they, as all other propertied persons, could claim privilege

ears cut off; 1 person - flogged through the streets; 2 persons - led through the streets as an ass; 7 persons - ordered to assist at the executions; 1 person - hanged at St. Joseph's
A detailed report on several of these incidents is given immediately following this list.

43. C.O. 295/8, "Report on the Government of the Island of Trinidad, 1804". Paper No. 1. Questions proposed by Lieut. Governor Hislop to Messrs. Nihell, Black, Begorrat and Langton. Also, *Recopilación* . . . . , Lib 7, Tit. 6, Ley. 15.

CHAPTER 5

under the status of *hidalgo* or gentleman. [44] By convention, privilege came to include all or nearly all whites. From time to time in Trinidad some whites were jailed. But they were put in specially provided rooms on the top storey of the jail from which exalted position the chief discomfort seemed to have derived from the stench below; or on being lodged below, they were spitefully informed that this untoward step had been taken as a proper punishment for their depravity. Actually, with little effort, a white man could avoid being imprisoned in the jail. Consequently, the only persons who could perhaps have effected an improvement in conditions had least cause to do so. Thus, the privileges and conventions operating as a positive prohibition against the incarceration of the most influential members of the community meant that the jail was regarded as an institution existing for the exclusive use of slaves, free coloureds and such whites as it might be salutary to discipline from time to time, with disastrous effects on its condition.

On the last Monday of January Fullarton visited the jail. He had announced his decision at a *Cabildo* meeting where strenuous attempts had been made to prevail on him to desist by Messrs, Black, Begorrat and St. Pé, all members of the *Cabildo* and two of them, Black and Begorrat, members of the Council. [45] Fullarton persisted, and with some ten other persons, including most of the officials who had accompanied him from England, embarked on his visit. He found the jail to be as foul and polluted as he had been led to expect; and he drew three conclusions which, in the light of current practices, further embroiled him with Picton. To be imprisoned in such a jail, he said, was itself a torture; to be detained there pending trials, as was often done with slaves, was to be horribly punished before sentence was even passed; to be detained and then to be freed on acquittal, or even without a trial as sometimes happened, was to suffer the ultimate injustice. [46]

44. *Recopilación...., Lib. 7, Tit. 6, Ley. 15; Lib. 7, Tit. 8, Ley. 14. In 1811, John Sanderson who was not a member of the *Cabildo* protested his imprisonment by Judge Smith on the ground that, as a lawyer and proprietor, he was an *hidalgo* and so exempt from ordinary imprisonment.
C.O. 295/26, Walker : Sanderson, 16.1.1811; enclosure.
45. C.O. 295/10, Fullarton : Hobart, 27.3.1804.
46. C.O. 295/10, Fullarton : Hobart, 27.3.1804.
Fullarton provides a clue to his reaction elsewhere. He writes: "The Prison itself was in such a state of Pestilential nastiness, with 30 or 60 wretches some in chains others naked and many of them nearly starved to Death, that I can hardly think it was a Serious offence to prevent others from being added to their number, without knowing the grounds of Their Commitment."
C.O. 295/4, Fullarton : Sullivan, 7.3.1803.
A private letter to Sullivan alleges that to look at the jail "was more than sufficient punishment for any ordinary offence".
C.O. 295/4, Fullarton : Sullivan, 19.2.1803.
In 1801, the condition of the jail was attributed to a chronic "want of funds", a continuing impecuniosity in the colonial revenues. The prison was then described as a building "whose remaining walls are in such delapidation, & decay — not a door, or window to the few cells — that the few prisoners, are constantly endanger'd in their lives by the walls mouldering and tumbling about their ears, owing to the want of means, to render it tenable. . ."
C.O. 295/25, S. Newman: G. Adderley,15.4.1810, enclosed in George Adderley: Jenkinson, 6.7.1810.

142

"THE MOST TRAGIC EXPERIMENT OF ALL"

This visit seems to have brought Fullarton face to face for the first time
with some of the evils of slavery, and he charged Picton, perhaps a little
unjustly, with the full cost of his experience. In the jail he found lying on
lengths of bare boards, bound and fettered, five slaves belonging to Baron
de Montalembert, a French planter. They were nearly naked, and had been
lying there for some time. On enquiring, he was told that a few days previously they had been sent to jail by their master on suspicion of having
poisoned other slaves and were soon to be tortured since that was the only
way to extract the truth from them. Hardly had he recovered from the shock
of this disclosure, volunteered by Begorrat, than on leaving the prison he was
accosted by the executioner, William Payne, with a request that Fullarton
should do something about his emoluments since he had only received two
joes for sixteen persons he had some time ago flogged, beheaded or burnt. [47]
The sum total of Fullarton's experience can be described as traumatic.
And his humour was neither improved by Picton's protests about his attendance at *Cabildo* meetings, which Picton himself had only done on rare and
special occasions, nor by Picton's comment that Fullarton's visits to the jail
could be interpreted as implying neglect on his, Picton's, part. To these
strictures Fullarton replied that his attendance at *Cabildo* was absolutely
necessary if he was to understand the working of that institution and make
recommendations about its future. As for the jail, a new one must be built.
It did not help matters either that Fullarton had his way on both counts.
He continued to attend *Cabildo* meetings and at a meeting of Council it was
decided to purchase a house to be used as a prison while a better edifice was
being erected. Similarly, Picton's attempt at imprisoning and depriving of his
licence one Hargreaves, the printer of the Island's other newspaper, for
advertising a meeting of British citizens for the purpose of petitioning for
British laws came to nought; the attempted imprisonment was vetoed by
Fullarton. [48] But Picton had the satisfaction of persuading Fullarton that
the time was inopportune for such a meeting.
Saturday the twelfth of February marked the beginning of the final
break between Picton and Fullarton. The occasion was provided when
Fullarton allowed Madame Duval, a mulatto woman, to visit the Island.
Picton for some reason had had Madame Duval deported from the Island
some time past. Now Fullarton, perhaps in ignorance, perhaps because he
felt no harm could come from permitting the visit, allowed the woman to
come to the Island to transact some business. Whatever was the basis of
Fullarton's action, Picton was quite sure that the first commissioner had
knowingly and deliberately countermanded an order given by him in his late

---

47. C.O. 295/10, Fullarton : Hobart, 27.3.1804.   C.O. 295/4, Fullarton : Sullivan, 4.3.1803.
   M'Callum in his *Travels. .. ,* p . 209, furnishes a copy of the list proferred by Payne to Fullarton. One
   Joe equalled ₤ 2 sterling or ₤ 4 currency.
48. C.O. 295/10, Fullarton : Hobart, 27.3.1804.

capacity as governor. Fullarton protested that he had not, since he had not known that Duval had been previously banished; and anyhow his action was, he asserted, in strict accord with the terms of the Peace of Amiens by which those intending to leave the Island because of the confirmation of British rule had three years in which to wind up their affairs before leaving.[49] Picton remonstrated and protested the grant of the permit, Fullarton insisted and refused to retract his order and, after some unpleasantness in which Woodyear seems to have played a far from honourable part,[50] Picton visited Fullarton's house where, before his family and some friends and officials, he upbraided him in the most violent and public manner for his actions since his arrival in the Island.

The split between the commissioners was now in the open, and Fullarton and Picton abandoned all pretence at subtlety and decorum. Asserting that the Duval affair had made it imperative for him to know the names of those who had been the objects of Picton's displeasure, lest he should unwittingly offend the second commissioner by countermanding another of his "orders", Fullarton moved in Council for a list of those who had been hanged, flogged, burnt, tortured, lacerated, exiled or in any way punished by Picton.[51] Picton, pleading as he always did the absolute necessity of whatever acts of severity he had employed, rebuked Fullarton for intriguing.[52] Fullarton then introduced into the minutes of Council a list which William Payne the executioner, himself a slave, had thrust into his hands at the jail when asking for a fairer accounting of his emoluments - a gory chronicle detailing the fate of sixteen unfortunates who had been brutally punished or executed on Picton's orders. Whereupon members of the Council, sensing that they were witnessing a spectacle unique in the annals of British colonial government, urged a reconciliation on the two men. As a result, Fullarton's assertions were expunged from the Council records. Fullarton, however, while accepting the suggestion of a reconciliation, insisted on the suspension of Woodyear for his part in the Duval affair. This nearly precipitated a new crisis, but by then both men were thoroughly peeved by the inconclusiveness of the struggle. They decided for remarkably similar reasons to await the imminent

49. C.O. 295/10, Fullarton : Hobart, 27.3.1804. Reference is to the 13th article of the Peace of Amiens.

50. The papers respecting the Duval affair are in C.O. 295/5. See also C.O. 295/4, Fullarton : Hobart, 3.3.1803 and enclosure — declaration of 12.2.1803 signed by Fullarton and Woodyear.

51. C.O. 295/5, Minutes of Council, 14.2.1803. Fullarton, *A Statement*, pp. 9, 44. Heaton Robinson, Pi cton's biographer, comments (Vol. I, p. 101): "It could not for one moment be doubted that this was a preliminary step towards an enquiry into the conduct of the late Governor, under whose sanction, and by whose directions, these little *désagrémens* were supposed to have been inflicted". Robinson's contrived tone of slight disbelief does not tally with Picton's ready admittance of having ordered these punishments - though Picton was wont to call them "severities" and not "little *désagrémens*." Picton never questioned Fullarton's attribution to him of any of the numerous crimes alleged by the latter. His defence was restricted solely to a rationalization of his acts in the light of his position in Trinidad.

52 Picton, *A Statement*. . . , pp. 11, 53-5; and Fullarton's reply in his *Statement*. . . . , pp. 60-8.

arrival of Commodore Hood before embarking on the next phase of their encounter. [53]

*　　　　　*　　　　　*

The arrival of Commodore Hood on the 22nd February was an event to which both Fullarton and Picton had looked forward with mounting expectation. Fullarton, though so far having had the better of the contest, was beginning to experience some difficulty arising partly from the fact that all the public officials, with the exception of those who had accompanied him from England, owed their appointments to Picton. In the *Cabildo* the relatively mild protests occasioned by his decision to visit the jail [54] had been replaced by a deep-seated resentment of what the *Cabildo* conceived to be Fullarton's interference in their lawful proceedings. This resentment had its focus in the tribunals of the *alcaldes.*

The *alcaldes* had grown accustomed to meting out rough and summary justice to the free coloureds and slaves with whom they were wont to deal in their courts. It had for instance been for some time the practice to send slaves to jail with no other detail pertaining to their commitment but a brief note instructing the jailer to hold them in prison until a charge was preferred. This was a practice frequently resorted to by owners as well as judges, and had become so widespread that *"Jusqu'à nouvel ordre"* - until further orders - was perhaps the best known and most widely used legal formula in the Island. Often, slaves were sent to jail for punishment without any indication of the exact offence for which they were being punished. When corporal punishment was ordered it was often unspecified, in which case Vallot the jailer, a vile and cruel monster, would administer thirty nine lashes, the maximum under the law.

Not surprisingly, the abuse of slaves had encouraged the abuse of free Negroes and people of colour as well. Early in February another incident had been touched off by the improper commitment of a mulatto man by Monsieur Noel, the commandant of the quarter at Carenage. Following a little local difficulty, Noel, on February 4, arrested and sent to prison the Mulatto, Durand - *"Jusqu'à nouvel ordre"* as he had done so often before. Two or three days later Fullarton visited the jail, and seeing Durand there enquired as to the reason for his confinement. On being told that no charge had yet been laid, Fullarton ordered him to be released. Durand, with less than perfect discretion, hurried back to Carenage spreading the news of the new dispensation, and, according to Noel, proclaiming to all who would

53. John Rigby, a local resident, made a singularly acute observation at this point which is certainly worthy of note: "the half-healed wound is for the Present closed but this Motley Government cannot possibly last". C.O. 295/6, Rigby : Baillie, 15.2.1803.
54. C.O. 295/10, Fullarton : Hobart, 27.3.1804.

listen that coloureds were no longer the inferiors of whites, that all freemen now stood on the same footing, and that Fullarton had taken the free people of colour under his protection and was determined that they should enjoy their rights as citizens.[55]

It is not quite clear that Fullarton intended to be the author of so drastic a revolution in the social relationships of the society then existing in Trinidad. He certainly had a more than usually liberal concept of what those relations should have been, but he also recognized some of the limits imposed by the slave system. Nevertheless, he felt that these limits, whatever they were, did not, and should not, extend to the perversion of the rule of law. Thus he corroborated the need for firm governmental control of the coloured population, but he remained aghast at the attitude of the planters who "generally consider any attempt to do justice, or Even to hear the Complaint of a Negro, or Mulattoe (sic) as a Direct Injury and Violation of the Rights of Europeans". [56]

It was quite possible, in his estimation, to observe the social distinctions deriving from the slave system without doing outright violence to the legal entitlements of those who suffered under that system. The impartial observance and enforcement of a properly regulated code of laws pertaining to the conditions of imprisonment would, in his opinion, have extended the protection of the law to coloured persons in the same degree as to whites but would have done little to affect the numerous other disabilities under which the non-whites laboured. Mere parity under law he correctly perceived to be among the least satisfactory of the various forms of equality.

This was a line of thought that did not find favour with the Trinidad ruling classes. Nor perhaps did it represent the expectations of the free Negroes and coloureds. In fact Durand, in so far as he had interpreted Fullarton's intervention as heralding a fundamental social reorganization, had himself faulted it. If the laws were impartially administered the free coloureds stood to gain more than mere parity under law. The whole system of coercion based on the unequal application of legal sanctions would crumble, and the free coloureds would, by their numerical superiority, in time obtain a social position more befitting their numbers.

The whites, by their own reckoning, had everything to lose. Noel's assertion that Fullarton's actions tended to "undermine the Basis of the Colonial System of Government in a Country, where the Coloured People are so numerous and the least relaxation of Subordination would produce the most serious consequences" [57] exactly described the reaction of the majority of whites to Fullarton's innovation. [58] But it was an assertion

55. C.O. 295/4, E. Noel : Commissioners, 25.2.1803, enclosed in Minute of Council. 2.4.1803.
56. C.O. 295/4, Fullarton : Hobart, 3.3.1803. This letter was written separately by Fullarton to put points of view with which his colleagues, who had that day addressed a joint letter with him to Lord Hobart, could not have been expected to agree. This was one of those views.
57. C.O. 295/4, E. Noel ; Commissioners, 25.2.1803, enclosed in Minutes of Council, 2.4.1803.
58. Cf. C.O. 295/6, Rigby : Baillie, 13.3.1803 enclosed in Baillie : Sullivan, 7.4.1803.

concerned more with the expedience of the system than with its justice or legality. Fullarton could not see why a community of free men, different only by their colour, should not enjoy the same legal advantages as other free persons in the society. The whites could not see why the fact of being free should be permitted to obliterate completely the distinctions and disadvantages that derived from a condition of slavery chiefly distinguished by the colour of the slaves.

Thus, by the middle of February, Fullarton found himself confronted with an open and growing opposition to his measures. Opposition was centered in the *Cabildo* and to a lesser degree in the Council, but the majority of white inhabitants shared in varying degrees the general antipathy to him. The only exceptions were his personal entourage brought out from England, from which Woodyear had already defected, and those among the British inhabitants who looked to him to facilitate the introduction of British laws and a British constitution into the Island. But, these elements, while providing Fullarton with a measure of moral support, were insufficient to bring about the final defeat of the Picton group. Fullarton, therefore, looked to the arrival of the third commissioner "as greatly contributing to the Objects for which the Commission was appointed", [59] hoping that Hood's authority, joined to his own, would facilitate the implementation of what he regarded as the essentials of good government.

Picton, too, anticipated Hood's arrival for a somewhat similar reason. Out-ranked and increasingly outgeneralled by Fullarton, he hoped that the third commissioner would tilt the balance in his favour, and help to uphold the policies which he regarded as necessary for the maintenance of a proper system of colonial government. His supporters in the *Cabildo* and in the Council had so far conducted a fairly successful holding operation on his behalf. The *Cabildo* at a series of secret meetings was soon to condemn Fullarton's "interference". [60] The Council, though acquiescing in Fullarton's measures, was altogether sympathetic towards Picton. But the Council's powers were so circumscribed that, without Picton's positive lead, open opposition of the first commissioner was impossible. As a Council of Advice its decisions were not binding, and Fullarton could refuse to accept its advice if he conceived it to be in the public interest to do so. Besides, in Hood's absence, Fullarton, as first commissioner and commissioner for civil affairs, possessed the ultimate sanction of dismissal of Council members, a prerogative which, in the circumstances, he would have been only too happy have found some excuse for exercising. While Picton enjoyed the Council's unspoken support, therefore, Fullarton's seniority was decisive. Already Picton's increasing frustration had driven him to offer his resignation to the

---

59. C.O. 295/4, Fullarton : Hobart, 3.3.1803.
60. C.O. 295/4, Fullarton : Sullivan, letters of 7th and 8th March 1803; and Council minute of 12.3.1803 containing a report on a *Cabildo* meeting of 9.3.1803.

CHAPTER 5

Secretary of State and to recommend the supersession of "a Commission whose Speculations and Experiments, may and probably will occasion a great deal of evil and disorder and certainly very little good".[61] For Picton too, as for Fullarton, Hood's arrival had become the key to the future determination of the situation. Fullarton, in Picton's estimation, had sown the seeds of civil discord manifested most strikingly in a growing coloured insubordination. "The arrival of Commodore Hood was," in Picton's opinion, "(to) put an End to Philanthropic Theories incompatible with the State of Society in this Country".[62]

Neither Fullarton nor Picton desired that Hood's coming should be the means of effecting their permanent reconciliation. Both recognized his arrival as an approaching crisis in their affairs, but each wished that the crisis should be resolved by the virtual elimination of the power and influence of the other. By this reckoning, the affair, far from drawing to a close, was destined to embark on a new embittered career of vengeful and disruptive partisanship. In the succeeding months the participants in this extravagant farce were to plumb the depths of the droll and the grotesque, tremble on the brink of open violence, and destroy forever all possibility of the successful operation of the Commission.

For reasons that are not quite clear Hood, after an initial period of uncertainty, veered to the unwavering support of Picton. If Hood is to be believed, Fullarton's own hamhandedness in his approaches to him was the main reason for his decision.[63] But while Hood's affiliation with Picton was a severe blow to Fullarton, it was not, as Picton had hoped, conclusive. Picton's expectations on this point were founded on a reading of the distribution of powers within the Commission that was quite mistaken. Nor did he give Fullarton enough credit for tenacity and resource. As events were to show, Fullarton and Hood might easily have eliminated Picton; Hood and Picton together could not overwhelm Fullarton.

The events of the next five months can conveniently be divided into four distinct phases. The first of these is distinguished by the departure of the first commissioner in April ostensibly for a tour of the Island by sea. In fact, once out of sight, the schooner *Start* on which he had embarked changed course for Union Island in the Grenadines, thence to dispatch George Adderley for England with first hand reports of the proceedings in Trinidad for the Secretary of State.

---

61. C.O. 295/4, Picton : Hobart, 18.2.1803. In offering his resignation, Picton charged Fullarton with intrigue, designing and subversion of the Island's police and government to the danger of the Island's inhabitants and property. He charged him, too, with "a specious Phillantrophy, which has the double object of showing off his own great humanity, and placing that of my Administration in an opposite point of view".
62. C.O. 296/4, Picton : Hobart, 30.3.1803.
63. See Heaton Robinson, *Memoirs of Col. Picton. . .* , Vol. 1, pp. 113-115; E.L. Joseph, *History of Trinidad*, p. 223, and Picton's *A Letter addressed to the Rt. Hon. Lord Hobart, His Majesty's Late Principal Secretary of State for the Colonial Department*, (London, 1804), pp. 10-14. An interesting sidelight

The two months following Hood's arrival were also to witness the complete isolation of Fullarton and his small band of adherents. Fullarton's declaration that he would see Picton brought to justice for his enormities had, if that were possible, further increased his own isolation. In the *Cabildo* and in the Council, the combined efforts and influence of the junior commissioners had consistently thwarted him. From the *Cabildo* had come an Address completely repudiating Fullarton's approach to the Island's government. [64] Inside the Council he had been regularly outvoted; outside of it, he had been denied the right to execute the Commission's decisions without continued reference to his two colleagues. He had to meet with them every day to decide the business of the day. [65] And he was denied any authority whatsoever over any species of armed forces in the Island, and the soldiers and militiamen were advised accordingly. [66] Council debates had become more acrimonious and disorderly, and the councillors and public officials, no longer fearing Fullarton's authority, had openly paraded their contempt. His request for the depositions of thirty-six cases tried by the judges under Picton's administration was followed by the arrest of de Castro, the *escribano,* who had given them to him. [67]

His position had become plainly untenable, and even his departure which, one might have thought, ought to have been the occasion of general rejoicing, had provoked a final contemptuous retort. After he had embarked on Wednesday, March 29, his little schooner, the *Start,* had lain at anchor in the harbour threatened by the guns of the sea forts whose occupants were under orders from Picton to blow it out of the water should Fullarton attempt to sail without the permission of the two junior commissioners. Hood, as naval commissioner, had given identical instructions to the armed brig that patrolled the Gulf. After four days, during which Port-of-Spain reeled at the prospect of Fullarton's demolition, a bitter protest from the ship's captain and a threat of legal action by its owners brought about the signing of the necessary papers, and Fullarton was allowed to depart. [68]

The second phase, beginning with Fullarton's withdrawal and ending

is the role of the distaff side of Fullarton's household in the squabbling among the commissioners. Joseph, *op. cit.,* p. 223, refers to a communication between Hood and Earl Camden of 1.9.(?) in which Hood alleged that Fullarton had tried to win him over by "every art", (and)*by means of his lady"*. Joseph himself, *op. cit.,* p. 219 describes Fullarton as living "under what in vulgar parlance is called petticoat government, being completely ruled by his wife and her sister, two of the most accomplished political intriguants that ever came to afflict a West Indian colony". Picton too hinted at the unfortunate reputation Mrs. Fullarton enjoyed with the junior commissioners. He once spoke of Trinidad as having been "delivered over to the manouvres (sic) of an artful cunning man, under the absolute direction of an intriguing woman". C.O. 295/4, Picton : Hobart, 6.3.1803.

64. C.O 295/4, Address of Cabildo of 21.3.1803 enclosed in Minute of Council of 24.3.1803.
65. C.O. 295/4, Fullarton : Sullivan, 4.3.1803.
66. C.O. 295/5, Fullarton : Grinfield, enclosed in Fullarton : Hobart, 25.6.1803.
67. C.O. 298/1, Minute of Council, 18.7.1803; M'Callum, *Travels.* . . . , pp. 223-5, 283-4; Robinson, *Memoirs.* . . . , Appendix, pp. 433-6; Fullarton, *A Statement.* . . , . p. 16.
68. C.O. 295/10, Fullarton : Hobart, 27.3.1804; M'Callum, *Travels.* . . . . p. 235.

with Hood's was marked mainly by the re-establishment of the harsh and stern administration normally associated with Picton. On this occasion the desire to discipline the most active of Fullarton's supporters predominated. Messrs. Burke and Proby, two of the officials appointed by Fullarton to vacancies in the Island's administration were roughly handled. [69] Pierre M'Callum the author of *Travels in Trinidad* and an outspoken Fullarton supporter was deported to North America allegedly "as a dangerous Person, who had attempted to seduce from their Duty the Militia of this Colony, and for other seditious practices." [70] Dr. Timbrell, a surgeon in the artillery, who had given Fullarton some evidence pertaining to the execution of a soldier in 1797, was imprisoned. [71] And the system of irregular imprisonemnt, and punishment by flogging, mutilation and exile were re-introduced. [72] But the greatest extravagance of all was directed against the first commissioner himself. In a proclamation issued on April 27, the two junior commissioners divested Fullarton of all authority because of his continued absence from the Colony. [73] As an executive measure this was clearly illegal; but, given the state of the relationship between the commissioners, it is at least understandable why Picton and Hood should have thought it expedient. Hood was about to leave for active service elsewhere in the West Indies and the confirmation of Picton's sole rule, which was the effect of Fullarton's divestment, seemed to be the best means of rendering Fullarton ineffective on his return. With Hood's departure on April 28 Picton entered for the last time on the sole "governorship" of the Island of Trinidad.

Picton's energies in the third phase of our summary seem to have been equally divided between preparations to resist Fullarton's anticipated attempt to return to the Island's government, and the collection of testimonials in support of his administration throughout its duration. In pursuit of his first objective he attempted to regulate the flow of shipping in and out of the harbour, the better to guard against an unheralded appearance by Fullarton, by proclaming an embargo on the movement of all vessels then in port. [74] Next, he issued garrison and militia orders withdrawing the sentry from Fullarton's house, through Fullarton's wife and

69. C.O. 295/10, Fullarton,: Hobart, 27.3.1804.

70. C.O. 295/5. The affair, of great importance for an understanding of Picton's *modus operandi*, took place between April 10 and April 15. M'Callum himself graphically describes his predicament in his book, pp. 236 ff.

71. M'Callum, *Travels*. . . . , p. 62 ff. Also, C.O. 295/4, Fullarton : Hobart, 27.3.1803, enclosure dated 23.3.1803 in which Dr. Timbrell's declaration with respect to the soldier Gallagher's hanging is contained. Another enclosure in this letter contains the papers detailing Picton's hounding of an Englishwoman, Mrs. Griffiths, and her daughters at the instigation of his mulatto mistress Rosetta Smith.

72. M'Callum, *Travels*. . . . , pp. 251-2, 253-4, 263-4. Also, C.O. 295/10, Fullarton : Hobart, 27.3.1804.

73. C.O. 295/6, Rigby : Baillie, 28.4.1803; enclosed in Baillie : Sullivan, 1.6.1803. C.O. 295/5, Minute of Council, 27.4.1803. C.O. 295/5, Fullarton : Hobart, 25.6.1803, enclosure. M'Callum, *Travels*. . . . , pp. 281-2.

74. M'Callum, *op. cit.*, p. 282.

her sister still occupied it, and he instructed the forces and townspeople in the measures they were to take in the event of a crisis.[75] Another order, dated April 28, informed the populace that the firing of three guns from the sea fort would proclaim the beginning of martial law;[76] a proclamation of May 13 carried the additional information that the termination of martial law would be signified by the firing of five salvos from the same fort.[77]

Picton's other task, the collection of testimonials describing the benefits of his government, was attended with solemn and deliberate ceremony. On Friday, April 28, the Council assembled at Picton's house.[78] Present were Picton himself and four other members, including the now reinstated Woodyear. Two members were absent, St. Hilaire Begorrat and Archibald Gloster, the attorney general. This was no indication of their disaffection; Picton rejoiced in the constant and unquestioning support of the two absentees. Begorrat was even then, according to Fullarton, making overtures to the countryfolk and preparing them to resist Fullarton's expected return.[79] Indeed it would have been impossible to single out any member of that Council, present or absent, whose confidence Picton did not enjoy. John Nihell, chief judge and senior member of Council, had some time in the distant past opposed some of Picton's lawlessness;[80] but that was long since forgotten. A period of suspension from the duties of his office had instructed Nihell in the proper appreciation of his interests and he, like John Black, the *alcalde* of the first election for 1803, and Philip Langton a personal friend of the ex-Governor's, were now numbered among Picton's firmest auxiliaries.

As Council assembled that morning Picton must have rejoiced in Fullarton's absence, for it was a circumstance that undoubtedly faciliated the performance of the business at hand. Under his watchful eye several documents elicited from various sources and intended for eventual transmission to England, were entered on the Council minutes testifying to the nature of his government. A letter from the bishop of Guyana, the spiritual head of Trinidad's Catholic community, written in all innocence on December 16, 1802, and penned in that spirit of camaraderie often used between high officials, and never more effectively than when they are totally unacquainted, was now pressed into service.[81] Four highly approving letters from the Catholic curates of Arima, San Juan Aricagua, San Fernando, and Savana

75. *Ibid.*, pp. 285, 351-4. Fullarton, *A Statement.* . . . , pp. 76-8.
76. C.O. 295/5, Fullarton : Grinfield, 23.5.1803, enclosed in Fullarton : Hobart, 25.6.1803. M'Callum, *op. cit.*, pp. 353-4.
77. M'Callum, *op. cit.*, p. 354.
78. C.O. 295/5, Minute of Council, 28.4.1803.
79. C.O. 295/10, Fullarton : Hobart, 27.3.1804.
80. M'Callum, *op. cit.*, pp. 177 ff. See also, P.C. 1/3557, Picton : Duke of York, 31.10.1803; enclosed in Duke of York : Hobart, 10.11.1803.
81. C.O. 295/5, Bishop of Guyana : Picton, 16.12.1802, enclosed in Minute of Council, 28.4.1803.

Grande testified to the excellence of Picton's character,[82] though the fact that four priests from four districts so distant from each other and from Port-of-Spain signed their declarations at the capital on the same day, April 28, suggests not spontaneity but constraint. A letter from the ex-commandant of the quarter of Cedros took its place in the Council minutes with one from a M. Cipriani,[83] whose report of a mutiny of his boat while enroute to Martinique in 1799 had occasioned the summary execution of the sole surviving mutineer. Thus ended the felicitations of the day, and Council dismissed. The rest of the day, which seemed to have been specially set aside for this important business, was given over to the less formal but equally important preparation of an Address signed by some two hundred and twenty-five subscribers. These subscribers, the most prominent and wealthy members of .the community, drawn from the British and foreign white communities, recorded their undying gratitude to the Governor "to whose energy we owe, under God, our lives and properties." Finally, they bestowed on him the ultimate accolade of presenting him with a sword which they had recently ordered to be prepared in London for his use.[84] A testimonial from twelve notables of St. Joseph, unaccountably delayed, arrived at Port-of-Spain on the 29th.[85]

While these preparations, testimonials and ceremonies were enlivening the humdrum existence of Port-of-Spain's citizenry Fullarton, away at sea, had been far from idle. Leaving Union Island, whence he had dispatched Adderley to England, he had proceeded to St. Vincent in search of General Grinfield, the commander-in-chief of the armed forces in the West Indies. His purpose had been to solicit Grinfield's support for the civil government in Trinidad which, in Fullarton's estimation, was vested solely in him and was in grave danger of subversion by his two colleagues.[86] Missing Grinfield at St. Vincent he had proceeded to Dominica, thence to Martinique, on to Guadeloupe, and back again to St. Vincent, this time "to take on board Dr. Anderson, the celebrated naturalist" who was to accompany him on the survey of Trinidad.

Towards the end of May, his odyssey nearly complete, Fullarton hove to in the harbour at Bridgetown, Barbados. There he dispatched letters to Grinfield and Hood, and intercepted the official mail outward bound from England to Trinidad.[87] As he had hoped a dispatch from Lord Hobart was

82 Enclosures, C.O. 295/5, Minute of Council, 28.4.1803. Also, Gloster, *A Letter to the Earl of Buckinghamshire*, pp. 161-8.
83. C.O. 295/5, Minute of Council, 28.4.1803, enclosure.
84. This Address, dated 28.4.1803, is in C.O. 295/5, Minute of Council, 7.6.1803. Also, M'Callum, *op. cit.*, pp. 289-91, for printed copies of the Address and Picton's reply.
85. Gloster, *A Letter to the Earl of Buckinghamshire*, pp. 181-3.
86. C.O. 295/10, Fullarton : Hobart, 27.3.1804; C.O. 295/5, Fullarton : Hobart, 25.6.1803, enclosure, Fullarton : Grinfield, 23.5.1803.
87. C.O. 295/10, Fullarton : Hobart, 27.3.1804.

included. In it the Secretary of State intimated His Majesty's willingness to accept Brigadier General Picton's resignation, and further specified in a menner extremely favourable to Fullarton the exact extent of the powers and authorities vested in the first commissioner. [88] Fullarton communicated the contents of the letter to Lord Seaforth, then Governor of Barbados, and to General Grinfield. He also copied its contents to Commodore Hood, to Colonel Hope the commander of the regular troops in Trinidad, and to Colonel Grant the officer commanding the Island's militia. The original he dispatched to Picton after keeping a copy for himself.

If Fullarton believed that Picton would meekly have resigned the government of the Island into his hands on receipt of Lord Hobart's letter, he soon appreciated his error. His return to Trinidad occasioned another humiliating scene similar to that which had attended his departure in April. Fullarton left Barbados on June 1 and, sailing leisurely up Trinidad's coast - ostensibly on a survey, really giving his messenger sufficient time to convey the fateful letter to Picton - anchored at Port-of-Spain on June 6. Immediately Picton sent him a letter signifying his determination to resist his disembarkation, and enclosing copies of the proclamation of April 27, and of the minutes of Council dated June 3 and 6, whereby Picton and the Council, Nihell dissenting, had decided to ignore Hobart's despatch and resist Fullarton's landing. [89]

In the moment of crisis Fullarton's good sense prevailed. Remarking that "as this is now reduced to a mere Question of Military Power it remains to be adjusted by the commander of the Forces", [90] Fullarton then wrote to Grinfield at Barbados earnestly and successfully requesting his intervention. On June 14 Brigadier General Maitland, dispatched by Grinfield, arrived from Barbados to relieve Picton of his command in Trinidad. During the night Picton slipped out of the harbour and turned his back on Trinidad for the last time. Three days later, on June 17, Fullarton returned to the government of the Island.

*   *   *

The fourth and final phase of the Commission's affairs in Trinidad following the arrival of Commodore Hood had now begun. It was to end with Fullarton's departure on July 20 and Colonel Thomas Hislop's assumption of the sole command of the Island's administration as lieutenant-governor. As in the second and third phases when first Picton and Hood, and then Picton

---

88. This dispatch was Hobart's important letter of 23.4.1803 outlining the division of powers among the commissioners. The original is in C.O. 295/4; a copy is in 296/4.
    See below, pp. 188 - 9 for some further details of the contents of this dispatch.
89. C.O. 295/5, Fullarton : Hobart, 25.6.1803, enclosures. M'Callum, op. cit., pp. 284-5.
90. C.O. 295/5, Fullarton : Hobart, 25.6.1803, enclosure, Fullarton : Picton in reply to Picton : Fullarton of 9.6.1803 informing the latter of his determination to resist his landing.

alone, had administered the Island's government, Fullarton's magistracy was attended by a certain amount of recrimination and rebuke of those who were now on the losing side. But Fullarton's methods were characteristically milder. Woodyear's part in the Duval affair was thoroughly aired in Council; so too was his oft repeated allegation that on the voyage from England Fullarton had, in his opinion, exhibited "the most rooted prejudice, against the Character of General Picton" and had contrived to make his fellow voyagers believe that his two colleagues in the commission were "mere Cyphers".[91] John Black, the *alcalde* of the first election, was closely interrogated about the part he had played in the arrest of de Castro, the *escribano*.[92] Woodyear, Black and others were questioned about their support of the *Cabildo's* accusations that Fullarton had subverted the Island's police by applying unwarranted prohibitions on the punishment of slaves and the imprisonment of persons of colour.[93]

Fullarton, by a relentless and practised cross-examination of these witnesses in Council, successfully controverted many of the allegations previously made against him. But he had not had things all his own way. The Council had, after all, struck the first blow. With the single exception of Judge Nihell its members had haughtily declined the first commissioners summons to a Council meeting at his house on June 20.[94] A detailed memorandum explaining their decision had deliberately baited Fullarton. Woodyear, too, entering fully into the spirit of revolt, and secure in his reinstatement as public secretary by Hobart's despatch of April 23, had cynically tendered his resignation.[95] Fullarton, unable to accept, had endured the taunt with as much grace as he could manage. But he reconstituted the Council. Sir James Bontein, James Rigby, Colonel John Rutherford the surveyor general John Smith and Andrew Wilson had replaced Messrs. Gloster, Black, Begorrat and Langton. Judge Nihell had retained his seat, as had Mr. John Nugent absent on leave in England. Begorrat was replaced by John Smith as commandant of the quarter of Diego Martin. And Gloster who enjoyed no immunity by reason of a secretarial dispatch was suspended from the attorneyship general.[96]

For the next month, while Fullarton compiled an impressive dossier of evidence against Picton for various misdemeanours,[97] some desultory attention was paid to the business of the Commission. In his disregard of his administrative duties Fullarton was not more culpable than his colleagues had

91. C.O. 298/1, Minute of Council, 13.7.1803. See also, Note 36, above.
92. C.O. 298/1, Minute of Council, 18.7.1803.
93. C.O. 298/1, Minutes of Council, 13th, 15th, 18th and 20th July 1803.
94. C.O. 295/5, Declaration from Messrs. Black, Begorrat, Langton and Gloster, dated 20.6. 1803, enclosed in Fullarton : Hobart, 25.6.1803.
95. C.O. 295/5, Woodyear : Fullarton, 17.6.1803, enclosed in Fullarton : Hobart, 25.6.1803.
96. C.O. 295/5, Motion for the suspension of the attorney general, no date, enclosed in Fullarton : Hobart, 25.6.1803.
97. *A Statement.* . . . , pp. 167-201.

been. They too had attempted to fulfil some at least of the objectives of the Commission, but only at intervals grudgingly appropriated from the main business of repelling and opposing Fullarton and all his works. Normal administration, such as it was, had become part and parcel of the continuing dispute among the commissioners. Few indeed were the decisions affecting the Island's administration which were not taken with the intention of furthering the partisan aims of the warring factions.

Before Fullarton's departure in April, the commissioners acting together had authorized the beginning of a marine survey by Captain Columbine. But Picton and Hood had later countermanded the order providing a sum of money for the surveyor's expenses and had refused to provide a schooner for the task.[98] They had also received some Dutch and German settlers and had begun with varying degrees of enthusiasm to make arrangements for their accommodation. All this was communicated to Lord Hobart in a letter of March 3.[99] Even so Fullarton had thought it incumbent on him to write a separate letter disclosing plans then being discussed with the Catholic missionaries for the use of Indian labour to build houses for the new settlers. He discussed too the feasibility of making the Caroni river more navigable, the fortification of Chaguaramas and various other pet schemes, with the clear implication that his colleagues did not share his zeal for some of these projects.[100]

During Fullarton's absence Picton and Hood had pushed on with the fortification of Chaguaramas. But they had recommended the scrapping of the surveyor general's department as being too expensive and staffed with incompetents, and had urged the abandoning of the settler scheme on the grounds that, "The German and other Settlers, who have been induced to come to this Island are, in general, people of loose dissolute Morals, without any habits of Industry".[101] They had also recommended a legislative Council "resembling that of Canada", and a gradual assimilation of Spanish law to English practices as observed in the other British West Indian islands as being best suited to the existing state of the Island. A *consulado* or commercial court had also been set up for the determination of commercial disputes, and the use of the English and French languages, as well as Spanish which alone had formerly been used, had been authorised in the Island's courts.[102]

But the plague of controversy blighted all normal business. The

98. C.O. 295/4, Fullarton : Hobart, 20.3.1803.
99. C.O. 295/4, Commissioners : Hobart, 3.3.1803.
100. C.O. 295/4, Fullarton : Hobart, 3.3.1803.
101. C.O. 295/5, Picton and Hood : Hobart, 25.4.1803. The commissioners also argued that if the French experience in Cayenne, where 30,000 European settlers had succumbed in the course of eighteen months, was anything to go by, the British Government should proceed slowly in introducing European settlers into Trinidad before comfortable accommodation had been prepared for their reception.
102. C.O. 295/5, Picton and Hood : Hobart, 25.4.1803.

CHAPTER 5

recommendation to abandon the surveyor general's department owed as much to the fact that that department was staffed with Fullarton cohorts, and was for practical purposes under Fullarton's control, as it did to its alleged expensiveness and other inadequacies. Fullarton's enthusiasm for the settler scheme provided at least as important a reason for its discontinuance in the minds of Picton and Hood as did Picton's own antipathy for it. If Picton's recommendation of a nominated Assembly in December 1801 is recalled his partiality for a legislative Council in April 1803, on Gloster's recommendation, and in the absence of Fullarton the civil commissioner, can be construed as an attempt to forestall what he regarded as the certainty of Fullarton's recommendation of the full fledged Assembly system.

Nothing illustrates the corroding influence of dissension among the commissioners on the Island's administration as does the dispute surrounding the three and one-half per cent duties on Trinidad's imports and exports. The three and one-half per cent duties provided the only source of revenue in the Island. Though convenient for the Island's government because it was easily collected, it was thoroughly unsatisfactory to large sections of the Island's proprietors. No section of the community felt the burden of this tax more than the merchants, and they were unanimous in their condemnation of it. In any proper evaluation of the Commission's tasks the propriety of the tax would have merited immediate and thoughtful consideration. This it never received. The merchants, the chief protagonists of the abolition of the tax, were, as we have seen, in the forefront of the demand for British laws and a British constitution. They were also, because they conceived that Fullarton's opposition to Picton's system of government bespoke a sympathy for British laws, generally devoted to the person and policies of the first commissioner. What should have been a straight policy decision was derogated to the level of a vituperative dialogue between the commissioners.

On February 3, 1803, Lord Hobart wrote instructing the commissioners, to exact the full impost of three and one-half per cent instead of one and one-half per cent which had so far been its average yield. But he counselled caution. The levy was to be gradually increased but in such a way that while the revenue benefitted, "the interests and feelings of the Community" would be least affected by the measure. [103] The problem thus posed for the commissioners was obvious if not simple: it was that they should produce a formula for reconciling the Island's inhabitants to the payment of a higher level of taxation. Or, failing this, that they should inform the Secretary of State of the precise reasons for their failure. Even if an amicable relationship between the commissioners had prevailed it seems likely that they would have had to resort to the second alternative. The point at issue here is not the commissioners' failure to exact the higher duty but the manner in which this failure, deriving from the attitude of the Island's inhabitants, was ex-

103. C.O. 296/4, Hobart : Commissioners 3.2.1803 (Draft).

156

ploited to further the interests of factional strife between the commissioners themselves.

On Tuesday, March 28, the day before Fullarton boarded the schooner *Start* to leave the Island, Attorney General Gloster pointedly presented a memorandum to the other two commissioners on the question of the tax. [104] While arguing that the tax was not supported by the terms of the capitulation nor by the various proclamations relating to the Island's trade issued immediately subsequent to the capitulation, nor even by Spanish precedents, he refrained from saying that it was illegally collected. An accompanying letter laid the responsibility for so saying squarely at Fullarton's feet. An obvious reference to the first commissioner alleged that, "as the suggestions respecting the illegality of these Duties *came from a certain quarter,* I shall not be surprised, at their failing altogether *immediately* as a source of permanent revenue". [105] But if, as Gloster maintained, Fullarton had connived at opposition to the tax, he was not alone among the officials in feeling that it should be exacted. Gloster's whole argument led logically to the conclusion that the tax was improperly imposed, but he preferred to charge Fullarton alone with responsibility for this opinion. He contented himself with stating that the collection was inexpedient because it acted as an imprudent restraint on the Island's trade.

Picton had little compunction in communicating to Lord Hobart a similarly distorted account of the reason why the full duties could not or should not, be collected. The full collection of the three and one-half per cent duty he described as a measure "which, probably, will make some Noise amongst the Merchants, at home, as a Clamour against it, *here,* has been secretly encouraged from authority". [106]

Fullarton, back in Trinidad in June, felt constrained to rebut these allegations. For this reason the tax ceased to be the object of his considered judgement. Despite his previous uncertainty about its efficacy he now gave his wholehearted support to the collection of the tax mainly, it would seem in order to refute the allegations of his enemies. His previous failure to promote its efficient collection he represented as being solely due to "various secret obstacles . . . . constantly opposed to its Success and it seems intentionally to have been suffered to Diminish in its Amount". [107] This last was a condition that Fullarton in his new-found enthusiasm could not allow to endure. Resolutions were passed in Council obliging all masters of vessels to produce exact manifests and invoices of their cargoes and an inspector was appointed to visit all ships entering at Port-of-Spain to enforce the new regulations. [108]

104. C.O. 295/5, Gloster : Picton and Hood, 28.3.1803, enclosed in Picton : Hobart, 30.4.1803.
105. C.O. 295/5, Gloster : Picton and Hood, 28.3.1803, enclosed in Picton : Hobart, 30.4.1803.
106. C.O. 295/5, Picton : Hobart, 30.4.1803.
107. C.O. 295/5, Fullarton : Hobart, 25.6.1803.
108. C.O. 295/5, Fullarton : Hobart, 25.6.1803; enclosure, Minute of Council, 25.6.1803.

This surprising turnabout can only be explained in terms of the bad relationship existing between the commissioners. In normal circumstances it is more than likely that the commissioners would have agreed to represent to the Secretary of State the difficulties opposed to the full exaction of the tax. None of them believed that the tax was proper or expedient. Picton had always levied it at much below the maximum; besides, as proprietor of a large sugar estate, he had every interest in maintaining a low rate of duty on plantation supplies, and in seeing that the Island's products were not priced out of the market by a burdensome duty on exports. Fullarton on arriving in the Island had been alarmed by the high level of prices that prevailed [109] and was easily persuaded that part of the blame attached to the existence of the three and one-half per cent duty on imports and exports. His bias in favour of the mercantile community provided the final spur to his belief. His later assertion that "the 3½ percent appears, If equally and fairly collected to have many advantages over any other likely to be substituted in its Place", [110] was an obvious rationalization.

Yet, Picton maintained that discontent among the inhabitants "secretly encouraged from authority" was the only bar to the full exaction of the duty; and Fullarton enacted local regulations to enforce its collection. How much the situation had been distorted is further indicated by the fact that the measures finally adopted by Fullarton were recommended by a committee of merchants who, no doubt urged by Fullarton, appeared in Council as the promoters of a policy they had so long opposed.

The Commission's business in Trinidad ended abruptly on the morning of Wednesday, July 20, with the arrival of Colonel Thomas Hislop to assume the reins of the government. [111] After the ceremonies attending Hislop's installation as Lieutenant Governor were over, Fullarton took his leave and departed from the Island. His departure was attended then, as it had been on another occasion, by another annoying incident. His determination to take the *escribano,* de Castro, to England as a witness in his projected prosecution of Brigadier General Picton was forestalled by the concerted action of Messrs. Black and St. Pé the *alcaldes ordinarios.* Exhuming an old Spanish regulation, the *alcaldes* arrested de Castro alleging that his books were not in order and refused to release him. Besides, de Castro's deputy, on whom the burden of his duties would have fallen in his absence, could not legally execute the duties of *escribano,* said the *alcaldes;* for, though he looked white his ancestry was uncertain and "he might have a portion of mulatto blood in his veins". [112] Fullarton could hardly have received a more pointed reminder of his failure in Trinidad.

109. See C.O. 295/4, Fullarton : Sullivan; 12.1.1803.   110. C.O. 295/5, Fullarton : Hobart, 25.6.1803.
111. C.O. 295/10, Fullarton : Hobart, 27.3.1804. Hislop had been appointed on May 20, 1803. See
C.O. 296/4, Hobart : Hislop, 20.5.1803.   112. C.O. 295/10, Fullarton : Hobart, 27.3.1804.

CHAPTER 6

THE SUM OF EXPERIENCE

With the departure of all the commissioners and with Hislop's succession to the administration of the Island's government the formal stage of the Commission's activities in Trinidad was brought to an end. It remains now to try and strike a balance between collapse and achievement in order to understand whether or not there was anything of value that the Commission did do.

It is all too easy to conclude, as all pertinent accounts have so far concluded, that the experiment in commission government contributed only negatively to the development of the infant community in which it occurred. All these accounts, not at all lacking in the scattered literature dealing with the subject, tend to emphasize the personality aspects of the conflict, and most of them encourage the belief that Fullarton single-handedly brought about the downfall of the experiment. Or better yet, they assert that Fullarton, with the certain connivance of John Sullivan the Under-Secretary of State for the colonies, and with the possible collusion of Lord Hobart, the Secretary of State, deliberately wrecked the Commission by embarking on a calculated persecution of Brigadier General Picton from the first moment of his arrival in Trinidad. Assertions of this belief range from the serious to the frivolous and scurrilous, and are largely responsible for the execration of Fullarton's name and the obliteration of the more laudable aspects of his character which followed on his term of public duty in Trinidad.

No less an historian than L.J. Ragatz has contributed to the general denunciation. Clearly believing that Fullarton was mainly to be blamed for the Commission's failure, Ragatz dismisses him as a "vain and over-bearing self-seeker, soon at outs with his fellow-officials".[1] This judgement, intended to provide a definitive explanation of the miscarriage of the experiment, is qualified only by an equally harsh but more deserving criticism of the Addington government for having displayed "a stupid, short-sighted disregard for the means of insuring administrative harmony, (Picton) was superseded without being recalled".[2]

The British *Dictionary of National Biography* laments the fact that Fullarton's memory has suffered by his participation in the protracted prosecution of Brigadier General Picton for the torture of Louisa Calderon. But it contributes to the condemnation generally inflicted upon him by suggesting that Fullarton began his attack on Picton's government "on alleged humanitarian grounds" some time before coming to Trinidad as first commissioner and, apparently, even before the Addington government had acceded to office. On Addington's elevation to the premiership, the argument continues, Fullarton's views prevailed and the Commission was instituted primarliy as a

1. Lowell J. Ragatz, *The Fall of the Planter Class in the British Caribbean,* (New York, 1928), p. 273.
2. *Ibid.,* p. 273.

means of investigating Picton's conduct.[3] This view, interesting though it is, is wholly unsubstantiated and seems to be totally unfounded.

E.L. Joseph asserts that the Commission was appointed "through the miserable intrigue of Downing-street . . .   in order to satisfy Lord Sidmouth (as Addington was known in later life) and his friends, for though not brilliant, they never could have been stolid enough to imagine three persons could have fulfilled the duties of an absolute Spanish governor".[4] Joseph further claims that he possessed at the time of writing conclusive evidence that Fullarton was sent to Trinidad to drive Picton out of the government, but excused himself from parading it on the ground that it was "too voluminous" for the scope of his work.[5] With such knowledge allegedly in his possession, Joseph's description of Fullarton is hardly surprising. "A man better calculated to put a secret manoeuvre into operation", he wrote, "could not be found; he had been educated in the Eastern school, and finesse and intrigue became a second nature to him; he was plausible and even eloquent, wrote well, and was as regardless of truth as most men whose characters come under the notice of history".[6]

L.M. Fraser in his *History of Trinidad* subscribes to the general view of Fullarton and, though refraining from expressing outright belief in the complicity theory, nevertheless concludes that Fullarton came to Trinidad "strongly prejudiced against the man he was to supersede". [7] The reason he gives is that Fullarton, as M.P. for Ayrshire between 1796-1803 must have received numerous complaints against Picton from his constituents some of whom "were connected with the very men who were most clamorous against Picton on account of his determination not to allow the recent settlers to carry everything with a high hand . . ."[8] Like Ragatz, he is impressed by the British government's inept handling of the Commission's appointment but construes it more sinisterly in that he conceives that a deliberate slight was offered to Picton by Fullarton's appointment which could only have been the result of "gross misrepresentations. . . . made to, *and credited by,* the King's Ministers . . . ."[9]

However this may be, the most comprehensive attempt at maintaining the theory of official complicity in the Commission's destruction had its origins in Trinidad and its sequel, in the classical manner, in the law courts of England. In February 1805, almost a year to the day before Picton's first trial for the torture of Louisa Calderon before the court of King's Bench on February 24, 1806, Archibald Gloster, Trinidad's attorney general, received a letter from a Dr. Frederic Lynch then resident in the Island.[10] In his letter Lynch maintained that before coming to Trinidad in early 1803 he had sought an interview with the Secretary or Under-Secretary of State. Eventually he had seen John Sullivan, the Under-Secretary, to whom he had enlarged his

---

3.   *Dictionary of National Biography,* see note on Fullarton, p. 1136.

4.   *History of Trinidad,* p. 218.   5.   *Ibid.,* p. 219.   6.   *Ibid.,* p. 219.   7.   Vol. I, p. 145, note.

8.   *Ibid.,* p. 145, note.   9.   *Ibid.,* p. 145, note.

10.   C.O. 295/13, Lynch : Gloster, 18.2.1805.

hopes and plans for settling in Trinidad. Towards the end of the interview Sullivan had asked him whether he had a letter of recommendation to the commissioners who would soon be administering the government in the Island. Lynch had replied that he had two, both to Brigadier General Picton. Thereupon, Sullivan had allegedly remarked that it would be to greater advantage if he had had one to Colonel Fullarton, since Picton would in all probability be ordered home within six months as Fullarton had been instructed to investigate his conduct in the administration of the Island. [11]

If this tale were true the allegation of complicity was of course proved; whether it materially explained the failure of the Commission is another matter. Insofar as a legal decision can be held to determine truth, the allegation seems to have been unfounded. For, in a trial which began on June 27, 1807, a Lieutenant Colonel Draper of the third regiment of foot who had, with more passion than good sense, taken up the cudgels on Picton's behalf, and published an attack on Sullivan alledging that he and Fullarton had masterminded the whole sordid mess, [12] was found guilty of libel, fined and bound over to keep the peace. [13]

The laws of libel being what they were Draper's assertions, stemming from Lynch's allegations, were indeed difficult to prove. Not being himself party to the alleged conversation he was forced, in Lynch's absence, to rely for his defence on several testimonials of good character given by eminent persons in his acquaintance among whom were Sir Stephen Cottrell, secretary to the Privy Council and, as he now was, Sir Samuel Hood.

Lynch himself had hesitated to come forward, but his reasons seem to have stemmed more from the difficulties of leaving his home in Trinidad and travelling to England than from a reluctance to sustain his allegation. When a suitable financial provision had been made he had journeyed to London and sworn an affidavit supporting his previous statements of Sullivan's guilt. [14] But this was after Draper had already been found guilty by a jury, and was of no avail in promoting a successful motion for a new trial. Later, however, in spite of Draper's fate, Lynch returned to the attack with a published pamphlet scathingly denouncing Sullivan for his continued prevarication [15] - a challenge made more obvious by Sullivan's signal failure to do anything about it.

Sullivan's behaviour throughout the affair invites condemnation. Though he was uncompromising in refuting Lynch's accusations, there is something faintly unconvincing about his reluctance to grapple with Lynch who was, after all, the real foe. Lynch's many affidavits urging Sullivan's guilt, one of which was sent to Viscount Sidmouth who was for a brief period Lord

11. Heaton Robinson, *Memoirs. . . .*, Vol. I, pp. 96 ff.
12. Lieut. Col. Edward Alured Draper, *An Address to the British Public on the case of Brigadier-General Picton . . . with observations on the Conduct of William Fullarton, Esq., F.R.S. and the Right Honourable John Sullivan*, (London, 1806).
13. Howell, *State Trials*, Vol. XXX, pp. 959-1062.
14. *Ibid.*, pp. 1033-6.
15. Dr. F. Lynch, *A Letter addressed to the Rt. Hon. John Sullivan, late Under Secretary to the Rt. Hon. the Earl of Buckinghamshire, and Member of the Board of Control*, (London, 1808).

President of the Council under Pitt,[16]   evoked denials but nothing like the determined action elicited by Draper's publication. The suspicion lingers that Draper was seized upon in an effort - unsuccessful in the event - to still the pen of a better circumstanced, and possibly abler, adversary in the person of Lynch.

Awareness of the manner in which the personnel of the Commission was recruited adds to the uneasiness one feels about the nature of Sullivan's denials. With the exception of Hood, Woodyear, and of course Picton, it is possible to trace a chain of connection through Hobart, Sullivan, Fullarton and several of the officials appointed to the Commission's service in England.

The exercise of influence and connection was of course the recognized method of gaining employment in eighteenth and early nineteenth century England. Places and positions existed to be dispensed to one's friends and acquaintances, or to the friends of one's friends and acquaintances. The risk of being badgered to death by anxious place seekers was a peril inseparable from the enjoyment of high public office; the higher the office, and the more sublime the dignity attached to it, the greater was the risk. No acquaintance was too slight nor any association too intimate to preclude the possibility of a request for some coveted position. Indeed, officials themselves encouraged the mendicant throng since the exercise of patronage was the exercise of a power as personally satisfying as it was socially corrupting. [17]

The appointment of the Fullarton wing of the Commission demonstrates the classic operation of the patronage system. Between John Sullivan and William Fullarton the strongest ties of friendship subsisted dating from the period 1782 to 1786 when they had both seen army service in India. [18] Between John Sullivan and Robert, Lord Hobart, later 4th Earl of Buckinghamshire, there existed an even closer bond of affection and interest. During the years 1794-1798, when Hobart filled the position of governor at Madras, John Sullivan, then, like Fullarton, a member of Parliament, looked after Hobart's public and political interests in England with the most solicitous

---

16. C.O. 295/13, Lynch : Sidmouth, 12.7.1805, enclosure.

17. The *Hobart Papers* are of course filled with begging letters from all sorts of people. Here is one with a difference which illustrates the cynicism with which the patronage system was administered. It is filed with numerous refusals to humble requests for jobs and favours from widows, the impecunious and the unemployed.

"Apprehensive that the weight of Taxes may fall inconveniently on your hospitable disposition, it has occurr'd to me that you might feel no objection to an appointment, which as I am informed after paying the Deputy by whom the duty would be performed, would yield to you at least seven hundred pounds a year — possibly enough to cover your Wine Merchants Bill.

The Office, or rather the offices in question are those of the Secretary and Receiver to the Settlement of Berbice one of our late Conquests.

It would *not* be necessary that you should go there to qualify, & the only trouble you would have, would be that of appointing a Deputy and receiving your money. Let me know your Sentiments upon this subject . . . . "

Hobart Papers, Bundle Y (C. 252), Hobart : Lord Westneath, 23.12.1802.

18. For details, see below pp. 171 - 5.

care. [19] He encouraged Hobart in his hopes of succeeding to the governorship general, and, when these hopes faded and Hobart was minded to resign out of pique, Sullivan urged caution and exerted himself in procuring a peerage for his disappointed friend - no mean feat considering that Hobart had made himself unpopular at India House by making "a number of appointments that are incompatible". [20]   These services Hobart repaid by inviting Sullivan to serve with him on his appointment to the secretaryship of state.

Fullarton it seems knew Lord Hobart well. At any rate he wrote to him in April 1801 following Hobart's appointment as Secretary of State offering his services in any capacity Lord Hobart might be pleased to employ him. [21] Hobart's warm reply assured Fullarton that his request gave him much pleasure and promised to do his best by him. [22]   In the following year the opportunity presented itself and Hobart, no doubt urged by Sullivan, offered Fullarton the civil commissionership in the proposed Commission of government for Trinidad.

Adderley, too, seems to have owed his appointment to a prior acquaintance with Hobart and Sullivan. He had served in India with Hobart and was, to tell the truth, one of the "incompatible" appointments that Hobart had made. [23]   In fact the Adderley family seems to have been part of the inner circle surrounding Hobart and Sullivan. Sullivan on one occasion enclosed two letters for Adderley in Hobart's mail. [24] On another he reminisced with pleasure about the interlude recently spent in the country with Adderley's brother, Richard, and other friends. [25]   And on Hobart's side at least it was nothing to address a letter to Adderley familiarly, "Dear George." [26]

Of the other officers appointed to the Commission, Woodyear alone seems not to have owed his appointment to Fullarton or his acquaintances. Woodyear was appointed on the personal recommendation of Prime Minister Addington who, following his first recommendation, [27] wrote about a week later requesting that Woodyear's appointment should be suspended until he could speak with Lord Hobart about the matter. [28] What hesitations he might have had were overcome or dispelled for, as we have seen, Woodyear accompanied the Commission from England.

During the operation of the Commission in Trinidad there were several evidences of the close connection existing between Fullarton and Sullivan on

19.   *Hobart Papers*, Bundle K (India).
20.   *Hobart Papers*, Bundle K (India), Sullivan : Hobart, 21.5.1797.
21.   *Hobart Papers*, Bundle Y, Fullarton : Hobart, 12.4.1801.
22.   *Hobart Papers*, Bundle Y, Hobart : Fullarton, 13.4.1801.
23.   *Hobart Papers*, Bundle K, Sullivan : Hobart, 17.2.1797.
24.   *Ibid.*, Sullivan : Hobart, 23.9.1794.
25.   *Ibid.*, Sullivan : Hobart, 5.8.1796.
26.   *Hobart Papers*, Bundle Y (C. 530), Hobart : Adderley, 16.4.1804.
27.   *Hobart Papers*, Bundle B, Addington : Hobart (Secret), 29.8.1902, postscript. No reason was given. The note read: "May I be allowed to recommend Mr. Woodyear, as Secretary to the Trinidad Commission? His Christian name & Place of Residence may be learnt by reference to Mr. Clavin, one of the Clerks of the Treasury".
28.   *Hobart Papers*, Bundle B, Addington : (Sullivan), 4.9.1802.

the one hand, and Hobart and Adderley on the other. Fullarton frequently and familiarly wrote directly to Sullivan, often after he had already written to Hobart,[29] sometimes without even troubling to do so?[29a] On one occasion Sullivan seems to have leaked some information pertaining to the intended supersession of the Commission, and was, as a result of Fullarton's comment in a later despatch, constrained to explain the leakage to Lord Hobart.[30]

Adderley regarded Lord Hobart as the maker of his fortunes and overwhelmed him with a profusion of thanks for having conferred on him the office of provost marshal in the Island. Of his appointment to this office, a new one in the Island's administration, Adderley wrote: ".... I have learnt enough to convince me that it will eventually be most productive if I am to believe some accounts I shall be rich beyond my most sanguine hopes . . . you have set Independance (sic) within my reach whether that Independance (sic) shall be accompanied by a Moderate competence or by affluence is but a secondary consideration you are equally . . . entitled to my warmest gratitude".[31]

Gratitude to Hobart seems to have inspired the correspondence which Adderley kept up with the Secretary of State throughout his stay in Trinidad from early January till Fullarton dispatched him from Union Island in early April. Adderley's accounts were anti–Picton, but in the light of events, not unnecessarily so. What is important and bears on the question of connivance is the fact that Adderley, a subordinate officer attached to the Commission, *was* writing privately to the Secretary of State, and, as he himself said, without Fullarton's knowledge. Equally important though is the fact that Hobart was in his own words "not prepared at present to say anything upon the subject of his (Adderley's) letters".[32] And apparently he never did.

Hobart in fact observed, throughout the Commission's existence, a scrupulously correct attitude to affairs in Trinidad. When Woodyear was suspended by Fullarton, Adderley immediately wrote asking Hobart to confirm him in the post of public secretary,[33] as did Fullarton on Adderley's

---

29. For example, C.O. 295/4, Fullarton : Sullivan, 4.3.1803 in which he enlarged on his separate letter to Hobart of March 3.

29a. Most notably, C.O. 295/4, Fullarton : Sullivan, 7th, 8th and 9th March 1803. It is also interesting to note that Fullarton broached the subject of the responsibilities of the individual members of the Commission first to Sullivan, and only to Hobart after an interval of about three weeks.
His letter to Sullivan he wrote on February 19; that to Hobart on March 3. Both are in C.O. 295/4.

30. C.O. 295/5, Fullarton : Sullivan, 10.7.1803. The first few lines of Fullarton's second paragraph read: "It appears to me, to have been a fortunate circumstance for the Character of ministers and for the Welfare of the Colonies, that the Messenger was Stopped at Buckingham House. Because if the intended Superseding which He conveyed, had taken place, it would have been considered by the West Indian Publick, as an official Declaration, that in this Country, it is more hazardous to Expose Delinquencies, than to commit them".
Sullivan in forwarding this letter to his superior, wrote alongside these lines, "I do not know what this can allude to".

31. *Hobart Papers,* Bundle Y (J. 268), Adderley : Hobart, 12.1.1803.

32. *Hobart Papers,* Bundle Y (J.289), Minute on Adderley's letter of February 18, dated 27.4.1803.

33. *Ibid.,* Bundle Y (J. 289), Adderley : Hobart, 18.2.1803.

behalf on several occasions.[34]   But Hobart, as we have seen, reinstated Woodyear.[35]   And if this was because Woodyear enjoyed Addington's protection, there is no evidence that Gloster who was reinstated[36] after his suspension by Fullarton was reinstated because of the protection of anyone. On the whole there is no evidence whatsoever to indicate that any decision taken by Hobart respecting the Commission's activities in Trinidad was determined by any other consideration but the objective good of the Commission as he understood it.

In a certain sense the Adderley-Hobart relationship was more sinister than the Fullarton-Sullivan connection. Yet it is on the latter that we must concentrate. Picton himself was quick to exonerate Hobart of the guilt of connivance. He believed as many others did that, "if there really was any secret understanding, it must have been wholly between Mr. Fullarton and Mr. Sullivan; they might, like true Indian politicians, have prepared two strings to their bow, and if the insult of degrading me from the high situation of Governor in Chief to that of Junior Commissioner did not excite my resentment, and occasion my immediate resignation, the other mode might have been reserved as an *ultimatum* to get rid of me at all events".[37]

Apart from the fact that the decision to "degrade" Picton must have been Hobart's and not Sullivan's, Picton's thesis raises one question which seems never to have been put, much less answered. It is this: if the intention was to investigate Picton's conduct and ultimately to dismiss him from the government, what possible advantage was to be obtained by retaining him as a member of the Commission instead of simply superseding him? Picton's dismissal as a prelude to the investigation of his conduct would have facilitated in every way the more effective pursuit of that investigation. His retention as a commissioner was, on any reckoning, bound to obstruct it.

If the intention really was to turn Picton out of the government, Fullarton was by no means sufficiently equipped for the task. In a suggestive passage which both infers that he might have been dispatched for this purpose and also indicates the extent of his inadequacy, Fullarton lamented the fact that ". . . without adequate Means I have been sent forth, unarmed, or at the utmost with a Simple Scrip (sic), and a Sling to contend against the Gigantick Power of a Goliath, who ruled this Settlement with unlimited

34.   For example, C.O. 295/4, Fullarton : Hobart, 19th and 20th March, 1803. C.O. 295/5, Fullarton : Hobart, 25.6.1803.
        Fullarton was of course anxious to get as many of his men into office as he possibly could. To this end Sullivan's aid was enlisted, Fullarton requesting him on March 9, to obtain Adderley's confirmation in Woodyear's post. (C.O. 295/4.) On March 20, Fullarton even suggested to Hobart that the Council might be reorganized, and furnished Hobart with the names of four persons who might be substituted for Messrs. Black, Begorrat and Langton, and for Nugent who was away in England. Fullarton's nominees were, James Rigby, Mr. Grant the collector of Customs, Dr. Arthur Robertson, and Mr. Solicitor Pigot.
35.   C.O. 295/4, Hobart Commissioners, 23.4.1803.
36.   Cf. C.O. 295/7, Hislop : Hobart, 16.8.1803. C.O. 298/1, Minute of Council, 22.7.1803.
37.   Lynch, *A Letter to the Rt. Hon. John Sullivan . . . ,* p. 3, Picton : Gloster, 20.5.1805, quoted.

Terror, and having frightened many Persons out of their Wits, prevailed upon his Coadjutor, to assure Ministers, that I had been reduced to the same Predicament".38

Fullarton was of course adept at seeing his problem in historical perspective. David and Goliath, Cicero and Verres, Burke and Hastings were all symbolic episodes of human wickedness that nourished his own indignation against Picton.39   But in any immediate contest of strength Picton had all the advantages. The members of Council were, in Adderley's truthful phrase, "all his creatures, all equally involved in every improper transaction . . ."40 So, too, were the members of the *Cabildo* the chief officials of which were personal friends of the ex-Governor. Of the twenty-eight commandants of quarters, about twenty-four were French royalist and were all appointed by Picton.41   Noel's reaction to Fullarton's "interference" with the customary processes of law enforcement was typical of this class. The two Black corps, among the best organized military formations in the Island, were officered by French royalists of an even more reliable breed than the most rabid English settler - men of the stamp of Colonel de Soter and the Baron de Montalembert.42   Picton was himself in undisputed command of the Island's military forces. And, less formally, Picton was by reason of long residence and business interests fully identified with the ruling planter class which was unwaveringly opposed to Fullarton.

To take the argument one step further it would seem that whereas Fullarton, as chief commissioner and as a newcomer to colonial government, would more likely than not have been eager to make a success of the Commission, Picton because of his obsessive concern with his "degradation" would have been predisposed to accept, if not actively to strive for, the Commission's failure. Fullarton had everything to gain by making a success of his first colonial administrative assignment.43   Picton's reputation, in Picton's eyes, could only have been rehabilitated by the continuation of his

38. C.O. 295/5, Fullarton : Sullivan, 10.7.1803.
39. Several of Fullarton's strictures on Picton's administration do in fact read like Cicero's orations against Verres, and Fullarton probably pictured himself as a Burke if not as a Cicero. His letter of April 24 to Hood, enclosed in Fullarton : Hobart of 25.6.1803 (C.O. 295/4), particularly pp. 16-7 is reminiscent of Cicero at his most indignant.
40. *Hobart Papers,* Bundle Y (J. 288), Adderley : Hobart, 15.2.1803.
41. C.O. 295/4, Fullarton : Sullivan (Private), 19.2.1803.
42. C.O. 295/4, Fullarton : Hobart, 3.3.1803; also Fullarton : Sullivan, 7.3.1803.
    Soter and Montalembert for a long time held high posts in the militia. In December 1803 they were confirmed as Adjutant General and Brigadier General respectively in that force. See C.O. 295/8, Hislop : Camden, 1.8.1804.
43. A fact that seemed to argue for discretion not rashness on Fullarton's part. Fullarton was always aware of the delicate situation into which his elevation over Picton had thrust him. Fullarton always claimed that he avoided all "retrospect" and examination of Picton's conduct until these had been unavoidably thrust upon him. In 1804, he expressed himself as having felt from the beginning "so much delicacy on the subject of the relative situation in which I was placed, by superseding Governor Picton, who had ruled the Colony with absolute power for six years, that I avoided everything that could wound his feelings". C.O. 295/10, Fullarton : Hobart, 27.3.1804.

policies under the Commission or, utlimately, by the failure of the Commission itself: hence Picton's determination to have Fullarton, in one of his first public acts, subscribe to the policies and appointments by which he had governed the Island. And when Fullarton refused, Picton, smarting at being reduced to a "Sulbaltern Situation" where once he had been governor-in-chief, interpreted this refusal as the beginning of a calculated attempt to discredit him.

The final judgement of the importance of the complicity theory as an explanation of the breakdown of the Commission must be made in the perspective of all the events associated with the Commission. When Fullarton was appointed to the first commissionership he must have discussed Picton and his government with someone at the Secretary of State's; it would have been cause for comment if he had not done so. It is more than likely that these discussions were with Hobart. But supposing that they had been with Sullivan. It would have been remarkable if Picton's rule had not been considered, particularly since Picton's conduct was then under fire from various sources because of his handling of the Wharton's Tavern affair. [44] Say, too, that as a result of these discussions an understanding had, as Lynch suggested, been arrived at to turn Picton out of the government at the first opportunity. Does this then alone, or even chiefly, explain the serious and irreparable conflict that erupted between the two men?

To say that the Commission failed because Fullarton calculatedly persecuted Picton is to ignore both the chronology and the significance of events. If Fullarton had had instructions to persecute Picton these instructions must have been given him in England before he came out to Trinidad. Yet his first letters to Lord Hobart, and indeed to Sullivan too, were full of praise for the manner in which Picton had received him and expressed the highest hopes for the successful working of the Commission. [45] Grant that, on Fullarton's part, this might have been the artful guile of a "true Indian. politician". What then of the serious differences of policy that fed the flames of the initial conflagration? It is to these we must turn for a truer explanation of the Commission's failure.

*   *   *

If it is arguable as so many have argued that the Commission failed because Fullarton plotted against Picton or because quite simply they disliked each other it is even more plausible that the conflict, whatever the cause, reflected the contradictions provoked in the metropolis and in the colony alike between the new currents of trusteeship and responsibility and the old,

44. See above, pp. 102 - 5.
45. See, for example, C.O. 295/4, Fullarton : Hobart, 12.1.1803; and Fullarton : Sullivan, 12.1.1803. At Draper's trial Sullivan also pointed out that his last letter to Fullarton before the latter left England spoke highly of the "Manly character of General Picton" and hoped that Fullarton "will quickly fall into habits of free communication" with him. Howell, *State Trials*, xxx, p. 1038.

167

unadulterated colonialism of a still recent era. The discussion, however, must begin with the examination of the contrasting personalities of Picton and Fullarton the two principal participants in the whole affair. In a sense all differences of policy were determined by the differing interests, intellectual equipment and moral sensibilities that Picton and Fullarton brought to the tasks in which they were both engaged. Between them both a fatal incompatibility existed. In this incompatibility as well as in events are to be found the ultimate causes of the sterility of the whole endeavour.

In outlook, disposition and circumstances, Fullarton and Picton were as dissimilar as it was possible for two men born in the same decade and in the same country to be. They were both, after their own fashion, products of their age, but they represented different and contrasting, even antagonistic, trends of that age. Fullarton was the antithesis of all for which Picton stood; Picton rejected everything in which Fullarton believed. Thrown into a situation that made cooperation the condition of success the two commissioners could, at best, permit themselves only a mutually grudging toleration; at worst, they bordered on the indecency of physical conflict.

Picton's was the less complicated character.[46]   He was to the manner born. Nothing quite became him like the military career to which he dedicated himself from his earliest youth. Tall and stern with piercing eyes and implacable look he was, in appearance, every inch the soldier. For a long time his efforts to make a success of his chosen career had, however, been unavailing. Born in 1758 a younger son of an undistinguished and equally uninfluential Welsh father, he was severely handicapped by the mediocrity of his birth. He possessed few of the advantages that determined success in eighteenth century Britain, but one of these, fortunately for him, was an uncle who was a lieutenant colonel and who for some time commanded the 12th regiment of foot. In this regiment, Picton at the age of thirteen was given an ensigncy. Six years later, in 1777 still in his uncle's regiment, he was gazetted with the rank of lieutenant. For five years he served in Gibraltar, where he acquired a competency in the Spanish language, returning to England in 1778 with the 75th regiment to which he had been transferred at his own request in the hope of seeing more active service. Instead, he had five years of quiet drudgery serving in English provincial towns and home garrisons.

In 1783, a reduction in the armed forces caused a mutinous commotion in the 75th, then at Bristol, and under threat of disbandment. Picton, with much energy and at some personal danger, almost singlehandedly dealt with the disturbance and effected the arrest of the ringleaders.[47]   For a while this

---

46.   These sketches of Picton and Fullarton have been drawn mainly from the *Dictionary of National Biography*. In addition, Heaton Robinson's *Memoirs* of Picton have also been used. Other sources used for Fullarton are indicated where necessary.
For Fullarton see, too Sir Lewis Namier and John Brooke, *The House of Commons, 1754-90*, (H.M.S.O., London 1964), three volumes, Vol. 11, pp. 475-6.

47   Heaton Robinson, *Memoirs . . .*, Vol. I, pp. 13-5; J.N. Brierley, *Trinidad: Then and Now*, (Trinidad, 1912), pp. 76 ff.

incident seemed to promise a change in his fortunes. But though commended by the King for his courageous action and promised the appointment to the first vacant position of major arising in the Army, on the disbandment of the 75th in 1783 Picton, then a captain, was pensioned off on half pay.

Bewildered by his continuing misfortune Picton retired to the family home in Pembrokeshire where for nearly twelve years he suffered the torments of unremitting idleness. Between the wars he found it increasingly difficult to obtain a military appointment. His frequent applications elicited nothing but unredeemed promises. Still a young man, he chafed at the end which circumstance seemed determined to put to his military career. Even the outbreak of war between Great Britain and France in 1793 brought no immediate change in his fortunes. Finally, more than disgusted with his position, he embarked for the West Indies in late 1794 on the strength of a slight acquaintance with Sir John Vaughan then commander-in-chief of the West Indian station.

In the West Indies his good fortune was as remarkable as his ill-luck had been in Europe. First under Vaughan, and then under General Sir Ralph Abercromby who succeeded Vaughan on the latter's death in Martinique in 1795, Picton not only saw active service for the first time in his career, but gained fairly rapid promotion. In Abercromby, who had known Picton's uncle and who took an instant liking to the eager young officer, Picton was especially fortunate. Promoted by Abercromby to the rank of lieutenant colonel he was given his own regiment, the 56th, and by his attachment to his benefactor soon earned for himself the sobriquet of "Abercromby's pupil.'[48] He took part in the reduction of St. Lucia and St. Vincent in 1795, accompanied Abercromby to England and, returning to the West Indies in 1797, was with Abercromby at the conquest of Trinidad in February of that year.

Exalted by Abercromby to the military command of Trinidad following its conquest Picton, at thirty nine, had reached that equivocal age when habit and experiment beckon with equal urgency. What he had not been taught in the army he was willing to learn in the West Indies. The army had taught him the lessons of discipline; in the West Indies he learned to indulge the conceits of power. Like most 'strong' men he was strong mainly in that he exacted an unquestioning obedience from his inferiors; but he was weak in that he often surrendered to the grossest frailities of self-indulgence. He worshipped authority whether in his own or in someone else's person, and he expected others to do the same. Bemused by the magic of authority he thought nothing of rushing headlong, sword in hand, into a barrack room of mutinuous soldiers; but he endured the depths of despair at the merest prospect of a superior's displeasure.

Much has been made of his frankness, his artlessness and his iimpetuosity. Even Joseph's phrase that Picton was "rather too much inclined to cut any knot he could not untie"[49] sounds, in its context, not like the stricture it

48. Brierley, *op. cit.*, p. 83.   49. Joseph, *op. cit.*, p. 219.

was doubtless intended to be, but like the small boy's grudging admiration for the village bully. The man who, in human affairs, prefers to cut the knot rather than untie it, lacks all comprehension of the complexity of human relations. Picton was, above all, sadly wanting in that awe and respect for human life which alone justifies the presumption of government; and in this more than in anything else he was the child of his age.

West Indian slave society further compromised Picton's moral fibre. On his own testimony he had left Britain "with a strong prepossession against the (slave) system",[50] but a residence of nine years in the West Indies had produced a complete change in his beliefs. The reason is not difficult to discover. Economic advantage had mollified his previous aversion to slavery. To an anonymous correspondent he confided that his own investments in slaves and sugar plantations had been greatly rewarding. An initial investment of £17,000, raised largely through credit had yielded a gross capital value on all his holdings of £50,000 by 1802.[51] His enterprise had not only yielded satisfactory profits, it had induced him in the process to underwrite all that he had formerly regarded as questionable in West Indian society. His attitude to slaves and slavery, the free coloureds and their rights, came to be determined less by the maxims of the administrator and more by the standards of the businessman and the slave owner.

The opportunity of power and domination reinforced by the arguments of economic interest had a profound effect on the behaviour of the planter class in the West Indies. In Picton, because he disposed of so much more power, the effect was correspondingly greater. Paternalistic in his attitude, Picton might well have been less stern if his paternalism had been allowed free rein. But contemporary Trinidad society was less restrained than it might have been and offered little scope for a paternalism founded on a conception of the unchanging social inequality of white and coloured. Thwarted, Picton became convinced that firmness was the only answer. Trinidad, governed by a code of Spanish law imperfectly understood and casually enforced, tinged with republican sentiment, peopled by men of various nationalities, profuse with people of colour and bristling with slaves, provided the exact state of confusion in which arbitrary government, untrammelled by law or convention, best flourishes. Picton solved the problem of temptation by yielding completely to it.

The material circumstances of their formative years provide the first and obvious point of contrast between Picton and Fullarton and explains in large measure the differing attitudes with which they approached the business of colonial government. It is of great significance, for example, that whereas Picton, when he came to the West Indies, was a man very much on the make, Fullarton on his appointment to the first commissionership was a man already made. He had in fact been very well circumstanced since birth, and came to

50. C.O. 295/2, C.O. 296/1, Picton : Hobart, 12.4.1802.
51. *Hobart Papers*, Bundle P (M. 68), Picton : no name, 17.2.1802.

Trinidad after a lifetime of somewhat distinguished endeavour as a soldier, author and member of Parliament.

Four years Picton's senior, Fullarton was born in 1754 the son of a wealthy Ayrshire gentleman. [52]   He had never known the lower middle-class penury that had embittered Picton's early years. Nor had he experienced, like Picton, the humiliation of continually entreating in vain for military appointments. With all the advantages of wealth and connection his future was in doubt only to the extent that he seemed to have had some difficulty in deciding exactly what he wished to do: his was the problem of too much opportunity, not too little. In his adolescence he went to Edinburgh University but left prematurely to become travelling tutor to William Beckford whom he accompanied on visits to Malta and Sicily. Later, out of deference to his father who intended him for a diplomatic career, he spent some time attached to Lord Stormont's embassy in Paris. But on his father's death and on his accession to the family estates, he came to England and successfully sought a parliamentary seat, being elected M.P. for Plympton in 1779.

Twenty five years of age and a member of Parliament, Fullarton turned, apparently for the first time, to a military career. Picton at a similar age and with twelve years' soldiering experience behind him had known, and was about to endure in greater degree,the frustrations of inactivity. Fullarton insured himself against disappointment and boredom by an expedient Picton could never have hoped to emulate: he raised and equipped his own regiment. With his good friend Thomas Humberstone Mackenzie, *de jure* Earl of Seaforth, who also undertook to raise a regiment on his Scottish estate, Fullarton approached the government with a plan for the capture of the Spanish Acapulco fleet. The government agreed, and on May 29, 1780, Fullarton was gazetted lieutenant colonel and the commandant of his regiment, the 98th. Circumstances altered, and the regiments, at first intended for Acapulco, were ordered to the Cape and thence to India to take part in the second Mysore War against Hydar Ali.

The India experience was vital in the evolution of Fullarton's personality. He arrived there in 1782 a full colonel in the army of the East Indies, and he left for Britain towards the end of 1784 having contracted a fever on a journey from Madras.[53]   Though he had only been in India for about two years, his venture had been an unqualified success. In May 1783 he had succeeded to the general command of all troops south of Coleroon and had, against all odds, waged a fairly successful campaign against the enemy. He had displayed the highest qualities of leadership and, as commander of the forces, had won many plaudits for his attention to his men's comfort and well-being and for the highly efficient methods he had devised of obtaining intelligence about the enemy. On every level Fullarton returned from India a much dif-

---

52.   As indicated in Note 46, this sketch owes much to the *Dictionary of National Biography.*

53.   *Hippisley Papers*, B.M. Add. Mss. 41,622, f. 302; Fullarton : Hippisley, 15.12.1784. For the events surrounding Fullarton's activities in India see, *Cambridge History of India 1497-1858*, (Cambridge 1921-1958), 6 Vols., Vol. V, pp. 273-93.

ferent man from the young tyro whose military career had begun with the fanciful longing to despoil the Spanish fleet at Acapulco. On the personal level India strengthened his quixotic sense of mission of which the Acapulco idea had furnished some early evidence. But India also gave him the stimulus and the confidence inseparable from success in high endeavour, while his contacts with officialdom on the sub-continent had made him very much aware of the shortcomings of British overseas rule.

On his return to England his Indian experience further facilitated his entry into the recondite confines of social and political power in eighteenth century England. As a successful Indian commander with an enviable record of achievement in a difficult overseas post Fullarton naturally commanded more respect than, as a wealthy young parliamentarian, he had done before. In India, too, Fullarton had made many acquaintances that were to stand him in good stead in his future life. Among these were Lord Macartney, governor and president of the Select Committee at Madras; John Sullivan, paymaster to the forces in India, one-time resident of the Southern Counties and later Under-Secretary of State to Lord Hobart; John Coxe Hippisley, acting resident of Tangore from 1782 to 1787 and later British minister in Rome; and William Burke, Edmund's kinsman, and commissary general to the forces in the East Indies after 1782, through whom Fullarton was introduced to the Burke family, Edmund included.[54] With Edmund Burke himself, as a result of this introduction, Fullarton seems to have made an enduring connection. In 1785 there was an exchange of letters between the two men.[55] Initiated by Burke it concerned the fortunes of his kinsman William, at that time in some difficulty in India because of the alleged misuse of commissariat funds. Apparently at about the same time, Fullarton, who obviously found much joy in the relationship, described himself to Hippisley as seeing Edmund Burke often. But Burke was only one of the several new contacts who, together with his wealth and his new found reputation as a soldier, facilitated Fullarton's entrance into the higher reaches of London's social and political life.

A Fellow of the Royal Institutes of London and Edinburgh, Fullarton was literate and enquiring, even gossipy in the way that many serious men are. In addition, he wrote well, he wrote much and he wrote on the slightest excuse.

---

54. For Fullarton's introduction to, and relations with, Edmund Burke I am indebted to Mr. P.J. Marshall of King's College, London, who provided several references at a very crucial stage of my research into Fullarton's activities on his return from India. On December 30, 1785, William Burke wrote to Richard Burke, Edmund's son, saying: "I rejoice exceedingly that Fullarton . . . went to you so soon, it was a kindness to me . . . I am glad you all like him".
Public Record Office, P.R.O. 30/8/116, f. 125.

55. On August 1, 1785, Burke wrote to Fullarton asking him to use his influence on William's behalf.
Mss. 580, No. 340, in the National Library of Scotland, to be printed in the *Correspondence of Edmund Burke*, Vol. 5.
On August 29, Fullarton wrote to Burke asking about "our valuable friend in India".
Fitzwilliam Mss., Northamptonshire Record Office, A. ii. 53.

His writings on the bread supply of London,[56] the appointments to judge-
ships in his native Ayrshire[57] and his several fulminations against Picton
testifv to the catholicity of his interests. His propensity for letters earned
him from Picton the disparaging description of "a man of Intrigue and of
Papers".[58] In India, as in England, and as he was to do still later in Trinidad
he thought nothing of coming in from a day's work and composing a lengthy
script to some distant official or acquaintance, copied perhaps for his own or
someone else's benefit. Through his voluminous correspondence at this time
one gets a picture of a man entering enthusiastically into the petty intrigues,
plots and counterplots that were inseparable from the political and social
life of his day. He exerted himself in cultivating the acquaintance of government ministers and was unsparing in trying ever to further his own and his
friends' interests.

For Hippisley, his constant correspondent during the years 1782-5, he
attempted in 1785 to get something "beneficial and permanent".[59] For
Sullivan he hoped to be instrumental in getting the governorship of Madras
on Lord Macartney's resignation; Macartney himself he preferred to see as
governor general in succession to Hastings.[60] He delighted in the constantly
shifting political scene at home and reported at length on the machinations
of the various parties over the appointment of a new governor general in
succession to Hastings in 1786. In the growing storm over Hastings himself,
he assessed and calculated the strength of the Hastings party - "or as they are
called the Bengal Squad" - in Parliament at a hard core of about thirty.[61] He
even found time to describe his own encounter with "a delightful little
Demoiselle" whom he met on his return to England,[62] and to lament the
confusion into which the Foxite Whigs were thrown by the rumoured
marriage of the Prince of Wales to Mrs. Fitzwilliam.[63]

In pursuit of his varied objects at this time Fullarton was brought into the
cloest contact with the new stream of liberal thought that was beginning to
grow out of Britain's enlarged responsibilities for a world wide empire. Next
to the issue of slave trade abolition nothing had so simulated this movement
as had the activities of the East India Company in India, and Fullarton had
been priviliged to witness these activities at first hand, India left him forever
curious about the nature of Britain's empire, the means of its maintenance,

56. *Pelham Papers*, Add. Mss. 33,124, ff. 39-42; Fullarton : Pelham, 11.7.1800. Also, *Ibid.*, ff. 43-4.

57. *Pelham Papers*, Add. Mss. 33,108, f. 454; Fullarton : Pelham, 15.12.1802.

58. C.O. 295/4, Picton : Hobart, 6.3.1803.
59. *Hippisley Papers*, Add. Mss. 41,622, ff. 305-6; Fullarton : Hippisley, 20.12.1785.
60. *Ibid.*, ff. 308-11; Fullarton : Hippisley, 11.2.1786.
61. *Ibid., loc. cit.*

62. *Hippisley Papers*, Add. Mss. 41,622, ff. 305-6; Fullarton : Hippisley, 20.12.1785.
63. *Ibid.*, ff. 308-11; Fullarton : Hippisley, 11.2.1786, postscript.

and the countervailing rights and responsibilities of overseas dominion. His acquaintance with men like Burke, moreover, sharpened his own latent dissatisfaction with the state of affairs in India.

The dissatisfaction he chronicled in his book "A View of the English Interests in India" published in 1787.[64] In it he argued that British principles and policies in India as witnessed in the activities of the East India Company had produced a "most pernicious instability" seriously endangering the prospects of Britain's permanent hegemony. Irreverence for local customs, arrogance in civil and military matters, and an insensitivity to local interests had forced the local powers actively to seek the extermination of British power in India: hence, for instance, Hydar Ali. Above all the transformation of the East India Company from a merchant company pure and simple into a seemingly soverign governmental authority had, far from strengthening British dominion in India, severely weakened it. "Capricious innovation" and "the continued operation of violence" in the interests of economic gain had greatly weakened the superstructure of British rule. The answer lay in the efficient overseeing of the Company's activities by the British government in the interests of the native population.

This point of view put Fullarton firmly with the small but influential minority who saw "the humane treatment of subject races" as a policy not only dictated, as Harlow has said, "by Christian ethics but. . .(as) a necessary condition of profitable business".[65] This new developing idea of trusteeship, of moral accountability for the welfare of dependent peoples was,in Harlow's phrase, one of the "formative influences" of late eighteenth and early nineteenth century imperial policy.[66] Its influence was probably best seen at work in the parliamentary debates on Fox's India Bill and on Pitt's own Bill which was finally preferred. Though the India Bill provided some of the most tawdry politicking of the reign of George III it also provided the opportunity for unequivocal statements of recognized moral obligation to overseas dependants by the greatest political figures of the day. Fox, Burke, Sheridan, and because of political tactics Pitt to a lesser extent, all concurred in the belief that political authority over subject peoples was in essence a trust that imposed duties and responsibilities as well as rights and privileges. In India the power of the East India Company had to be curbed: Fox and Pitt disputed the method of enforcing control and the degree of its enforcement,

---

64. *A View of the English Interests in India*, (London, 1787). By William Fullarton, M.P. F.R.Ss. of London and Edinburgh, and the late Commander of the Southern Army on the Coast of Coromandel, pp. 5-9.
   Another book which he proposed writing entitled *"Constitutional and Comparative Commentaries on the British Empire and the other states of Europe"* was put aside, probably on his appointment to the first commissionership in Trinidad, and was never finished.
   See *Pelham Papers*, Add. Mss. 33,107, Fullarton : Pelham, 1.8.1802.
65. *Cambridge History of the British Empire*, Vol. II, p. 143.
66. *Ibid.*, p. 143.

but they were at one in agreeing that control, in the interest of the native population, was necessary.[67]

Imperial trusteeship was also the idea that inspired Burke's prosecution of Warren Hastings for mis-rule in India - a trial that seems to have exercised a profound influence on the mind of Fullarton. The impeachment of Hastings began in the same year, 1787, that saw the publication of Fullarton's book on the English interests in India, and dragged on for eight long years. During these years the publicity attending the trial plus the increasing agitation for the abolition of the slave trade, thoroughly acquainted the British public with the notion of trusteeship as a factor in imperial relations even though it did not convert them all to its acceptance. Influenced by the most liberal minds of his day, impressed by Burke's assaults against Hastings, and impelled by his own intellectual conviction, Fullarton was decidedly a disciple of the new philosophy.

The conflict between Picton and Fullarton, then, was one of ideas as much as of personality. Picton represented the school of thought, still influential, still powerful, for long destined to be a factor in British political life that held, like George III, that it was impossible in overseas territories like India and, by implication, the West Indies "to carry on business with the same moderation that is suitable to a European civilized nation" [68] George III might have been the most exalted but was neither the only, nor the last, protagonist of this view. The acquittals of Hastings, of Picton himself, and of ex-Governor Eyre of Jamaica in the late nineteenth century, adequately illustrate the recurring strength of this belief.[69]

As representatives of antagonistic streams in British political thought Picton and Fullarton shared no common ground. Picton exhausted every device to promote his own point of view and to show how unreasonable Fullarton's was. His own trial and prosecution he depicted as an attack on the integrity and freedom of action of every military officer who, because of his profession, might be called to the governorship of an overseas colony. Pursuing this argument in a letter to the Privy Council in 1804, he described himself as "the Representative of the British Army: of every Officer who has

67. *Ibid.*, pp. 139-43 for a full discussion on the Indian Bill. Also, *Parliamentary History*, xxiv, pp. 322-7; 378; 420. And, G.R. Mellor, *British Imperial Trusteeship, 1783-1850*, (London, 1951), pp. 22-5, for a brief discussion on the genesis of the idea of trusteeship.
   Erich Eyck, *Pitt versus Fox Father and Son, 1735-1806* , (London, 1950) pp. 250-4, 257, 266-9 adequately deals with the "tawdry politicking" attending the passage of the Indian Bills.
68. *Cambridge History of India*, Vol. VI, p. 308. Quoted from Stanhope, *Life of William Pitt*, I, p. 480. The remark was occasioned by Pitt's vote to impeach Hastings on the Chait Singh charge. Conceding that Pitt had no doubt acted according to his conscience, George III argued that conscience was one thing in Britain or Europe and quite something else in the colonies.
69. Bernard Semmel, *The Governor Eyre Controversy*, (London, 1962), particularly Chapters V and VI, discusses the prevailing sentiment among the British upper classes towards overseas native peoples and shows how upper class attitudes towards the British labouring classes led naturally to the justification in the minds of upper class Britons of the employment of terror as a normal method of colonial government.

been in similar Situations, or may be so in future; and . . . I have come forward, alone, unsupported, with every thing inimical . . . to the Discussion of a Question of the greatest Importance to the Service . . . The Question is. . . whether an Officer Commanding in an Enemy's Country, under extraordinary Circumstances of Difficulty and Danger, may safely make use of extraordinary Means for the support of His Majesty's Government, and the Preservation of His Post?" [70]

Not surprisingly Fullarton asked a different question. He was interested in establishing the limits which he believed the conventions of British justice imposed on the behaviour of British administrators and governors towards overseas dependents of the Crown. The occasion for his query was provided by the rumour that Picton had been given command of a regiment about to embark for India, and by the news that Lord Castlereagh, as Secretary of State, had presented Picton to the King. Both these occurrences seemed extraordinary to Fullarton, particularly since Picton had not yet been cleared of the crimes imputed to him and indeed stood under the cloud of having been found guilty at his first trial of unlawfully torturing Louisa Calderon. Referring to these incidents and Lord Castlereagh's part in them, Fullarton observed that: "So far as Lord Castlereagh is concerned, his conduct has brought to a specific issue the important Question on which I have been so long and so earnestly engaged - What modes and measures of severity those who govern in the King's name, may inflict upon his Majesty's subjects in the distant possessions of the Crown? He (Lord Castlereagh) seems labouring to establish, that Military Commandants and Governors abroad are to be exempted from obedience to the principles of British justice, to the Laws of these Realms, or to the Municipal Institutes of any Civilized Society - In other words, that our Colonial Rulers are henceforth to be at liberty to commit Individuals without specifying any offence - to confiscate their Property and Banish them, without assigning any reason - to inflict Torture, Mutilations and Death, in the most summary and cruel forms, without trial or any means of defence . . . and remain beyond the power of refutation". [71]

These two questions stemmed from irreconcilable points of view, and Picton and Fullarton were irreconcilable antagonists. Their individual circumstances admirably fitted them for the role each had elected to play. Picton after nine years' residence in the West Indies during which his personal position had undergone a remarkable and satisfying change not unnaturally regarded the trappings of a slave society, its repressions and inequalities, as indispensable to the enjoyment of civilized leisure by the enfranchised white classes. Never having been exposed to liberal influences he was supremely sceptical of all philanthropic theories and found it impossible to respond favourably to Fullarton's liberalizing innovations. His residence in the West Indies had moreover coincided with the increasing agitation of the abolitionists

70. C.O. 295/10, Picton : Privy Council, 8.10.1804.
71. C.O. 295/17, Fullarton : Duke of York, 15.6.1807.

176

against the slave trade. If, in England, the effect of this agitation had been to assist in the creation among the British public of what Semmel has called "a kindly view of the native races",[72] the effect in the West Indies had been wholly different. Picton's instinctive rejection of the settler scheme was in part an indication of the parallel development which had taken place in the West Indies, namely, the hardening of West Indian planter opinion against all efforts at liberalizing the slave system.

Fullarton, uncorrupted by long residence in the West Indies, could not view the problem in the same way. Even India, his only other colonial experience, was not quite as bad as the West Indies. He was genuinely shocked by the presumptions and injustices which, deriving from the slave system, transcended the relationships between supposedly free sections of the society. The conventional proscription of the whole coloured class filled him with dismay. His solemn determination "to render Every Man's Condition better and more prosperous without, if possible rendering any Man's Condition Worse"[73] was undoubtedly made in good faith. But it was this same determination that caused Picton to regard him as "the most fatal present that could possibly be made to this unfortunate colony".[74]

In another sense there can be little doubt that Fullarton and Picton conformed to the "liberal aristocrat-poor white" syndrome now regarded as a sociological commonplace in the discussion of relations existing between Europeans or other whites and non-European subject races. Fullarton was undoubtedly the liberal aristocrat. A man of independent means he could fraternize with free coloureds without, as it were, losing caste. With his Scottish estates, his well-placed connections, and his parliamentary background, he could be liberal without fearing the possibility of suffering by his liberalism. Not so with Picton, the poor white. Every assault on the West Indian planter position, every attempt to erode the foundation of injustice and inequality on which that society was based, was construed by Picton as a grave threat to his own carefully constructed material and social position. It was an unfortunate chance that the Commission of government for Trinidad happened to provide the backdrop to this conflict of ideals and personality.

The unfortunate fact though was that history was on Picton's side. The British West Indian islands in the early nineteenth century were ruled by whites, but it was increasingly by a class of poor whites. All the historical development of the few preceding decades, economic hardship, revolution in the West Indies, absenteeism, the attack on the slave trade, the growing challenge from the free coloureds and, finally, the psychological effects of an awareness of impending change, had made white West Indian society an embattled, poor white one. In relations with the Negroes this meant a preference for firmness and intransigence rather than for humanity and accom-

72. Semmel, *op. cit.*, p. 20.
73. C.O. 295/4, Fullarton : Sullivan, 8.3.1803.
74. C.O. 295/4, Picton : Hobart, 6.3.1803.

modation. And it was this mood that Picton so correctly represented. Thus, the suggestion that Trinidad's social system should be remodelled by the introduction of free white small holders, possibly as a prelude to introducing men of the same kind into the rest of the West Indies, was one of the most revolutionary suggestions that could have been made in the context of the period. It is no accident that it was this one question which continuously surfaced in discussions of such policy differences as were exhibited between the commissioners. Constitutional change and the 3½% duties seem never to have claimed their attention in the way that the settler scheme did, for, in its essential aspects, it heralded not merely a change in patterns of labour or of land holding but a change in society itself.

In many ways the attempt to introduce a class of free white small-holders into Trinidad was an attempt to revert to a form of society the West Indies had already known and had already discarded. The social conditions of the West Indies in the early nineteenth century had been more than three centuries in the making. The rigorous labour demands of the early West Indian environment had first produced, and then eliminated in turn the Indian labourer, the white indentured worker and the white small-holder. Whereas the disappearance of the Indian labourer had been fairly permanent, the white man's disappearance as a worker had been succeeded by his re-appearance as proprietor and manager and had been symptomatic of the profoundest economic and social changes. For though at first white labour had given way to Negro slavery on mainly economic grounds 75 the prejudices of race, class and caste which had developed from the imprint of Negro slavery had become more important than the economic factors which were supposed to underwrite the existence of that institution. Slavery had become more important for the social attitudes which it nourished and sanctioned than for the economic objectives it was originally intended to serve, particularly if, as some writers were beginning to say, slavery was expensive, wasteful and inefficient.76 In the long run, expense, waste and inefficiency were to play their part in demolishing the institution, but such factors were powerless to modify the essentials of the social system that

75. See Eric Williams, *Capitalism and Slavery*, (Chapel Hill, 1944), p. 9 ff., and especially pp. 19-20, 23-24. Williams writes that Negro slavery "had to do not with the color of the labourer, but the cheapness of the labour". And again, ". . . the colonies needed labour and resorted to Negro labour because it was cheapest and best".
See also, M.L. Hansen, *The Atlantic Migration 1607-1860*, (Harper Torchbook edition, 1961), pp. 41-2. Speaking of the substitution of Negro for white labour in Barbados, Hansen writes:—
"The Negroes, numbering sixty-four hundred in 1643, totaled over fifty thousand in 1666, and for nearly every one who came, an Englishman, Scotchman or Irishman had to depart". Many of the departing whites were smallholders and one-time indentured servants.
Also, V.T. Harlow, *A History of Barbados 1625-1685*, (Oxford, 1926), pp. 42-4, 292, 309, 338.

76. For example, Adam Smith, *The Wealth of Nations*, (Everyman edition, 1958), Vol. I, pp. 72, 345-6. And as indicated above, p. 134, note 25, the arguments of Layman. See also the pamphlet of a contemporary of both Smith and Layman. (James White), *Hints for a Specific Plan for An Abolition of the Slave Trade and for Relief of the Negroes in the British West Indies*, (London, 1788).

slavery had called into being. Slavery as an institution had come to rest on timeworn and specific assumptions pertaining to the functions and attributes of the various racial groups composing West Indian society. And the presence of a large white labouring class in a West Indian colony would have been as menacing by its existence as the abolition of slavery itself.

Picton was, as we have seen,[77] contemptuous of the settler scheme from the very beginning, partly because it was predicated on the need to stop the slave trade to Trinidad. Doubtlessly he construed this as an encroachment on the rights and privileges of the Trinidad planter, made more invidious because it abrogated one of the terms of the implied contract between government and planter in a new colony, namely, the adequate and continuing supply of slave labour. But, more fundamentally, Picton was also concerned with the preservation of the historic role of the European in the West Indies, a role that he and all West Indian whites from Trinidad to Jamaica knew and well understood.

Thus he railed against the belief purveyed by "Raynal and . . . other picturesque Historians" that cocoa had been easily cultivated by the Spaniards in tropical colonies[78] and, according to Hobart, could be profitably grown in Trinidad by small white farmers. If indeed Spaniards had done so, said Picton, they were Creoles not Europeans and only at the cost of the best years of their lives. Planting cocoa was much too arduous an activity for whites. So too was the breeding of cattle, another occupation recommended by Hobart for the special attention of prospective white settlers. Cattle breeding Picton also ruled out on economic grounds. To make Trinidad a self-sufficient producer of livestock would be to cut off one of the great articles of trade between the Island and the Venezuelan mainland and would ultimately lead to a diminution in the flow of currency into Trinidad. It mattered little to Picton that the purchase price was high. "The higher the price of Cattle, and of all supplies drawn from the Spanish Main," he argued, with scant regard for the pockets of the colonists, "the more advantageous to the Commerce of Great Britain, as a greater proportion of her Manufacturers will be disposed of in payment".[79]

77. See above, p. 155. In March 1803, Adderley was firmly of the opinion that Picton loathed the settler scheme and was "resolved it should fail". The Dutch settlers who had arrived from Surinam sometime prior to Fullarton's arrival had been neglected by Picton and had, according to Adderley, fallen into "a condition of the most deplorable wretchedness". They sold their rations for rum, lay dead drunk in the streets and had become "woeful objects of disease . . . The barrack where they are lodged is an absolute nuisance".
Picton, Adderley concluded, was "decidedly hostile" to the settling of a white peasant population. *Hobart Papers*, Bundle Y (J. 310), Adderley : Hobart, 19.3.1803.
78. C.O. 295/10, "Report on the State and Affairs of Trinidad" by Col. Picton. February 1804.
79. C.O. 295/10, "Report on the State and Affairs of Trinidad" by Col. Picton. February 1804.
What Picton is arguing here is that, since the trade between Trinidad and the Spanish Main was largely a barter trade, Trinidad was an excellent outport for British manufactured goods to the Main and, the dearer Spanish supplies were, the higher the exchange value which could be set on exported manufactured goods.

Similarly, the same settler who could not, with the help of his family, eke out an existence by growing cocoa on his allotment of land, would become an efficient producer of cocoa if he had but "five or six Negroes".[80] And cattle breeding was rejected not only because it was hostile to the true interests of the Mother Country, but because it only promised to the settler the "patient expectation of remote advantages" and guaranteed him nothing but a bare livelihood.[81]

This was not what the European expected from the West Indies. For him the Caribbean still wore the beguiling shimmer of *"El Dorado"*, and the promise of quick and easy wealth. This was not merely reflected in the highly selective form of economic enterprise in which he participated. In Trinidad, at least at the beginning of the nineteenth century, there were sound economic motives for the traditional emphasis on sugar to the detriment of other crops. Sugar prices were high, returns enormous, and few could be bothered with the slow profits accruing from coffee, cocoa and cotton. Whereas 14,164,984 lbs of sugar were produced in 1802, only 278,271 lbs of coffee, 138,669 lbs of cocoa and 190,210 lbs of cotton[82] were produced, mainly by Spaniards and small French planters with few slaves and insufficient capital for sugar cultivation.[83] In 1803, Fullarton described cocoa production as not being fashionable because its profits were too slow for "the Impatient Activity of English and French Colonists".[84] But European enterprise in the West Indies was conditioned not only by notions of profit but by less tangible though equally real concepts of how a white gentleman should live in the tropics. Thus Picton could say that, "The European, to stimulate him to Labour in these relaxing Climates, must have something before his Eyes, that he can almost touch with his hands. The near prospect of Ease and Independance (sic) alone, is capable of exciting to such exertions".[85] Similarly, he could recognise the possibility of employing a considerable number of Europeans in Trinidad, but not as labourers. Opportunities existed for their employment as "Managers, Overseers, Drivers etc. who when they have acquired a small Capital by their Industry, and the necessary knowledge to convert it to advantage, may become useful settlers without any expence to the state, or to humanity, as by that time, they will have been seasoned to the Climate, without going through the firey (sic) ordeal of Manual Labour".[86] The idea did not originate with Picton, but the strategy of European enterprise in the West Indies was never more clearly stated.

Depressed groups of whites - "poor whites" in a different sense - were to be found in the West Indies in the early nineteenth century, but the term

80. *Ibid.*   81. *Ibid.*
82. Sanderson, *Political Account. . .* , p. 100.   83. *Ibid.*, p. 62.
84. C.O. 295/4, Fullarton : Sullivan, 12.1.1803.
85. C.O. 295/10, "Report on Trinidad. . . ." by Col. Picton. February 1804.
86. *Ibid.*

"poor whites" is in itself a sufficient comment on the rarity of the phenomenon. In Barbados, George Pinckard encountered such a group at the end
of the eighteenth century. He described them as "obscure individuals, remote from the great class of merchants and planters" obtaining a meagre
livelihood breeding poultry and cultivating a small patch of earth. Pinckard
was so stunned by his experience that he could only attribute their condition,
in many ways similar to that of the free Negroes, to "misfortune, or misconduct, in some of the race. . ."[87]   In the Leewards, whites worked as
hucksters, tradesmen, cryers and craftsmen, as did some of the free people of
colour. Others purchased a slave or two and lived by hiring them out as
domestic servants, lightermen or any of the various other jobs performed by
slaves in the towns.[88]   But with the possible exception of the Barbados
"poor whites" who were an ostracized class and among whom by the end of
the eighteenth century poverty already seemed to have been endemic, white
society in the West Indies was remarkable for its mobility, its homo-
geneity and its enthusiasm, characteristics founded in large measure on the
justified expectation of the individual white that he would some day become
richer. Huckster, craftsman, small slave-owner, overseer, manager: these
were the occupational gradations of a society continually on the move, the
object being ownership of the plantation and as Professor Goveia has said,
"leadership in the islands or . . . the even giddier heights of wealthy· absenteeism in England".[89]

Social and economic depression was the least enduring characteristic of
the lower white classes. If a white settler could not succeed in one island he
simply moved to another, carrying with him what Fraser has called "the
colonial patent of nobility"[90] - his white skin - and began claiming and exercising his privileges all over again. If his ambitions had no upper limit - in the
heyday of sugar he might even like William Beckford have become lord mayor
of London or, failing that, have excited the King's curiosity by the splendour
of his carriage - his starting point was always at least one rung removed from
the foot of the ladder. The lowest grade of West Indian labour, the toilsome
drudgery of the field hand, could never again blight his existence. And the
highest reaches of power and influence were his if he could only lay claim to
the opulence which was for him the sole condition of success.

Lord Hobart's concept then of a white yeomanry permanently forming
the basis of a reorientation of the labour force in Trinidad made necessary by
the imposed restriction of African slave imports would very probably have
fallen flat. The further depression of the free coloured class and the servitude

87. George Pinckard, *Notes on the West Indies*, Two volumes. (Second edition, London, 1816), Vol. II, p. 309.
88. Elsa V. Goveia, *Slave Society in the British Leeward Islands, 1780-1800.* (Yale University Press, 1965), Chapter IV.
89. Elsa V. Goveia, *Slave Society in the British Leeward Islands, 1780-1800.* (London University Ph. D thesis, 1952), p. 167.
90. *Op. cit.*, Vol. I, p. 313.

CHAPTER 6

of the Chinese immigrants would have been more likely consequences. As far as the Chinese were concerned, this was a development that Hobart seemed to have anticipated with more than becoming equanimity. His observations on this point put the whole scheme of Chinese immigration in a new light. Referring to this suggestion in his unsigned memorandum to the commissioners he commented:

> "In the preceding observations the object principally in view has been to suggest the means of introducing and establishing a white Yeomanry in Trinidad: it must be acknowledged that the Cultivation of the Island, though it might be improved by the intelligence, could not be much advanced by the Individual labour of Europeans or their unmixed descendants - To effect this to any extent by other means than the employment of Slaves, we must have recourse to the Chinese. . . ."[91]

Chinese labour, then, and by implication the labour of the mixed descendants of Europeans, were to provide the leaven with which the benign intellect of European convicts, soldiers, indentured servants and other settlers was to mould the economic prosperity of the Island of Trinidad. Lord Hobart seems to have been among the first to anticipate the failure of his scheme.

* * *

The division of powers and responsibilities among the commissioners further minimised the prospects of the Commission's survival. The most careful reading of the Commission and Instructions issued to the commissioners on their appointment does little to provide an unequivocal interpretation of the Secretary of State's intentions on this score. The bare bones of his proposals we already know. The Commission was to consist of three officials respectively distinguished by the title of civil, military and naval commissioner. The commissioners were vaguely intended to cooperate in the Island's administration. The civil commissioner was the most senior among them, the military and naval commissioners ranking next in that order. Beyond this the Secretary of State said little, but much more needed to be said.

Three questions of interpretation suggest themselves. Was it intended, for instance, that each commissioner should solely and exclusively exercise a complete jurisdiction over the separate branch of administration reserved to him, whether civil, military or naval? Or, alternatively, were the three commissioners intended to cooperate on the administration of all things civil, military and naval, the separate jurisdiction extending only to the execution of agreed decisions pertaining to the commissioner's special field of reference? And, what precisely were the powers of the first or civil commissioner as head of the Commission? Vagueness on points like these need not have been fatal given conditions of concord and amity between the commissioners. But in the actual conditions that prevailed, such ambiguity, though not the prime

91. C.O. 296/4, Hobart : Commissioners, 16.10.1802, enclosure No. 20.

182

cause of the dispute among the commissioners, could not but help to extend the area of conflict and increase its overall effects.

The Secretary of State in describing the division of powers among the commissioners seems to have favoured the latter of the two alternatives outlined above. The commissioners were collectively regarded as the equivalent of a single governor and were expected to exercise their powers as a governor would. Thus the responsibility for everything affecting the Island's welfare and administration was to be "conjointly" exercised [92] The only concession made to the novelty of the experiment was the formulation, frequently repeated in the format of the enabling Commission, that the commissioners acting together, or any two of them, could legally exercise the prerogatives of the Commission. [93] Thus official cognisance was taken of the possibility that the "governor" could theoretically be divided within himself. But the idea of a single "governor" was not taken to its logical conclusion and several questions remained unanswered.

The role of the Council in the operation of the Commission was not specifically discussed in the Commission and Instructions but an enlarged Council was instituted with the Commission. [94] From subsequent events it seems to have been intended that discussions of proposals for the Island's administration, and military and naval defence, should take place in Council. Decisions would have been taken by a simple majority of votes of Council members and junior commissioners voting together, the civil commissioner as chairman of the Council having a casting vote only. What would have happened in the event that two commissioners opposed a measure passed by a majority of the Council was not said. Technically, since the Council's powers under the Commission, as under the governorship that preceded it, extended only to advice, and executive power was vested in the commissioners, the vote of any two commissioners against a proposal assented to by a majority of Council votes should have counted as a veto. In effect, this would have meant that, as in the case of the governor's veto, such a "decision" would have been negatived pending the decision of the Secretary of State.

The most reasonable construction of the Commissioner's powers would seem to be that executive action ought to have been preceded by a discus-

92. The word "conjointly" was often used in the Commission and all powers were granted to "you the said William Fullarton Thomas Picton and Samuel Hood. . ." Even such a clause as No. 20 of the Instructions seemed to grant the commission of vice-admiral, with powers to appoint judges etc. to the vice-admiralty court, to all three commissioners.

93. This formulation was predicated on the need to provide for the absence, sickness or death of one of the commissioners - and of course for normal disagreement on policy. Later the junior commissioners were to interpret it as enabling them together to implement the Commission in such a way as to exclude the first commissioner from any effective participation in it. This was not the intention of the Commission which was framed on the reasonable expectation that amity would prevail among the commissioners.

94. Instructions, clause 3. Membership of the Council was increased from five to seven.

sion of the subject involved by the commissioners in Council. The decision then arrived at would have been implemented by the commissioner concerned depending on whether the issue was civil, military or naval. A majority of votes would have decided the issue, providing no two commissioners held inflexible objections. But it the dissident commissioner were adamant, then execution of the intended measure would have had to be suspended, the dissident commissioner forwarding their reasons to the Secretary of State.

This system of voting would admittedly have destroyed the advantage that Lord Hobart hoped to derive from having an expert commissioner responsible for each of the three sections of the Island's administration; but the destruction would have been less complete than under a system by which voting in Council decided once and for all what policies were to be implemented. It would have reconciled the advisory role of the Council with the executive and administrative powers of the commissioners. A majority vote of the seven ordinary Council members could not have overwhelmed a majority opinion of the commissioners, and the commissioner whose special responsibility was being discussed would have had to gain the support of one of his commissioner colleagues and not a majority of the whole Council on a contentious subject. For it was not entirely inconceivable that, say, the military commissioner could have been outvoted in Council on a military matter. But if this happened then his proposal would have failed to win not only the majority support of ordinary Council members but also the support of at least one of his colleagues in the Commission. This would have made the performance of an immeasurably distasteful task, in his role of executive officer, a bit more palatable. This system if followed would also have placed the highest premium on consultation among the commissioners prior to the ordinary discussion of issues in Council.

In fact, however, owing to the course of events, attention focussed not on the relations of Council and Commission but on the distribution of power within the Commission itself. This necessitated the adherence to a certain view of the commissioners' powers, and from the inception of the commissioners' rule a conflict of views relating to their respective powers prevailed. According to Woodyear, largely because of Fullarton's efforts aboard ship, there existed among the officers who accompanied the civil commissioner on the journey from England, "A pretty general opinion . . . that Colonel Fullarton was the sole Governor, as to Civil Matters, and that His opinion on those Subjects was to determine any point".[95] In the public imagination too, before the interpretation of the commissioners' powers became a matter of urgent partisanship, Fullarton was regarded as the "Chief Governor".[96] But a sufficient apprehension of impending confusion

95. C.O. 298/1, Minute of Council, 13.7.1803.
96. C.O. 295/6, Rigby : Baillie, 15.2.1803. A phrase used by Rigby and attributed chiefly to some members of the French and Spanish communities.

existed for *Cabildo* members to feel that the appointment of the Commission just "would not answer".[97]

In the Council, in the absence of Commodore Hood, the naval commissioner, there was a general concurrence in the belief of Fullarton's supremacy. Aware of the weakness of their position and of the insecurity of their tenure, Council members voted, in spite of their personal feelings, for those measures introduced by Mr. Fullarton who, as first and civil commissioner, outranked Brigadier General Picton, his colleague. The only occasion on which there was a recognizable opposition in Council to Fullarton, on the motion for the suspension of Woodyear from the public secretaryship on February 19, opinion was divided and the matter was decided by Fullarton's casting vote.[98]

But the general acquiescence in Council cloaked the strength of feeling against Fullarton. Moreover, it obscured a vital facet of the Council's interpretation of the commissioner's powers. Council members did not believe that Fullarton was the "Chief Governor",· but only the senior of the two commissioners then present. On Hood's arrival, believing that the combined votes of the two junior commissioners eclipsed the authority of the civil commissioner, the Council consistently opposed Fullarton and supported Picton and Hood. Here the Council's interpretation of the commissioners' powers was vital. For the Council supported the junior commissioners not only because its members agreed with their policies, but because they were convinced that Picton and Hood acting together were constitutionally more powerful than Fullarton, chief commissioner though he was.[99] It is not too cynical to say that had the Council conceived that the balance of authority lay on Fullarton's side their support for Picton and Hood would have been less forthcoming in the early stages of the dispute. For the majority of Council members it was as important to support the more powerful faction as it was to aid in the promotion of their own favoured policies; that they acquiesced in the policies pursued by Picton and Hood only added to the satisfaction felt at the discomfiture of the first commissioner.

Following from the Council's adherence to the junior commissioners there arose certain developments that soon forced a discussion of the commissioners' powers at the highest level. Apart from presiding at Council and *Cabildo* meetings Fullarton, in effect, was stripped of all function or influence which ought to have derived from his being the first as well as the civil commissioner. The theory of his colleagues' combined authority being in every way superior to his stripped him not only of power but of the pre-

97. C.O. 298/1, Minute of Council, 18.7.1803. Assertion of Mr. Black, the *alcalde* of the first election, under cross-examination by Fullarton in Council.
98. C.O. 298/1, Minute of 13.7.1803. Examination of Woodyear. The relevant Minute of Council of 17.2.1803, enclosed in C.O. 295/4, Fullarton : Hobart, 3.3.1803, does not give details of the voting.
99. This was a point of view shared even by those sympathetic to Fullarton. Rigby, writing to Baillie at the time of Hood's departure, remarked as follows:—
    "I think the departure of the Commodore, a measure calculated to throw the Colony into commotion, if any thing could, for whilst he was here, *there was no doubt but the majority of the Commission had authority to act. . .*" My emphasis.
    C.O. 295/6, Rigby : Baillie, 28.4.1803, enclosed in Baillie : Sullivan, 1.6.1803.

rogatives of pre-eminence and, in the final analysis, threatened the existence of the civil government itself.

By the very nature of things the powers of the civil commissioner were severely weakened. He could no longer prevail in Council; hostility to him in the Council was universal, with the exception of Adderley who, in succeeding Woodyear as public secretary had for a while also supplanted him in the Council.[100] Even Fullarton's ability to influence Council decisions was small; as chairman of the Council he had only a casting, not an original, vote. Besides, the layman, and the councillors were laymen, more readily accomodates himself to the view that experts exist in almost any field of human activity but that of civil government. It is easier to believe in the notion of an expert in military or naval affairs than in an expert in government. Not that examples of this rare species have never existed. It is only that government is much too partial and subjective a thing to foster the dispassionate acceptance of another's competence on which the concept of expertise thrives.

Because of this and because of the hostility which his measures engendered, Fullarton's every act or proposal was subjected to the closest scrutiny, while his colleagues were free to do very much as they pleased in their respective fields. John Rigby's doleful expostulation and prophecy uttered at this stage of the Commission's affairs echoed the public dismay at the antics of the commissioners, and aptly described the diminution which Fullarton's powers had undergone. "For God's sake", wrote Rigby, "what were Ministers about when they formed such a Government. General Picton commands the Army - Commodore Hood the Navy exclusively, and the civil power they divide with Colonel Fullarton who alone knows any Thing of the Requisites of Civil Government. A House divided against itself must fall."[101]

Secondly, since civil government was proportionately more involved in the running of the Island than strictly military or naval business every impediment arising out of the worsening relations between the commissioners weighed more heavily on the civil commissioner than it did on the other two. Even after decisions affecting the Island's civil government were taken, it was necessary, as Fullarton ruefully remarked, "to meet every Day except Sunday in order to guard against the Interruption of Executive and Deliberative detail to prevent any one of us, from having to complain that any order is Discussed or issued without His participation".[102] The occasions on which military or naval matters were discussed between the three commissioners

100. Appointed to the Council by Fullarton after Woodyear's suspension on February 17, 1803, Adderley was removed on a motion of Picton's on March 10, on the ground that the office of provost marshal and the position of member of Council were incompatible·
C.O. 295/4, Minute of Council 10.3.1803.
101. C.O. 295/6, Baillie : Sullivan, 7.4.1803; enclosure, Rigby : Baillie, 13.3.1803.
102. C.O. 295/4, Fullarton : Sullivan, 4.3.1803.
C.O. 295/4, Fullarton : Hobart, 20.3.1803 indicates that this was a change instituted on Hood's arrival and countermanded Fullarton's successful motion in the Council on February 17, in Hood's absence, to have the "daily detail of executive business" performed by the senior commissioner being

were rare indeed; the daily meetings were in fact necessitated by the junior commissioners' desire to maintain the closest possible vigilance on what Fullarton was doing. Frequent meetings in the interest of a tolerable relationship acted in restraint of the proper exercise of Fullarton's powers as civil commissioner.

Thirdly, as relations between the commissioners became progressively worse, supervision of Fullarton's actions was increased to the point of rendering him totally ineffective. Concurrently, he participated less and less in the discussion of military and naval problems, and was finally excluded altogether. The furthering rift meant that the civil government was denied the protection and support that, of right, it ought to have obtained from the military. Indeed, the military and naval forces under the control of the junior commissioners were ranged against the civil power represented by Fullarton. The confusion existing between strictly military forces and civilian forces bearing arms further exacerbated the position of the civil government. Picton tended to regard any one bearing arms as belonging to the military - a contention fairly easily maintained in the confused situation where all able bodied men were required to bear arms at some time.

After sentries had been removed by Picton's order from duty on the seafront [103] and military assistance had been refused to the deputy *alguacil mayor* when attempting an arrest, [104] Fullarton attempted to confer some authority on his government by establishing his control over the militia. [105] His efforts were rebuffed and were the ultimate occasion of his complaint to Lord Hobart on March 3. "Your Lordship", he wrote, "will no doubt Direct in what manner the Militia are to Receive Detail orders and Commissions, and who, is to Command, Inspect, or Review Them! At present it does not appear that any one of the Commissioners, is sufficiently authorized to undertake these Duties, which from their nature cannot be Executed by three Persons. Of course they will remain with several other Executive operations Either not performed at all, or very ill performed untill your orders shall be received".[106]

present in the Island. Fullarton's motion, incidentally, accorded with Hobart's own directive in his letter of April 23. Indeed, a comment on the back of the Minute of Council, a copy of which was enclosed, described the motion as being "perfectly consonant with the instructions of Government".

103. C.O. 295/5, Fullarton : Hobart, 25.6.1803; enclosure, Fullarton : Grinfield, 23.5.1803. C.O. 295/4, Fullarton : Sullivan, 9.3.1803, enclosure.

104. C.O. 295/4, Fullarton : Sullivan, 9.3.1803, enclosure. M'Callum, *Travels.* . . . , p. 225.

105. In a previous letter of February 19, Fullarton had written to Sullivan elaborating a plan for raising a force of Black Pioneers part of his purpose being to provide "a standing and really operative Colonial Force for defence — responsible to the Civil and Colonial Government". C.O. 295/4, Fullarton : Sullivan (Private), 19.2.1803.

106. C.O. 295/4, Fullarton : Hobart, 3.3:1803.
This also explains his desire to leave the Island. On 23rd May he wrote to Grinfield informing him of his determination to "abstain from any interference in the detail transactions of the Port of Spain, until I shall ascertain and possess sufficient powers to afford effectual protection and to quell violence". Fullarton obviously felt his frustration very keenly.
C.O. 295/5, Fullarton : Hobart, 25.6.1803, enclosure.

CHAPTER 6

On the following day, Thursday March 4, coming straight from a Council meeting where once more he had had an extremely rough passage, Fullarton penned a hasty letter to John Sullivan, the Under-Secretary of State, while a ship, delayed by his order, waited for the anxious missive. In this letter Fullarton described the fundamentals of the position that confronted him, and confronted the administration in England. Thus he wrote, "Whether the Reign of Terror or the Rules and Principles of British Government are to be the order of the Day for this Colony it is Extremely Requisite that the Lieges should know what they are to Expect or to apprehend - For my own part I shall use every Effort to preserve Matters, as much as possible in a State approaching to pacification untill the orders of Lord Hobart be Received - If I attempt to act at all in any Case I shall be accused of assuming powers of which I only hold a part. If I were to give any opinion on a Case between a European & a Colored Person, I should on the one Hand be accused of Encouraging dangerous Presumption of the Tawny orders or on the other, of neglecting the principles of Justice & Protection to which all Persons under the British government are apt to Refer".[107]

By the time the Secretary of State was able to sort out the ticklish problem of jurisdiction the Commission had, as we have seen, collapsed in disorder despite Fullarton's avowal that he "would strain every nerve to make the machinery Hang together, being Convinced that the great point is, to make the Mill go well, without considering whether it turns by Wind or Water".[108]

As far as the command of the militia was concerned Lord Hobart was of the opinion that it "should be held solely by Mr. Fullarton in like manner as it is held by the several Governors in the West Indies. . ." On the more general question of the duties of the commissioners it was ruled that the executive government of the Island should be vested in the hands of the civil commissioner subject to the deliberations of the commissioners-in-Council, and "subject to the Control of the Majority and making the opinions of such Majority duly recorded upon the minutes of Council, the rule of his Conduct".[109]

Between Council meetings all orders pertaining to the Island's government were to proceed from the civil commissioner, irrespective of whether or not

107. C.O. 295/4, Fullarton : Sullivan, 4.3.1803.
Adderley writing to Lord Hobart about two weeks later was of the opinion that, ". . . no talents however comprehensive can make the Machine work constituted as it is at present". *Hobart Papers,* Bundle Y (J. 310), Adderley : Hobart, 19.3.1803.
Soo too, was Baillie, Rigby's London correspondent. Writing to Sullivan on 19.5.1803 he ventured the opinion that "no three men that can be appointed, will draw together, and that it will be found necessary to fix upon one immediately, who is equal to the undertaking — I am confident that Colonel Fullarton's appointment to this office, would be highly agreeable to all the respectable Inhabitants and Merchants connected with the Island of Trinidad". Later he was to write: "I need not urge you to memorialise for British Laws and a single Governor, and I give you my fixed opinion, when I say that by no means can unanimity be restored here but by a removal of all the Parties. . . ." Rigby : Baillie, 28.4.1803, enclosed in Baillie : Sullivan, 1.6.1803. (C.O. 295/6.)
108. C.O. 295/4 Fullarton : Sullivan, 7.3.1803.
109. C.O. 295/4; C.O. 296/4, Hobart : Commissioners, 23.4.1803.

the issues involved had been previously discussed in Council. Orders on subjects not previously discussed in Council could however be revoked. Whether revocation was to be effected by the combined action of the other two commissioners acting outside the Council is unclear from the script. In the light of what preceded, however, it seems certain that the intention was that the process of revocation was intended to be exercised by discussion within the Council. As for command of the military forces, in the absence of the military commissioner from the Island, the civil commissioner, no other general officer being present, acceded to the command of the Island's forces "in like manner as it has been provided for in all His Majesty's Governments in the West Indies".[110]

These instructions came too late to save the Commission. Fullarton, as we have seen, intercepted this despatch at Barbados at the end of May, when Hood had already left the Island after entrusting full command of the administration to Picton who, in his turn, was busily preparing to resist Fullarton's expected return.[111] Even so, it is doubtful whether the despatch could at this stage have retarded the process of decay that had already set in. Nothing was said about the responsibilities of the military and naval commissioners *per se*. It was also unlikely that the junior commissioners would readily have acquiesced in the substantially enlarged powers thus bestowed on the civil commissioner. It is doubtful too whether these powers were in any case sufficiently adequate to ensure the stability and authority of the civil government. The role of the Council, which the Secretary of State was careful to emphasize, was clearly calculated to establish some stability in the relations between the commissioners in the interests of good government. This was predicated on the belief that the Council was an impartial body capable of arbitrating between the factions. But as we know, and as Lord Hobart apparently did not, the Council was itself implicated in every phase of the dispute.

The despatch fulfilled its purpose only after the Commission had ceased to function as a corporate body. Lord Hobart, unable to hold this rickety structure together, had, in the same despatch, intimated his willingness to accept Picton's proferred resignation. But he seemed still willing to persevere with the experiment for he promised to fill the vacancy on the Commission as soon as possible. [112] But the departure of commissioners Picton and Hood which alone gave the Commission some chance of functioning under its new regulations was attended, as we have seen, by circumstances which forced its supersession by the appointment of Colonel Hislop as Lieutenant Governor of the Island.

The disintegration of the Commission of 1802 meant the abandonment of all the ambitious plans for settlement and redevelopment which were associated with it. But even more than this it greatly embittered the struggle for

110. C.O. 295/4; C.O. 296/4. Hobart : Commissioners, 23.4.1803.
111. See pp. 150-3
112. C.O. 295/4; C.O. 296/4, Hobart : Commissioners, 23.4.1803.

constitutional change in Trinidad. White society was profoundly affected by the abject failure of the experiment. The Commission had come and gone and the constitutional problem was no nearer a definite solution. The Assembly system had not been introduced, a legislative Council had not been tried, nor for that matter was the *status quo* confirmed; in fact the partisan views of neither side had prevailed. The Island continued as it had done since the conquest, very much in a state of constitutional expectancy; the general feeling prevailed that something should and probably would be done, but when and what no one knew.

Following the departure of the commissioners, faction reigned supreme. In addition to the many highly significant social, economic and political variables, such as nationality, occupation, class and political beliefs that divided white society, there was now added an even more significant new distinction. People came to be distinguished, often pre-eminently so, by their partisan adherence to one or the other of the late commissioners: they were in fact either "Fullartonians" or "Pictonians". Partisan sentiment cut the community like a scythe. The commissioners having departed, the constitutional question became the battleground on which the competing claims of the factions were to be fought. To be a disciple of Fullarton or of Picton connoted a commitment to or disapproval of the introduction of the representative system and British laws. Political activity became heavily tinged with personal animosities, and the bitterness engendered by the Commission envenomed the relationship between the factions and complicated all future discussion of constitutional change. The story of the next few years chronicles the manner in which this divided society, after a period of bitter strife, finally achieved a sort of unanimity which enabled it, in 1810, to present a united demand for an Assembly system of government and for the introduction of British laws.

In fact between 1803 and 1810 the history of Trinidad can conveniently be divided into two periods. The first period, 1803 to 1808, is the history of domestic faction and of its operation among two white groups contending with equally unprincipled rapacity for the fruits of place and power. The second period, 1808 to 1810, was marked by yet another disastrous experiment following on the decision of the British government to make Spanish law fully operative in the Island. The chosen method had to do with the institution of a chief justice burdened with all the powers usually attaching to the person of an *oidor* and to the institution of an *Audiencia* in the Spanish system. [113] The resulting creation was a legalistic monstrosity with powers so wide and far-reaching that conflict with nearly every other constituted authority in the Island, including the Governor, was virtually inevitable.

113. For a discussion of the *oidor* see C.H. Haring, *The Spanish Empire in America,* (New York, 1947), *passim.*
See also, the *Recopilación,* Lib 2, Tit 15, for a general statement of the *oidor's* duties. Also, Lib. 3, Tit. 3, Ley. 34, and Lib. 2, Tit. 16, Ley 16; Lib 3, Tit. 2, Leyes 10, 11.
For the *Audiencia,* see pp. 37 ff above.

Thereafter ill-will and petty colonial intrigue completed the dissolution of that experiment. The attendant circumstances were such, however, that the free coloured, faced with the seeming certainty of the grant of the conventional representative system and British laws, in a context which would have rendered their position even more untenable, acted decisively to avert that danger.[114]

Throughout these periods Trinidad remained an Island of experiment with a form of government that was neither one thing nor the other. This constitutional ambivalence was in due course to be soundly condemned by the critics. Yet, viewed in the perspective of time it is not now as easy to acquiesce in this general condemnation. If the British government thought itself committed to a particular task of reassessment and innovation in Trinidad then the failure of the Commission had made it even more imperative to retain effective political power in the hands of the Crown. This it was that angered the critics most. Yet there can be little doubt that, in terms of the interests of the majority of the Island's residents, that is of the slave and free coloured populations, this was a fairer prospect than that which would have ensued on the grant of a representative system of government administered in the pursuit of a very sectional interest.

The failure of the Commission of 1802 had then this positive advantage. By splitting the white community into two temporarily irreconcilable factions it promoted the development of strong local interests in favour of two different models of constitutional advance. This provided the British government with the opportunity of prolonging the period of direct supervision precisely at that time when the legitimacy, if not the expediency, of so doing was still to be established. The withholding of the representative system later permitted the British government to indulge in a series of serious official experiments intended to set the pace for amelioration of the slave system in the West Indies.

The major ameliorative schemes applied to the Island, namely, the registration of the slaves, the House of Commons proposals for relieving the condition of the slave population in 1823, and the apprenticeship scheme in the interval between abolition and emancipation later took place in a context of increasing metropolitan acceptance of the legitimacy of direct rule in the colony. The internal history of the operation of amelioration, abolition and emancipation is yet to be written. When it is written, however, it seems that its details will confirm the view that Trinidad's role in aiding the speedy liquidation of slavery in the British West Indian colonies was momentous and effective. The failure of the Commission of 1802, by effectively postponing decision on the Island's future, and by providing an acceptable basis for prolonging the period of imperial supervision at a crucial stage, contributed immeasurably to the fulfilment of this later role.

114. With some immediate success; see C.O. 296/4, Liverpool : Hislop, 27.11.1810.

ctures and Plantations, such as Sugar,

or 320 Acres.

SERVATIONS.

it for Coffee and Cocoa only.
oil, flat Land, and communicates with the River Caroni.
y be made into Sugar Plantations, from the facility of cutting Canals.
ns; having a light Soil, it may be extended into the Vallies of the Northern Mountains.
drained, and Navigable Canals made through it.
re.

} nearly the whole of these Quarters are suitable for the Culture of Sugar Canes.

Hills are in Ridges, near each other; fit for Coffee.
e, except Cotton.
of the Ortoire, and is not very hilly; these three Districts may be enlarged.
able River Ortoire; the Soil is good and well drained.
account of the Navigation of the Ortoire.
able for all sorts of Plantations.

st Sugar of the Colony; hath two navigable Rivers.
Interior of the Land is sandy, having a white Sand to the depth of three Feet, and red Sand under it.
for Sugar and Coffee.
e of a superior Quality for the Culture of Sugar Canes and Coffee.
ly in the Interior; it is fit for Sugar and Coffee only.
l in the Neighbourhood of Icaque is damp and marshy.
e, on account of the easy Communication with both Coasts.
it for every Sort of Culture.
a, and is capable of being enlarged.
onveniency of the Landing Places, is fit for every kind of Culture.
otton and Coffee only.
ight Bank of the Ortoire, but on approaching to Guayaguay, the Cultivation becomes more laborious, and the
er are high; a Canal might be made, which would communicate with Mayaro.   Land more rugged.
ed, and hath a fruitful Soil.
h an *Embarcadaire,* or Landing Place, at his Entrance, and another at the Point Mancenille.
ng a Navigable Canal, to open a Communication between the Rivers Oropuche and Caroni.
Coffee, and the low Lands for Cocoa; the Soil is very productive.
ng hilly and rugged; it has two *Embarcadaires,* or Landing Places, and communicates with Matura.
towards the East Coast only.
tions might be established in this Quarter, the Soil being very good, but has little depth.

e North Coast, are covered with all kinds of incorruptible Wood, fit for Ship Building; the
, Chogaray, Erino, Quemada, Cedros, Irois, Guapo, la Brea and Naparima, abound in
or Crapa Wood.

rinidad. By Captain F. Mallet, dated July 1797, and published at London, 1802.

TABLE III

ABSTRACT OF POPULATION SHOWING THE NUMBER OF WHITE
AND COLOURED MEN IN THE ISLAND OF TRINIDAD FOR THE YEAR 1803

QUARTERS	WHITE				COLOURED				TOTAL
	English	Spanish	French	Total White	English	Spanish	French	Total Coloured	
St. Anna	4	3	39	46	2	3	94	99	145
Tragarete	3	-	6	9	-	-	1	1	10
Mucurapo	6	1	7	14	3	7	5	15	29
Maraval	2	5	4	11	2	26	36	64	75
Diego Martin	21	1	22	44	9	11	42	62	106
Carenero (Carenage) & Bocas	21	8	39	68	4	20	126	150	218
(La) Ventilla	3	-	10	13	2	4	48	54	67
Cimaronero	3	1	2	6	1	2	18	21	27
Sta. Cruz	2	10	6	18	6	65	35	106	124
Aricagua	7	5	13	25	3	3	8	14	39
St. Joseph	5	21	18	44	-	63	13	76	120
Maracas Valley	2	14	2	18	2	26	-	28	46
Tacarigua & Arouca	28	-	8	36	5	-	5	10	46
Arima & Guanapo	3	11	3	17	-	6	6	12	29
Toco & Salive (Salibia)	8	-	3	11	2	2	10	14	25
Mayaro	-	-	15	15	-	-	27	27	42
Guayaguayare	-	-	16	16	-	-	8	8	24
Hidcos & Gallos	5	-	12	17	1	-	10	11	28
Cedros	7	-	5	12	2	.	18	20	32
La Brea & Erin	10	-	23	33	40	-	29	69	102
Oropuch	6	-	-	6	3	-	10	13	19
Naparima - South	23	-	27	50	9	-	13	22	72
Naparima - North	26	2	10	38	6	-	25	31	69
Punta de Piedra	5	2	12	19	1	-	38	39	58
Cuva & Savanetta	45	2	7	54	16	13	-	29	83
Chaguanas & Carony	-	-	2	2	-	1	-	1	3
Las Cuevas & Maracas	-	-	1	1	-	2	1	3	4
Port of Spain	250	83	175	508	163	36	296	495	1003
TOTAL	495	169	487	1151	282	290	922	1494	2645

Source: C.O. 295/8, Hislop: Camden, 9.7.1804, Appendix No. 1.

TABLE IV

ACCOUNT OF THE QUANTITIES OF PROVISIONS IMPORTED INTO TRINIDAD
FROM THE UNITED STATES OF AMERICA IN AMERICAN VESSELS, AND FROM THE
BRITISH COLONIES IN NORTH AMERICA IN BRITISH SHIPPING, 1802 - 1805.

Years		Feet Lumber	Shingles	Staves	Hoops	Bls. Beef	Bls. Pork	Hhds Fish	Bls & Boxes Fish	Bls. Flour	Bls. Rice	Bls & Bags Bread	Cattle	Sheep	TOTAL
1802	American	5,079,550	4,337,887	858,572	131,882	2260	1253	1505	5504	25,843	144	1659	113	579	
	British	233,013	187,000	397,200	-	-	-	567	1255	1,321	261	-	-	-	
1803	American	5,216,513	6,764,855	592,549	162,700	4267	2244	2433	3730	23,129	338	2872	396	789	
	British	880,080	185,000	-	-	-	-	1327	1180	2,400	323	-	9	-	
1804	American	3,108,000	2,403,220	524,000	748,000	4878	3462	1466	3594	25,532	1380	2210	252	348	
	British	178,000	105,700	-	-	-	-	466	204	1,216	-	-	-	-	
1805	American	3,002,050	3,467,000	671,500	185,465	7840	1449	2161	5209	19,603	424	393	466	985	
	British	61,000	22,000	43,500	-	-	-	901	1251	68	106	-	-	-	
1802 to 1805	American	16,406,113	16,972,962	2,646,621	1,228,047	19,245	8408	7565	18,037	94,107	2286	7134	1227	2701	
	British	1,352,093	499,700	440,700	172,000[1]	-	-	3261	3,890	5,005	690	-	9	-	

Source: C.O. 295/14, Hislop : Windham, 28.10.1806, No. 44, enclosure.

[1]As indicated in note at the end of the table in the original.

TABLE V

ABSTRACT OF POPULATION FOR THE ISLAND OF TRINIDAD FOR THE YEAR 1810
SHOWING THE RATIO BETWEEN ADULTS AND CHILDREN OF WHITE AND COLOURED
PERSONS OF DIFFERENT NATIONALITIES

	WHITE						COLOURED						TOTAL
	ADULTS			CHILDREN			ADULTS			CHILDREN			
	Men	Wo-men	Total	Boys	Girls	Total	Men	Wo-men	Total	Boys	Girls	Total	
BRITISH	514	223	*737*	231	214	*445*	462	803	*1265*	872	906	*1778*	4225
SPANISH	178	156	*334*	71	57	*128*	523	491	1014	207	137	*344*	1820
FRENCH	353	261	*614*	42	71	*113*	560	851	*1411*	161	111	272	2410
MALTESE	5		5										5
CORSICANS	21		*21*										21
ITALIANS	26		*26*										26
PORTUGUESE	6		6										6
DUTCH	2		2										2
GERMANS	23	14	*37*										37
SWISS	8		8										8
AMERICANS	8		8										8
RUSSIANS													-
CHINESE							23		*23*				23
DANISH							14	3	17				17
SWEDISH							10		*10*				10
AFRICANS							88	47	*135*				135
	1144	654	*1798*	344	342	686	1680	2195	*3875*	1240	1154	*2394*	8753

Source: C.O. 295/24, General Return of Population for the year 1810. This is an exact representation of the data provided. The figures do not agree with those provided in the general return where total whites were said variously to amount to 2595, and 2487, total free coloured to 6264, total slaves to 20861, and the grand total was said to be 31144. In point of fact only the free coloured total was correct. Yet, it must be pointed out that the figures for the free coloured given above add up to 6269 - the kind of error only too often encountered in Statistical accounts of the Island's population.

TABLE VI

ABSTRACT OF ADULT MALE AND TOTAL WHITE, COLOURED, SLAVE AND INDIAN
POPULATION OF THE ISLAND OF TRINIDAD AT 31.12.1810.

QUARTERS	COMMANDANTS	ADULT MALE WHITE	TOTAL WHITE	ADULT MALE COL- OURED	TOTAL COL- OURED	SLAVE	INDIAN	TOTAL
1. Carenage & Bocas	John Gloster	41	97	68	231	1199	5	1532
2. Diego Martin	John Smith	41	82	88	291	1275	-	1648
3. Maraval	Thomas Mathurin de Gannes	9	22	99	373	447	-	842
4. Mucurapo	Jacob Simons	7	12	1	26	173	-	211
5. Tragarete	R. La Deveze	12	26	10	26	216	-	268
6. St. Ann's	J.E. Maingot	34	66	110	362	737	-	1165
7. La Ventilla	Vt. Patrice	12	17	75	229	354	-	600
8. Cimaronero	H. La Coste	4	7	25	60	351	-	418
9. Sta. Cruz	Ant. Portel	28	74	108	382	644	-	1100
10. Aricagua and St. Juan	Francis Derieux	21	45	36	186	821	-	1052
11. St. Joseph	Guisepy and German	43	130	48	175	552	4	861
12. Valley of Maracas	Francis Farfan	22	63	52	177	256	1	497
13. Tacarigua and Arouca	Richard Joseph	34	68	37	133	1335	1	1537
14. Arima and Guanapo	Manuel Sorzano	33	70	54	205	403	833	1511
15. Toco and Cumana	Wm. Thornhill	6	7	19	55	107	230	399
16. Mayaro	(Jn. Bte. Durafour	11	24	28	61	365	1	451
17. Guayaguaydre	(	10	12	26	88	225	12	337
18. Hicacos and Gallos	Ch. St. Bresson	15	32	22	75	225	-	332
19. Cedros	Francis Massiany	14	20	5	29	374	3	426
20. La Bray	Joseph Rivers	33	73	41	106	732	117	1028
21. Oropuch	Duval Desrivieres	11	19	15	39	302	108	468
22. South Naparime	John Outen	37	72	31	122	1562	-	1756
23. North Naparime	Robert Mitchell	50	106	35	101	1124	336	1667
24. Point a Piedra	La Source Mondilhon	22	45	27	68	712	-	825
25. Cuva and Savoneta	Ths. Drape	43	49	70	139	2329	-	2517
26. Las Cuevas and Maracas	Valentine Basanta	2	2	3	5	107	-	114
27. Carony	Col. de Soter	6	11	3	6	253	-	270
28. Chaguanas	Ant. Cipriany	12	17	2	4	227	-	248
The 4th (sic) Alcaldes de Barrio of Port- of-Spain		526	1227	542	2510	3414	32	7183
		1139	2495	1680	6264	20821	1683	31263

Source: C.O. 295/24, General Return of Population for the year 1810. This
table furnishes yet another example of the uncertainty of the
statistics. The data must be regarded as valuable in that it offers a
reasonable approximation of the Island's population. Final, accurate
figures are exceedingly difficult to obtain. These ones are probably
the most serviceable of the lot.

TABLE VII

ABSTRACT OF WHITE AND COLOURED POPULATION FOR THE ISLAND OF TRINIDAD BY
NATIONALITY AND RACE, 1802, 1806, 1810.

	WHITE				COLOURED				GRAND TOTAL
	BRITISH	FRENCH	SPANISH	TOTAL	BRITISH	FRENCH	SPANISH	TOTAL	
1802[1]	663	1093	505	2261	599	2925	1751	5275	7536
1806[2]	792	940	542	2274	1568	2447	1386	5401	7675
1810[3]	1182	727	462	2495[4]	3043	1358	1683	6264[5]	8759

Sources: [1]C.O. 295/6, Return of Population at 1.10.1802.
[2]C.O. 295/16, Return of Population at 31.12.1806.
[3]C.O. 295/24, Return of Population at 31.12.1810.
[4]Including other whites as in Tables 5 and 6.
[5]Including other coloured as in Tables 5 and 6.

TABLE VIII

ABSTRACT SHOWING CHIEF CROPS, ACREAGE UNDER CULTIVATION AND PRODUCTION FIGURES
IN THE ISLAND OF TRINIDAD - 31.12.1810.

CROP/COMMODITY	ACREAGE OR NUMBER OF TREES	SIZE OF PRODUCTION
SUGAR	13,560 acres	21,746,775 lbs.
COCOA	818,301 Trees	726,173 lbs.
COFFEE	1,721,260 Trees	295,443 lbs.
COTTON	629 Acres	114,980 lbs.
PLANTAINS	2,376,370 Trees	-
RUM	-	463,870 Galls.
SYRUP (Molasses)	-	82,163 Galls.
PROVISIONS	6,856 Acres	-
PASTURE	10,538 Acres	
AMOUNT OF LAND GRANTED	145,227 Acres	

Source: C.O. 295/24, Return of Population, 31.12.1810.

TABLE IX

ABSTRACT OF POPULATION FOR THE ISLAND OF TRINIDAD
FOR THE YEARS 1782, 1789, 1797, 1802, 1806, 1810.

DATE	WHITES	COLOUREDS	SLAVES	INDIANS	TOTAL
1782[1]	126	295	310	2082	2813
1789[2]	2151	4467	10100	2200	18918
1797[3]	2151	4476	10009	1082	17718
1802[4]	2261	5275	19709	1232	28477
1806[5]	2274	5401	20761	1607	30043
1810[6]	2495	6264	20821	1683	31263

Sources:

[1] L.M. Fraser, *History of Trinidad*, Vol. 1, p. 289.

[2] Fraser, *op. cit.*, p. 289.

[3] Capt. F. Mallet, *Descriptive Account . . .*, July 1797.

[4] C.O. 295/6, Return of Population on October 1802, dated March 1803.

[5] C.O. 295/16, Return of Population at 31.12.1806.

[6] C.O. 295/24, Return of Population at 31.12.1810.

TABLE X

PRICES OBTAINING ON IMPORTS AND EXPORTS AUGUST - DECEMBER 1811

COMMODITY	AUGUST & SEPTEMBER	OCTOBER	NOVEMBER	DECEMBER
		IMPORTS		
Beef per barrel	£14. 8. 0	£12. 12. 0	£13. 10. 0	£13. 10. 0
Pork ” ”	£16. 4. 0	£18. 0. 0	£18. 0. 0	£15. 6. 0
Boards per 1000	£22. 10. 0	£22. 10. 0	£18. 0. 0	£27. 0. 0
Shingles per 1000	£ 2. 5. 0	£ 3. 3. 0	£ 3. 12. 0	£ 1. 16. 0
				(Boston Shingles)
Staves, White Oak, per 1000	£22. 10. 0	£31. 10. 0	£31. 10. 0	£45. 0. 0
Staves, Red Oak, per 1000	£20. 5. 0	£22. 10. 0	£22. 10. 0	£22. 10. 0
Hoops, per 1000	£22. 10. 0	£18. 0. 0	£18. 0. 0	£31. 10. 0
Clapboards, per 1000	£16. 4. 0	£22. 10. 0	£18. 0. 0	£22. 10. 0
Codfish, per quintal	£ 3. 12. 0	£ 3. 3. 0	£ 2. 5. 0	£3. 12. 0
Scale Fish, per quintal	£ 3. 3. 0	£ 1. 16. 0	£1. 16. 0	-
Port Wine, per doz.	£ 3. 12. 0	£ 4. 10. 0	£ 4. 10. 0	£ 4. 1. 0
Flour (Superfine) per barrel	£ 6. 6. 0	£ 8. 2. 0	£ 7. 4. 0	£ 7. 4. 0
Oats, per 16 bushels	£ 9. 0. 0	£18. 0. 0	£18. 0. 0	-
Sheep	£ 2. 14. 0	£4. 10. 0	£ 4. 10. 0	£ 3. 3. 0
Cattle	£27. 0. 0	£31. 10. 0	£31. 10. 0	£31. 10. 0
		EXPORTS		
Sugar, per cwt.	£1. 16. 0	£1. 16. 0	£1. 16. 0	£ 1. 11. 6
Cotton, per cwt.	£ 7. 4. 0	£ 8. 2. 0	£8. 2. 0	£ 6. 6. 0
Coffee, ” ”	£ 2. 14. 0	£ 3. 12. 0	£3. 12. 0	£ 3. 12. 0
Cocoa, ” ”	£ 3. 3. 0	£ 3. 3. 0	£ 3. 12. 0	£ 2. 5. 0
Indigo, per lb.	£ 0. 9. 0	£0. 2. 3	£0. 2. 3	£ 0. 12. 0
Fustick, per ton	£ 9. 0. 0	£10. 16. 0	£10. 16. 0	£11. 14. 0
Lignum vitae	£ 9. 0. 0	£ 8. 2. 0	£ 8. 2. 0	£ 6. 6. 0
Rum (Improved) per gall.	£ 1. 2. 6	£ 0. 9. 0	£ 0. 9. 0	-

Prices are quoted in £ currency, that is at roughly one-half of the £ sterling.

In November and December the £ sterling exchanged at 192½ per cent of the £ currency.

One Spanish dollar = 9/- currency.

Source: C.O. 295/26, List of Prices current enclosed in Munro: Liverpool, 13.10.1811.

PART THREE

TOWARDS A SOLUTION

CHAPTER 7

STRIFE BY OTHER MEANS

If, as has often been said, war is the continuation of diplomacy by other means then government in the Island of Trinidad in the post-Commission period was the pursuit of faction in another guise. As we have seen, the manner of Trinidad's settlement from 1783 onwards, together with the effects of war and revolution in the West Indies, and later the conquest of Trinidad itself, contrived to bring together in notably trying circumstances people of various nationalities and aspirations, thereby laying the basis, though not at once promoting the formation, of faction. Faction, however, was the peculiar legacy of the activities of the Commission of 1802. Before the Commission came to Trinidad in early 1803 there existed a multitude of aims. After 1803, apart from the free coloureds and slaves whose role in the ensuing events is a minor one, there existed two white groups deeply divided by political rivalry and imbued with a strong sense of the perfidy and villainy of their antagonists.

The factions were distinguished by two factors, partisan loyalties to the departed commissioners and differences over the Island's future government. These two factors were never quite separate. They were, and for a long time remained, closely interrelated. To the extent that one predominated over the other, however, personal antipathies and loyalties deriving from adherence to the commissioners can be said to have prevailed during the first half of the period under discussion, say from the middle of 1803 until the end of Picton's first trial in 1806; thereafter, the purely constitutional issue predominated.

Apart from explaining the genesis of the factions, the presence of these two factors conveys some impression of their composition and numerical strength. Considered as an expression of personal adherence to the commissioners, the Fullarton faction was more British dominated than the Picton faction was. The impression that Fullarton favoured the interests of the British against those of the foreigners, and that Picton favoured the foreigners to the detriment of the British tended to embitter the partisans of both commissioners. Writing at a time in the Commission's affairs when Picton's star was ascendant, Rigby voiced the popular feeling among the majority of the British when he averred that, "The British & Spaniards are the most oppressed people, whilst French & Corsican Exiles of every description are in full possession of the Island".[1] Fullarton who, as an administrator, was sensitive about the implications of his partiality towards the British citizens felt obliged to defend his attitude towards them.[2] But his sensitiveness did not prevent him from appointing a Council completely comprised of Britishers on his return to the Island in June 1803.[3]

1. C.O. 295/6, Rigby : Baillie, 28.4.1803; enclosed in Baillie : Sullivan, 1.6.1803.
2. See for example, C.O. 295/5, Fullarton : Hood, 24.4.1803; enclosed in Fullarton : Hobart, 25.6.1803.
3. See C.O. 295/5, Fullarton : Hobart, 25.6.1803.

STRIFE BY OTHER MEANS

A perusal of the two Addresses voted to Picton and Fullarton on their respective departures from the Island clearly reveals the composition of their support. [4] Picton's Address, signed by 225 subscribers, included the most prominent Frenchmen on the Island and almost all the office holders in Council, *Cabildo,* and the public service, most of these office holders being British. The list of subscribers was studded with names from the French upper and middle classes, the British planting and professional classes, and about half a dozen Spaniards of social eminence but of little wealth. The ratio between the French and British subscribers was about three to two.

Fullarton's Address on the other hand was signed by 219 persons, over-whelmingly British. The number of foreigners hardly exceeded a dozen and a half, and though there were two *Chevaliers* among them, those apart, there were no more than two or three others who could be identified as prominent foreigners. The British subscribers were, as was to be expected, mainly merchants, small businessmen, artisans and shop assistants, with a small sprinkling of planters, and office holders like Colonel John Rutherford, the surveyor general, and John Smith, an *alcalde de barrio.* [5]

If the factions are considered as expressions of plain political sentiment it is overwhelmingly obvious, on the basis of the evidence provided by the several petitions for British laws, that the majority of persons desiring those laws were themselves British. The political Addresses voted between 1803 and 1810 petitioning for a representative Assembly and British laws differ only marginally in the extent to which they reflect the preponderance of British interest. Sanderson's remark apropos the 1801 'Wharton's Tavern' Address that foreigners' signatures were not solicited and if offered were not accepted "as that address was from the British inhabitants alone", [6] seems to have described the rule generally adopted by the British during the years 1801 right up to 1810. The British attitude to the constitutional question was that the old British system was something to be obtained almost exclusively by British effort. Until the attitude was abandoned, sympathetic foreigners could do little to help the British party who were alone to be blamed if their antagonists continually represented themselves as the champions of the foreigners who, it was frequently said, were all opposed to the introduction of the representative system.

The correspondence that Fullarton and Picton maintained with individuals in Trinidad after their return to England also facilitates the identification of some of the principal members of the factions. This evidence, besides con-firming the general thesis pertaining to the national composition of the

4. Copies of the Fullarton Address, dated 16.6.1803, are in C.O. 295/6, and C.O. 298/1. A copy of the Picton Address, dated 28.4.1803, is in C.O. 295/5, Minute of Council of 7.6.1803.
5. For the purpose of identifying the factions the Addresses are particularly useful because there is no duplication of subscribers; one either signed one or the other. Nihell, who was singularly adept at surviving among the factions, signed Picton's first, and though he might have wished to, was precluded by this from signing Fullarton's thereafter.
6. *Political Account,* p. 150.

193

factions, also indicates how much the existence of these factions depended on the sense of allegiance to Fullarton or to Picton.[7]

Immediately after his departure Fullarton was kept informed of proceedings in Trinidad by Rutherford, Andrew Wilson and James Rigby, all members of his last Council, who wrote to him on the specific question of the Council's reconstruction by Hislop.[8] Rigby who wrote at the same time of his failure to get de Castro shipped off to England as a witness against Picton, almost certainly continued his correspondence with Fullarton. Fullarton might also have corresponded with Thomas Higham. When, in 1804, the Island was threatened with the outbreak of party spirit in a new virulent form, it was because Fullarton, informed by Higham who was then in London, wrote to the Under-Secretary of State alleging that torture was still being used in Trinidad, and that a coloured man, Modeste, had been tortured.[9] In the same year, Lieutenant Governor Hislop was constrained to protest to the Secretary of State about the circulation in the Island of Fullarton's latest book on the Picton affair with some very uncomplimentary references to Hislop's government.[10]

Picton, like Fullarton, contrived to stoke the fires of partisanship in Trinidad. Writing to Begorrat about the Modeste affair in 1804, he expressed annoyance at the resignation from the *Cabildo* of John Black, one of the *alcaldes*, for his part in the torturing of Modeste. He lamented Black's rumoured decision to leave the Island, and observed that,"he ought not to have yielded to the miserable remains (of) a stinking beggarly faction despised by everyone here . . . People of their description always regard Moderation as a Symptom of Fear. There is but one successful mode of Governing them. Those who recur to others will be disappointed".[11] Many of Picton's other friends were, like Begorrat, foreigners. On the same occasion he asked Begorrat to convey his regards to "my old friends Bontur, Farfan, the Portels, Padre Royer of Arima etc. etc."[12] In another letter he showed that he was aware of, and encouraged, the continued feuding among the parties: "I hope Gloster Langton and you will continue to pull well together," he wrote, "and not allow those Rascals to succeed in any of their remaining Projects".[13]

Apart from these formal advances to their adherents in Trinidad, the two principals managed to keep the spirit of party strife very much alive in the Island merely by engaging in the much more serious business that claimed their attention on their return to England. Arriving in Scotland at the

7. One has to be a little bit cynical about these attachments. As Judge Smith was to say in 1809, the names of the two commissioners were often involved to cloak purposes "never good & often wicked" that had little to do with the commissioners themselves, C.O. 295/22, Smith : Cooke, 28.10.1809.
8. C.O. 295/5, Rutherford : Fullarton and Rigby, 25.7.1803, Andrew Wilson : Fullarton, 29.7.1803; all enclosed in Fullarton : Hobart, 1.10.1803.
9. C.O. 295/10, Fullarton : Cooke, 6.6.1804; Higham : Camden, 5.10.1804. See also, C.O. 295/8, Hislop : Camden, 3.9.1804 and enclosures; C.O. 296/4, Camden : Hislop, 18.7.1804; C.O. 295/9, Camden : Hislop, 24.11.1804 (Draft).
10. C.O. 295/8, Hislop : Camden, 4.9.1804.
11. B.M. Add. MSS. 36,870, Picton : Begorrat, 16.8.1804.
12. Ibid.
13. B.M. Add. MSS. 36870, Picton : Begorrat, 20.9.1804.

beginning of October, 1803, Fullarton immediately hastened to London there to lay before Lord Hobart a long list of charges for various criminal misdemeanours against Brigadier General Picton. [14] These accusations Hobart in turn referred to the Privy Council for investigation. [15] The Privy Council, impressed by the gravity of the charges, had Picton arrested in December, 1803, and bailed in the sum of £40,000. [16] Meanwhile, various aspects of the affair continued to be discussed by the Privy Council until, convinced that much more information was needed, the Lords of the Council issued a commission to Robert Brietzke Deane, a barrister-at-law, to proceed to Trinidad there to ascertain and enquire into charges that Picton had illegally issued commissions for the trial and execution of slaves on suspicion of sorcery and poisoning. [17]

Little is known about Deane's activities in Trinidad, [18] but it needs no inspired guessing to assume that his visit must have contributed to the general avidity with which the progress of events in England was being followed. Of much greater interest from this point of view is the fact that, prior to Deane's visit, a mandamus had been issued in England for the collection of evidence in Trinidad relative to the charge of torture of Louisa Calderon alleged against Picton. [19] In Trinidad a court under the presidency of Lieutenant Governor Hislop sat intermittently from November 11, 1804 to September 6, 1805. There were no wild unruly scenes but there was much ill-feeling beneath the surface. Francisco de Castro, *escribano* to the *Cabildo* at the time of the alleged offence, declared that he could not truthfully answer questions put to him by the prosecution because of threats against his person. [20] After a spell in jail for contempt he was persuaded to make a few innocuous statements, but could apparently not even be coerced into identifying his persecutors. [21] Father Joseph Maria Angeles, the Catholic curate of Port of Spain, perjured himself in giving testimony about the age of Louisa Calderon, and was described by his superior, the vicar-general, as a thorough scamp whom he had "never believed to be a man of good faith from the first day I saw him". [22] Nihell, accustomed to handling delicate affairs with authority, wrestled successfully with his conscience. His evidence

14. C.O. 295/5, Fullarton : Hobart, 1.10.1803.
15. *Hobart Papers*, (Bundle B), Hobart : Attorney General (Private) Draft, 31.10.1803.
16. C.O. 295/13, Picton : Camden, 17.1.1805; Heaton Robinson, *Memoirs. . .* , Vol. I, p. 155.
17. C.O. 295/13, Cottrell : Cooke, 22.11.1805. For some of the activities preceding the appointment of Deane, see *B.M. Add. Mss.* 38,241, 38,358 (Liverpool Papers) pp. 282-7 and 270 respectively.
18. Deane's report has not been seen. He arrived in Trinidad about February 1805 and had left for England by July. Hislop had almost nothing to say about him; he only reported his departure. (C.O. 295/14, No. 36 Hislop : Windham, 31.7.1806). For a sweeping attack on Deane's terms of reference see C.O. 295/15, Fullarton : Windham, 22.7.1806.
19. Howell, *State Trials*, XXX, pp. 226-31.
20. *Ibid.*, p. 253.
21. *Ibid.*, pp. 253-58 ff.
22. Howell, *State Trials*, XXX, p. 270. For Angeles' evidence see pp. 266-68. See also. Picton, *Evidence taken at Port of Spain, Island of Trinidad in the Case of Louisa Calderon. . . .* (London, 1806). And several letters to the Secretary of State calling for the punishment of the curate for attempting to incriminate him. e.g. C.O. 295/13, Picton : Cooke, 15.9.1805; C.O. 295/15, Picton : Windham, 25.7.1806; C.O. 295/15, Picton : Shee, 9.9.1806; C.O. 295/11, Hislop : Castlereagh, 15.11.1805.

was as devious as ever and led to the totally unexpected conclusion that Picton had been an unqualified boon to the Island.[23] Begorrat, Langton, and Picton's other friends were as reliable in his defence as they had always been in supporting his transgressions.[24]

*   *   *

To pursue the consideration of the factions in Trinidad it is necessary to turn now to a consideration of the Council. In many ways, the history of the constitutional struggles of the next few years is the history of the Council. Instituted in 1801 on Picton's appointment to the civil governorship, the Council at first played a significantly small part in the Island's administration. Under Picton, meetings were few and far between, and if minutes were kept they were not preserved, and no indication of the frequency of Council meetings now exists.[25] With the coming of the Commission, however, the Council entered on a new stage of development which was destined to be further enhanced by the dissensions among the commissioners.

The reasons for this development are fairly obvious. Partly because he was less familiar with the Island's affairs, and partly because his disposition suggested a more constitutional, perhaps even a more officious approach to the Island's government, Fullarton had summoned the Council much more frequently than his predecessor had done. From his arrival in January to his first departure in April Fullarton held a Council meeting on an average of more than once a week. After his departure the Council, under Picton and Hood, tended to meet just as frequently; and on Fullarton's return in June the Council indulged in a spate of furious activity, sometimes meeting as often as three times a week.

Then, too the frequency of Council meetings was directly related to the growing acrimony among the commissioners: the more bitter the dispute among them, the oftener the Council met and the more important it became. The Council was the one place where the dispute could be pursued with any semblance of decorum; and in the pursuance of charge and counter charge the Council was the vehicle through which the details of partisan activity could be transmitted to England free from the embarrassment of overt and sometimes unpleasant exposition.

There was too the question of legality. It was not only that the Council's interpretation of the commissioners' powers was vital, but that the Council provided the ultimate sanction of right that Trinidad could provide. The Council's agreement to the dismissal of a public officer disguised if it did not

---

23. *State Trials*, XXX, pp. 310-16.
24. Begorrat's evidence is in *State Trials*, XXX, 286 ff. Langton's evidence is in *Ibid.*, p. 317 ff. Farfan's evidence is in *Ibid.*, p. 299 ff.
25. C.O. 298/4 contains one of the very few records of Council meetings held by Picton prior to the institution of the Commission. See, Minutes of Council of 18.4.1810, enclosing Extract of Minutes of Council of 7.12.1801. The question discussed is that of the appointment of an Agent.

obscure the strongly partisan reason for his dismissal, just as the Council's co-operation could make a proclamation stripping a commissioner of his office plausible if not legal.

For all these reasons the Council, at the break up of the Commission, had undergone a very remarkable change. It had become a permanent and indispensable organ of government, no longer existing, as it were, by sufferance of the Island's governors, but subsisting by a right of its own. The Council could of course be organized and reorganized virtually at will as both Picton and Fullarton had shown, but government without its constant participation was no longer possible.

The Picton prosecution in England also emphasized the importance of the Council. In Trinidad the prosecution was represented as raising the question of the legality of the Island's laws and of the extent to which a Governor could safely be guided by them in the execution of his duty. [26] For this reason Lieutenant Governor Hislop was more than willing in his own defence to share with the Council the responsibility for all his acts. "By and with the advice of His Majesty's Council" became the standard phrase with which Hislop informed the Secretary of State of any act the absolute legality of which was, or possibly could be, in doubt. [27] In 1806, Hislop himself stated the principle on which he invariably acted in such circumstances. Questioned about his handling of the Dickson case, [28] he vowed that,

"In Mr. Dickson's business *as well as in every other when unusual Circumstances have demanded extraordinary proceedings, I have invariably advised & Consulted with His Majesty's Council.* No step has ever been intemperately or inconsiderately taken by me. The existing laws and His Majesty's instructions, have on all occasions assisted with legal advice determined my conduct."[29]

26. The intensity of feeling held by Hislop, the Council and the *Cabildo* on this score can be gleaned from a study of the following documents:- C.O. 295/14, Hislop : Windham, 3.5.1806, No. 24; C.O. 295/15, Hislop : Windham, 11.11.1806, No. 31. These two despatches were occasioned by the passing of a verdict of guilty on Picton for having acted without the sanction of Spanish law in torturing Calderon. The authorities in Trinidad represented the verdict as a sweeping indictment of the Island's laws. Hislop wrote that the current belief in Trinidad was "that there are no laws existing here for the punishment or prevention of Crimes. . ." This was an overstatement as the law officers of the Crown correctly maintained in a legal opinion on the matter. (C.O. 295/17, Piggott : Shee, 6.1.1807 and 26.1.1807. These were sent out in C.O. 296/4, Windham : Hislop, 26.1.1807, No. 10.) The fact that, as the court had incorrectly maintained, no law existed in Trinidad to support the legal application of torture was very far from saying that no law existed for the punishment or prevention of crime. It was part of the strategy of the Picton faction in Trinidad to represent his trial as undermining the rule of law in the Island in order to force a verdict favourable to him. Another despatch of Hislop's (C.O. 295/12, Hislop : Castlereagh, 13.12.1805) alleged that slaves accused of poisoning others now went unpunished "so great is become the reluctance of the Magistrates to take Cognizance of Matters of this Kind".
27. Hislop's despatch relative to the slave "insurrection" of 1805 provides a typical example of this reaction. C.O. 295/11, Hislop : Castlereagh, 19.12.1805. See also, Fraser, *History of Trinidad,* Vol. I, pp. 268-72.
28. See pp. 214 ff. below.
29. C.O. 295/14, Hislop : Windham, 31.7.1806, No. 36. The emphasis is mine.

Far from wishing to govern without a Council, the Governor was eager to govern with the constant advice and consultation of one.

With Hislop's accession to the lieutenant governorship the Council attained its maturity as an organ of government. Under Picton it had been relegated to a position of unrelieved obscurity. Under the commissioners its obscurity had been exchanged for the precarious existence of a weapon in the armoury of factional feuding: it became in fact the plaything of the commissioners. Under Hislop its participation as a full and equal partner in the process of government was eagerly encouraged.

Hislop's first act presaged the increasing pre-eminence and authority of the Council. Rightly conceiving his first task to be that of exorcising the demon of party spirit, Hislop descried in the Council the means of doing so. His plan for the reconciliation of the factions was simple. He decided to "call into the Council the most respectable Persons, who had distinguished themselves for their attachment to the two parties. . . judging. . . that from their unity of action in the Government a principle of reconciliation would extend itself throughout all who were supporters of their former conduct".[30] Thus Rigby, Rutherford and John Smith, though unanimously and vigorously protesting, were joined in the Council by Archibald Gloster, now reinstated as Attorney General, St. Hilaire Begorrat and John Black.[31] Nihell, agile as usual, declared himself to Hislop as belonging to neither party and became the seventh councillor.

In the ensuing months the Lieutenant Governor was to report the success of his plan. His assurances to the Secretary of State were climaxed in November, 1803, by the statement that it was a pleasure to work with the Council among whose members there was then no evidence of the differences that formerly existed. As for the public he added, "If differences of opinion on the former Circumstances of the Colony are entertained they are on no Occasion intruded in Society and Consequently are unknown. I am certain a stranger would not suppose that ever a division of Sentiment had taken place".[32]

Hislop, author of the plan, had a vested interest in its success, and his assurances must be treated with great circumspection. In the absence of any records of the votes in Council his assertion is difficult to refute. Moreover, membership of the Council was a highly prized perquisite; few would have wished to mortgage their membership in a futile pursuit of sectional interests. As we have seen Rutherford, Rigby and Smith though disgusted at being joined in the Council by Gloster, Begorrat and Black nevertheless refrained from resigning their positions. Besides, the Council was particularly ill-suited to the active representation of conflicting community interests. The pre-

---

30. C.O. 295/7, Hislop : Hobart, 16.8.1803. Also, C.O. 295/7, Hislop : Hobart, 25.7.1803.
31. C.O. 295/7, Hislop : Hobart, 16.8.1803. C.O. 298/1, Minute of Council, 22.7.1803.
32. C.O. 295/7, Hislop : Hobart, 16.11.1803. Also, C.O. 295/7, Hislop : Hobart, 24.11.1803. Also, C.O. 295/23, Hislop : Liverpool, 19.4.1810 (Private).

dominance of the Governor's role, his powers of appointment and dismissal, his veto, and often his very involvement in the advocacy of one or other interest to the near exclusion of another, made the Council a forum not so much of intelligent discussion as of artful sycophancy. The Council, organized as it was, could function only on the basis of unanimity or not at all. The concept of a continuing struggle between opposing groups within the Council introduces into the consideration of the Council an essential attribute of democratic government which the Council did not possess. The Council was an organ of autocratic control, not a platform for democratic debate.

Much more important a consideration is the fact that the Council's unanimity could only have existed on the basis of the capitulation of the Fullarton faction. Hislop himself was undoubtedly a Picton man, and had more in common with the Picton group than with their opponents. He saw an obvious parallel between himself, who, as Governor, might have to resort to some of Picton's methods, and Picton. When asked in 1805 to furnish copies of the commissions under which Picton had had slaves tried and executed for sorcery and poisoning, he entered into a detailed defence of the latter, commenting that severe measures of justice were inseparable from the government of a slave society.[33] His statement read in fact not only as a defence of Picton, but also as a justification of any acts of severity he might himself in future commit.

Even a strict counting of heads within the Council reveals a preponderance of pro-Picton sentiment with predictable implications of social and constitutional beliefs. The Governor, Gloster, Begorrat and Black, together with Nihell who soon came down on the official side, outnumbered the Fullarton group five to three. Of these three, only Rigby possessed sufficient wealth and position to maintain some independence: he was to be Higham's ally in the Modeste affair of 1804[34] and to sign a petition for British laws in 1805.[35] Rutherford, as surveyor-general, was head of a heavily indebted department the existence of which was beginning to be a matter of debate between the Governor, the Council and the Secretary of State.[36] He possessed little real independence and apparently was easily prevailed upon to forgo his old allegiance. So, too, was Smith whose highest post, before entering the Council under Fullarton, had been that of an *alcalde de barrio,* a minor position with nothing like the status attached to membership of the Council.

33. C.O. 295/11, Hislop : Castlereagh, 13.12.1805.

34. C.O. 295/8, Hislop : Camden, 3.9.1804. Higham was nearly prevented by the Governor from leaving for England. Rigby stood security for his return should he be required to stand trial for any of the various offences of public mischief alleged against him.

35. The petition is enclosed in C.O. 295/11, Hislop : Camden, 5.2.1805. It is analysed by Sanderson in *Political Account...*, p. 151 ff.

36. Cf. C.O. 296/4, Camden : Hislop, 19.7.1804.

CHAPTER 7

Hislop's assurances about the state of society as a whole, the peace and absence of strife that prevailed, though supported by other commentators,[37] were much too sanguine. As he himself said, at about the same time, the merchants were protesting against the 3½% duty in a manner which suggested that they aimed at its complete abolition. [38] This was in fact what they were doing. And their protest was political and factional in that it aimed at the substitution of new laws for old ones in a community where such agitation was by nature factional. In the new year, significantly, formal petitions against the duty were lodged by the merchants and manufacturers of Glasgow trading in Trinidad. [39] Glasgow was the port, it must be noted, from which the cargo of goods that provoked the protest in Trinidad, had arrived. The consideration of the constitutional struggle that began once more to assume new life will show how wrong Hislop was.

*   *   *

In January 1804, being assured that peace prevailed once more among Trinidad's warring factions, Lord Hobart addressed Lieutenant Governor Hislop on the constitutional issue. Adverting to the Commission's failure to devise and recommend a constitution for the Island, he urged the Governor to prepare as a matter of urgency a report on the Island's government and to submit recommendations for its constitutional change. [40]

In his despatch Lord Hobart set the limits within which the Governor was expected to operate. As he had intimated to the commissioners in 1802, the grant of an Assembly was not for the moment to be considered. It was his firm belief that "the Constitution of the Old British Colonies can (not) at present be expedient or even practicable in Trinidad". [41] On the other hand, however, the possibility of a legislative Council was noted and conceded.

A legislative Council would not meet all the objections to the present system of government, but, said Lord Hobart, it would offer some succour to those who felt, like the London merchants, that Spanish laws were "an insurmountable obstacle to the advancement of the Commerce and Cultivation of the Island."[42] This it would do by facilitating the gradual introduction of some of the laws of England, particularly those relating to the preservation of the subject, the administration of civil and criminal justice and the recovery of debt.

Another despatch about a month later revealed that Lord Hobart had firmly opted for a policy of gradualism. The immediate object was to give

---

37. Cf. C.O. 295/10, William Greene : John Sullivan, 31.5.1804, and Sanderson, *An Appeal. . .*, pp. 56-7. For a contrary and more correct view, see, C.O. 295/22, Smith : Cooke, 28.10.1809. Smith described the attempt as having "failed altogether".
38. C.O. 295/7, Hislop : Hobart, 10.10.1803.
39. C.O. 295/9, Boyd Alexander : Secretary of the Privy Council, 2.1.1804.
40. C.O. 296/4, Hobart : Hislop, 9.1.1804.
41. *Ibid.*   42.   *Ibid.*

Trinidad "a form of Government as nearly approaching to that which subsists in His Majesty's other Colonies". [43] Thus, the Assembly system was not forever abandoned, only indefinitely postponed.

To aid Hislop, Lord Hobart outlined the constitutional variants possible of application in the colonies. There were three: the Assembly system itself; a legislative Council; and the system then prevailing in Trinidad with the Island ruled by its ancient laws with all authority, legislative and executive, entrusted to the Governor. To the last two the Governor's attention was particularly drawn. He was given drafts of the Commissions and Instructions issued to the Governors of Quebec when that province had had a legislative Council, and he was invited to consider carefully the clauses empowering the Governor to constitute courts of justice and to consider the extent to which it might be necessary to abolish the existing courts and construct new ones.

These despatches left the Governor little room for manoeuvre. The issue was clear cut and his recommendation of a legislative Council was not surprising. The detailed work on the proposals for its institution was Gloster's, and his recommendations were transmitted untouched to Earl Camden, Secretary of State in succession to Lord Hobart from May 1804.[44] Gloster, undoubtedly the most comprehensive critic of the Assembly system who ever lived, argued against its introduction into Trinidad very much as if that point was at issue. An Assembly, he said, was inadmissible in a community such as Trinidad where the numbers of white foreigners were substantially greater than those of British descent.[45] Not only were the foreigners more numerous, they possessed a considerably larger proportion of the Island's landed property.[46] So that whether the Assembly was elected on an equal franchise of all adult white males or on the basis of the possession of landed property, the foreigners were sure to provide the majority of electors, with most likely a corresponding majority of the Assembly's representatives: this possibility Gloster dismissed as "monstrous (sic) and absurd!" To try and evade such a result by tampering with the franchise would be to court the dangers of turbulence and strife; hence an Assembly was out of the question.

His own experience in the West Indies, he said, had made him "doubt the propriety of investing any of the *petty* Colonies with such powers, from the inconvenience I have seen arising from them. . ." In a new colony like Trinidad with its "motley and pyebald (sic) Crew of English, French, Spanish, Italians, Genoese and Corsicans . . . needy adventurers, men of desperate fortunes and uncultivated intellects. . .", the dangers likely to attend the

43. C.O. 296/4, Hobart : Hislop, 2.2.1804.
44. C.O. 295/8, Hislop : Camden, 9.7.1804. This letter with its enclosures contains the Report on the Island's government and the documents recommending a legislative Council, one of which is a sketched bill of the form the legislature should take.
45. C.O. 295/8, Gloster : Hislop, 4.7.1804, enclosed in Hislop's letter quoted above. All references and quotations in the ensuing discussion, except where indicated, are from this letter. See also, C.O. 295/13. "Mr. Gloster's observations for a new Constitution. . . submitted to Lord Castlereagh." Dated 28.12.1805. Emphases where indicated are Gloster's.
46. Cf. C.O. 295/24, Smith : Liverpool, 14.2.1810.

precipitate grant of representative institutions were even greater. Such men as he had described were "the last persons, *surely,* to be selected, to discharge the important duties of the Solons and Lycurgus's!" Looking at the issue in perspective, he lectured the British **government** on having, by the indiscriminate grant of legislative Assemblies, permitted "the seeds of democracy to be planted, and to grow so thickly in the various provinces of North America. . . America would not, perhaps have been lost, had the Provinces been governed by Prefects and Proconsuls". As for security it was his opinion that, "A deliberative power in an Army or Garrison would be a very strange phenomenon, - and I regard a conquered or ceded West Indian Island, *in time of War with the state of its black Peasantry since the french revolution,* to require nearly similar discipline and superintendence, as a Military body."

Gloster also rejected on the ground of impolicy the consolidation of the Island's legislative and executive government in the hands of the Governor. Such a system would inevitably lead to despotic rule: not, he hastened to say, a possibility under the benign administration of Lieutenant Governor Hislop - who should in fact be made a Governor as soon as possible - but who knew what the future might bring? "The Sceptre that graced the hand of Trojan and Antoninus was a dreadful instrument wielded by Nero and Caligula."

A legislative Council, on the other hand, would provide the Governor who was often a military man, with precisely the type of advice and help that a Council of the Island's citizens sharing with him the onerous responsibility of lawmaking would be able to provide. The citizens themselves were best circumstanced to legislate for their needs. Finally, he argued, a local legislature was needed if only to infuse life and vigour into the Island's government.

As proposed by Gloster, the legislative Council was to consist of thirteen members with a quorum of nine, and a privy council of five of the most senior members as advisers to the Governor. [47] Members were to be nominated from amongst the most opulent and respectable planters. A few merchants were to be included: "(being also landed proprietors)". Councillors should hold office during pleasure, should be allowed full freedom of debate, and should not be liable to dismissal at the will and caprice of the Governor. Dismissal should only be on the establishment of "good and sufficient cause", and then with the assent of a majority of the Council, signified after a formal debate of the charges against the councillor concerned.

The Council should have wide legislative powers and should make laws subject to the assent of the Governor and the ultimate sanction of the Crown. The purpose of such legislation should be to facilitate the gradual transition from Spanish to English law. The Council should have powers to tax. Such a power, already in Gloster's opinion safeguarded by the device of having as legislators those who would in all likelihood bear the brunt of taxation,

47. C.O. 295/8, Gloster : Hislop, 4.7.1804; enclosure, "Sketch of Bill", Articles 1 and 3.

should be further protected by the publication of proposed money bills well in advance of their enactment in order to facilitate the adequate consideration of such public protest as might be made. [48]

A court of common pleas should be instituted to determine all causes of debt, contracts, personal wrongs, torts, damages, and questions of commerce and revenue. The court's jurisdiction should not extend to causes originating before the Island's conquest and cession and involving a dispute over real property, nor in any case where one or more of the parties was foreign. The temporary continuance of the Spanish courts was therefore envisaged. Ejectment cases involving British subjects alone, and dating from a period subsequent to the conquest and cession, were to be removed to the court of common pleas. The problem of uniting the functions of this new court with the already existing Spanish ones was admitted by Gloster to be nearly insurmountable, but deferring the attempt could only add to the difficulty. [49]

Trial by jury in civil cases was also proposed: a system which, Gloster argued, though liable to many objections in Trinidad, would eventually prove to be as beneficial to the foreigner as to the British-born subject. Free blacks and people of colour were to be excluded from jury service: "they are not (jurors) in the other Islands, nor should they be in this. . . . They can feel no jealousy or offence at not being called to a task, in general coerced by fine and trouble, of no emolument, and from which they must know they are carefully excluded in the other Islands". [50]

A court of chancery consisting of the Governor and two councillors was also suggested. [51] The purpose of this court would be to determine bankruptcy cases, the aim being to establish a practical mean between the English and the Spanish systems: no *concurso* of creditors was to be called as in the Spanish system, but the debtor was not obliged to settle with the first creditor making a demand to the detriment of other creditors as in the old British islands. The question of mortgages was indeed so serious that Gloster thought it best taken up in the British Parliament, "to make the Bill more palatable in London, and the other great commercial Cities". Meanwhile priority should be given to mortgage claims according to the date of their registration. For this purpose the registry should be thoroughly reorganized. And the Act 5. Geo. II, cap. 120, for the more easy recovery of debt in the colonies should be extended to the Island, Spanish law notwithstanding, as long as the debt was contracted after the conquest and cession. [52]

It was Gloster's opinion that the English criminal law should be introduced; but so grave were the objections of the Spanish judges and of Chief

---

48. C.O. 295/8, Gloster : Hislop, 4.7.1804; enclosure, "Sketch of Bill", Article 2.

49. See "Sketch of Bill", Articles 13, 14; and Gloster's covering letter to Hislop of 4.7.1804.

50. Gloster's letter of July 4.
51. "Sketch of Bill", Article 8.
52. "Sketch of Bill", Article 15.

Justice Nihell to its introduction [53] that the question, in his opinion, was one that ought to be referred to His Majesty's ministers. Nevertheless, argued Gloster, the transition to British forms of judicial administration was not as difficult as commonly supposed. Much of the apparatus already existed. Commandants of quarters performed functions much like those of English lords-lieutenants and sheriffs of counties; *alcaldes de barrio* were like the English justices of the peace; *alguaçiles* were constables, and the *alguaçil mayor* was the equivalent of the provost marshal or jail keeper in the old British islands.

Freedom of worship should be granted to Roman Catholics and others. [54] Religious belief should not be a bar to participation in the legislature or other public office. The Roman Catholic clergy's subordination to the Bishop of Angustura should however be superseded by the appointment of a bishop from among the respectable parish clergy, or by the British government's appointment of a suitably qualified Spanish minister from England to fill the post. Appointments to vacant benefices in the Catholic and Protestant churches had to be authorised by the Governor. Acts passed by the legislative Council for the regulation of religious observance in the Island should not come into force until the royal assent was obtained. [55]

Finally, Gloster suggested that certain laws should be enacted by the Council as soon as it should have come into being. Proposed legislation should, therefore, comprise: a permanent bill for the salary of the Governor and other public officials; [56] a bill erecting new courts of civil and criminal jurisdiction as suggested in his letter; a bill substituting a revenue tax for the 3½% duty on imports and exports; a bill appointing an Island Agent in London; a bill to encourage the immigration of white British and German protestant settlers; a bill prohibiting masters of vessels from taking debtors and their slaves and other property off the Island without permission; a bill regulating the procedure of the registry office; a *habeas corpus* bill; a bill for regulating the treasurer's salary and reorganizing the public treasury; and a bill, in effect, for establishing the Church of England.

*   *   *

Gloster's Bill, the first detailed proposal for the Island's government since the cession, became the immediate focus of bitter controversy. The pro-

53. C.O. 295/8, Reports of Begorrat, Black and Langton, and of John Nihell on the Island's government; enclosed in Hislop : Camden, 9.7.1804.
54. "Sketch of Bill", Article 16.
55. "Sketch of Bill", Article 7.
56. These are at the end of Gloster's letter to Hislop. Gloster's attitude to W.I. Assemblies was partly due to their cavalier treatment of the salaries of public officials. When appointed Chief Justice in Grenada in 1810 he remonstrated against the appointment saying that he did not like to be entirely dependent on a colonial legislature. He heard Grenada was very reluctant to make a permanent grant for the post, and it was "incompatible with the dignity of the situation of His Majesty's representative in the Seat of Justice, to accept it, so shackled". C.O. 295/22, Gloster's memorial, 18.5.1810, enclosed in Hislop : Liverpool, 19.5.1810, No. 18.

tagonists of the Bill were fortunate in that the Secretary of State's acquiescence in its broad principles seemed assured. Ex-Governor Picton, writing from London in August, after the Bill had been despatched from Trinidad but before it had arrived in England, informed Begorrat that several conversations with the Secretary and Under-Secretary of State had been attended with most encouraging results.

"There is no Idea of introducing the System of the Old Colonies", he wrote. "There are insuperable (arguments) against it in the Nature and Composition of (the) Colony, which the most superficial Politician must be sensible of, even on a Cursory Examin(ation). The Plan will be to Vest in the Govr. & Council the Power of making Regulations which on receiving his Majesty's assent will (have) the force of Laws. This is what I recommended in my Report, and what I have reason to think will be ultimately adopted. They will however do nothing until they receive Genl. Hyslop's (sic) Report, which they are in daily expectation of."[57]

Early in September Hislop's despatch containing the new recommendations arrived in England. The Secretary of State made no immediate comment, but Picton whose interest persisted, criticised the proposals on two counts. His first criticism foreshadowed Lord Liverpool's definitive pronouncement on the Island's constitution in 1810.[58] Contrary to what he had previously believed, Picton could now see no possibility of ever introducing the representative system into Trinidad. To the chief clerk at the War Office he expressed the opinion that the present proposal should be regarded not as a temporary expedient but as a final settlement of the question; the arguments that prevailed in favour of a legislative Council now, would be even more appropriate in the future. "If it should be thought imprudent to Establish a free elective Govt. when there were but 7000 free People of Color," he reasoned, "will the danger become less when they exceed 30,000?"[59]

Picton objected, too, to the proposal for the introduction of trial by jury. In his opinion it was not feasible for the same reason that made the Assembly system unworkable. If trial by jury was introduced, one would be faced with the necessary exclusion of the free coloured, thus rendering them at once dissatisfied and dangerous.[60]

Picton's arguments were, according to premises then current, impeccable, but they were off target. The constitutional question in 1804 did not involve a consideration of the role of the free coloured. If the contending parties of white inhabitants were able to agree among themselves, they would have blithely recommended an Assembly and let the free coloureds 'go hang', as indeed they were to do in 1810. Gloster had not considered free coloured

---

57. *B.M. Add. Mss.* 36870, Picton : Begorrat, 16.8.1804.
58. C.O. 296/4, Liverpool : Hislop, 27.11.1810.
59. C.O. 295/10, (Memorandum) Picton : Chapman, 4.9.1804.
60. C.O. 295/10, *Ibid.*

sentiment an important element in Trinidad's dilemma. His arguments against an Assembly were, as we have seen, that the foreign white element was too large; that the majority of British and foreign inhabitants were too crude; and that "democracy" in a conquered West Indian colony in time of war was a luxury that could be ill-afforded.[61] In discussing trial by jury he had mentioned the possibility of coloured participation, but had dismissed it as an aberration not worthy of serious study.[62] As an essay in political engineering the proposed legislative Council must be construed as an attempt at reorganizing the Island's government in order to conciliate the mercantile community, while at the same time consolidating political power in the hands of the planters. It was essentially a concession from a ruling class to a class of would-be usurpers. It remained, however, a proposal for the reform of the structure of government that deliberately avoided the re-distribution of political power.

Criticism centered on the Bill's inability to ensure the recovery of debts by the merchants. A petition from the London merchants in January 1805 remonstrated against the proposal because they feared that, "by the unqualified adoption of the measures now proposed, the *recovery of debts* would *depend upon* such laws as might be enacted by *this council,* composed in a great measure of *the very inhabitants to whom these advances have been made,* and who, your petitioners humbly conceive, ought not at the same time, to be *judges* and *parties".* [63]

In Trinidad, a petition for British laws signed by 236 subscribers of whom 182 were British described the Bill as an evil device fashioned without their consent and calculated to shield "the fraudulent debtor from the just claim of the fair Creditor". It was, too, a blatant attempt at prolonging the existence of the Spanish code, a system so abused and misunderstood in Trinidad that it had, in addition to cramping and stultifying the Island's economy, destroyed "the vestige of faith between man and man". [64]

Indeed, few stones were left unthrown at the proposal. In the passage of arms between the parties the Bill was denounced as an attempt to reincarnate the "hideous ogre" of taxation without representation,[65] and to reimpose the oppressive and tyrannical government that had once flourished under Picton. Sanderson, the most consistent protagonist of the Assembly system, could, despite his bitterness, even see comedy where comedy was not. Claiming that the legislative Council was the invention of one Judge Stokes who had presided in the state of Georgia prior to the American Revolution, he ventured the opinion that, "the greatest advantage that could be derived from a constitution framed according to the principles of Mr. Stokes, would

61. See above pp. 201 - 2.   62. See above p. 203.
63. Sanderson, *An Appeal to the Imperial Parliament* . . . (London, 1812). Quoted, pp. 72-3. Petitioner's emphasis.
64. Petition for British laws from some of the Inhabitants of the Island of Trinidad, enclosed, C.O. 295/11, Hislop : Camden, 5.2.1805.
65. Sanderson, *An Appeal.* . . . , pp. 68-9.

be in banishing from Great Britain all the dissatisfied politicians, to live under such a government in Trinidad; whence they would return, after a few years of purgatory and expiation, perfectly satisfied with what they had formerly complained of; and would declare, that, 'to be free, is to be born and live under the English Constitution'." [66]

Some stones of course were thrown back. Lieutenant Governor Hislop damned the Trinidad petition describing it as unrepresentative of the landed interest, (an interest it did not set out to represent), or of the general wish or sense of the community. It represented, he said, the views of a British clique and a few disreputable foreigners, and could only have been devised to "give . . . Countenance to the extraordinary petition presented some time ago to His Majesty by the London Merchants . . ." [67]

Gloster, savagely attacked, replied with verve and vigour. Joseph Marryat, an eminent London merchant destined in future years to be the leader of the Trinidad lobby in England, intemperately drew attention to himself by forwarding to Hislop a copy of a petition presented in London describing Gloster's Bill as a device "to shelter the embarrassed and unprincipled at the expence of the independent and honorable (sic) part of the community . . ." [68] On him Gloster turned the full force of his venom. He professed considerable pain and astonishment at the precipitation and ignorance evinced by the framers of the petition and enclosed a few clauses of the Bill for their benefit, pointing out that far from wishing to promote fraud the Bill had been designed to facilitate the recovery of debt. Another letter from Marryat said by Gloster to abound in "libellous animadversions" was repelled even more strenuously. Among the allegations was one that Gloster had interpreted the Spanish laws favourably to himself in order to defraud a creditor. This drew a savage riposte and a promise from Gloster, if he should meet in London the man who had inspired the story, one Paull, a Trinidad merchant, to "go to the expense of an Horsewhip and convince him that although slander may be pleasant it is not safe. . ." [69] This extravagance of expression Hislop, in forwarding Gloster's letter to the Under-Secretary, excused by describing Gloster as a man then labouring "under the keenest impression of suffering unmeritted (sic) Calumny, for having punctually discharged his duty". [70]

*   *   *

The debate on Gloster's Bill had till then been dominated by considerations relating to the recovery of debt. Economic conflict was not, how-

66. Sanderson, *Political Account. . .* , pp. 160-161.
67. C.O. 295/11, Hislop : Cooke (Private), 7.2.1805. See note 68.
68. The petition itself has not been seen. It was apparently presented in October, 1804. Marryat's letter, not seen either, was written, according to Gloster on October 4. In his letter Gloster quotes the above, presumably from the petition. C.O. 295/11, Hislop : Cooke (Private), 9.1.1805; enclosing Gloster : Marryat (copy), 3.1.1805.
69. C.O. 295/11, Gloster : Marryat, 16.12.1805; enclosed in Hislop : Cooke, 21.2.1805.
70. C.O. 295/11, Hislop : Cooke, 21.1.1805.

ever, the main issue; the main issue was political domination. Sanderson said as much when he described the Bill as emanating from a group of men who "possessed official power" and was "desirous of keeping it". [71]

The official party in Trinidad had no misgivings about its continuing right to rule; as a landed class it conceived that ruling was not only its right but its duty. Merchants could crash the legislative Council only if, as Gloster said, they first qualified as landed proprietors. Hislop echoed the same sentiment in his strictures on the Trinidad petition of 1805: the petitioners were unrepresentative of the landed interest and should therefore be ignored. Not only did the planter class maintain its right to rule, but looking around, as Gloster did, at its adversaries, it proclaimed that it alone had the ability to rule.

To the extent that the "right to rule" was the real question the official party, overwhelmingly representative of the planter class, could deal with it with more assurance than its opponents could. Convention and interest, in Britain as well as in the West Indies, still favoured the landed class. The planter class in the West Indies was the traditional ruling class; merchants were the interlopers. In the other West Indian islands the antagonism between the groups had been resolved by the development of a community of interest on a wide range of issues, the gradual conversion of the merchant class into a land-holding class, and the equally gradual infiltration of merchants into positions of power. [72] In Trinidad this could not be. The problem demanded an immediate solution. The merchant class was new, homogeneous and bitterly hostile to the planters. By its connection with the British mercantile houses it represented an absentee creditor interest against the interest of resident planters who were, by and large, debtors. Concessions of political privilege to local merchants would avail little as long as the real creditors were abroad; a merchant sitting in the legislative Council was still a merchant who was responsible, in the last analysis, to his European principal. Anyhow, if, as the merchants were saying, the continuation of Spanish law put them, as creditors, at a disadvantage with the planters, their debtors, then the law could be modified. But this was no reason to concede the merchants a prominent role in the Island's government. Indeed, if the recovery of debt was to be facilitated, then the planters in their own defence needed more than before to conserve their political ascendancy.

It was here that the merchants saw their opportunity. They asked the natural question: could a legislature dominated by planter interests be trusted

71. Sanderson, *An Appeal...*, p. 68. Sanderson was of course right. It is clear, for instance, that Gloster's proposal of a privy council of five of the most senior members was intended to reinforce control of the old cadre of administrative officers. It is doubtful that merchants even if they gained access to the legislature, would have been admitted to the privy council. See, Wight, *Op cit.*, p. 38, where the illegal introduction of such a device into Quebec by its first Governor after the Quebec Act of 1774 is discussed. For its introduction Sir Guy Carleton the Governor concerned was reprimanded and the device was abolished.

72. See, Pares, *Merchants and Planters, passim* and especially p. 44, where the point is made that "merchants resident in the islands, as a class, dwindled in importance or disappeared during the eighteenth century".

to pass laws which, by facilitating the recovery of debt, would lead to the probable ruin of many planters? And if such laws were passed, could the courts be expected to enforce them? No matter what new courts were created, as long as the judges remained, as seemed likely, representative of the planting interest, the merchants could expect little justice from them.

By dint of repetition the merchants attracted attention to this aspect of the problem. The argument was a powerful one. A list of mortgages [73] provided by Gloster as an appendix to his Bill showed that Chief Justice Nihell owed £16,663. 19. 4d. sterling to one Lawrence Nihell who may or may not have been a relative; if he was it made little difference, for Nihell's fortune was ruined by 1809. [74] Archibald Gloster owed £3,800 sterling to William Manning one of the London merchants who had petitioned against the legislative Council in 1805. John Nugent, an ex-councillor, owed £6,000 sterling, and, like Nihell, was financially embarrassed in later years. [75] There were two mortgages held against planters for sums of £20,000 and over; several for amounts varying from £10,000 to £20,000, and one for £5,000. Rigby and an associate held a note for 3,280 dollars from a Susannah Phipps. Joseph Marryat held two for a total of about £3,000. But what is really revealing is that almost all the mortgages, totalling more than £ 200,000 sterling, were held by Trinidad or metropolitan British merchant houses. And this list represented only those mortgages contracted between January 1, 1802 and June 15, 1804. Mortgages prior to these, and listed in Spanish, were not provided, not being then ready for despatch to England.

In discussing the political aspect of the controversy the merchants were much less ingenuous. If a legislative Council dominated by planters was rightly regarded as a poor guardian of legitimate mercantile interests, it is difficult to see how an Assembly *per se* could be a better one. It was moreover taking a rather big hammer to crack a rather small nut. The relevant questions are: why did the merchants, knowing the Secretary of State's objections to the grant of an Assembly, not fight for a more adequate representation in the proposed legislative Council? And, what sort of Assembly were they really after?

In answer to the first question it is eminently arguable that the intensity of party spirit ruled out all question of compromise. This is what a discussion of the legislative Council proposal would have amounted to. And it was a *tertium quid* which, if considered by the merchants, was discarded with abhorrence as stripping them of their rights as British citizens and conceding too much to their hated opponents. It would have involved too, in any combination of forces acceptable to the planters, the undoubted continuation of planter predominance. And though a modification of the legislative Council

73. C.O. 295/8, Gloster : Hislop, 4.7.1804; enclosed in Hislop : Camden, 9.7.1804, Appendix No. 3.
74. C.O. 295/21, Nihell : Hislop, 27.5.1809, enclosed in Hislop : Castlereagh, 29.5.1809, No. 60.
75. C.O. 295/17, Nugent : Castlereagh, 31.10.1807.

CHAPTER 7

was probably considered by the British merchants in London, who only protested against "the unqualified adoption of the measures now proposed",[76] it was certainly never considered by the Trinidad merchants.

As for the second question, Sanderson provides the clue as to how, by winning the grant of an Assembly, the Trinidad merchants hoped to alter the basis of political power in their favour. The question was: what sort of Assembly did the merchants want? According to Sanderson, they wanted first of all a Governor drawn from civilian ranks. Like Mrs. Carmichael, they believed army officers to be unsuited for the "deliberative character of a civil governor".[77] Military men in the view of Sanderson, for example, tended to be violent and imprudent, and what was worse could be depended on to form a natural alliance with the class of persons most antagonistic to the Assembly system in Trinidad.[78]

Judges and law officers should as far as possible be excluded from political functions. Judges should have legal training, be permanently appointed and well paid so as to render them independent of local interests. They should travel throughout the Island holding circuit court in the various districts. Commandants of quarters should be replaced by English justices of the peace; thereafter, foreigners should be excluded from the system, not knowing anything about it. The judicial functions of the Council should be abolished and should not be duplicated in any of its successors, whether the upper or the lower house. The Governor should retain his judicial authority, hearing appeals in civil and criminal cases, and as a tribunal of first instance in chancery cases.

Lastly and most importantly, membership of the Assembly should be mainly determined by the candidate's ability to speak and write English, in which language all Assembly business was to be conducted. Sanderson's observation on this score is a masterpiece of disguised menace. Religion should not be a bar to the enjoyment of civil rights, but, "as the great body of the Roman Catholics in Trinidad, consists of persons who do not speak or understand the English language; such as Spanish, French, Italian etc. these may be ineligible to the Assembly on account of their *language,* though not of their *religion*".[79] Language, not religion or nationality, mattered.

At one stroke then, the Governor was to be removed, not being a civilian, and replaced by someone presumably more sympathetic to civilian problems.

76. See p. 206 above.
77. See, Mrs. Carmichael, *Domestic Manners and Social Condition of the. . . Population of The West Indies,* (London, 1834). Second edition. Two volumes. Vol. II, pp. 54-5.
78. Sanderson, *Political Account. . . ,* p. 173. His recommendations relative to an Assembly are on pp. 197-203. These proposals were presented as a series of recommendations for the improvement of the system throughout the West Indies. Trinidad could thus become the proving ground for some of the improvements which Sanderson suggested. What began as a general critique of the West Indian system soon turned to a specific examination of Trinidad's position. His recommendations re judges and commandants of quarters were specifically intended for Trinidad.
79. *Political Account. . . ,* pp. 168-9.

All the existing judges were to be dismissed not having had legal training. Rural administration and the administration of justice in petty suits were to be placed in the hands of English justices of the peace, thus getting rid of a foreign-dominated cadre of administrators. The political functions of judges, and of legal officials like the Attorney and Solicitor General, were to be extinguished. And having thus emasculated the anti-British party, the issue was to be decided on the ability of assembly-men to speak and write the English language. The relevant factor would then not be the relative proportion of whites who supported or opposed the Assembly system, but the proportion of *British* whites who did. In such a contest every advantage of numbers and influence was on the side of the merchants.

*   *   *

The debate on Gloster's Bill achieved two positive results, both pertaining to the Council. For the first time the Council had committed itself to a policy of constitutional change. It was true that, as Gloster said, the proposal for a legislative Council was the Lieutenant Governor's personal policy, not the decision of the Council.[80] In a formal sense this was indeed so. The Council as a body had not been consulted; but the majority of its members had been. Nihell, Black and Begorrat, and Langton, a councillor under Picton, had between them produced two papers on the Island's courts, institutions, and general administration under Spanish law.[81] Gloster, as we have seen, was the architect of the Bill. And though the Chief Justice, like the *alcaldes,* did not favour the introduction of the English criminal law, there was general agreement on the wider principles of the Bill. Rigby, Rutherford and Smith do not seem to have been consulted. If they were, it is probable that Rigby alone disagreed with the proposal, since he signed the petition in 1805 repudiating the Bill.[82] On the whole, however, there can be little doubt that the Council, or the majority of it, favoured the establishment of a legislative Council.

The second result was that the Council became from henceforth the public and recognized spearhead of the attack on the British party. Henceforth, the Council was committed to the support of a policy in opposition to the wishes of the majority of British settlers. In recommending the Gloster proposals the government of the Island, comprising Governor and Council, abandoned its uncomfortable role as arbiter between the factions. It was, for all to see, itself an integral part of one of the factions.

A definite pronouncement on the Island's constitution by the Secretary of State was the one expected result that did not ensue. In July 1805, Pitt's cabinet was reshuffled, and Earl Camden was succeeded by Viscount Castlereagh as Secretary of State for War and the Colonies. The departure of

80. C.O. 295/11, Gloster : Marryat, 3.1.1804; enclosed in Hislop : Cooke, 9.1.1805.
81. C.O. 295/8, Reports of Begorrat, Black and Langton, and of John Nihell on the Island's government; enclosed in Hislop : Camden, 9.7.1804.
82. See Petition enclosed in C.O. 295/11, Hislop : Camden, 5.2.1805.

211

CHAPTER 7

Camden and the arrival of Castlereagh led to the postponement of any decision relating to the Trinidad constitution. Indeed the coming and going of various Secretaries and Under-Secretaries of State is one of the factors that helps to explain the British government's indecision on the constitutional question prior to 1810. And in the absence of a decision, the Trinidad Council not only reigned but ruled.

As a consequence affairs in Trinidad got very much worse before beginning to get better. The years 1805-1809 were one long period of savage in-fighting between the factions in which the British party was severely worsted. This period saw the Council at the zenith of its power; it was never so powerful again, and was indeed to be firmly suppressed under Governor Woodford. Lieutenant Governor Hislop, elevated to the governorship partly by the exertions of the Council,[83] repaid its members by an even closer identification with them. In this his recruitment to the planter class as a proprietor in his own right undoubtedly played some part, as James Stephen was to point out in 1810.[84] Of some importance, however, was the fact that in the struggle with the British party he became more and more prone to acts of unmitigated high-handedness, thereby increasing his dependence on the Council whose connivance, and the doubtful warrant of Spanish law, were often presented in vindication of his actions.

With the active collusion of the Governor, the Council acquired and exerted all the influence and command of the representative Assemblies in the old British Islands, more so indeed since in Trinidad there was none of that fretful dissension between Governor and Council that often marked the proceedings of the Assemblies in the other islands. A network of committees run by eager councillors transacted the Council's business. There were at various times committees for examining the public accounts, for handling its correspondence, for considering petitions to the Governor, and for implementing the numerous *ad hoc* regulations made for the Island's management.[85] By performing such tasks councillors acquired stature and import-

83. Hislop was appointed Governor in July 1806. See C.O. 295/14, Windham : Hislop, (draft), 3.7.1806. More than a year earlier the Council had petitioned that he be given the rank of Governor. See, C.O. 295/13, Baillie : Marryat : Camden, 20.3.1805, enclosing the petition. The definitive reason for his elevation was, however, the Secretary of State's decision to revoke Fullarton's commission. (See, C.O. 296/4, Windham : Fullarton, 17.2.1806.) Till then the Commission of 1803 was held to have been suspended, and Hislop was regarded as acting head of the Island's administration.

84. It was Stephen's opinion that a Governor, by becoming a planter or by otherwise becoming involved in the "peculiar private interests" of a slave colony ran the risk of acquiring prejudices which thoroughly unsuited him for the post of Governor. For this reason he recommended that Governors and other high colonial officials like the Chief Justice should be barred from becoming planters. And for this reason too, he recommended Hislop's recall. C.O. 295/25, Stephen : Liverpool (Private) 1.9.1810.

85. The minutes of Council are strewn with examples of the working of such committees. The personnel of the committees kept changing but certain committees seem to have had an almost continuous existence. Such a one was the Committee of Public Accounts which in 1805 consisted of Messrs. Rigby and Gloster. While Gloster was in England from late 1805 till the middle of 1807 as Island Agent a Committee of Correspondence, consisting of Begorrat and James Piggott, the Solicitor General, was appointed to correspond with him on the Island's affairs, Cf. C.O. 295/15, Gloster : Shee, 23.4.1806, enclosure, Begorrat & Piggott : Gloster, 1.2.1806. C.O. 298/2, Minute of Council, 2.2.1805 contains an example of the Committee for the consideration of Petitions at work.

ance, became addicted to the exercise of power, and were less willing to suffer in silence the barbs of their attackers.

Not only did the Council dominate the Island's political life, it dominated its judicial processes too. With the Governor the Council functioned as an appellate court [86] and as a superior tribunal of first instance for the examination of persons accused of insurrection, rioting and subversion. [87] The Governor himself possessed a little used right of hearing cases as a court of first instance, and with his *Asesor* constituted the Court of Intendant for the trial of cases involving the rights of the Crown. [88] Then there was John Nihell, the Chief Justice, whose powers had been greatly enhanced by a proclamation of 1806. [89] By this proclamation the authority of the *alcaldes* over criminal cases was abolished. Nihell became the sole judge for criminal cases, and in civil cases any matter of long standing or of dispute in the *alcades* courts could be transferred to the Chief Justice by petition to the Governor, Spanish law notwithstanding. From Nihell appeals were allowable only to the Council, with whom the Governor now shared his right to hear appeals, and thence to the King-in-Council. In 1807, on the death of James Piggott, Solicitor General and councillor since November 14, 1805 and judge of the vice-admiralty court, Nihell added the judgeship of that court to his other appointments. [90] There was also the Attorney General who, though not trained in Spanish law, and despite the existence of an official *Asesor,* was, at this time, *de facto,* the *Asesor* to the Governor. [91] And various members, as *alcaldes* or *alcaldes de barrios* or as commandants of quarters, performed functions directly relating to, or impinging upon, the administration of justice. [92]

This concentration of administrative and judicial powers in the same hands would have tried the wisdom and restraint of a Solomon. In the

86. See for example, C.O. 298/3, Minutes of Council, 9.3.1808 and 23.3.1808. Also, C.O. 295/14, Hislop : Windham, 1.4.1806.

87. Such an occasion was the Council's trial of the slaves suspected of attempted insurrection in 1805. Hislop described the Council as a Superior Tribunal "before which Crimes of this description are alone Cognizable and in which only the power is Vested to proceed summarily by dispensing with the forms of law used in Common Cases". The Council's powers derived from association with the Governor who possessed the authority to try such cases. Spanish law had of course made no provision for the Council's judicial authority. C.O. 295/11, Hislop : Castlereagh, 19.12.1805. See also, Fraser, *History of Trinidad,* Vol. I, pp. 268-72.

88. Charles Reis, *A History of the Constitution of Trinidad,* (Trinidad, 1929), Two volumes, Vol. I, p. 154. Also, *Parliamentary Papers,* House of Commons, 1826-27, (551) XXIII, p. 7.

89. C.O. 295/14, Hislop : Windham, 6.5.1806, No. 26.

90. C.O. 295/16, Hislop : Windham, 7.2.1807, No. 37.

91. A Spaniard Don Gaspar de la Guardia was at this time the *Asesor,* but it is clear that he had nothing like the influence the Spanish law intended the *Asesor* to have. Gloster, who was much closer to the Governor and on whose advice the Governor most often relied, has much stronger claims to be regarded as the *Asesor,* in fact if not in name.

92. John Smith was an *alcalde de barrio* in 1803. Black was *alcalde* of the first election in 1804. John Smith, Archibald Gloster, and John Gloster who succeeded to the deputy-clerkship of the Council in November 1806, were all commandants of quarters in 1807. In addition some of them held commissions in the militia. In 1808 Archibald Gloster was a colonel of militia in addition to being aide-de-camp to the Governor. And his brother who was later to become deputy registrar to the court when George Smith was appointed Chief Judge, was a lieutenant colonel in the militia in 1805.

hands of an oligarchy closely knit by ties of interest and sentiment, and involved in a bitter struggle with an uncompromising and defiant foe, it became a frequently used weapon of factional assault.

The case of George Dickson, senior partner of a local firm of merchants, George and William Dickson, is an apt illustration of this point. In the early months of 1805, the arrival of a French fleet in the West Indies gave rise to persistent rumours of the threatened invasion of the Island.[93] The invasion never materialised, but two prolonged periods of martial law and the maintenance of a state of preparedness throughout the Island resulted in an enormous public expenditure.[94] Among the bills presented for settlement at the end of the crisis, and passed on for scrutiny to the Committee for Public Accounts, was one from the Dickson firm for a sum of £4,001. 1. 7d. currency. After a preliminary examination the Committee advised that payment should be withheld.[95] And a further examination revealed that some of the supplies for which payment was claimed had not only never been supplied but had not yet arrived in the Island.

Dickson, commissary general in the militia, was first courtmartialled, found guilty on two of the four charges of fraud alleged against him, dismissed from his post and reduced to the ranks.[96] Then the Council, although Dickson had not been paid a cent in respect of the bill he had presented, arraigned him before the *alcaldes* for the recovery of civil damages;[97] later the sentence was to be reviewed by the Council itself acting in the character of a court of appeal.[98] Dickson protested against these proceedings, called attention to the fact that the Governor himself had given evidence against him at the court martial,[99] and pointed out that he was being tried at every stage by his own accusers. Less wisely, he asserted his rights as an Englishman to be tried by English instead of Spanish law, and begged leave to proceed to England for that purpose.[100] In this his merchant colleagues supported him, pointing to his plight as dramatizing the need for the immediate grant of British laws.[101]

With these sallies by the British party the affair was held by the Governor and Council to have passed on to forbidden ground. Dickson's protest that he could not properly be tried by Spanish law, nor for that matter be

---

93. C.O. 295/11, Hislop : Camden, 22.3.1805; 31.3.1805; 3.4.1805; 5.4.1805; 23.5.1805; 24.6.1805.
94. Martial law was declared for the following periods: February 25, 1805 - April 10, and May 19 - July 16. Total expenditure amounted to £12,997. 4. 8d. sterling. See, C.O. 295/11, Hislop : Camden, 26.4.1805 and 23.5.1805.
95. Hislop : Camden, 18.5.1805, and enclosed in Minute of Council, 15.5.1805.
96. C.O. 295/11, Hislop : Camden, 21.7.1805. The proceedings of the court martial are fully reported in C.O. 295/12.
97. C.O. 295/11, Hislop : Castlereagh, 8.9.1805.
98. C.O. 295/14, Hislop : Windham, 1.4.1806.
99. C.O. 295/13, Dickson : Camden, 17.8.1805.
100. C.O. 295/11, Hislop : Castlereagh, 28.9.1805, No. 6, enclosing a detailed statement from George Dickson protesting the proceedings against him on nine points of which this was one.
101. C.O. 295/11, Hislop : Castlereagh, 28.9.1805, No. 5.

adequately represented by a Spanish lawyer since there was none, was deemed to be seditious. [102]   He was imprisoned and condemned to pay a fine amounting to three times the sum he would have acquired by his attempted fraud. [103] A letter written on his behalf by his friends to the Commercial Committee, a merchant's organization, was the pretext for the intimidation of all those who had signed it by examination before the Council. [104]   Charles Augustus Hayes, the lawyer who had written it, was banished. [105]   His real crime seems to have been, however, that he had been prosecution lawyer for the collection of evidence against Picton when the mandamus had been sent out in 1804. He was also a staunch proponent of British laws.

Fortunately for Dickson, just as the government was preparing to divest him of his property, he made his escape to New York and thence to London. There, while Hislop protested in vain that "so audacious a Violator of the Laws" should appear at large "in the metropolis of the Empire", [106] Dickson enlisted the aid of an influential merchant to his cause. [107] Hislop's request for his extradition to the Island was found to be unwarranted by the British law officers. [108]   And Dickson had the extreme satisfaction of being able to inform Hislop, in a letter of malicious sarcasm, that his conviction had been reversed on appeal to the Privy Council: an act of justice for which he warmly thanked the Governor, since "the foundation . . . was laid by your Excellency without whose aid my case could never have found its way to the Privy Council. . ." [109]   The affair ended with the payment to Dickson of damages and costs totalling £1604. 4. 8d. sterling. [110]

Not content with having thus ignominiously wrecked themselves on Scylla the Governor and Council contrived to come to grief on Charybdis too. In 1806, the East Indiaman *Fortitude,* in fulfilment of Lord Hobart's plan for the introduction of Chinese settlers and the diversification of the Island's trade and production, arrived in Trinidad with 192 Chinese settlers and a cargo of East Indian goods some of which was intended for re-export. [111] The Chinese immigrants were welcomed with open arms but, unfortunately, the ship and cargo were seized by Lieutenant Briarly in command of the Royal Navy brig stationed at Trinidad, for contravention of the navigation laws prohibiting direct trading between the colonies. [112]

102. C.O. 295/11. Hislop : Castlereagh, 8.9.1805.
103. C.O. 295/14, Hislop : Cooke (Private), 20.2.1806.
104. C.O. 295/12, enclosures of Hislop : Castlereagh, 28.9.1805, No. 5.   The despatch itself is in. C.O. 295/11.
105. C.O. 295/12, *Ibid.* Minutes of Council of 24th, 28th September, 1805. Also, C.O. 295/17, Hayes : Cooke, 23.12.1807.
106. C.O. 295/16, Hislop : Castlereagh, 24.6.1807. Also C.O. 295/16, Hislop : Cooke (Private), 23.6.1807.
107. Charles Bartrum of London. See, C.O. 295/14, Windham : Hislop, 5.6.1806. C.O. 298/2, Council meeting of 23.7.1806.   C.O. 295/15, Fawkener : Shee, 2.12.1806.   A memorial from Bartrum on Dickson's behalf is in C.O. 295/15, dated 9.5.1806.
108. C.O. 295/17, Fawkener : Cooke, 13.10.1807, and enclosures.
109. C.O. 295/20, B. Ward : Cooke, 21.8.1808; enclosure, Dickson : Hislop, 6.4.1808.
110. C.O. 295/21, Hislop : Castlereagh, 14.9.1809.
111. C.O. 295/14, Hislop : Camden, 26.10.1806, No. 44.
112. C.O. 295/14, *Ibid.*

The story of the *Fortitude* interesting as it is need not detain us here. Suffice it to say that it was a good and proper seizure. [113] Almost at the same time that the seizure was being made in Trinidad, the Board of Trade was writing to the Secretary of State for the Colonies warning him of the possibility that the ship, though sailing under official instructions might be seized. [114] And suffice it, too, to say that Briarly, whose motives were admittedly not of the purest, earned the undying hatred of the Governor and the Council for this direct challenge to their authority in a sphere where they were forced to tread carefully. [115]

For Governor and Council the opportunity for revenge soon came. In August 1807 when the American ship *Addams* arrived at Trinidad with a cargo of lumber, foodstuffs and tobacco, trading between America and the West Indies lay under one of those periodic restrictions which Britain, partly out of pique with the former colonies and partly in an attempt to stimulate the trade of British North America, imposed from time to time in defiance of all commercial logic. [116] Stringent conditions regulated the import and export of goods in foreign ships, and were to be relaxed only for specified periods of six months at times of crisis, and then only for the importation of foodstuffs and lumber, and the exportation of rum and molasses. [117] Tobacco would, on the most careful examination, not seem to belong to any of these categories. Yet the Council, petitioned by the consignees of twenty-five hogsheads of tobacco, decided otherwise. And the Governor allowed the importation on the very implausible ground that the long dry season had led to a scarcity of provisions for the slave population and thus made the importation of tobacco necessary for their support. [118]

Briarly, a most interested spectator of these deliberations, was not impressed, and when the *Addams* began to discharge the tobacco both ship and tobacco were seized. [119] On this occasion Briarly discovered that there was no disposition among Trinidad's officials to permit his seizure. The collector of Customs into whose keeping the ship was supposed to be entrusted refused to take charge of it, regarding the seizure as illegal. [120] The Attorney General for the same reason refused to initiate legal proceedings. [121] And

---

113. James Piggott, Judge of the Vice Admiralty, declared in his judgment of December 10, 1806. C.O. 295/17, McQueen : Windham, 2.1.1807, enclosure.
114. C.O. 295/15, Fawkener : Shee, 17th, 24th November, 1806.
115. Hislop's inaction over the *Fortitude's* seizure was partly explained by the fact that he had not received his commission as Vice Admiral and was unsure of his authority. He wrote for this commission in the new year. (C.O. 295/16, Hislop : Windham, 7.2.1807, No. 37.) But he does not seem to have had it when the *Addams* was seized.
116. For the attempts of British North American trading interests to obtain more of the colonial trade for themselves see: G.S. Graham, *Sea Power and British North America 1783-1820: A Study in British Colonial Policy*, (Harvard, 1941), Chapter XI. For details of the Addams' cargo, see C.O. 300/16, Returns of Shipping Inwards, July 6 to October 6, 1807.
117. Ragatz, *op. cit.*, pp. 298 ff. Also, C.O. 324/103, Circulars of September 21, October 3, 1806.
118. C.O. 295/16, Hislop : Castlereagh, 15.8.1807, No. 13.
119. C.O. 295/16, *Ibid.*
120. C.O. 298/3, Minutes of Council, 7.8. 1807 and 8.8. 1807.
121. C.O. 298/3, Minutes of Council, 7.8. 1807, and 10th and 12th August, 1807.

Hislop whose mortification at the seizure of the *Fortitude* still rankled (though not enough to prevent him from later claiming his share of the prize money) [122] summoned Briarly to appear before the Council. When Briarly finally made an appearance he found himself very much the accused. He was made to endure a long interrogation by Governor and Council at the end of which he was found guilty of defiance of the government, contumacious conduct and insubordination, and jailed for a month. [123]

Questions of law concern us here only as far as they help to sustain the presumption of good or bad faith on the part of the main participants. It was by no means clear that Briarly had acted improperly or rashly, though Nihell chose to believe so. For when, on his release from prison, Briarly brought an action in the vice-admiralty court, Nihell found for the defendants, abused George Knox, Briarly's lawyer, and commended Gloster highly for his handling of the case. [124] His judgement was based on the proposition that the Governor had the right to permit the importation of tobacco as "an essential article of life . . . contributory in the highest degree to the health of the unfortunate white and coloured settlers, and particularly so to the slaves. . ." [125]

James Stephen, humanitarian and staunch supporter of the Orders-in-Council regulating the trade with the neutrals, declared the seizure to be "illiberal" and "disreputable", though he confessed that he could find no legal principle on which the acquittal of the American captain could be supported. A colonial Governor, he argued, could not permit importations contrary to the Acts of Parliament except on the conditions specially enunciated in those Acts; and it was difficult to see how tobacco could fairly be described as a provision - a presumption indeed so ridiculous, he said, "as hardly to bear serious discussion". Yet he thought it unconscionable that a foreigner should be deprived of his vessel and part of its cargo after importation had been allowed by the Governor and port authorities. He therefore agreed with the acquittal. [126]

This was, though, essentially a compassionate opinion, possibly the only one uttered by Stephen that ever found favour with Trinidad's officialdom. It was not, however, the view of the High Court to Admiralty which reversed Nihell's judgement, on Briarly's appeal, [127] on the ground that no case had been or presumably could be made for the necessity of the importation. [128] The propriety of the importation was, if not wholly questionable, sufficiently

---

122. C.O. 295/16, Hislop : Castlereagh, 11.7.1807. C.O. 295/19, Hislop : Cooke, (Private letters), 5th, 7th July 1808.
123. C.O. 298/3, Minute of Council, 19.8.1807.
124. C.O. 295/19, Hislop : Castlereagh, 26.7.1808; Nihell's judgment, dated 5.7.1808 enclosed.
125. C.O. 295/19, *Ibid.*
126. C.O. 295/21, Hislop : Castlereagh, 28.3.1809; Stephen's opinion of 18.1.1809 enclosed.
127. C.O. 295/22, Bishop : Cooke, 24.4.1809.
128. C.O. 295/27, Charles Robinson : Liverpool, 14.8.1811. On the contrary the judge had found abundant evidence that the transaction had "the complexion of artifice, and fraudulent Evasion of the known regulations of the Law".

doubtful to make Briarly's imprisonment before the matter had even been referred to the vice-admiralty court a most extraordinary proceeding. What had followed was equally so. At the trial Gloster had defended the American Skipper, Tubbs, free of costs, [129] a manifestation of justice at its highest if one could be convinced that justice was the aim of the Governor and Council; and later, the Council had guaranteed Tubbs' bond in case the appeal should go against him. [130]

In preparing to meet the appeal the execration of Briarly's character was unhesitatingly resorted to by the Governor. Hislop represented him as an unprincipled adventurer whose sole interest was the prize money derived from his seizures. A series of damaging innuendoes assaulted his character, his manner of living and his financial integrity. He was a squanderer who, coming penniless to the Island in 1804, was now a substantial proprietor; a paradox that was easily resolved by attributing to him a variety of fraudulent and unscrupulous enterprises that had succeeded "in a particular degree" in attracting the attention of the Navy Board, [131] and had in addition led to his being "detained for debt" by the Governor. [132] In addition the Secretary of State was urged to exert all his influence to ensure that Briarly's appeal should fail. And a letter written by Hislop to the Island Agent in London suggested strongly that an attempt should be made through Sir William Grant, Master of the Rolls, whose brother Charles Grant, collector of Customs at Trinidad, was then in London, to procure a judgment favourable to the Trinidad government. [133]

These were by no means the only occasions on which Governor and Council acted against the spirit of common justice. Usually they quoted Spanish laws and precedents in support of acts which on any reckoning reeked of prejudice and ill intent. So they did in Dickson's case. [134] Briarly's case is important because Spanish law did not cloud the issue. Legal or illegal importation was decided solely with reference to the navigation acts, the propositions of which Governor, Council and law officers knew well. It is not at all surprising, therefore, that Sir Alexander Cochrane, on the occasion of the seizure of the navy transport *Resource* in obvious reprisal for Briarly's two seizures, was moved to describe Trinidad as a colony in which "there is

129. C.O. 298/3, Minute of Council, 12.8.1807.
130. C.O. 295/27, Hislop : Lt. Col. Bunbury, 22.10.1811. C.O. 295/27, Harrison : Peel, 30.9.1811. An amusing note is provided by Hislop's insistence that "Any informalities or deviations from the letter or spirit of the Law, are alone to be Ascribed to the Opinion which that Officer (Gloster) express'd at the time of the transaction and which had its influence on the Minds of the Members of the Council in advising me to permit the importation with reference to the Collector of the Customs". C.O. 295/27, Hislop : Bunbury, 31.10.1811.
131. C.O. 295/19, Hislop : Castlereagh, 1.8.1808, No. 39.
132. C.O. 295/17, Hislop : Cooke (Private), 14.7.1808.
133. C.O. 295/22, Maling : Cooke, 25.4.1809; enclosing Hislop : Mailing, 23.2.1809.
134. C.O. 295/19, Hislop : Castlereagh, 8.10.1808, No. 44. C.O. 298/3, Minutes of Council 27.7.1808. The Council held that the success of Dickson's appeal was due to the Privy Council's misconception of Spanish law.

neither Law, nor persons capable of administering the Laws, if they had them . . . The Judge (is) a man who knows nothing of the Law - before whom it is reported Mr. Gloster pleads, and afterwards assists in passing the Sentences" [135]

A few public officers found the strain of continued prostration before Governor and Council too demanding. James Piggott, appointed Solicitor General in October 1804, and brother of Sir Arthur Piggott, Attorney General in the "Ministry of All the Talents", was perhaps one of these. His judgment against the *Fortitude,* ("There is no suspension of the Law, and by the law I am bound."), [136] reads like a defiance of local officialdom. His death in 1807 saved him further embarrassment.

George Knox was another. He had been recruited as King's Counsel during the absence of Gloster and Piggott from the Island. [137] Knox was no rebel. His father who had been the Island's first Agent urged his confirmation in the post, describing him as one whose chief wish was "to avoid being employed on the democratic side". [138] But barely six months after Hislop had announced Knox's temporary appointment, he was announcing his dismissal, just when Piggott's death had made his permanent appointment possible. The reason, Hislop insinuated, was wholly political: Knox had seen fit "in the most unequivocal terms to avow himself my *political* Enemy, at the same time adopting a line of Conduct establishing the Sincerity of his professions . . ." [139] He might have said that the breach had also been caused by Knox's disagreement with the attitude he, Hislop, had taken to Briarly's seizure of the *Fortitude.* Knox was to urge his point with greater vehemence when he represented Briarly in the *Addams* case.

William Holmes, captain in the third West Indian regiment and deputy clerk of the Council from August 1804, was to cause Hislop not a little worry in future years. Holmes, who was on leave from the army and was due to return to active service anyhow, was haughtily dismissed by Hislop "for having attempted to refute the solemn assertions of the Senior Member of this Board, and Chief Judge of the Island, respecting a Conversation which he Capn. Holmes, particularly addressed to him in this very Council Chamber . . ." [140] Holmes left the Island and returned not to the army but to England, where his talents seemed to have been so appreciated that he became a member of Parliament and highly skilled Tory whip. His name became a byword

135. C.O. 295/22, Commissioners for conducting His Majesty's Transport Service : Castlereagh, 1.6.1809, enclosing Cochrane : Commissioners, 12.4.1809.

136. C.O. 295/17, enclosed in MacQueen : Windham. 2.1.1807.

137. C.O. 295/14, Hislop : Windham, 29.9.1806.

138. C.O. 295/15, William Knox : (Shee?), 19.4.1806.
139. C.O. 295/16, Hislop : Windham, 7.2.1807, No. 37.
140. C.O. 298/2, Minute of Council, 26.11.1806.

for dexterity in party management and skill in dispensing patronage; and for Hislop a cause of unremitting trepidation. [141] It took Hislop several years to realise that, absorbed as he was in his work, Holmes had no time for seeking vengeance on a petty-minded Governor of a small island possession.

*   *   *

Throughout the years 1805 to 1808 the constitutional question imparted purpose and volition to men and affairs in Trinidad. And yet in one sense these were the lost years in the struggle for constitutional change. The continued exertions of the two parties evoked nothing but a wooden silence on the part of the imperial government; and when finally this silence was broken it was to the discomfiture of both. It was not that unpleasant or unacceptable decisions were taken; ministers, preoccupied with Napoleon's rapidly extending imperium in Europe, for a long time took no decision at all. Ministers followed each other in and out of office with the same conspiratorial silence on the Island's constitutional affairs. Between 1805 and 1808 three different ministries followed each other in and out of office, and there were four successive changes in the office of Secretary of State for War and the Colonies. Lack of continuity meant lack of decision, and it was no chance that the deadlock was finally resolved by Viscount Castlereagh, Secretary of State from 1805 to 1806 and again from March 1807 to October 1809. The solution was not Castlereagh's; it was rather the work of George Smith, soon to be appointed to high office in Trinidad. [142] But only a minister long familiar with the Island's problems could have spared the time to impose a solution, whether his own or not.

In the face of such discouragement the tenacity of the parties, and not least of the Governor and Council, excites the imagination. Saddled with the burdens of government, the Governor and Council were embarrassed by the continuing indecision, though not always as acutely as they pretended. The arguments advanced by the Trinidad government in support of the immediate grant of the legislative Council were often, to put it at its most charitable, extremely dubious. Gloster, dispatched to London towards the end of 1805 as Island Agent extraordinary, [143] displayed an amazing virtuosity in marshalling such arguments. During his eighteen months' sojourn in the metropolis he submitted several letters and memoranda to the Secretary of State and the Treasury on the constitutional problem. No opportunity was lost to urge again and again the absolute necessity of granting a legislative Council with all possible speed. Of all his correspondence only his observations to the

141. Cf. C.O. 295/19, Hislop : Cooke (Private), 5.7.1808. C.O. 295/19, same to same (Private), 13.10. 1808. A little denigration was also tried, as in the case of Briarly. Cf. C.O. 295/19, Hislop : Maling, 31.7.1808; and enclosure. This time however it drew a sharp rebuke from Castlereagh, Secretary of State. Cf. C.O. 295/21, Hislop : Cooke (Private), 23.10.1809.
142. See below, pp. 228 ff.
143. C.O. 295/11, Hislop : Castlereagh, 8.9.1805 and enclosures.

Secretary of State in December 1805, which was a restatement of his earlier views submitted to Hislop in 1804, stand up to serious scrutiny.

His memorandum of March 5, 1806 is an outstanding illustration of the pitfalls of uncontrolled enthusiasm. [144] Referring to the slave "insurrection" of December 1805 which had occurred since his departure from the Island, he ascribed "the origin and progress of this intended insurrection to the example of insubordination and opposition to his Majesty's government there manifested and avowed by a set of men of a *white* complexion, who have been employing every means in their power to enfeeble and render nugatory the constituent authorities in existence, and preaching a doctrine that Spanish Law did not exist, which is, in fact, to hold out, that all Civil government in Trinidad was paralyzed, and no restraint could be laid, *by Law,* upon the most insolent and boundless pretensions of the most unruly classes of that Society". The blacks, he said, were only completing what their "patrons in Iniquity" had begun.

Seizing on a more familiar and not quite as implausible argument, he said that the verdict of guilt on ex-Governor Picton, which had just then been handed down, had destroyed the basis of law and social order in the Island. Referring to Louisa Calderon he lamented the fact that, "A person of *colour* of the vilest character, aided by persons as *vile"* had called to account "his Majesty's representative for infliction. . . of punishment according to the Spanish Law". Trinidad was now a "British Colony where British Laws dont extend, and where crimes of all descriptions may be committed without tryal (sic), and consequently without punishment". [145] Only the swift grant of a proper constitution to this "extensive and most interesting colony" could stem the advance of such decay.

On March 23, he returned to the attack, forwarding a letter from Trinidad telling of the worsening financial situation, which, he said, suggested that the most interesting question of the Island's constitutional future must be quickly answered. [146] A few days previously he had argued that the decision to exclude Trinidad because of its form of government from the operation of the bounty system relative to the importation of salted fish was most unjust. [147] If Trinidad had been granted a legislative Council, it would have been able to pledge itself to repay the bounties advanced by the

---

144. C.O. 295/15, Memorandum, apparently to the Secretary of State, dated 5.3.1806.

145. This argument was intended to serve another purpose apart from that indicated above. Gloster's mission to England was closely connected with Picton's trial. He gave evidence for Picton *(State Trials,* XXX, p. 509 ff.) as did John Nugent (p. 506 ff) and played an active part in getting Lynch to come to England to help Draper in his defence of the libel alleged against him by Sullivan. His efforts for Picton were complemented by those of the Council in Trinidad. Immediately the verdict was known the Council met to collect evidence to refute the assumption that Spanish law did not permit torture as had been successfully argued by the prosecution at Picton's first trial. Cf. *State Trials,* XXX, pp. 568 ff; and C.O. 298/2, Minutes of Council, 1st, 2nd, and 3rd May 1806.

146. C.O. 295/15, Gloster : Shee, 23.4.1806, enclosing Begorrat and Piggott : Gloster, 1.2.1806.

147. C.O. 295/15, Fawkener : Shee, 7.4.1806, enclosing, Gloster : Auckland, 7.4.1806. Also, C.O.

CHAPTER 7

imperial government and raise the sum by taxation. The fault was not Trinidad's, he said, but the British government's. In the Treasury at least this note struck an answering chord: George Harrison, Under-Secretary of the Treasury, wrote to the Secretary of State suggesting that the constitutional question in Trinidad be settled as soon as possible. [148]

Throughout these years the most telling argument for the swift settlement of the Island's constitutional affairs centered on the government's inability to raise revenue by taxation. Revenues were completely dependent on the 3½% duty. In Picton's day as we have seen, this duty yielded sufficient revenue to meet all the normal expenses of government and yet leave a healthy balance in the colonial chest. The coming of the Commission had put an end to this. Enormous expenditure on the various projects of the Commission, and especially on the surveyor general's department, had left a legacy of great and increasing debt. Not only was the Island bankrupt, but the several charges upon its revenue ensured that it would stay bankrupt if they were all admitted.

From year to year the financial problem got steadily worse. In 1804, the Council moved a series of resolutions praying the imperial government to absolve the Island from the responsibility of meeting the charges arising out of the Commission's activities; these were in excess of the Island's yearly income and, if paid, would leave nothing with which to meet normal administrative expenditure. In particular it wished to be freed from the burden of continuing payments to the commissioners and the officers appointed to serve with the Commission. [149]

In 1805, the French scare and the burden of debt which resulted underlined the Island's insolvency. The militia, permanently on duty throughout the crisis, received not " a farthing of pay or recompense of any Kind." [150] In July a committee of the whole Council recommended that several public buildings should be sold in view of the depleted state of the finances. A suggestion by the Governor that the government slaves should be sold was not however approved by the Council; they were in fact to be increased. [151]

295/16, Hislop : Castlereagh, 7.9.1807.
148. C.O. 295/15, George Harrison : Shee, 30.5.1806.
149. C.O. 295/9, Hislop : Camden, 25.12.1804, enclosures, Minutes of Council, 8th and 12th December. The yearly income was estimated at £12,000 sterling. The salaries of the Commissioners, the surveyor and his assistants equalled £12,000. 5s. sterling. The Council was not absolutely correct in its estimate. Both Picton and Hood had resigned and were no longer charges on the Island's revenues. Salaries to the Commissioners meant in fact, salary to Fullarton alone, since as he said (C.O. 295/10, Fullarton : Camden, 10.7.1804) he was the only person in whom the Commission could then be conceived to exist. Subsequently, when Fullarton's claims for continued payment of salary were admitted, Picton (C.O. 295/13, Sturges Bourne : Cooke, 21.5.1805 and enclosure) and Hood (C.O. 295/17, Mary Hood : Windham, 6.1.1807) then also claimed the right to be paid. The salaries to the subordinate officers of the Commission some of whom had accompanied Fullarton to England were still a charge against the Island. Those in England were paid by the Treasury after much haggling on the understanding that the Island should ultimately re-imburse that department. Cf. C.O. 295/13, Fullarton : Castlereagh, 24.8.1805; C.O. 295/17, Harrison : Cooke, 4.5.1807; and Treasury auditors report on the Commission expenses in C.O. 295/15.
150. C.O. 295/14, Hislop :Castlereagh, 8.1.1806, No. 15.
151. C.O. 298/2, Minutes of Council, 25.7.1805.

The Island began to lean heavily on the British Treasury and continued to do so. [152] Even this had its drawbacks. Imperial responsibility for local expenditure could never be assumed, and imperial money was never paid without stern warnings and long delays. The general feeling of crisis was exacerbated by rumours then current, allegedly originating in Barbados, that bills drawn on the Treasury by the Trinidad government would not be met. As a result there was a depression of confidence and trade in the Island. Loans became more difficult to obtain, and the rate of exchange increased. Whereas a bill of exchange for £100 sterling fetched credit worth £195 currency in Barbados, the corresponding figure in Trinidad was only £185. [153] Indeed, it was this developing financial crisis which had paved the way for Gloster's dramatic visit to England in late 1805.

By the beginning of 1806 there was hardly anyone who had been or then was in the Island's employ whose salary was not well in arrears. Sir Charles Cameron, Agent for Trinidad between his commissionership in Malta and his governorship in the Bahamas, was not yet paid for his efforts though three full years had elapsed. [154] His successor, a Mr. Maling, received his first pay-packet only after he had been five years in the Island's service. [155] John Rutherford, the surveyor general, on leave in England, not only failed to procure the arrears of several years but suffered the additional misfortune of having his commission revoked owing to the expenses of his department. [156] Fullarton, canny Scot that he was, successfully insisted on his right to be paid by the British Treasury; to be paid, as the auditors insisted, out of Trinidad's revenues was not to be paid at all. [157] From Trinidad the Governor echoed the tale of woe. A letter described "the absolute penury of this Government for the Want of funds sufficient to pay the unavoidable expences thereof in Consequence of which every Officer and other person having claims thereon are very Considerably in Arrears and myself among those principally so." [158]

Even worse was to follow. The Colony had followed with bated breath the ups and downs of the movement for abolition of the slave trade. Gloster had loudly applauded a temporary reversal in the fortunes of the abolitionists, and hoped "to find the dreams of Enthusiasm and folly upon this topic,

152. Cf. C.O. 295/11, Hislop : Camden, 18.5.1805.
153. C.O. 295/11, Hislop : Castlereagh, 8.9.1805; enclosed Minute of Council, 5.9.1805.
154. Mr. (as he then was) Charles Cameron was appointed Civil Commissioner in Malta in May 1801, Agent for Trinidad in early 1802 and Governor of the Bahamas in February, 1803. Even as late as 1809 he seems not to have been paid (Cf. C.O. 295/22, Memorial of 14.11.1809 and C.O. 295/24, Memorial to the Treasury, 22.4.1810) which was probably his own fault since Hislop seemed willing and able to remit his salary in 1808. See note 155.
155. C.O. 295/19, Hislop : Castlereagh (Private), 14.7.1808.
156. C.O. 295/11, Hislop : Cooke, 17.5.1805; C.O. 295/17, Huskisson : Cooke, 13.4.1807. C.O. 295/20 Rutherford : Castlereagh, 13.1.1808 and Memorial of 31.10.1808.
157. C.O. 295/13, Fullarton : Cooke, 23.7.1805; C.O. 295/15, Fullarton : Shee, 16.8.1806, enclosing Castlereagh : Fullarton, 5.11.1805. For letters pertaining to arrears to other Commission officers see, C.O. 295/17, Fawkener : Shee, 7.2.1807; Huskisson : Cooke, 4.5.1807.
158. C.O. 295/14, Hislop : Cooke, 6.3.1806.

speedily *abolished* also". [159]   But the abolitionists had triumphed; May 1807 saw the abolition of the slave trade. [160]   Frantic efforts by the British planting and mercantile interest connected with the Island to show that Trinidad, because of the recency of its plantation development, would be peculiarly and disastrously affected by the proposed abolition, had failed. [161] And even after discounting the exaggerations indulged by the planters, it must be admitted that abolition did much to sharpen the Island's financial crisis. Slaves were after all a large part of the Island's imports and exports; and the decrease in the trade was soon to be reflected in a diminution of the duties received from the 3½% tax, with a corresponding fall in revenue. [162]

The interference of the Orders-in-Council with the American trade was another source of grave financial embarrassment to the Island's government. Patriots like Layman and Sanderson and M'Callum [163] could rail against the trade and plot to extinguish it, but the government and public of Trinidad could hardly have existed without it. The Order-in-Council of September 17, 1806, [164] prohibiting the import of salted provisions from the United States of America and the export of sugar and other plantation produce in American ships, aggravated the increasing trend of diminishing duties and revenue; and this at a time when the Island was already protesting about other restrictions on the trade with neutrals. [165]

Restrictions on the American trade not only affected the government's ability to pay its way, it increased the financial difficulties of the inhabitants and made traders less able to turn to meet the duty payments imposed in normal trading.   A glut of sugar on the British market, indebtedness to British merchants, and the chronic scarcity of money had increased the colonists' dependence on the American trade; for foodstuffs and other supplies the colonists were wont to barter their sugar and such produce as the Americans could take. [166] So important was this trade that the Governor, on receipt of the Order-in-Council of September 1806, had suspended its operation at the certain risk of a sharp ministerial rebuke. [167] But to obey

159. C.O. 295/11, Hislop : Cooke, 28.4.1805, enclosing Gloster : Hislop, 27.4.1805.
160. 47 Geo. sess. 1, cap. 36.
161. See, Fraser, *op. cit.*, Vol. I, pp. 278-82. Also, *Journal of the House of Commons*, Vol. 62, p. 148.
162. C.O. 295/16, Hislop : Cooke (Private), 23.6.1807.

163. Layman, *Outline of a Plan. . .* , pp. 57-8, argued that the likelihood of the West Indies being rendered self-sufficient in foodstuffs and so independent of the American trade, was one of the major reasons for his plan to introduce Chinese labour into Trinidad and ultimately to the other territories. Sanderson, *Political Account*, p. 69 ff. M'Callum, *Travels*, pp. 56-7. The American trade he, Layman, called a "predatory Proceeding".

164. C.O. 324/103.
165. C.O. 295/13, Picton : Cooke, 26.10.1805; and C.O. 295/15, Cottrell : Shee, 16.4.1806 enclosing, Gloster : Board of Trade, no date, and a Memorial of 12.3.1806. Both Picton and Gloster represented the hardship imposed by the trading restrictions on the imports of low priced wines and oils of France from the Danish and Swedish West Indies.
166. C.O. 295/17, Marryat : Castlereagh, 29.4.1807, and enclosures.
167. C.O. 295/15, Hislop : Windham, 4.12.1806.

the order was not only to snub a customer who often himself paid the export duty on the sugar he took away, [168] but also to force the inhabitants to trade with other suppliers who often demanded cash for their goods, [169] and to increase substantially the chronically high cost of living. [170]

The effect of restrictions on the American trade is graphically illustrated in a contemporary letter from a Trinidad planter.

"It would be in vain for me to attempt to describe our situation; which ever way I turn I see nothing but ruin staring us in the face; nothing helps us in vis vitae but the supplies we receive from the United States, and should we be deprived of that, and the subsequent means of bartering our produce for the necessaries of life, we must abandon entirely the culture of cane, and manufacture of sugar, and turn our estates into pens for a subsistence. . . in the mean time, beef, which was current at 20 dollars, rose instantly to 40; butter from 18 to 30; pork from 24 to 64; and fish from 10 to 16. In this dilemma the governor and council considered themselves justifiable in suspending the effect of the King's order, until the expiration of the proclamation issued in Oct(ober);[171] by which the faith of government was pledged to the public, for the admission of the articles therein ennumerated until the 22nd April. By the fagg end of that proclamation we now subsist. . .

"The London, Liverpool, Glasgow and Irish merchants say send no sugar home; give it away rather - Government say, you shall not send it to the United States to be sold and remitted to England; nor shall you barter it with foreigners for the necessaries of life; at least if you do, those foreigners shall not carry it away.

168. Sanderson, *Political Account. . .* , p. 74. This meant of course that he paid the planter so much the less for it. But it was a help, since the planter often was short of cash and the duty was not payable in kind.
169. Such as the traders who infrequently came from British North America. These were themselves in difficult financial straits. The discrimination in their favour was intended to build them into rivals to the Americans, and to eliminate the difficulties which, they argued, faced them as fairly new suppliers of the West Indian market, and as citizens of a young country. They thought it unfair, for example, that the West Indians should buy from the Americans merely because they sold their goods cheaper; after all, a new British colony should be encouraged in every way. Ironically this was the same argument that the Trinidadians were urging without success as a reason for permitting them to trade with the Americans; they were a young country too. See, for the Canadian argument, Graham, *Sea Power. . .* , pp. 185-190.
170. Cf. *B.M. Add. Mss. 36,499*, Cumberland Papers, Vol. IX, pp. 101 ff. C.O. 295/4, Fullarton : Sullivan, 12.1.1803. Fullarton described Port of Spain as "chiefly supplied with Provisions from the Spanish Main. But the doctrine that prices find their level, has not been verified here. For although near One Hundred Launches and Pirogas have arrived from the Continent within the Last Month, Besides quantities of flour and Indian Corn from North America, still the price of living and lodging is so Exorbitant, that a Blacksmith asks three Dollars for shoeing a Horse, and a Merchant frequently pays. Five or Six Hundred Pounds a Year for the Rent of a House and Stores". Also, Baron de Montlezum, *Souvenir des Antilles. . . .* , (Paris, 1818). Two volumes. Vol. I, p. 271.
171. C.O. 295/15, Hislop : Windham, 4.12.1806 and enclosures. The proclamation dated October 19, was one of a series permitting trade with the Americans in a large range of goods for successive periods of six months.

"There is a dilemma - and to crown it all we'll abolish the African trade; you shall have no more slaves, and we will endeavour to starve to death those you have -

"Better and better! there is philanthropy for you! Well done Mr. Wilberforce!" [172]

Another letter written in the same vein began ominously: "I landed here on Friday, and found all things very dull. Sugar selling at 2½ dollars" [173] the hundredweight; the normal price was around eight dollars. [174] Steadily falling prices for export produce complemented a steadily diminishing revenue and contrasted sharply with the spiral of rising prices.

Ultimately the Island's parlous economic position stirred the imperial government out of its languorous indifference, but not before the continuing crisis had set the stage for the reconciliation of the factions. For all the Island's ills the government, burdened with the responsibility for the Island's welfare, had so far had one palliative. The grant of a legislative Council, it was argued, would at least enable the government to tackle the existing problems, if not to solve them. But Gloster back from England had had only failure to report. Meanwhile the economic situation grew worse and worse until, by the middle of 1807 there was not *"literally speaking . . .* a single farthing in the Colonial Chest". [175] The fire of March 1808 which reduced much of Port of Spain to smouldering ruins was to complete the picture of desolation and woe.

In despair the government made its last throw. Governor Hislop suggested that the imperial government should make a direct grant for the Island's up-keep after the manner of the Spanish government in the latter years of its dominion over the Island. [176] And Gloster prepared a "Case" for the Secretary of State. This time he suggested that the King's prerogative should be used to introduce local taxation. The 3½% duty he baldly stated to be illegal, and was in any case insufficient for the Island's needs. He recommended a 3½% duty on exports, a 2½% duty on British imports, a four per cent tax on house rents, and a poll tax of twenty shillings per head on white persons, thirty shillings on free coloureds and five shillings on slaves. If the King's prerogative could not be used to introduce taxation, he again urged the immediate grant of a legislative Council. [177]

From this time on however the government's advocacy of a legislative Council began to wane, if at first only imperceptibly. And as it waned an increasing amity between the Island's government and the London merchants

---

172. C.O. 295/17, Marryat : Castlereagh, 29.4.1807, enclosure, dated 5.2.1807.
173. C.O. 295/17, Marryat : Castlereagh, 29.4.1807, enclosure dated 3.3.(1807).
174. Fraser, *op. cit.,* Vol. I, pp. 301-2. Letter from Marryat to Gov. & Council (no date), quoted.
175. C.O. 295/16, Hislop : Cooke (Private), 23.6.1807.
176. C.O. 295/16, Same to Same, same date.
177. C.O. 295/16, Hislop : Castlereagh, 4.8.1807, No. 12; enclosing Minute of Council, 3.8.1807 containing a copy of a case made out by Gloster on the doubtful legality of the 3½% duty.

became the first fruit of imperial indifference and financial insolvency. While the parties were still tearing at each other's throats in Trinidad, the government in despair was looking outwards to the allies of the British party, the merchants of London and the other great cities, for help in solving its problems.

In Britain the central figure in this development was Joseph Marryat, one of the most successful London merchants, a member of Parliament from 1808 to 1824 and at his death chairman of the Committee at Lloyd's. A West Indian by sentiment and interest though not by birth, Marryat's long residence in Grenada in his youth gave him an enduring interest in West Indian affairs. His first relations with the Trinidad government were, as we have seen, [178] rather bitter. He had considerable interests in Trinidad, had suffered substantial loss in the Colony, [179] and, after reading Gloster's 1804 Bill, regarded the Governor and Council as a clique of defaulters, if not worse. Their attachment to a legislative Council undoubtedly strengthened his own determination to foster the introduction of the Assembly system into the Island. Yet by 1807 the Governor and Council had come increasingly to rely on Marryat to represent their views in London.

Marryat's own insistence in concerning himself with the Island's affairs and his obvious qualifications (apart from his political views) are factors that help to explain this development. By August 1805 he had so far overcome the first objections to him that the Council had been induced to recommend him for the job of Agent. [180] The recommendation was later cancelled only because Gloster was himself dispatched as Agent in September. The other factor was Maling's obvious unsuitability and incompetence. Not only was he incompetent, he had no taste for the task either. He had been appointed Agent mainly because his daughter was espoused to Lord Mulgrave, Chancellor of the Duchy of Lancaster in Pitt's last ministry and Lord of the Admiralty in Portland's, and a suitably remunerative and socially acceptable position had to be found for him. [181] But he regarded his situation, in the best nineteenth century manner, as a sinecure, and could not be stirred to exertion. Marryat was infinitely more interested and knowledgeable, was not afraid to haggle with the Secretary of State, and it was he who, unofficially at least, served as the Island's Agent in London.

It was Marryat who had represented the Island's views on the impending abolition of the slave trade. [182] It was Marryat who, when abolition had seemed certain, had pleaded with British ministers for compensation for the Island's plantation owners. [183] It was Marryat, too, who kept the Island in-

178. See above, pp. 97-8
179. With Fullarton's help, he alleged. See, C.O. 295/10, Marryat : Camden, 6.8.1804, enclosure Marryat : Hobart, 10.10.1803.
180. C.O. 298/2, Minute of Council, 3.8.1805.
181. C.O. 295/15, Sidmouth : (No name), 5.8.1806.
182. Fraser, *op. cit.*, Vol. I, p. 282, Marryat : Hislop, 21.2.1807 quoted.
183. Fraser, *op. cit.*, Vol. I, p. 282, Marryat : Hislop, 21.2.1807 quoted.

formed of the progress of the constitutional discussions in England; and, if his aim was different from that of the Governor and the Council, it was some consolation to know that someone was actively striving for a solution. In February 1807 he was reporting that his Majesty's ministers "are seriously occupied in deliberating upon a constitution for Trinidad. The Attorney General . . . has given his opinion in favour of a Council and a House of Assembly rather than a Legislative Council, preferring experience to experiment. . . ." [184] On Gloster's "Case" of 1807 he expressed the view that ministers would sooner "give the Colony a Constitution at once than resort to the exercise of the King's prerogative. . ." [185] and argued with Spencer Perceval, then Chancellor of the Exchequer, that he should "not think it necessary to take the opinion of the Law Officers of the Crown whether His Majesty can by his prerogative impose taxes on the inhabitants of Trinidad treating it as a conquered country, when the alternative is before you of enabling them to tax themselves by giving the Colony a British Constitution". [186]

Later Marryat had to report the failure of his endeavours to obtain a British constitution for the Island. But, he said: "At any rate you have the satisfaction of knowing that the situation of the Colony is now fairly before His Majesty's Ministers and will be attended to in some mode or other". [187] And so indeed it was. At long last a decision had been reached. As usual, Marryat reported it. In early 1808 he wrote that the British government's concern over Trinidad was at last manifested: "the office of Chief Judge has been given away by Lord Castlereagh to Mr. Smith, late Chief Justice of Grenada, who came home to apply for the vacant situation of Judge of the Admiralty at Barbados, but finding the office disposed of before his arrival, he applied for the Chief Justiceship of Trinidad, in preference to resuming that situation in the island of Grenada". [188] And Smith was successful.

By such chance was the constitutional dilemma temporarily resolved. If the price of a solution were the introduction of an Assembly into the Island, the Governor and Council would have been half willing to pay it. [189] To use Hislop's words apropos the reconstitution of the Council in 1804, a "principle of reconciliation" had begun in England which was soon to spread to the factions in Trinidad. But this did not guarantee the acceptance of the

---

184. *Ibid.*, p. 281, Marryat : Hislop, 19.2.1807 quoted.

185. Fraser, *op. cit.*, Vol. I, p. 299, Marryat : Governor and Council, 8.10.1807 quoted.

186. *Ibid.*, p. 299, quoted, Marryat : Perceval, 1.10.1807, enclosed in Marryat : Governor and Council, 8.10.1807.

187. *Ibid.*, pp. 301-2, Marryat : Governor and Council, no date (certainly late 1807).

188. *Ibid.*, pp. 302-3, Marryat : Governor and Council, no date. See also for general comment, Murray, *op. cit.*, pp. 74-82.

189. As Hislop's comment on the Address of 1808 for British laws shows. In fact it's his absence of comment that is striking. He said he would comment only if asked to do so. C.O. 295/19, Hislop : Castlereagh, 6.3.1808, No. 26.

solution now imposed. Events were to show that the appointment of George Smith as Chief Justice was to hasten the process of reconciliation, but in a manner that brought little joy to harassed British ministers. The second great experiment in the constitutional affairs of the Island was destined to heal the factional breaches created by the first.

CHAPTER 8

'AN INSUPERABLE OBJECTION'

The appointment of a new Chief Justice for Trinidad in 1808 in the person of George Smith ushered in the second experiment in the Island's constitutional history. Like the first, this experiment was also fated to end in bitterness and confusion. Smith was, in time, to be stripped of his judicial authority by the Governor and Council,[1] and to flee the Island aboard a vessel secretly lying off Macqueripe to receive him.[2] Nevertheless, this second experiment was to provide the background to a definitive pronouncement about the Island's future, thus putting an end to the speculation which had so much been a part of its constitutional history.

The macabre end of the Smith experiment, reminiscent in more ways than one of the disintegration of the Commission of 1802, was rivalled only by its beginning. In June 1811, Joseph Marryat, introducing a debate in the House of Commons on the administration of justice in Trinidad, was to provoke gales of laughter on Opposition benches by describing the manner in which Smith obtained his appointment. He was to paint a picturesque sketch of Smith "being taken into the office of the noble colonial secretary, who, with a brush of his magical wand, like the metamorphosis of Ovid, transformed the barrister into a Corridor (i.e. *Corregidor*), an Alcalde, and a supreme judge of the Audiencia. . ."[3] As pungent as this criticism was, however, it conveyed only one-half of the irony of Smith's appointment.

Smith, to an extent beyond the ken of most public officers, was a creature of his own creation. A *protégé* of Lord Castlereagh, the Secretary of State, Smith was permitted to write his own Commission and Instructions. An abrasive and officious little man, he had previously benefitted by Castlereagh's indulgence and regarded him with justice as "the Parent & first Patron of my better Fortunes".[4] In 1805 Castlereagh had been Secretary of State for War and the Colonies for the first time and he had, at that time, made Smith Chief Justice in Grenada.[5] But a salary of about £1,120 sterling plus fees averaging between £800 and £1,000[6] did not exactly correspond to Smith's sternly held views of lucrative employment. He therefore resigned his office and returned to England in 1808 in search of the judgeship of the vice-admiralty of Barbados carrying an expectation of well over £5,000

1. C.O. 295/26, Hislop : Liverpool, 25.3.1811, No 62, and enclosures.
2. C.O. 295/26, Hislop : Liverpool, 18.4.1811, No. 66, and enclosures.
3. *Parliamentary Debates,* Vol. XX, p. 611.
4. C.O. 295/22, Smith : Hislop, 20.11.1809; enclosed in Hislop : Castlereagh, 21.11.1809, No. 78. Smith's *Laws of Grenada,* published in 1808, was also dedicated to Lord Castlereagh described by Smith as his patron.
5. C.O. 102/18, p. 99, Castlereagh : Maitland, 21.10.1805, No. 2.
6. C.O. 295/20, Smith : Castlereagh, 28.12.1808.

annually. Failing in this, and determined not to return to the "comparatively trifling Colony of Grenada", he successfully put forward a claim for the chief justiceship of Trinidad.

Appointing Smith head of the judiciary in Trinidad was much less complicated a task than deciding exactly what he was to do there. Lord Castlereagh agreed on the appointment as early as January 1808, but it was not until early 1809 that the role of the new Chief Justice was finally decided. The intervening period was dogged with uncertainty and indecision, the main problem being that of coupling Smith's appointment with a decisive change in the Island's constitutional affairs.

Three different alternatives were considered. One of them, certainly the most amenable to the Island's inhabitants, was reported by Picton in February 1808. From London he wrote St.Hilaire Begorrat thus:

"I have this morning seen your Chief judge, Mr. Smith; I think you are fortunate in having such a man. He appears to have the abilities and *decision* necessary for such a situation, and I am told he is most indefatigable in his attention to business. Your new *constitution* is nearly completed, and Mr. Smith will probably be the bearer of it out. There are to be no exclusive privileges, people are to be equally admitted to all situations and offices, without respect to religion or nation. The Roman-catholic clergy and the Protestant to be equally provided for by Government without any distinction.

"An Assembly will be formed consisting of about 17 members, to be nominated by the proprietors in their respective districts all to have a qualification in land and slaves, *60 slaves and 200 acres* to entitle any one to a seat in the Assembly. Thus far I have been able to collect, and, upon the whole, I think the arrangement is rather a satisfactory one; and I most sincerely hope that it will bring along with it a disposition to good humour which will set the spirit of faction at rest."[7]

If in early February, as Picton reports, it was decided to give the Island an Assembly, this idea, for reasons that are not clear, was soon discarded.[8] Smith himself might possibly have played some part in the shelving of the plan. He held Assemblies in poor esteem, did not think Trinidad was ready for one, and thought that Spanish law, scrupulously enforced, was all that

---

7. *Parliamentary Papers.* 1831-2, (212) XXXI, pp. 11-12. Extract of a letter Picton : Begorrat, 5.2.1808, enclosure No. 1, Marryat : Goderich, 30.12.1831. This Marryat, also Joseph, was the son of the Marryat with whom we are more familiar.
8. One of the reasons seems to have been, contrary to what Picton implied, the complexity of devising a constitution for the Island. On October 20, 1808 (C.O. 295/20, Smith : Castlereagh) Smith wrote that Stephen who was preparing the new constitution, feared that "many many months" would elapse before it was ready. Later, Stephen himself (C.O. 295/25, Stephen : Adam Gordon), 1.9.1810, spoke of having prepared a paper on "an interior Legislature" for Trinidad. But the reference is not clear and might have had something to do with the petition of 1810 for a British constitution from the Island.

the Island needed. Besides, he seems to have favoured a slightly larger field for his energies than that offered by Trinidad alone. He thought the administration of justice in the West Indies to be inadequate and farcical, and singled out the incompetence and partiality of West Indian judges as the most important factors calling for an urgent reorganization of the system. Accordingly, he put forward a plan for the amalgamation of the Windwards and Leewards into three judicial districts to be served by fully qualified and independent judges at suitably rewarding salaries. One of these districts composing Trinidad and the islands to the south of Martinique, Barbados excepted, he selected for himself. For such an appointment he suggested a salary of £4,000, taking care to point out in justification of this astronomical sum that the duties of such an office would be "laborious & unceasing" though, he modestly confessed, the burden of the appointment was with him "one of the strongest motives for seeking it. . ."[9]

This plan like the first was promptly shelved. It was finally decided to continue the operation of Spanish law in the Island and to charge the new Chief Justice with the administration of that law. In arriving at this decision the Secretary of State was prodded into action by Smith who, after long months of inactivity, wrote on October 20, setting out his views on the Trinidad situation and urging the need for haste. "At present the Colony has not the benefit either of English or Spanish law," wrote Smith,"& this arises from the suspension of the Court of Audiencia whose officers & their powers have been most imperfectly supplied by the Authorities which have been acting by a sort of substitution since the British Government prevailed." [10] While a final settlement of the constitutional question was being determined, it was necessary to remove all uncertainty from the Island's legal system by enforcing a properly regulated code of laws. This, Smith suggested, could be done by resurrecting in its entirety the Spanish system. He therefore suggested that he be given a temporary commission to establish an *Audiencia* and the other judicial offices inseparable from the proper organization of the Spanish legal system, and offered, if his plan should be approved, to draw up such a commission himself.

Lord Castlereagh, still in a quandary about Trinidad, must have been highly gratified by Smith's continuing display of initiative and resource. He gave him the necessary authority and within a fortnight the drafts of the Commission and Instructions were ready. [11] Smith conferred on himself all the powers previously residing in the *Audiencia* at Caracas and, since the conquest, fitfully exercised by the Island's Governors. In addition he created himself an *oidor,* an *alcalde del crimen* and *fiscal,* thus uniting in his person the highest judicial offices operative under Spanish law. He laid claim to all "the powers authorities and jurisdiction whether appellant or original, which were heretofore enjoyed and exercised either collectively or individually over the Province or Vice Royalty of the Carraccas (sic) or any part thereof

9. C.O. 295/20, Smith : Castlereagh, 28.3.1808.   10. C.O. 295/20, Smith : Castlereagh, 20.10.1808.
11. C.O. 295/20, Smith : Cooke, 3.11.1808; enclosures.

by the Members of the Audiencia of the said Province or such of them as were known to the Spanish law by the names of Oidores, Alcaldes del crimen and Fiscales. . ."[12] He claimed an original jurisdiction over all cases civil and criminal and an exclusive appellate jurisdiction over all matters whatsoever. He extinguished the Governor's right to hear appeals; from the Chief Justice's court appeals were to be allowed only to the King-in-Council if, in civil cases, the sum involved exceeded £500 sterling. But capital sentences were to be approved by the Governor before execution; and the Governor and the *alcaldes ordinarios* were suffered to continue to judge cases as courts of first instance.

He bestowed on himself the power to make rules governing the procedure and practice of all the Island's courts. He abolished torture on the principle that only such punishments as were employed in England were to be employed in Trinidad. Fees payable to judges and other legal officers were regularized. A docket of standard fees was prepared, and the penalty of suspension from office was prescribed for all those found to be overcharging for legal services.

The *oidores* of the *Audiencia,* besides being judges of appeal were also advisers to the Viceroy charged with responsibility for ensuring that the edicts and ordinances of the Council of the Indies were properly executed. [13] Though the *oidores* were forbidden from interfering in matters of government,[14] they had precise political functions. One of these permitted the senior *oidor* to preside over the Council of government in the Viceroy's absence. [15] Accordingly, Smith claimed a right to membership of the Island's Council ranking in precedence next to the Governor. He claimed the right to preside in the Council and to take over the reins of government in the Governor's death or absence.[16] His right to preside over the Council in such circumstances was later conceded, but his claim to act as Governor's deputy was not entertained, and was excluded from the final Instructions. Finally he enjoined on himself the duty of always paying due respect and deference to the Governor and not interfering in the business of government except by giving advice as a member of Council.

As was to be expected, Smith had his critics. Joseph Marryat, continuing his burlesque in the House in June 1811, left an imperishable description of Smith going about his duties in Trinidad.

"Mr. Smith decided in the lower courts", he said, "then went and sat in the higher court of Audiencia, dressed not as in the inferior courts, in a plain dress, but in a superb Spanish dress. Therefore

---

12. *Ibid.,* enclosure No. 1. See also, C.O. 380/134, No. 24.

13. *Recopilación*, Lib. 2, Tit. 15 for a general statement of the duties of the *oidor.*

14. *Ibid.,* Lib. 3, Tit. 3, Ley 34.

15. *Ibid..* Lib. 2, Tit. 16, Ley 16; Lib. 3, Tit. 2, Leyes 10, 11.

16. Smith also argued that this right was sanctioned by English practice in the West Indies where presidents of the Council were known to assume office in the Governor's death or absence.

all the salutary checks which the laws imposed were done away,
  the offices being united in the person of Mr. Smith"[17]
Marryat attacked the method. Others, on the lunatic fringe, contested the
right of the British government to have inaugurated such an experiment.
Richard Adderley, George Adderley's brother, argued that the maintenance
of a Spanish code of laws subsequent to the cession was "a subject of high
Impeachment. . ." Smith he described as being "greater than our law can
make him. He is a branch larger than its Trunk; he is a creature more mighty
than his Creator . . . Oh! What a subject is here . . . Sooner or later in parliament and out of parliament this large question will be largely discussed..."[18]

*   *   *

The temptation to view the history of Trinidad after the conquest as a
series of eponymous epochs is strong and persistent. Picton, Fullarton and
Smith were all men of strong and dominant personalities. Besides them
Hislop is almost an anonymous figure chiefly remembered for his long
governorship and for his bitter feud with Smith in the last year of his administration. The new Chief Justice or, as he was most frequently called,
the "Chief *Oidor,*" was a different proposition. Shrewd, energetic and uncompromising, he affected the Island like a catalyst and soon laid bare its
innermost impulses while remaining himself steadfastly set in his ways. He
came to the Island at a time when the Secretary of State was beginning to feel
the need of a new and authoritative point of view on the Island's problems.
As the person destined to provide this point of view Smith was a fortunate
choice.

On the other hand, however, the new Chief Justice carried with him the
aura of controversy. A man of undoubted ability, he was unconnected to
any local interest and he had the confidence of Government ministers who
felt assured of his impartiality. He was a good observer and a good writer.
He saw everything, missed nothing, and, like Fullarton, was an indefatigable
correspondent. He had a lucid and penetrating style, and his lawyer's training
enabled him to get directly to the heart of the most complicated problem.
But he lacked finesse. He had the uncanny ability of being able to unite the
most implacable enemies in opposition to himself on the very briefest
acquaintance.

In addition he had very firm notions about the society to which he had
come, and though he invariably tended to a certain liberality in outlook, his
motives were not always free of suspicion. He possessed in the highest degree
that haughtiness and arrogance of spirit which metropolitan whites frequently
exhibited on contact with the brash, sensuous and uninhibited societies of
the West Indies. If he was impartial in his dealings with the various social
groups in the Island, he was partial in that his keenest instincts made him

17. *Parliamentary Debates*, Vol. XX, p. 611. 18. C.O. 295/22, Adderley : Perceval, 11.12.1809.

bitterly opposed to West Indian society as then constituted. Taken by itself this was undoubtedly a good thing. But even impartiality in the West Indies of the nineteenth century was an important political position: impartiality between whites and coloureds had been, in the eyes of Trinidad's white society, Fullarton's besetting sin. Smith had not the good sense nor the desire to profit by Fullarton's experience and to tread as carefully as he might have done.

A man less headstrong than Smith, and more judicious, would have nimbly avoided the embarrassing *dénouement* towards which the swift flow of events was eventually to carry him. He would have suspected, for example, that in any crisis the Governor, whose long residence had inextricably entangled him with local interests, was more than likely to oppose him. He would have guessed that his conglomeration of powers, if too readily asserted, would inevitably bring him into conflict with the Governor, without whose aid his jurisdiction could easily be blunted. He would have taken special care not to alienate too many interests at once. But he would also have been a very cunning and artful man. He would probably not have been a good judge either. Most certainly he would not have been Smith.

George Smith arrived in Trinidad sometime in May, 1809.[19] His arrival marked an abrupt change in the Island's affairs. Several despatches had preceded him informing the Governor of his appointment and of the changes attendant thereon. The first despatch outlined the extent of Smith's jurisdiction and the way in which it had affected the Governor's judicial authority. The Governor was informed that his appellate jurisdiction was revoked though he could continue, as before, to hear cases as a court of first instance. Smith's salary was fixed at £2,000 sterling per year to be paid out of the Island's revenues. A specimen docket of fees was enclosed and the Governor instructed to establish a scale of charges on the same pattern for use in the courts. The termination of Nihell's appointment was announced, as was his supersession by George Smith as senior member of the Council.[20]

Two other despatches informed the Governor that His Majesty's Government would willingly consider compensation of the ex-Chief Justice for his abrupt dismissal,[21] and that ministerial policy for the time being aimed at the proper administration of Spanish law in the Island.[22] A private letter of the same date outlined Smith's special role.[23] He was to determine, with the help of the Governor and Council, a form of government suitable to the permanent administration of the Colony. And lastly the Governor's attention was drawn to four specific points.

19. C.O. 295/21, Hislop : Castlereagh (Private), 28.4.1809.

20. C.O. 296/4, pp. 346-50, Castlereagh : Hislop, February, 1809.

21. C.O. 296/4, pp. 351-2, Same to Same, 6.3.1809, No. 9.

22. C.O. 296/4, pp. 352-3, Castlereagh : Hislop, 6.3.1809, No. 10.

23. C.O. 296/4, pp. 353-4, Same to Same (Private), same date.

Steps were to be taken to achieve the eventual establishment of the Church of England, and to facilitate the religious instruction of mulattoes and slaves. A regular and abundant supply of slave provisions was to be provided for. All rights and privileges to which the Negro slave was entitled by Spanish law and the terms of the capitulation should be secured to him; to this end a liberal code of slave laws should be enacted. The condition of the free people of colour should be improved; their privileges should be increased and their education facilitated, since "it is considered that upon the fidelity and attachment of this Class of Inhabitants the Security & Prosperity of the West India Islands may hereafter greatly depend".[24]

The appointment of the new Chief Justice then was not only intended to lead to the reorganization of the judicial system and the determination of the Island's constitution. It was also intended to contribute to the amelioration of the condition of the free coloured and slave population. The moral and legal status which the free coloured and slave inherited under Spanish law was to be extended to them once again. Religious instruction was to be provided for and the social position of both groups was to be improved. The resurrection of Spanish law was therefore intended to affect not only the formal proceedings of the courts but the social relations of the main groups of the Island's society. Both the letter and the spirit of Spanish law were to be observed.

It must be said at once that nothing was done to implement these proposals. As with the Commission of 1802, an ambitious programme of reform failed because the prospects of its implementation were soon blighted by the venomous struggle that broke out amongst the Island's leading officials, in this case, the Governor and the Chief Justice. Besides, the War Office again changed hands in October 1809. Lord Liverpool succeeded Lord Castlereagh, and what had begun as a promising movement of reform died in obscurity somewhere in a ministerial cubby-hole. Metropolitan indifference and colonial dissension had once again been the death of good intentions.

The new experiment began under the happiest of auguries. Judge Smith opened his court on May 25[25] and took his seat on the Council ranking as senior member next to the Governor in precedence. Nihell, superseded as senior member, nevertheless retained his seat, deferring only to the Governor and the new Chief Justice. The Governor expressed himself well pleased with the new experiment and regretted that it had not occurred sooner: he would, he wrote, have been saved a lot of unnecessary bother had Smith accompanied him "with the same Authorities as he possesses when I was sent out to this Government".[26] The Chief Justice regarded the Governor with equal favour: the latter was "everything that is excellent and amiable as a man" if a trifle too inclined to weakness in government.[27] Indeed, an almost embarrassing

24. C.O. 296/4, pp. 353-4, Same to Same (Private), same date.

25. C.O. 295/22, Hislop : Castlereagh, 4.10.1809, No. 77. Return of Offices.

26. C.O. 295/21, Hislop : Cooke, 1.7.1809.   27. C.O. 295/22, Smith : Castlereagh, 4.10.1809.

amiability prevailed. Nihell, severely put out by his dismissal, [28] was recommended for a pension of £1,000 sterling by Smith, who was regarded by all as being exceedingly influential at home. [29] By the end of the year, the Governor, with Smith's cooperation, temporarily assuaged Nihell's feelings by appointing him *alcalde* of the second election in an effort to make the *Cabildo* respectable. [30] John Sanderson, soon to be among the most determined opponents of the Chief Justice, was recommended by him for the post of King's advocate in the vice-admiralty court. [31]

Soon, however, the storm clouds were beginning to gather. Everything about Smith conspired to alienate the support of those upon whom, in normal circumstances, he could probably have depended. The Governor, despite his effusive welcome of the Chief Justice, felt himself denuded of much of his authority by the very extent of the other's powers. And though Smith, during the first year of his appointment, took every opportunity to affirm his subordination to the Governor, the latter remained keenly aware of Smith's potential as a rival. Moreover, it was all too plain that Smith's assertions of subordination were intended to emphasize his determination not to encroach on the Governor's administrative authority in the hope that he would himself be left in the undisputed enjoyment of his awesome judicial prerogatives.[32]

Every legal and judicial authority whose function Smith had completely or partially usurped also had an axe to grind. Nihell was not the only one nursing a grudge. Archibald Gloster, the Attorney General, was rendered practicably unemployable by the new appointment; the wonder was that his office was still in existence. Three months after his arrival Smith, in pursuit of his brief, wrote to the *Audiencia* of Caracas requesting a complement of Spanish trained lawyers and the latest books on Spanish law.[33] Soon the legal establishment was placed on a regular footing with a complement of four Spanish lawyers, one of whom was *Asesor* to the Governor, another assistant to the Chief Justice, while the other two functioned as public practitioners. [34] Gloster soon suffered the mortification of being transferred on promotion as Chief Justice to Grenada - an honour that he would dearly have loved to decline - and the emoluments of the office of Attorney General were substantially reduced.[35]

28. C.O. 295/21, Hislop : Castlereagh, 29.5.1809, No. 60; enclosing Nihell : Hislop, 27.5.1809. See also, C.O. 295/21, Hervey : McNamara, no date, and enclosures.
29. C.O. 295/24, Smith : Jenkinson (Private), 2.3.1810.
30. C.O. 295/22, Smith : Cooke, 28.10.1809; C.O. 295/23, Hislop : Liverpool, 7.1.1810. *Alcaldes*, as we have seen in Chapter II, were usually elected by the *regidores.*
31. C.O. 295/23, Hislop : Liverpool, 2.1.1810, No. 6; enclosing, Smith : Hislop, 19.12.1809.
32. C.O. 295/25, Smith : Jenkinson (Private), 28.6.1810.
33. C.O. 295/24, Smith : Jenkinson (Private), 2.3.1810; Appendix No. 6.
34. C.O. 295/24, Smith : Jenkinson (Private), 2.3.1810.
35. C.O. 296/4, Liverpool : Hislop, 14.3.1810, No. 4; C.O. 295/23, Hislop : Liverpool, 19.5.1810, No. 18, enclosing, Extract of Minute of Council, 18.5.1810 containing Gloster's petition against his transfer. The salary of the post was reduced from £500 to £200 sterling per year.

CHAPTER 8

The judicial reorganization materially affected the emoluments attaching to such offices as the provost marshal's and the deputy registrar of the courts. Compared with Smith's growing prosperity - in his first five months he earned 4,300 dollars by way of fees[36] alone - these two offices, supporting deputies as well as principals, soon ceased to support either. The fault was not all Smith's as Sylvester Newman, the deputy provost marshal, pointed out.[37] Yet even he selected Smith's "system of Tyranny & oppression un-controll'd" as one of the causes for his and his principal's increasing pauperisation.[38] Richard Adderley was not as restrained, and frankly blamed Smith for robbing his brother's "all", by "hastening through the long arrear of causes and putting my brother's fair perquisites into the pockets of others".[39] Archibald Gloster, furious at the prospects of having to depend for his salary in future on Grenada's fractious Assembly, cursed at Smith for having interfered to procure a diminution in the emoluments then attaching to the Attorneyship General, and drew attention to the Chief Justice's own salary of £2,000 sterling plus fees.[40]

The public too were beginning to rue the day when the Chief Justice had arrived in the Island. Smith had lost no time in dealing with the large back-log of cases awaiting his attention. During his first six months in office he settled some seven hundred cases many of which had been pending *"under influence for years"*.[41] Debtors who had long evaded their creditors had been forced to pay up. Their groans, said Smith, had provided "a source of general amusement and laughter" during the first two months of his ad-ministration.[42] Soon, however, the general amusement turned to an equally widespread dismay. Smith's overbearing manner had caused a certain amount of dissatisfaction. But the discovery that the firm execution of the laws pertaining to debt could harm even those who had been most insistent in demanding such firmness caused even more. In Smith's capable hands it was soon demonstrated that Spanish law, properly administered, could help and not necessarily hinder the recovery of debt. Surprisingly enough, this led to a totally unexpected clamour against his administration.

The fact was that if Spanish law shielded the debtor against the creditor, debtors and creditors were no longer to be found in the exclusive compart-ments to which they had once belonged. Debtors were no longer only, or

36. C.O. 295/22, Hislop : Castlereagh, 4.10.1809, No. 77. Return of Offices.
37. C.O. 295/25, George Adderley : Jenkinson, 6.7.1810, enclosing Newman : Adderley, 15.4.1810. Also, C.O. 295/21, Hislop : Castlereagh, 30.5.1809, No. 63, enclosing Smith : Hislop, 29.5.1809; and C.O. 295/22, Hislop : Castlereagh, 21.11.1809, No. 78, enclosing Smith : Hislop, 20.11.1809 where Smith makes the same point. See also, C.O. 296/4, Castlereagh : Hislop, 26.9.1809, No. 14, and C.O. 296/4, Liverpool : Hislop, 22.12.1809 for ministerial queries respecting the decreased revenues of the provost marshal's office.
38. C.O. 295/25, George Adderley : Jenkinson, 6.7.1810, enclosing Newman : Adderley, 15.4.1810.
39. C.O. 295/22, Perceval : Liverpool (Memorandum), 13.12.1809, enclosing Adderley : Perceval, 11.12.1809.
40. C.O. 295/24, Gloster : Liverpool, 21.5.1810, and enclosures.
41. C.O. 295/22, Smith : Cooke, 28.10.1809.   42. *Ibid.*

mainly planters. Between 1802 and 1809 there had been some significant changes in the patterns of property ownership. Several local merchants had invested in plantations, and had been as unscrupulous in their evasion of their creditors as the planters had reputedly always been. Some merchants, agents of overseas firms, had collected debts on behalf of those firms and, while continuing to represent that Spanish law prevented the recovery of the debt, had quietly turned the proceeds to their own ends. A confused system of laws, improperly and even corruptly administered, had created the conditions in which deceit and sharp practices thrived. The community had learned to live with its sins and, as Smith said, the new dispensation obviously did "not suit a number of persons . . . who themselves never possessed a shilling of property, and are now rioting in the spoils of their deceased friends whose families or heirs they have plundered of the property they ought to have protected. The Spanish law is singularly efficacious against such gentry, who certainly do not feel quite at ease while it is not only in force *but enforced*".[43]

A singular efficiency in dispensing justice was matched by a characteristically individual approach to the Chief Justice's relations with the community. Convinced that every effort would be made to influence his legal decisions, Smith completely isolated himself from his environment:

". . .like the General who destroys the roads to prevent the approach of the enemy's artillery I determined to adopt for my guide the (precaution) against Influence provided by the Spanish Law, which forbids any intimacy between the Judge and the Community. I gave public notice that the prevailing practice of private applications to the judge if attempted with me would be considered as a personal insult. This notice was once disregarded and I turned the party down stairs. The offence has not been repeated. I occasionally receive at my own table the principal members of the Community but I accept myself no invitations but those of the Governor".[44]

Such a rule of conduct, inflexibly observed by Smith, had already brought him into conflict with the *Cabildo* whose members took offence at his rough handling of one of the *alcaldes*.[45] Smith, however, was not disturbed. He took every care to confine his actions within the limits of the authority conferred on him, never exerting his authority, as he himself said, "without the law in my hand to support it"; but within those limits he was inexorable. A few months after assuming office he was

"at high war with the two Brothers Glosters (sic) the Attorney General & the Deputy Register. They have both estates at a dis-

43. C.O. 295/22, Smith : Cooke, 28.10.1809.
44. C.O. 295/22, Smith : Cooke, 28.10.1809. For a discussion of the principle involved here see, Parry, *The Audiencia of New Galicia in the Sixteenth Century*, p. 153. Also, *Récopilación*, Lib. 2, Tit. 16, Leyes. 52, 55, 82.
45. C.O. 295/22, Smith : Cooke, 28.10.1809.

tance from town, which in the case of the Atty. Genl. is directly Contrary to law, & from their repeated absences the public business in many instances stand still. They say they have no notion of being obliged like schoolboys to ask leave of absence & I insist that a public officer shall not under me postpone the business of the public for his private affairs".[46]

It seems, too, that the alienation of the legal and judicial officers and the Chief Justice's own isolation were already beginning to affect the administration of justice. Smith was plainly not receiving the assistance to which he was entitled. Among the court officials there was a general laxity in executing his orders and sentences. The Chief Justice was driven to complain of the "slavery" of his situation which had become unbearable, not because of the burdens incidental to it, but because

"I am so miserably supported by those who are about me, that if I am compelled to pass sentence of death I shall be obliged to be my own Jack Ketch. The only two warrants I ever issued about which I was at all anxious the Provost Marshal let both parties escape; more or less thus it is in every thing".[47]

As far as support of the judiciary was concerned the crucial relationship was that between the Chief Justice and the Governor. Wide as his powers were Smith, in the last resort, could only exercise them with the Governor's willing assistance, and this was not forthcoming. Smith, whose misfortune it was completely to misread Hislop's motives, explained the deficiency in terms of the Governor's weakness, a fault which was entirely of Smith's own imagining. Hislop, he said, was much too kind a man to bring to heel the "weak and tremulous creature who holds the Police department." What was needed was a "peremptory hint" from home.

"A hint from you," he counselled, "would set all right, because I know the consequences would be that he (the Governor) would either consult with me & depute me to manage the Police & as I care not one pinch of snuff for the opinion of any one here & look for no better reward than to obtain your approbation by doing credit to your appointment of me I wd (sic) take care that the laws are enforced & that we had a better police here than in any other English Island."[48]

Contrary to Smith's beliefs the Governor's attitude was not a passing phase nor was it for that matter the result of "weakness" or indecision. Even two years earlier Smith would have found Governor Hislop a willing accomplice in whatever acts of coercion he wished to indulge, provided of course that they could have agreed on the choice of a victim. In 1809, however,

46. C.O. 295/22, Smith : Cooke, 28.10.1809.

47. C.O. 295/22, Same to same, same date.

48. C.O. 295/22, Smith : Castlereagh (Private), 4.10.1809.

the attitudes of both men were conditioned by the manner in which each viewed the agitation for British laws which was once more gaining momentum. Smith was convinced that the continued agitation of the constitutional question was factious and unnecessary, and that as far as public order was concerned the British party harboured the greatest offenders against the law. Hislop on the other hand had ceased to regard the British party with an automatic abhorrence, and Smith's pleas for firmness in the government fell upon deaf ears.

* * *

Smith's appointment as Chief Justice with the powers of *Audiencia, oidor, fiscal,* and *alcalde del crimen,* with instructions to enforce Spanish law had, in fact, fortified the determination of the British party to be rid of that law for ever. The British party of 1809 and 1810 was not, however, the much maligned and abused merchant party of 1802 to 1808. From the time of the cession up till 1808, as we have seen, the protagonists of the Assembly system had had much the worse of an encounter confined, in its bitterest stages, to two groups struggling for domination of the Island's government. Largely because of imperial indecision neither party had triumphed. The same indecision, however, had had the effect of narrowing the gap between the factions. Plagued with financial worry and the difficulties of government, the official party had mollified its previously intransigent stand against the Assembly system. The idea of a colonial Assembly, if not yet acceptable to all, no longer evoked the intense hostility of bygone years.

Paradoxically, at the very moment when official opinion in the Island had reconciled itself to the growing prospect of representative government and a possible shift in the political balance, the British government had initiated an experiment equally reprehensible to both parties. The Smith experiment found favour with none of the main contestants. It substantially decreased the power and prestige of the incumbent officials without increasing the influence of their opponents. Victory for either side became at once equally remote and, in the light of later events, the significant contribution of the Smith experiment was the unification of the erstwhile contestants for political power.

In 1809, however, the movement for British laws was not yet a popular movement, nor did it, as it later did, yet enjoy the unstinting support of the Governor or of the foreign members of the community. Overt advocacy of British laws was still confined to the British party, the organization of which was still in the hands of the few whose names had been associated with it since 1802; the main difference was that the party now operated in a generally more receptive atmosphere. At the top, leadership was shared by John Sanderson, Dr. Alexander Williams, and George Knox described by Smith, during Sanderson's absence in England, as "The Captain General of the Insurrection".[49]

49.   C.O. 295/22, Smith : Castlereagh (Private), 4.10.1809.

CHAPTER 8

In London itself, there was the old firm of Marryat, Inglis and Lushington. For these diehards the Smith experiment was a brief interlude in the progress towards representative government. On May 4, while Smith was yet at sea on his way to the Island, Inglis met with Lord Castlereagh in London. They discussed the Island's constitution and Inglis flourished a draft of a bill containing the outlines of a British constitution. Castlereagh, it seems, was somewhat impressed, but he declined to act until he had heard from Smith who was expected to report on the Island's government.[50]

In Trinidad itself what was to be the most impressive demand for British laws so far began to take shape in August 1809. A meeting convened at the home of Dr. Alexander Williams on the twenty-sixth of that month passed a number of resolutions on the subject of a British constitution.[51] An Address was voted to the King and every precaution was taken to represent this latest prayer for a British constitution as the desire of British born and adopted subjects alike. The subscribers requested a constitution making no distinction as to privileges on any ground whether national or religious,[52] and expressed the view that the implementation of British laws should be without prejudice to any past agreements or contracts made under the sanction of Spanish law.[53] It was also decided that a committee of twenty persons comprising equal numbers of adopted and natural born subjects should be formed to promote the Address. Vacancies arising on the committee were to be filled on the same fifty-fifty basis. Meetings of the committee were to be valid if attended by seven members,[54] and George Knox was to be appointed the Island's emissary in London to promote the Address there.[55]

The Chief Justice who was well aware of these arrangements looked upon them with suspicion and disapproval. It was his belief that *"at present nothing is wanting to this Colony but more energy* in the administration of its Government".[56] The agitation for British laws and a British constitution he represented as the work of a small, least independent, and most insignificant part of the community.[57] He hoped that the movement would disintegrate in rivalry and confusion, and looked to the approaching arrival of

---

50. Sanderson, *An Appeal. . . .* , p. 90. Sanderson himself was later to state what was perhaps the extreme view of the constitutional problem. In a letter to Lord Liverpool of January 3, 1811, (C.O. 295/26) he expressed the view that since Trinidad was by cession "a part of the British Dominion the subjects are certainly entitled to be governed by the Laws of the Land. . . they are *British Subjects* to all intents and effects; and by no maxim in the British Constitution, to which they have sworn Allegiance, can they as *British* Subjects be governed by Spanish laws".

51. C.O. 295/22, Copy of a Circular dated 12.9.1809.

52. *Ibid.,* Second Resolution.   53. *Ibid.,* First Resolution.

54. *Ibid.,* Third Resolution. It is not, of course, unusual for a quorum to consist of roughly one-third of a constituted body. But in the absence of any stipulation of the required composition of the quorum itself it is clear that the leadership, which was all British, could have acted without the participation of any of the foreigners.

55. *Ibid.,* Fifth Resolution.

56. C.O. 295/22, Smith : Castlereagh (Private), 4.10.1809.

57. *Ibid.*

John Sanderson from London to produce a "perfect schism" over the prospective appointment of himself or Knox as the Island's representative abroad.

Smith's dire prognostications were unfulfilled. Sanderson arrived, the party did not disintegrate, and Knox, saddled by Smith with the sobriquet "Ambassador of the Malcontents", departed for England. Nevertheless there had been difficulties. Smith, who alone records the detailed events of these hectic days, claims that there were many defections at the meeting of August 28, and that several of the persons nominated to the Committee withdrew.[58] Of the twenty committeemen finally chosen only three, he said, could be described as being of independent means. The rest were "either distressed merchants or men indebted to the extent or beyond their means, or men *whose funds are not their own".*[59]

It was clear, however, that already the greatest threat to the British party was the growing hostility of the Chief Justice. As yet no public act of his had signified his disapproval. Now, on Knox's departure, he publicly announced his determination to prepare the Secretary of State for the emissary's arrival. And he wrote the Under-Secretary stating his decided opposition to the grant of an Assembly to the Island.

His objection for the time being rested on two grounds. The first was the need to protect the slave population from their masters. Thus he wrote,

"If you mean to ruin the Colony you will give us the British Constitution a form of Government, whose foundation resting on general liberty becomes an absolute caricature in a community, where four fifths of the whole population are slaves; and in which of course the rights of humanity can only be guarded by an executive government holding over the master an authority bearing some proportion to that which he claims over his slave, and the want of which in the other English Colonies is the true cause why in those colonies the slaves are treated with less humanity than those of France and Spain. And I will venture to predict, from the peculiar circumstances of this Colony that here such a form of Government would become the worst of those caricatures by casting the authority of resisting the Executive into the worst hands".[60]

The second ground of opposition was that the grant of an Assembly would deter foreigners from migrating to the Island. In Smith's view few immigrants could in future be expected from the old British islands. But the unsettled state of the French and Spanish colonies could yet induce many of their inhabitants to settle in the Island. To such persons, a colonial Assembly would seem to be a means of their oppression, and only "imperious necessity" would induce them to take refuge in the Colony under a British constitution.[61]

58. C.O. 295/22, Smith : Cooke, 28.10.1809.

59. *Ibid.*

60. C.O. 295/22, Smith : Cooke, 28.10.1809.

61. C.O. 295/22, Smith : Cooke, 28.10.1809.

CHAPTER 8

Compared with the Chief Justice's attitude, Hislop's can be described as oscillating somewhere between a slightly amused tolerance and a determination not to become personally involved in the proceedings. But he was equally determined not to prohibit the various meetings, subscriptions and public discussions with which the British party sought to keep the constitutional issue alive. Smith, on the other hand was all for repression, and his wish for a firmer police was conditioned as much by a desire to contain the British party as by a longing to improve the general efficiency with which justice was administered.

January 1810 witnessed a decisive change in the Island's affairs. Governor Hislop, summoned by the commander of the forces to aid in the reduction of Guadeloupe, was temporarily succeeded by Lieutenant Colonel Henry Tolley.[62] Hislop's departure corresponded with a sudden sharpening in the controversy over a British constitution, and in the Governor's successor Judge Smith found an easy convert to the principle of firmer government. The change in administration corresponded, too, with a despatch from the Secretary of State on the Island's constitution.[63] Representations had been received on the question in London, and though there was yet no intention of acquiescing in the demand for a British constitution, the Secretary of State was anxious that causes of discontent should be eliminated by making the existing system as perfect as possible. To this end it was suggested that the police be reorganized in order that the judiciary should be made more effective.

The new directive merely served to intensify the process of reorganization which was already well in train. The acting Governor and the Chief Justice embarked on a series of regular visits to the jail, sometimes releasing prisoners who, in their opinion, had been unnecessarily confined. Licences on the retailing of spirits were increased, as were the fines payable on infringement of the regulations.[64] The *Cabildo* was enjoined to keep proper financial accounts, and an attempt was made by the Chief Justice to curtail the jurisdiction of the *alcaldes*. The *alcaldes* were instructed to take cognisance only of cases originating in Port of Spain. Outside Port of Spain, in St. Joseph and the rural districts, the commandants of quarters were to exercise an ordinary jurisdiction in cases formerly dealt with by the *alcaldes*.[65]

The Council, too, came in for scrutiny. A radical change in its membership was suggested. It should be enlarged, said the Chief Justice, to a total membership of not less than nine nor more than twelve. Some of the existing members should be retired and the foreigners should be given a more adequate representation. The Spaniards in particular had been neglected in the past. Yet, Smith argued, they were among the best of His Majesty's sub-

62. C.O. 295/23, Hislop : Liverpool, 9.1.1809, No. 8.
63. C.O. 296/4, pp. 362-3, Liverpool : Hislop, 20.1.1810.
64. C.O. 295/23, Tolley : Liverpool, 7.3.1810, No. 5.
65. C.O. 295/24, Smith : Jenkinson (Private), 2.3.1810; and enclosures, particularly Appendix No. 1.

jects and should be suitably rewarded. In any case the Colony would never prosper until "it is apparent that it is governed by a *strong* and an impartial government which . . . . knows no distinction of nation". [66]

In pursuit of his objective of infusing the Island's government with permanent vigour the Chief Justice suggested that the commission of civil Governor should be temporarily added to his other appointments.

"To govern this Colony", he wrote, "requires a firmness very different from military courage. It requires a firmness in the exercise of a coercive system which while it avoids all acts of cruelty is not to be deterred by the clamours of a faction or by the fear of unpopularity from necessary acts of vigour nor appalled. . . by threats of prosecution in the court of king's bench. It requires that the Governor should separate himself from all intimate connections in the Colony by which alone he can escape from involving himself in a party or becoming the tool and the dupe of men for whose cunning his probity will be no match." [67]

Smith, in his own opinion, possessed all the qualities necessary to undertake the burdens of governorship.

While Hislop was abroad, however, and the administration remained in Tolley's hands, the Chief Justice found no cause for complaint. The continued agitation of the constitutional question attracted the very special attention of both officials. The foreigners had taken fright at the activities of the British party, and the *Cabildo,* in an Address of February 15, had urged that no decision should be taken on the Island's government until the sense of the community had been carefully ascertained. [68] The Council, on a motion by the Chief Justice himself, had expressed similar sentiments. [69] As a result, and because of the growing warmth attending the constitutional debate, the acting Governor prohibited all public discussion of the subject. The newspapers were instructed to desist from printing all letters, articles or editorials pertaining to the subject. One editor decided not to publish anything at all. The other, Matthew Gallagher, editor of the *Trinidad Weekly Courant and Commercial Gazette,* continued to publish in defiance of the ban and was jailed as a result. [70]

All this time Smith was pursuing a very high-powered discussion with the Secretary of State on the Island's government. It was largely due to this that, though he lost all the immediately ensuing battles, he was destined in the end to win the war. Perhaps the most persuasive of his many despatches

66. C.O. 295/24, Smith : Jenkinson (Private), 2.3.1810; and enclosures, particularly Appendix No. 1.
67. C.O. 295/24, Smith : Jenkinson (Private), 2.3.1810.
68. C.O. 295/23, Tolley : Liverpool, 15.2.1810, No. 2.
69. C.O. 295/23, Tolley : Liverpool, 15.2.1810, No. 4. See also, C.O. 298/4, Meeting of 15.2.1810. Of the seven members present at the meeting only one, John Nugent, dissented.
70. C.O. 295/23, Tolley : Liverpool, 7.3.1810, No. 5. Also, C.O. 295/24, Tolley and Smith : Liverpool, 28.2.1810; and C.O. 295/24, Smith : Jenkinson (Private), 16.5.1810, and an enclosed pamphlet entitled *Letters and Documents relative to the Imprisonment and Discharge of Matthew Gallagher. . .*

was that written to Lord Liverpool on February 14.[71] It was written at the time when, both in London and in Trinidad, the tide of constitutional agitation was beginning to flow most strongly. In London, at a meeting of West Indian merchants and planters held on February 8, it had been decided to petition the House of Commons for a British constitution for Trinidad. A Committee consisting of Messrs. Inglis, Manning, Marryat and Lushington had been appointed to carry the meeting's resolutions into effect, and to press for an early meeting with the Secretary of State.[72] In Trinidad, the British party, undaunted by the ban on public discussion, was busily circulating an Address and soliciting signatures for a renewed petition for a British constitution.

Smith's despatch of February 14 falls naturally into three parts. The first part is a general statement of his views on the inapplicability of representative government to the British West Indies taken as a whole. His views, he said, were formed long before coming to Trinidad, but what he had observed since his arrival had reinforced his determination to oppose the extension of the Assembly system to the Colony. This he had decided for two reasons. The representative system, he said, was "incompatible with the vital principle of colonial existence". Also, it was incompatible with the stage of physical, moral or intellectual development so far achieved in the West Indies.

"The vital principle of Colonial Existence," he wrote, "is Slavery in which State are to be found five Sixths of the Inhabitants of every Colony. Freedom is an exception in favour of two thirds of the remaining sixth and Liberty, as we understand it, a privilege only attaching to the remainder. Such is the picture of our Population, 5/6 Slaves, 2/3 of the remaining sixth free people of Color in a state of degradation & the remainder free White Inhabitants, reducing the latter description to about one eighteenth of the whole population and after deducting the number of women and children leaving the adult male population of free white Inhabitants not more than one thirtieth part of the whole.

"The general principle of the British Constitution is Liberty to all who live under it; and the object of all its regulations is to secure to all alike the benefit of that general principle . . . . . The House of Commons in England represents the whole people and has but one common interest with its constituents. A Colonial Assembly represents only a very small part of the Inhabitants whose feelings and interests are in direct opposition to the feelings and interest of the remainder; and it is owing to this vital, this irremediable defect in the legislative body of the English Colonies that our slaves are proverbially worse treated than in other Colonies.

71. C.O. 295/24, Smith : Liverpool, 15.2.1810.
72. C.O. 295/24, Inglis : Jenkinson, 16.2.1810.

"In the present circumstances, of our Colonies, deprived by the Abolition of the Slave Trade of all resources for encreasing the number of their labourers save that of encreasing by their own population, Policy not less than Humanity calls aloud for such a system of Government as may insure to this class of human creatures that protection which is essential to their encrease, a practical not a nominal protection: This protection can only be afforded by an authority over which the Master of the Slave has no control and to which he must submit; & certainly he who claims himself a right over his fellow creatures not merely repugnant but in direct opposition to every principle of the British Constitution has no ground in reason or justice for complaint if his exercise of such a right is at least overlooked by an authority which tho' it may be in extent unknown to our Constitution is not more so than the principle on which he holds his own power over his slave. . . and let it be further recollected that these clamorous advocates for the introduction of British Laws while they call for so much as suits their own purpose as loudly resist the admission of any principle favorable to the rest of the community."

The representative system, he continued, was also inapplicable to the West Indies because Britain lacked the physical strength to enforce its principles, and the West Indians lacked the moral and intellectual fibre to obey them. As long as the representative system existed Britain could do little to effect the impartial administration of justice, and in the West Indies, interest and connection, the "laxity of morals & the general absence of education" made the English constitution in such hands nothing but the instrument of injustice and oppression.[73]

Adverting to the specific difficulties attendant on the introduction of an Assembly into Trinidad, Smith referred to the language problem. Ignorance of English would operate as an automatic disqualification of most foreigners, or else a "confusion of tongues" will be admitted in the legislature and the jury box which must impede the proper functioning of both.

The preponderance of foreign economic interest in the Island was another problem. The foreigners would be very dissatisfied with any system of government that conceded the reality of political power to the British

73. For comparison see Lord Brougham's statement on the extension of English law to the West Indies, made in the House of Commons in 1811. *Parliamentary Debates*, Vol. XX, pp. 615-6. Brougham was generally sympathetic to Smith and argued that the Spanish slave code was more humane than the British, and that a change at the time that Smith was appointed could hardly have been for the better. And so he argued that: "When we talked of English law, we talked of it by reference to English judges, to English juries, and to English feelings and principles. . . . It was a mockery to talk of transplanting the English law to the West Indies when only the name was carried thither, and all the true English feeling was left behind. Then the law of England served only as the engine of fraud and oppression, rendered doubly disgraceful, because carried on under the pretence of law and justice. This was under the pretence of justice to the whites, to load the other miserable wretches with oppression unbounded. . . . to substitute oppression and injustice for benevolence. The British constitution was to be found in no other part of the world but in this country."

citizens. An analysis of the economic wealth of the British and the foreign sections of the society[74] led the Chief Justice to the conclusion that the British interest in anything else but coffee "is nothing, and in that article they grow about one fifth of the whole crop. The French & Spaniards grow all the Cocoa and the French and colored People grow all the cotton. So that it appears that in the sugar cultivation the foreigners with less *Capital* and less *strength* than the English produce more sugar and are almost exclusively the promoters of all the other articles cultivated by the Colony".[75]

Lastly, Smith reaffirmed his faith in the propriety of the existing Spanish system. The merchant, he said, might well bemoan the absence of English law which in the other British colonies had operated to bring "irredeemably within his grasp" half the property of those Islands. But the Spanish law was of inestimable value to the long term prosperity of the Colony. By lessening the planter's credit it forced him into habits of frugality and independence, diminished the temptation to extravagance and promoted the general economic well-being. The English law, by facilitating credit, fed the planter's "natural habits of expence" and tended eventually to convert his estate "once the residence of an opulent and respectable proprietor into a mere sugar farm worked by the overseer of a London Merchant for the benefit of his absent master".[76] And once again calling attention to the injustice inseparable from a system of laws under which "planters act as the judges & soldiers as the Chancellors", Smith concluded that "the Spanish Code . . . is more practically calculated than our own for the narrow limits of a Colony".[77]

All Smith's arguments had been designed to prompt the Secretary of State into making a swift and authoritative pronouncement scotching once

74. A precis of Smith's analysis shows that: 92 sugar estates and 25 coffee estates, cultivated by 7,210 slaves were in English possession. 154 sugar estates, 167 coffee, and 78 cocoa estates, cultivated by 8,600 slaves were owned by foreigners. Production on the English sugar estates, slave population 6,877, equalled 12,927,573 lbs. On foreign sugar estates, number 154 and employing 6,342 slaves, production totalled 13,023,355 lbs. So that foreign production amounted to 95,782 lbs. more though 535 slaves less were employed. On the other hand the English estates were, on average, larger than foreign ones. Cotton production was almost exclusively in the hands of small French proprietors and people of colour, with 246 cotton estates employing 2,492 slaves. Smith also estimated that inclusive of cotton estates and town Negroes, foreigners and people of colour controlled 13,592 slaves as against 8,390 controlled by the British. According to these figures it would seem that though foreigner and free coloured ownership out-stripped British ownership, Englishmen were, on average, proprietors of larger holdings than their foreign and free coloured counterparts. The political significance of this would have been, if one takes Picton's dictum of 60 slaves and 200 acres as the criterion of political participation, and excludes the operation of other considerations, that an Assembly elected on this or a higher property franchise would have been dominated by Englishmen. See also, C.O. 295/23, Hislop : Liverpool, 16.4.1810, No. 15.
75. C.O. 295/24, Smith : Liverpool, 14.2.1810.
76. *Ibid.* See also, C.O. 295/27. A copy of a petition from *"Les Nouveaux Sujets de Votre Majesté"*, the original of which is in C.O. 295/24, Hislop : Liverpool (Private), 12.10.1810. George Knox, commenting on the petition (p. 5) virtually concedes Smith's point. He describes the English planter in the old islands as obtaining advances on mortgage "until he almost sinks into the Manager of the Merchant".
77. C.O. 295/24, Smith : Liverpool, 14.2.1810.

and for all the belief that the grant of a British constitution was still negotiable, and could be obtained if sufficient pressure were exerted. Long before the Secretary of State had decided on such a pronouncement, however,
and indeed before he could have properly digested Smith's most recent
despatches, events in the Island took a decisive turn.

Hislop returned to the government on March 21 after an absence of about
two months.[78]   While at Guadeloupe reports had reached him of the progress of affairs in the Island and of what he was later to describe as the
considerable agitation among the populace in consequence of "Certain
Measures Adopted by the Executive Government".[79]   His return effectively
put a stop to the firmness with which Tolley and Smith had administered the
Island during his absence, and an effusive and emotional welcome by the
inhabitants set the stage for the very momentous events that were to follow.

Under pretext of welcoming the Governor back to his administration, an
Address was voted requesting once again the grant of a British Constitution.[80]   In comparison with previous Addresses on the subject, this one was
by far the most representative. Much could of course be said in criticism of
it, and much was said, particularly by Smith, who, while associating himself
with the general sentiments expressed on Hislop's safe return, was intensely
critical of the Address and the manner in which it had been subscribed.[81]
Many of the persons who signed had done so, as Smith said, in the belief that
they were merely signifying their satisfaction at the Governor's return. They
had had no wish to petition for British laws, but neither had they wished to
offend by refusing to sign what they believed to be primarily an Address of
welcome. Others had been persuaded to sign who "however respectable in
their humble or even menial stations, are as improperly placed in regard to
the political part of the address as would be the villagers Shopkeepers Shop-
man in one of a similar tendency presented by the freeholders of an English
County to our Sovereign. . . . .".[82]

It was indeed quite clear that the Address was the product of cunning
and artifice as well as of solicitude and relief at the Governor's safe return.
As its date shows it had been prepared for some time; it was far from being a
spontaneous effusion of loyal sentiments. And by combining sentiments of
welcome with the prayer for a British constitution, it had drawn much wider
support than it otherwise might have done. The other effect of the device
was to implicate the Governor himself in the petition. Addresses had
previously been directed to the King or to Parliament. This one was not; it

78. C.O. 295/23, Hislop : Liverpool, 21.3.1810, No. 9.
79. C.O. 295/23, Hislop : Liverpool, 9.4.1810, No. 10.
80. C.O. 295/23, *Address to His Excellency Major General Thomas Hislop etc.,* dated 21.2.1810.
81. C.O. 295/24, Smith : (Jenkinson), 16.4.1810, enclosing Smith : Hislop, 30.3.1810; and C.O. 295/24,
    Smith : Jenkinson, 13.5.1810. Also, C.O. 298/4, Minute of Council, 24.3.1810. Addresses were
    voted to the Governor by the *Cabildo* and the Council. These were limited to welcome only, and the
    Council Address was read in the chamber by the Chief Justice.
82. C.O. 295/24, Smith : (Jenkinson), 16.4.1810; enclosing Smith : Hislop, 30.3.1810.

was a direct appeal to the Governor in circumstances that disposed him to a favourable response. The ruse was eminently successful. The Governor, flattered by the profusion of his welcome, became the most distinguished recruit to the movement for British laws. Henceforward he was, by reasons of his position, to be its automatic leader.

Even after admitting the employment of manoeuvre and finesse in the preparation and presentation of the Address, it must be conceded that a significant change in public opinion had been registered. Of the four hundred and fifty one subscribers, about one-third were foreigners drawn from the most respectable sections of the French and Spanish populations. Foreign participation in what had hitherto been primarily a British effort was significant. So too, of course, was the number of the petitioners. Artifice apart - and some persons signed in their own right as individuals and then as partners of commercial houses - four hundred and fifty one was an impressive figure, nearly double the subscribers to the 1805 petition, the largest till then.[83]

Several explanations suggest themselves. Of these, dissatisfaction with the Spanish system as then administered, and in particular with the Chief Justice himself, was of prime importance. The Address had in fact specifically referred to the duress under which the inhabitants had laboured since Hislop's departure. The subscribers had "fondly" anticipated a return to "that Harmony and Confidence, which heretofore existed under your benign Auspices".[84] Indeed, if the subscribers had anything approaching a common plank underwriting their demand for British laws, it was their opposition to Smith. It was this that probably accounted for the large number of public officials who signed the Petition,[85] though, as with everyone else, it is difficult to ascertain whether they acted out of courtesy to the Governor or from a desire for a British constitution.

The dogged determination of the British party must also be recognized. It was partly responsible for the exasperation which was a potent conditioning influence among the foreigners. Disgusted with the continued agitation of the constitutional question the foreigners, after long years of resistance, were willing to capitulate merely in order to end the whole affair.[86] Besides, though they were well aware of the partisan objectives of the British in desiring an Assembly, time had mollified their objections to the system. Among the foreigners too were many refugees who had fled from the revolutions that had convulsed the islands to the north and east. They set a high price on security and social stability. The Spanish American mainland

83. Two hundred and twenty nine subscribers.   84. C.O. 295/23, Address of 1810, preamble.

85. These were mainly the subordinate public officials. Only one member of the Council, John Nugent, signed. Some, though not all, members of the *Cabildo* signed. For members of these two bodies it was easier to avoid the charge of discourtesy to the Governor if they did not associate themselves with the Address since both bodies presented separate Addresses of welcome. At any rate, as we shall see, the Council and the Cabildo were by no means yet converted on the constitutional question.

86. See Petition from *"Les Nouveaux Sujets de Votre Majeste"*, C.O. 295/24, enclosure in Hislop : Liverpool (Private), 12.10.1810.

was even then witnessing the struggle that was to end with the independence of the Spanish colonies. Looking at the revolutions taking place on the neighbouring continent, Trinidad's foreign population conceived that Trinidad could only be saved from similar upheavals by uniting on the constitutional question and thus eliminating the risks involved in the continued public discussion of political subjects. [87]

Hislop's own conversion is easily explained in terms of the developing conflict between himself and Smith. Even so it was clear, even before Smith's arrival in the Island, that the Governor was slowly moving towards an accommodation with the British party. There is little doubt that among the British community the idea of an Assembly still had a wide popular appeal. It was a much more appealing vision than that of a legislative Council. And the Governor, living in conditions of continued intimacy with some of the chiefest proponents of the idea, men like Samuel Span now resident in Trinidad and John Nugent, surrendered to its blandishments. In 1810, Hislop had been Governor for six years. Few West Indian Governors were ever able to hold out for prolonged periods against the insistent pressures of local interest. Capitulation nearly always ensued. But capitulation could be sullen and grudging as with Balcarres in Jamaica in 1799,[88] or it could be an active and convinced acquiescence in an entirely new line of action. Hislop's was the latter.

In recommending the Address of February 1810 the Governor stressed four points. He said that the assurances frequently given of a constitution for the Island had kept alive the inhabitants' expectations. Secondly, circumstances had combined to make a British constitution the one form of government most acceptable to the colonists. Besides it was the only constitution that would have the effect of removing "those existing jealousies, which the English part of the Community Cannot divest themselves of and which I believe the foreign proportion is in general desirous of seeing effaced". [89] Thirdly, he could conceive of no time more suitable than the present at which the change should be made. Future years would witness no significant change in the national composition of the population and, from this point of view, the Island was as ready for a change from Spanish to English laws as it ever would be. Lastly, he did not think the community could stand the stresses and strains incidental to another prolonged period of uncertainty on the constitution.[90]

As has already been indicated, the Council and the *Cabildo* carefully avoided a premature commitment to the renewed appeal for British laws. As usual they played their careful calculating game and waited to see the Governor's reaction to the Address. Once it was plain that he intended a favourable reply, it was only a matter of time before the Council and the *Cabildo* made

87. *Ibid.*   88. See above, pp. 94 ff
89. C.O. 295/23, Hislop : Liverpool, 9.4.1810, No. 10.
90. C.O. 295/23, Hislop : Liverpool, 9.4.1810, No. 10. Also, C.O. 295/23, Hislop : Liverpool, 16.4.1810, No. 12.

the necessary adjustments. The Council, having on February 15, on Judge Smith's motion, petitioned that constitutional change should be preceded by the most minute examination of the "sense of the community", expressed the view on April 11, that the Address had provided a sufficient indication of the "real sentiments and wishes of the inhabitants".[91] This view was further reinforced by a formal Address of the Council at a meeting of May 18 asking His Majesty to grant the Island "a change of laws and systems with such modifications as local circumstances may require".[92] George Smith, whose ability to influence the Council had drastically declined since the Governor's return, protested in the most vehement terms. He denied that any evidence existed to warrant the change in the Council's attitude. If the change had been occasioned by the recent Address to the Governor, it was his duty to observe that of the four hundred and fifty-one subscribers to that Address "more than two Hundred and fifty from their station in the Community have no right to interfere in any political question", and one half of the remainder had been duped into signing a political Address which it had not been their intention to support.[93] Nevertheless Smith's was a lone dissenting voice. Moreover the *Cabildo* soon gave its own support and, like the Council, became henceforth a willing participant in the measures subsequently adopted to further the aims of the constitutionalists.

The latest secretarial despatch arrived just in time to confer a spurious authority on the fevered activity then taking place in the Island. Writing on March 15, Lord Liverpool had referred to the recent meetings and discussions with the West India planters and merchants on the subject of Trinidad's constitution. He pronounced himself still very much reluctant to concede the demand for an Assembly for the Island, but indicated that he was willing to consider the views of the Governor and other informed persons on the subject.[94] To the Governor and the British party this was a godsend. Given the state of opinion in the Island such an invitation could have only one result.

The Secretary of State did not, of course, know of the Governor's conversion to the constitutional camp; his despatch had in fact been written before this event had taken place. Yet, thanks to Smith, he had had some

---

91. C.O. 298/4, Minutes of Council, 11.4.1810. This motion was moved by John Smith, no relation to the Chief Justice, and seconded by Archibald Gloster. George Smith and St. Hilaire Begorrat dissented.

92. C.O. 298/4, Minutes of Council, 18.5.1810.

93. C.O. 298/4, Minutes of Council, 18.5.1810. Begorrat also dissented on this occasion because he felt, as Smith did, that the sense of the community had not been properly ascertained. However, he acquiesced in the introduction of British laws subject "to such modifications as are essential to the local state and circumstances of the Colony". There is every reason to believe that Smith and Begorrat were right. The motion of February 15 had been motivated by the actions of the British party who were then collecting signatures for the very Address which was now held to be proof of the prevailing desire for British laws. On the other hand, the Council, nothing if not subservient, might well have assented to the motion only because of Tolley's and Smith's support for it.

94. C.O. 296/4, pp. 364-5, Liverpool : Hislop, 15.3.1810, No. 5.

intimation of the likelihood of such a development; the Governor's conciliatory attitude to the agitators had been the subject of frequent comment by
the Chief Justice. From this point of view Liverpool's invitation was certainly
inept. James Stephen, a close personal friend of Spencer Perceval the Prime
Minister, and an official adviser on Trinidad's affairs, was severely critical.
"The Governor and Council of Trinidad," he observed bitterly, "are to be
consulted on or rather desired to furnish a plan of constitution and laws by
which the statesmen of every Party, successive Administrations and parliament stand solemnly pledged before God and man to exclude the oppression
of the Old Sugar Colonies and the influx of slaves i.e. the very abuses
in which every one of these referrees is actually engaged". [95]

The despatch arrived in Trinidad just 'as the Council had reversed its
previous stand on the constitution; its contents were in fact intimated to
councillors at the very meeting of May 18.[96] And on the following day the
Governor wrote to the Secretary of State informing him that the councillors
had been invited to comment separately on Gloster's Bill of 1804 recommending a legislative Council. Their comments would, in due course, be forwarded.[97] The matter was not, therefore, to be discussed in Council. The
Chief Justice was to be given no opportunity for ribald public comment.

Hislop's purpose in flourishing this ancient recipe is obscure, unless it
was his intention to get a specific repudiation of it to bolster the Island's
claims to an Assembly. The promised comments were never presented nor
transmitted. Two comments were made, one by Smith who thought that
Gloster's plans for a legislative Council were as ill-advised as the constant
clamours for an Assembly.

"The materials of such a legislature as he (Gloster) proposes",
wrote Smith, "are as difficult to find as the materials for an
Assembly unless he is content to place the legislative authority
solely in the hands of the Foreigners. We have but one Independent
Planter among the English in the Colony. The rest are over head
and ears in debt." [98]

And Gloster, torn between his new-found allegiance to a British constitution
and loyalty to his Bill of 1804, opted for the latter on the ground that a
colonial Assembly was "not much encouraged in his Majesty's Cabinet", nor
was it a safe undertaking for a colony like Trinidad in a time of war. [99]

The Secretary of State had requested the Governor's views on the constitutional question. He had also suggested that, if the Governor thought
proper, reference should be made to "the members of the Council either

95. David Murray, *op. cit.,* p. 78, Stephen : Perceval, 19.4.1810. Quoted.
96. C.O. 298/4, Minutes of 18.5.1810.
97. C.O. 295/23, Hislop : Liverpool, 19.5.1810, No. 19. This was probably a snap decision. At the
meeting the previous day Hislop had suggested that the Liverpool despatch could be discussed at the
next Council meeting. This meeting occurred on June 20 when no such discussion took place.
98. C.O. 295/25, Smith : Chapman (Private), 8.7.1810.
99. C.O. 295/25, Smith : Chapman (Private), 8.7.1810, enclosure, Gloster : Hislop, no date, but about
June 1810 according to Smith.

collectively or individually".[100] In pursuit of this directive the Governor now embarked on the sounding of popular opinion on the subject. Circulars were sent out to the commandants of quarters instructing them to solicit the views of white males in their districts.[101] The returns showed 388 persons in favour of British laws, 24 favouring Spanish laws and 22 undecided; two persons consulted refused to give any opinion whatsoever.[102] Of the eighteen individuals signifying a wish for British laws in the quarter of Diego Martin, seven wished that substantial modifications suitable to local conditions should accompany the change.[103] Late returns transmitted to the Governor after the compilation of this first list boosted the number of white citizens in favour of British laws to 425, those in favour of Spanish laws to 25, with 43 undecided and the number of blank refusals the same as before.[104]

Ignoring for the moment the impropriety of these investigations[105] the returns certainly did not provide the evidence of widespread support that the Governor had hoped. Not even the July figures showed a numerical support for British laws at least as large as the number of persons signing the Address to the Governor on his return. In addition a study of both sets of returns reveals that, in the two weeks elapsing between June 20 and July 8, several persons who had expressed themselves as being in favour of British laws had changed their minds[106] - in the circumstances an act indicative of even greater conviction than that displayed by signing.

The most telling indictment springs however from a comparison of these figures with those of the adult male population. Among whites there were 1,147 adult males in the Island,[107] which means that less than half of this number was actually consulted. The remainder could hardly all have belonged to the great unwashed. And if they did then the argument for an Assembly was so much the weaker. Nor could the discrepancy be explained solely on the basis of the physical difficulties of consultation in the country

100. C.O. 296/4, pp. 364-5, Liverpool : Hislop, 15.3.1810, No. 5. See also, C.O. 296/4, pp. 378-82, Jenkinson : Smith (Private), 13.3.1810.
101. A copy of the circular is enclosed in C.O. 295/23, Hislop : Liverpool, 8.7.1810, No. 27.
102. C.O. 298/4, Minutes of Council, 20.6.1810.   103. *Ibid.*, note.
104. C.O. 295/23, Hislop : Liverpool, 8.7.1810, No. 27.
105. Smith objected on two grounds both of which were undeniably true. Liverpool's despatch, he said, did not disclose a "wish that the *Populace* of Trinidad should at all be brought into the discussion". The Governor was in fact treating the constitutional issue as a popular question for the first time. All his arguments previous to this had centered on the opinions of the *respectable* members of the community. In his eagerness he forgot that in his day, even among whites, for political purposes some men were much more "equal" than others. Secondly, Smith protested on the ground that "the foreigners have very generally signed not from conviction but in compliment to the Governor & had Co. Tolley & myself conceived ourselves warranted in such a step, our known opinions would have probably induced an opposite signature, nearer perhaps to their real sentiments tho not deserving of much more attention". C.O. 295/25, Smith : Jenkinson, 10.7. 1810.
106. On the other hand it must be pointed out that the second list contained no returns from Toco, Cedros, Pointe a Pierre and Las Cuevas. The first three of these had together two persons in favour of British laws according to the June list. No figures were given for those against or undecided.
107. See C.O. 295/24. Return of Population for 1810.

districts. [108]   Port of Spain had a white adult male population of 526. The June figures show 201 in favour of British laws, the July figures 197; roughly 300 persons were never consulted.   How explain the discrepancy here, particularly when one considers that the British population was very heavily concentrated in Port of Spain and was the section of the population most in favour of British laws?   The impression remains that the surveys showed not only a substantial proportion of those consulted as being in favour of British laws, but also that some care was taken to produce this result.

Meanwhile, the Governor, acting for all the world like a politician with a mandate, instituted a public discussion of the type of Assembly the Island should have. A committee consisting of the Council, some of the members of the *Cabildo* and eight nominees of the Governor's was set up on July 10 under the chairmanship of John Nihell. [109]   Its function was solely to consider the constitutional problem and make recommendations for the Island's future government. To guide the Committee's deliberations two papers were submitted for its perusal. One of these was Gloster's 1804 Bill, which received scant attention and was perfunctorily dismissed in the last of seventeen clauses drawn up by the Committee, [110] and the other was a memorandum entitled "The Assembly" submitted by John Sanderson. It was around this latter document that discussion revolved for the three days from July 10 to July 12 during which the Committee sat.

During the debates on the form of the proposed Assembly, Sanderson's proposals were somewhat modified to accommodate the participation of the foreigners in the legislature. His proposal that an ability to speak and under stand the English language should be an "indispensable qualification" for membership [111] was thrown out; whereupon Sanderson, Samuel Span and Charles Harrison who formed the nucleus of the radicals entered a formal protest. Similarly, Sanderson's wish that English law should become the sole law of the land once the Assembly was introduced [112] was not granted. A

108. Some of the differences between the numbers of persons resident and the number of persons consulted in particular districts are quite large. For example, in La Brea, 33 white males, 14 for British laws, none against, none undecided; St. Joseph, 43 white males, 6 for British laws, 8 against, 3 undecided; South Naparima, 37 white males, 15 for, 1 against, none undecided; Santa Cruz, 28 total, 12 for, 3 against; Diego Martin, 41 total, 17 for, none against, none undecided.

109. C.O. 295/23, Hislop : Liverpool, 19.7.1810, No. 31, enclosure No. 2. There were eighteen members of the Committee. Fourteen actually took part in the discussions, three members of Council, Black, Begorrat and Nugent, and William Lockheed one of the nominated members being absent. Gloster was a surprising absentee, the more so because his absence was not explained. Those who attended during the three days of discussion were: John Nihell and John Smith of Council; Valantine Basanta, Samuel Span, James Cadett, Benjamin de Castellet and Joachim Aristumunio of the *Cabildo;* Charles Farrill, Dr. Alexander Williams, Matthew de Gannes, Mathew Herbert, John Sanderson, Patrick O'Brien, Antoine Portel, all nominated. Chief Justice Smith was, for a very special reason which we shall soon discuss, absent from all discussions. Of the members attending, seven were British and seven foreign born.

110. C.O. 295/23, Hislop : Liverpool, 19.7.1810, No. 31, enclosure No. 2, clause 17.
111. *Ibid.,* Enclosure No. 1.
112. *Ibid., Loc. cit.* See also, enclosure No. 2, clause 4.

complicated system was adopted whereby Spanish law would continue to be operative in a specified number of cases after the adoption of English law. [113] And Sanderson's demand that a distinction be made between foreigners and free coloureds resident at the conquest and those coming to the Island afterwards[114] was substantially modified. He had proposed that foreign whites and free coloureds who had immigrated after the conquest should be naturalized only by individual Acts of the Council and Assembly. Instead, the Committee decided that all whites whether British or foreign-born should enjoy equal status as citizens.[115] The free people of colour should continue to enjoy such rights as they possessed under the existing laws irrespective of origin.[116]

Even with these modifications it was clear that the new system of government would be weighted in favour of the British. Though the foreigners still were in the majority among the white population,[117] representation in the Assembly was to consist of equal numbers of British born and adopted subjects.[118] This was however to obtain only for the first election to the Assembly. Thereafter the Assembly would draw up its own rules for future elections and the electoral boundaries, based on the Island's twenty-eight quarters for the first election, would be re-defined.[119] Also, it was proposed that the senior member of the Council should, as President, administer the Island in the Governor's absence or death and that he should be British born. Should the senior member not be British, the office of President was to be entrusted to the senior British member of the Council.[120] Also, it was envisaged that the Protestant Church would be established.[121]

The foreigners were well aware that the proposals for an Assembly merely papered over the divisions between themselves and the British community until the day when the grant of representative government would set the

---

113. *Ibid.*, enclosure No. 2, clause 4.
114. *Ibid.*, enclosure No. 1, under the heading "Political Privildges" (sic). See also, Sanderson's *An Appeal. . .*, p. 128, and Dr. J.B. Phillip's *Address by a Mulatto*, pp. 11-2 in which Phillip criticises Sanderson's attempt to distinguish between the rights of the free coloureds according to whether they were resident at the conquest or not.
115. C.O. 295/23, *Ibid.*, enclosure No. 2, clause 2.
116. *Ibid., loc. cit.*, clause 13.
117. The Return of Population for 1810 (C.O. 295/24) showed 514 British males as against 633 foreign. In the total white population the figures were 1,177 foreign as against 968 British - apparently only a marginal difference. But, as George Smith pointed out (C.O. 295/24, Smith : Liverpool, 14.2.1810) the British population was inordinately increased by the expedient of classifying all children born since the conquest as British, a system with obvious deficiencies when the national composition of the population is, as in this case, relevant. Thus, the statistics show that 514 British men and 223 women had 231 children; 178 Spanish men and 156 women had 71 children; and 353 French men and 261 women had 42 children. In the coloured class the figures were even more contrary: 1,265 British adults had 1,778 children; 1,014 Spaniards, 344 children; and 1,411 French adults, 272 children - an amazing fecundity on the part of the British.
118. C.O. 295/23, Hislop : Liverpool, 19.7.1810, No. 31, enclosure No. 2, clause 3.
119. *Ibid.*, Clause 12.
120. *Ibid.*, Clause 8.
121. *Ibid.*, Clause 9.

struggle going in earnest. They were aware of the political, economic and social differences that still divided both communities, and therefore they carefully enunciated the minimum modifications of the Assembly system which were needed to safeguard their interests. They were above all dominated by the fear of economic exploitation and did everything possible to guard against it. In the Address from *"Les nouveaux subjects de Votre Majesté"* to which reference has already been made, they saw themselves as representing a predominantly agricultural interest centred in the countryside, opposed to a British mercantile interest largely concentrated in Port of Spain. [122] For this reason they argued that no assemblyman should be chosen to represent an electoral district in which he had not lived as a proprietor for at least two years; and he should be in possession of at least thirty slaves. In addition, no elector should be allowed to vote unless he fulfilled an equivalent residential qualification and possessed at least ten slaves. Thus, the agriculturists would be represented by men of their own class and the merchants of the towns and villages by merchants.

They wished also to obtain safeguards against the introduction of laws permitting the separation of slaves and moveable property from the soil. Here self-interest made common cause with humanity. The plantation proprietor would be protected against the exactions of his creditors which, in the old British Islands, greatly contributed to the break-up of sugar estates. And the slave would be protected in that partial seizures for debts contracted by the proprietor was one of the most frequent causes of the separation of slave families.

They wished also to be assured that all transactions under Spanish law would be regarded as valid and that no civil or criminal cases decided under sanction of those laws, or of appeals of such cases, could be reviewed under British law. For some time after the introduction of British law facilities for the hearing of appeals under Spanish law should be maintained; expensive perhaps, they said, but necessary. In addition an arbitration tribunal consisting of two planters, two merchants, and a president chosen in alternate years from each group should be set up. This tribunal should resolve without costs or fees all disputes arising between planters and merchants, and disputes should only be taken to court on the specific recommendation of the tribunal.

In a passage that seemed to anticipate the failure of the call for an Assembly, the foreigners called attention to their under-representation in the Island's existing institutions and proposed that the number of foreigners in the Council should be increased. They requested also that the Catholic clergy be properly salaried out of the Island's revenues and, with their eyes on assimilation, put forward a plan for the establishment of a college for the education of the young where English should be taught free of cost. Finally ,

122. This Address, in French, is as already indicated, in C.O. 295/24, Hislop : Liverpool (Private), 12.10.1810.

to further the interest of the agricultural community they recommended that a department of agriculture should be established to carry out research and develop the agricultural resources of the Colony.[123]

Though not stated as grievances this Address reveals a number of points about which the foreign community was obviously unhappy. There was, to be sure, a substantial feeling of malaise among the foreigners who were very much alive to the fact that the movement for an Assembly was only the first of many intrigues which would, if unchecked, eventually erode and devour their rights. These rather substantial differences between the British and foreign white communities could have been exploited to wreck the deliberations of the constitutional Committee that met, as we have seen, to determine the form of the constitution in July. However, the one man who had the ability and the interest to do so, George Smith the Chief Justice, was not there.

* * *

The pace of the constitutional struggle necessarily relegates the story of Smith's increasing embarrassment to the background. But his embarrassment was a substantial fact that exercised what might be called a negative influence on the course of events. For, at the very time when Smith's opposition was most needed to stem the growth of constitutional fervour, he was at his most impotent.

Since Smith and the constitutionalists were so diametrically opposed, it was perhaps inevitable that the high point of success for those who urged a British constitution should have corresponded with the ebb of Smith's fortunes. What in fact happened to him however owed much more to design than to the chance effect of countervailing fortunes. The Chief Justice's jurisdiction had been directly attacked. Gallagher the printer, after an imprisonment of seventy days, had been released by the Governor without reference to the Chief Justice.[124] His licence had been restored although he had persistently refused to make amends for his insolence to Smith. In another case, possibly more notorious, the Governor had refused to protect the Chief Justice when the latter was most violently attacked by William Lockheed, a planter whose acquaintances we have already made. Lockheed's letter to Smith criticising the latter's use of his authority is a classic in invective and would have broken a man of lesser spirit. "When I prefix (the Hon'ble) to your name," wrote Lockheed, "remember, it is not that I address

123. It is of interest to note that this Address contained the signatures of the most influential foreigners of the community. Begorrat was a subscriber, as was Bartolomé Portel, the curate of Port of Spain and two or three other French priests. The total number of subscribers was about one hundred many of whom had signed the February Address to the Governor. For comments on this Address by a leading British member of the constitutional movement, George Knox, see C.O. 295/27 which contains a copy of the Address.

124. See, C.O. 295/24, Smith : (Jenkinson), 16.4.1810, and enclosures. C.O. 295/24, Smith : Jenkinson (Private), 16.5.1810, and enclosures.

you as a Member of His Majesty's Council, a Board which I respect. It is merely to distinguish you from a Gentleman of the same name in Port of Spain, who would blush to be taken for you".[125] Hislop, appealed to by Smith, pointedly failed to read in the Lockheed letter any insult to the Chief Justice.[126]

The fact was, as Smith himself said, that "an extraordinary rebellion" had broken out against his authority "with the Governor at the head of it".[127] The Sablich case, involving Anthony Sablich a merchant whose property Smith had placed in the custody of the court, was the first significant attack on the Chief Justice's jurisdiction. The Council, dubbed a pretentious and upstart body by Smith over the Agency question,[128] laid claim, with the Governor's active prodding, to a power of review over the Chief Justice's judicial decision. Thus, Smith, like any other offender in the bad old days of factional strife, was summoned before the Council to explain his judgement. And this, though not the least nor the last indignity that worthy was fated to suffer, had resulted in his withdrawal from the Council[129] and his absence from the centre of affairs while the debates on the Assembly were taking place.

From June 22 when he withdrew to September 9 when he returned to his seat on the Board, the status quo point of view which he normally represented found no champion. While Smith awaited a ministerial ruling on the Sablich affair, and fretted at the delay,[130] the Governor, as we have seen, proceeded with his plans to further the object of representative govern-

125. C.O. 295/24, Lockheed : Smith, 28.4.1810; enclosed in Smith : Jenkinson (Private), 16.5.1810. See also, C.O. 295/23, Hislop : Liverpool (Private), 20.5.1800, and enclosures. James Stephen, commenting on this incident some time later when he had been asked to give an opinion on the tangled state of affairs in the Island described this incident as "peculiarly reprehensible" on Hislop's part and the outstanding example of the means by which he attempted to humiliate publicly the Chief Justice. See, C.O. 295/25, Stephen : (Adam Gordon) 1.9.1810 and Stephen : Liverpool (Private), 1.9.1810.

126. C.O. 295/23, Hislop : Liverpool (Private), 20.5.1810; enclosure, Hislop : Smith, 11.5.1810. Also enclosure D, C.O. 295/24, Smith : Jenkinson (Private), 16.5.1810.

127. C.O. 295/25, Smith : Jenkinson (Private), 28.6.1810.

128. C.O. 298/4, Minutes of Council, 11th and 18th June 1810. Also, C.O. 295/25, Smith : Chapman (Private), 8.7.1810. On Maling's death the Agency question had come up again. Marryat who had been joint Agent with Maling regarded himself as heir to the entire office: Lord Liverpool insisted on associating one Mr. Willimot with him. The Council upheld Marryat, and Smith, alone of all the councillors, protested the Council's decision calling their action an upstart usurpation of the imperial authority, and read them the same lesson that Castlereagh before and Liverpool afterwards was to read them relative to their constitutional position.

129. C.O. 295/23, Hislop : Liverpool, 30.6.1810 and enclosures. Smith's withdrawal, which was a heaven sent opportunity for the Governor, facilitated Nihell's appointment as chairman of the Constitutional Committee as senior member of Council.

130. C.O. 295/25, Smith : Chapman (Private), 8.7.1810.

ment. Smith's plight was not a happy one;[131]   but if he had no influence in the Island, ministerial ears were still open to him and he poured his woes and a constant stream of condemnation of local activities into them. One point he never tired of making was the irreconciliability of the various interests who had hastily concluded this political *mariage de convenance*.[132]   But influence in ministerial circles was of little import as long as the initiative remained with the local authorities. It was in Trinidad that the vital constitutional struggles were taking place, and in Trinidad, Smith, isolated and distraught, was a spent force. It was at this point, however, that the free coloureds made a decisive intervention in the constitutional debate.

*   *   *

Since 1797, the free coloured population had played an ambivalent role in the Island's politics. Proscribed by convention from active participation in civil and political life, and intimidated by an increasing number of laws regulating their social behaviour, they had nevertheless exercised a powerful influence on the course of the constitutional debate right up to 1810. Picton, as we have seen, opposed the grant of an Assembly and continued to do so until the early months of 1808 on the ground that its introduction, accompanied by the exclusion of the free coloureds, would make them a disaffected and dangerous class. Fullarton, dismayed by the conventional proscription under which the whole coloured class laboured, aspired after a form of society which would "render Every Man's Condition better and more prosperous without, if possible rendering any Man's Condition Worse".[133] Smith, wary of the conflicts of passion, prejudice and interest that operated to the detriment of the coloured community in the West Indies, was willing to raise his voice "to its upmost pitch" against the grant of a system of government which, in the circumstances, could be nothing but "a mischievous and inhuman caricature" of the British constitution.[134]   And Lord Castlereagh, as we have seen,[135] urged the amelioration of the free coloured position on the ground that the future prosperity and security of the West Indies depended on the loyalty and affection of this class.

---

131. He graphically described his position in a letter to Chapman quoted above. "The favor I ask of you is to urge either an immediate and decisive order for the support & independence of my judicial Character or a six months leave of Absence *under the sign manual* untill the Question is decided: for it is not a pleasant thing to be **pelted like** a man in the Pillory by the rabble with mud and rotten eggs . . . even tho one has the strong·shield of conscious innocence to oppose as a cover and protection ."
    On another occasion he said that the Governor was trying to make his tribunal "a bear (sic) garden and place the Judge on a level with every blackguard in a Community in which every prentice boy thinks himself a gentleman and every Merchant's clerk is dubbed an Esquire". C.O. 295/24, Smith : Jenkinson (Private), 16.5.1810.
132. See especially, C.O. 295/24, Smith : Jenkinson, 13.5.1810.
133. C.O. 295/4, Fullarton : Sullivan, 8.3.1803.
134. C.O. 295/24, Smith : Jenkinson, 13.5.1810.
135. See above, p. 236.

While others debated their role in the Island's affairs the free coloureds themselves had remained silent, largely because the British party, whom they most feared, had never seemed likely to succeed in its avowed aim of extinguishing Spanish law and establishing the law and government of the old British islands. In July 1810, however, with Smith reduced to impotence and the Governor himself the shield and bulwark of a triumphant British party, it was obvious that something had to be done. Further silence by the free coloureds seemed likely to lead to the triumph of a hostile and reactionary political interest. Much better, they thought, to state their case even at the risk of official displeasure than to lose all by default.

On July 5, therefore, a petition signed by 236 free coloured inhabitants and addressed to the Governor sought permission to address the King in order to win for themselves some measure of participation in whatever system of government might be granted to the Colony. [136] The petition avoided all discussion of the merits of the Assembly system or of any other system, but forthrightly laid claim to a share in any system that might be introduced as a result of the recent agitation.

On receipt of the petition, the Governor replied, through his secretary, demanding to be told what precisely the free coloured wished to obtain from the Crown. [137] This was far from being the innocent request that it seemed, and the free coloureds replied with the greatest circumspection. They could not, they said, outline their objectives. Having always considered any specific claims or pretensions on their part as being "highly unbecoming" they had never discussed or encouraged any discussion on this subject. Nevertheless, since it was clear that a new form of government was being actively considered, they wished to petition for the introduction of a "moderate and consistent plan" for the improvement of their condition. [138]

In reply, [139] the Governor asserted that the measures so far adopted for bringing about a change in the Island's government had avoided all detailed discussion of what the system should be. Thus, he continued, an Address from the free coloureds would be premature. It would, he said, also be harmful in that it would provoke the suspicion that the proposals so far made had overlooked the interests of the free people of colour. Finally, he recommended that the intended Address to the Throne should be deferred until the free coloureds should have "just grounds of complaint", and uttered the pious hope that such an occasion should never arise.

The Governor's reply served only to confirm the fears of the free coloureds. Hislop's assertion that the details of the Island's government had

136. C.O. 295/23, Petition from the People of Colour to Governor Hislop, 5.7.1810.
137. C.O. 295/23, Thos. Walker : The Committee of the free coloured inhabitants, 7.7.1810. The Committee numbered three persons: Desir Fabien, Wm. Versepuy, and John Welsh Hobson. This is the first indication of the identity of the coloured leadership in the Island. See also, Fraser, *op. cit.*, Vol. 1, p. 306 ff. And, Sanderson, *An Appeal,* p. 128 ff.
138. C.O. 295/23, Committee of the free coloureds : Walker, 7.7.1810.
139. C.O. 295/23, Hislop : Committee of the free coloureds, 10.10.1810.

not yet been discussed was technically correct, but only just. On the same day that he wrote this letter, July 10, the Constitutional Committee was beginning its deliberations on the form of the proposed legislature. It was to end these deliberations three days later with scant attention paid to the free coloured position. As we have seen, [140] one brief clause suggesting that they should continue to enjoy such rights as they then possessed was the only stipulation made concerning their plight. And the free coloured feeling that their continued exclusion from political power would, under a representative system of government, only result in their further degradation was certainly justified.

Besides, there was no division of opinion among the white inhabitants about the role the free coloureds were to play in civil and political life; they were all agreed that this role should be as small as possible. George Knox had once favoured the enfranchisement of the free coloureds. [141] But this had been at a time when opinion in the Island was still divided on the grant of an Assembly. The threat of coloured participation was to be a ploy used to batter the opposition into submission. And Knox who was more politically sensitive than most was perhaps already beginning to sense that only the enfranchisement of this majority group, however limited, could have overcome the persistent reluctance of the British government to grant an Assembly.

But Knox's was certainly a minority view which he could hold precisely because, being neither planter nor merchant, he had, as a lawyer, a vested professional interest in the Island's conversion to British laws. In addition he possessed neither the conservatism of the planting classes nor the built-in illiberalism of the majority of the white population. Nevertheless, as Smith said, the price at which he was willing to purchase an Assembly made every other colonial settler shudder. [142] And in any case, unanimity among the white population on the constitutional issue soon removed the tactical advantage that might have been gained from offering the free coloureds some measure of participation in government.

The Governor's actions had so far contained only a mere hint of his displeasure at this coloured intrusion; now the mask of faint disapproval was dropped and his anger, full-blown and vengeful, was revealed. Faced with the demands of the free coloured the whole machinery of intimidation was once more brought into play, this time against a new foe. At an extraordinary meeting of the Council summoned on July 18, the free coloured petition was discussed. [143] The Governor's conduct of the affair was unanimously approved, and it was decided to have the petitioners once more re-

---

140 See above, p. 256
141. C.O. 296/4, pp. 378-82, (Jenkinson)´: Smith (Private), 13.3.1810.
142. C.O. 295/24, Smith : Jenkinson, 13.5.1810.
143. C.O. 298/4, Meeting of 18.7.1810.   Also, C.O. 295/23, Hislop : Liverpool, 19.7.1810, No. 30, enclosure.

quested to state their precise objectives. A committee of three of the most senior members of the Council, Messrs. Nihell, Black and Gloster, was appointed to ascertain the character and description of all the subscribers of the petition. The committee was instructed to distinguish between those who were natural born subjects and those who were not. The latter were to be thoroughly investigated and were to be required to state the circumstances under which "they had intruded themselves here & what may have been their Characters & Conduct" in the foreign countries from which they had come.[144]

The same Council that had frequently testified to the loyalty and affection of the coloured classes in the past, and had done so as recently as July 11,[145] now sought to revive the bogey of coloured fractiousness and discontent. A coloured man, Lucas Prieur, who was in jail for an alleged assault against a white man was brought before the Council, deemed a revolutionary, rogue and vagabond and sentenced to deportation to Martinique.[146] His escape from jail a few days afterwards became the occasion of an organised witch hunt among the coloured classes. At a new meeting of the Council[147] measures were decided upon for the organized persecution of the free coloureds. Free people of colour who were thought to be dangerous to the safety and tranquillity of the Colony were to be deported. Those who were thought to have aided Prieur's escape were summoned before the Council and interrogated. The committee of three was dispensed with. The entire Council became a permanent Board of investigation.

The investigation of various allegations[148] against coloured persons formed an uneasy background to the more formal discussions still taking place between the free coloured leadership and the Governor. In reply to the Council resolution of July 18 calling on them for a precise statement of their objectives, the free coloureds forwarded an explanatory petition on July 28.[149] They disavowed any intention to force themselves on the attention of the government, but averred that the spectacle of one class of the Island's inhabitants assiduously struggling to obtain such a radical change in the government as would "promote *their* happiness" had moved them to the serious consideration of their own. They had no complaint with things as they were, but they were exceedingly anxious to ascertain that no change in the Island's laws and system of administration would operate as a bar to their future freedom and industry. They were particularly anxious to secure to posterity the fruit of their labour, and to protect themselves "from the establishment of any future Law (which having no reference to any necessary

---

144. *Ibid.*
145. C.O. 295/23, Hislop : Liverpool, 19.7.1810, No. 31, enclosure No. 2, clause 13.
146. Minute of Council meeting, 18.7.1810.
147. C.O. 298/4, Meeting of July 25.
148. See C.O. 298/4, Minutes of Council, July 30; August 2; 22, 24 and 29 September,
149. C.O. 298/4. enclosed in Minute of Council meeting of July 30.

political object) might possibly be calculated solely to vex, and personally to degrade us in our individual capacities". Finally, they embraced the opportunity to state their chagrin and mortification at the reaction occasioned by their recent petition and lamented the assumption that their actions had been inspired by any improper or untoward motive.

In return[150] Hislop proclaimed himself as not feeling "authorised by his Instructions" to forward a petition from the free coloureds to the King. He offered however his own and the Council's services in safeguarding their future interests, rebuked them for having admitted improper persons to their counsels and reminded them that the success of a petition depends "on the respectability of the subscribers". Rather than exercise the doubtful privilege of appearing before the Council to state their case, as the Governor invited them to do, the free coloureds decided to await the arrival of the code of laws which, they were informed, was then being framed for the Island.[151] Later they could protest.

In future months, while he awaited the new constitution which he felt certain was coming, Hislop engaged in some not very discreet self-congratulation on the manner in which he had handled the free coloured petition. He reminded his London superiors that that was the way revolution had begun in St. Domingue, and sought their esteem for having so adroitly nipped incipient revolution in the bud.[152] Blunt soldier that he was, Hislop was singularly adept at taking the wrong view of what was essentially a political situation. He had never believed that the free coloureds could be loyal and deserving British subjects. In 1805, when the Island had been threatened by French invasion and the free coloureds had shown themselves as such, Hislop had attributed their courage to the issue of new clothing with which as he pointed out he had had the good sense to provide them.[153] Now, in 1810, it was beyond him to discover in the coloured petitions any other principle but that of intended insurrection; or to see the widespread coloured uneasiness as anything else but the result of the mischievous mis-representations of a disaffected minority. Hislop's, like Picton's, was a military mind, and the question was one of revolution and its suppression, not of political accommodation.

Fortunately, this was not the view taken in England. Lord Liverpool's despatch of November 27, 1810,[154] refusing the Island's plea for an Assembly, summarises the reasons for this refusal. It is one of the definitive documents of British colonial history and not only indicates an answer to the very particular problems existing in Trinidad, but provides an up to date statement of general British colonial objectives in the light of the historical groundswell of the times.

150. C.O. 298/4, enclosed in Minute of Council meeting of July 30.
151. C.O. 298/4, Minutes of 2.8.1810; reply from the free coloured enclosed.
152. C.O. 295/24, Hislop : Liverpool, 6.11.1810, No. 46.
153. C.O. 295/11, Hislop : Camden, 24.6.1805.
154. C.O. 296/4, pp. 369-75, Liverpool : Hislop, 27.11.1810

The question of Trinidad's constitution, said Lord Liverpool, revolved around two points. First of all there was the question of the desirability of introducing a British constitution as established in the old West Indian islands. Secondly, there was the question of introducing a British system of laws without any fundamental change in the constitution.

On the first point he refused to admit that there was a necessary connection between the old West Indian islands and Trinidad. Circumstances in Trinidad were not the same. But even if they were, current ministerial belief was such as to frown upon the extension of the Assembly system to Trinidad. Neither the Crown nor Parliament was willing to surrender such rights as they already enjoyed in respect of the Island's government. This being said, however, it must be admitted that the strongest argument against the establishment of the representative system in Trinidad derived from its dissimilarity from the other islands.

Trinidad was different in that of all the British West Indian islands, Dominica excepted, it possessed a free population consisting overwhelmingly of free people of colour. [155] In the West Indies, political rights and privileges had so far been enjoyed exclusively by whites. While this could be defended in the other islands on the ground that whites were in the majority among the free population, it could not be defended in Trinidad where they were not. The exclusion of free coloureds from political rights in Trinidad under a representative system of government would be regarded by them as a grievance, and would be directly contrary to the spirit of the capitulation.

Secondly, in the other islands British institutions were implemented by natural born British subjects who formed the majority of the population. "They have been educated, or supposed themselves to be educated" in the use of these institutions. This was not so in Trinidad. Here, said Lord Liverpool, the majority of whites were foreign. Among these there could certainly be no prejudice either of education or of habit in favour of the Assembly system. Even if there were, "the partial and exclusive principle" upon which the introduction of the Assembly was founded, that is, the exclusion of the largest section of the free population, "appears to defeat the object of it, and to constitute in point of justice and upon the very principles of the· system itself a decided and insuperable objection against it".

Thirdly, the question of an Assembly for Trinidad could not be viewed simply as a question concerning the internal government of that Colony. The abolition of the slave trade by Parliament "imposes upon the Government the necessity of keeping within itself every power which may be material for rendering this measure effective".

"It is essential for this purpose that in a new Colony the Crown should not divest itself of the power of legislation, and that neither the Crown nor Parliament should be subject to the embarrassments

155. In 1810, the free coloured population numbered 6264 as against a white population of 2495. Of male adults there were 1,680 coloured as against 1139 whites. C.O. 295/24, Return of Population.

CHAPTER 8

which on such an occasion might perhaps arise from the conflicting views of the Imperial Parliament and a subordinate Legislature."

For these reasons it was decided not to introduce an Assembly into the Island. The question of changing the Colony's laws was reserved for future discussion. In fact, they were thereafter to be only slowly and partially modified. The failure of the constitutional movement of 1810, and the events associated with it, most notably the highhanded usurpation of Smith's authority as Chief Justice by the Governor and Council, resulted in a greater exercise of imperial authority than had previously prevailed. The year 1810 witnessed the beginning of what was to prove to be a long struggle for civil rights by the free coloureds; it witnessed also the end of ministerial indecision about the Island's constitution. Henceforth, and until the introduction of the partially elected legislative system of 1925, Trinidad's future was to be that of an unmitigated Crown Colony.

APPENDIX

GLOSSARY OF SPANISH TERMS

Most, if not all of these, have been explained in the text. They are repeated for convenience.

alcalde de barrio	police supervisor of a ward or district in the town;
alcalde del crimen	a high court criminal judge and member of the *Audiencia;*
alcaldes ordinarios	the two leading members of the *Cabildo,* one being the *alcalde de primer voto,* or *alcalde* of the first election, the other *alcalde de segundo voto* or *alcalde* of the second election;
alférez real	standard-bearer;
alguaçil	constable;
alguaçil mayor	chief constable;
audiencia	superior court of justice and appeal court, also possessing administrative functions;
asesor	judicial adviser to a high administrative official for whose acts, based on his advice, he was legally culpable;
cabildo	town council;
cédula	decree issued by the Crown or on its authority;
consulado	commercial court;
corregidor	local official, like a Governor, with judicial and administrative authority, subordinate to Viceroy and *Audiencia;*
encomienda	a grant of land made to the early settlers in Spanish America;
escribano	notary, scribe; official notary attached to the *Cabildo,* or *Audiencia;*
fiscal	attorney for the Crown, usually two in an *Audiencia,* one for civil and one for criminal cases;
maravedi	very small Spanish coin, by contemporary reckoning, about 230 to 270 to the dollar;
oidor	judge of the *Audiencia;*
procurador	solicitor;
procurador general	also *sindíco;* watch dog of public interest in the *Cabildo;*
real	Spanish silver coin, eight to the dollar or *peso.*
regidor	councillor, member of *Cabildo;*
requirimiento	a quota of Indian labourers given to a settler in early Spanish America;
residencia	judicial review of an official's conduct at the end of his term of office;
sindíco	see *procurador general.*

267

BIBLIOGRAPHY

This book has been written on the basis of material originally consulted for a Ph.D thesis from manuscript and printed records available in England. These sources remain the foundation of the work; official Trinidad collections for this period where euphemistically they can be said to exist, imperfectly duplicate the metropolitan collections, or else for practical purposes simply do not exist.

Where possible, printed Spanish documents have been used. Original records in Spain or in Venezuela have not been consulted. Some recent publications have helped to close the gap which existed at the time the thesis was written, and these have been consulted. In any case since the main object of the work is to elucidate a problem of British colonial history such documents might well have aided the discussion in the early Chapters without contributing much to the development of the central theme.

SOURCES

I. **Bibliographies and Guides to sources.**

The most valuable of these were:

Bell, Parker *et al*, *Guide to British West Indian Archive Materials, 1926.*

L.J. Ragatz, *A Guide for the Study of British Caribbean History, 1763-1834*, (Washington, D.C. 1932).
Check List of House of Commons Sessional Papers relating to the West Indies, 1763-1834, (London, 1923).
Statistics for the Study of British Caribbean History, (New York, 1927).

M.S. Guiseppi, *A Guide to the Manuscripts preserved in the Public Record Office.* Two volumes, (London, 1923-24).

E.V. Goveia, *A Historiography of the British West Indies to the end of the nineteenth century*, (Mexico, 1956). This is, as its name implies, not a bibliographical guide; nevertheless it contains much useful comment on the bibliography of the West Indies.

R.A. Humphreys, *Latin American History: A Guide to the Literature in English*, (Oxford University Press, 1958).

Monroe N. Work, *A Bibliography of the Negro in Africa and America*, (New York, 1928).

The New York Public Library, *List of Works relating to the West Indies, (New York, 1912.)*

Lists and Indexes of the Public Record Office.
Indexes to the Publications of the Trinidad and Tobago Historical Society.
Indexes to Accounts and Papers and Parliamentary Papers.
Catalogue of the Library of the West India Committee.

II. Original Correspondence.

a. The bulk of these is drawn from the Public Record Office records, principally from the following:

C.O. 295/1-28	In-Letters to the Secretary of State.
C.O. 296/1-3	Precis of In-Letters.
C.O. 296/4-5	Copies of Out-Letters from the Secretary of State.
C.O. 298/1-9	Sessional Papers of the Council, Trinidad.
C.O. 380/134	Commission Book for Trinidad, St. Lucia and British Guiana.

In addition other miscellaneous papers have been used of which these are the main ones.

C.O. 300/16	Shipping Returns Trinidad, 1804 onwards.
W.O. 1/86	Invaluable for the period of the capitulation and just after, in Trinidad as well as in the other West Indian Islands.
W.O. 1/93-94	Contains many of Picton's early letters and statistical returns not found in the C.O. 295 series.
Adm. 1/315; 1/4169; 1/4170	
H.O. 30/1-2	
C.O. 318/76	A mine of information on the free coloured in Trinidad and elsewhere in the West Indies.
P.C. 1/3557	Unbound papers. Contains several documents and copies of documents on the Picton affair and related events in Trinidad.
C.O. 318/25-7	
C.O. 140/78 ; 89	Journals of the Jamaica Assembly.
C.O. 138/42	Out-letters to Jamaica.
C.O. 137/103-4	In-Letters; Governor of Jamaica to Secretary of State.
C.O. 101/21	In-Letters: Governor of Grenada to Secretary of State, containing St. Laurent's report on Trinidad.

b. The British Museum's *Additional Manuscripts* collection was also used. The following were particularly useful:

Additional Manuscript 36,320. This is a collection of seventeenth century Spanish transcripts on the Spanish colonies off the northern coast of South America. Several papers on Trinidad are included, one of which is the report on the *residencia* conducted by Don Sancho de Alquiza on the Island's Governor, Don Fernando de Berrio, in early 1612.

Additional Manuscript 36,870. Contains a miscellaneous collection of very interesting correspondence between ex-Governor Picton and various individuals in Trinidad, but particularly with St. Hilaire Begorrat.

Additional Manuscripts 36,499. Volume IX of the *Cumberland Papers.* On pp. 93-106 there is a very informative letter on the state of Trinidad at the beginning of 1802.

Additional Manuscripts 38,241 and 38,358 contain on pp. 282-7 and 170 respectively some correspondence on Privy Council proceedings against Picton.

Additional Manuscripts 37,883; 37,884; 37,885; 38,354; 38,356; 38,737 contain various accounts of Trinidad and references to some of the Island's affairs. Nos. 38,356 (pp. 5-6), and 38,354 (pp. 319-22), contain interesting descriptions of the Island and its prospects. Such descriptions abound in the private papers of the period.

Additional Manuscripts 49,173-7; and 49,184-7. The papers of Spencer Perceval.

c.   *Other Manuscript Sources.*

These included the *Hobart Papers* which are lodged at the Aylesbury Record Office. These are an invaluable source of information for the intrigues which formed the background to the Commission and contain much information from various sources of Picton's early years in the Island. Bundles K, P, S, and Y were the ones used.

Also used were the *West India Committee Records:*

Minutes of the Committee of West India Merchants, March 1794 to December 1802;

Minutes of the Committee of West India Planters and Merchants, February 1805 to March 1822;

Minutes of West India Merchants, September 1804 to July 1827.

III.   Printed Sources.

a.   *Parliamentary Papers*

Parliamentary Register, Lords and Commons, 3rd series, Volumes 17 and 18.
Cobbett's Parliamentary Debates, Volumes XIX and XX.
Parliamentary Debates, New Series, Volume VII.
Journal of the House of Commons, Volume 62.
Parliamentary Papers.
Of these the most important were:
Parliamentary Papers, House of Commons, 1826-27, (428), XXIII.
Report of the Commissioner of Inquiry on the Subject of Titles to Lands in the Island of Trinidad.
Parliamentary Papers, House of Commons, 1826-27, (551), XXIII.
Report of the Commissioners of Legal Enquiry for the Island of Trinidad.

Both these collections contain invaluable background information on the Island's economic, social, political and institutional development.

Parliamentary Papers, House of Commons, 1831-32, (212), XXXI. Papers relative to the Legislative Council in Trinidad.

Also, *Trinidad and Tobago Historical Publications.* Published between 1935 and 1951 by the Trinidad and Tobago Historical Society, this collection of about 1,000 documents reproduces in English many of the most important Spanish documents on the Island's early history. A set is contained in the British Museum, and in Trinidad at the Central Library, Port of Spain, and the Library of the University of the West Indies, St. Augustine.

T.B. and T.J. Howell (compilers): *Cobbett's State Trials.* Volume XXX contains the account of the Picton trials in England and much incidental information on the Island. It also contains the records of the trial of Edward Draper for libel arising out of allegations pertaining to the appointment of the Fullarton Commission.

b. Collections of Laws and Commentaries.

Recopilación de los reynos de las Indias, (Madrid, 1791). Reproduced in three volumes, Consejo de la Hispanidad, (Madrid, 1943).

Juan de Solórzano y Pereyra, *Politica Indiana,* (Madrid, 1647). Reproduced in five volumes, Compañía Ibero-Americana de Publicaciones, 1930.

José Febrero, *Libreria de Escribanos, Abogados y Jeuces.* Six volumes, (Circa 1797).

Alonso de Villadiego Vascuñana y Montaya, *Instruccion Politica Practica Judicial,* (Madrid, 1766). First published Madrid, 1641.

IV. Contemporary Pamphlets and Polemical Works.

The majority center on the Picton-Fullarton controversy. Nevertheless they do throw some light on the Island's affairs. Outstanding among these are:

"Decius", pseudonym
of the Rt. Hon. Thomas
Peregrine Courtenay,   *Letters. . . in answer to the criticism upon the "Political Account of Trinidad", and upon the defence of the crimes of Governor Picton, in the Anti-Jacobin Review, under the title of the "Pictonian Persecution".* (London, 1808).

Edward Alured Draper,   *An address to the British Public, on the Case of Brigadier-General Picton, Late Governor and Captain General of the Island of Trinidad: with Observations on the Conduct of William Fullarton, Esq. F.R.S. and the Right Honourable John Sullivan.* (London, 1806).

William Fullarton,   *Colonel Fullarton's Answer to Colonel Picton's Pamphlet. A Refutation to the Pamphlet which Col. Picton lately addressed to Lord Hobart.*

(London, 1805).

A Statement, Letters and Documents respecting the Affairs of Trinidad: including a Reply to Col. Picton's Address to the Council of that Island; submitted to the Consideration of the Lords of His Majesty's Most Honourable Privy Council. (London, 1804).

Archibald Gloster,

A Letter to the Right Honourable the Earl of Buckinghamshire. Late Secretary of the Colonial Department, Respecting Affairs in Trinidad in 1803, and in Answer to William Fullarton, Esq. (London, 1807).

Pierre M'Callum,

Travels in Trinidad during the months of February, March and April, 1803, in a Series of Letters addressed to a Member of the Imperial Parliament of Great Britain. (Liverpool, 1805).

M'Callum's work, like all the others, is unashamedly polemical. Nevertheless, the incidents he records are by and large accurately reported. Violently anti-Picton, M'Callum writes with some bias, but not as much as Brierley, in his *Trinidad: Then and Now,* p. 92 ff, pretends. C.O. 295/5 substantiates in every detail one of the most outrageously incredulous sections of his book (p. 236 ff) where M'Callum deals with his own treatment by Commissioners Picton and Hood.

Thomas Picton,

A Letter addressed to the Rt. Hon. Lord Hobart, His Majesty's Late Principal Secretary of State for the Colonial Department, (London, 1804).

Evidence taken at Port-of-Spain, Island of Trinidad in the Case of Louisa Calderon . . . with a Letter addressed to Samuel Hood, K.B. (London, 1806).

Heaton Robinson,

Memoirs of Lt. General Sir Thomas Picton. Two

Of a different kind are: volumes, (London, 1836).

Fortunatus Dwarris,

The West Indian Question Plainly Stated: and the Only Practical Remedy Briefly Considered; in a letter to the Right Hon. Henry Goulburn Chancellor of the Exchequer. (London, 1828).

A very informative work. Dwarris was one of the Commissioners of Legal Inquiry to Trinidad in 1826-7, and his book is based on his experiences in the Island.

W. Layman,

Outline of a Plan for the better cultivation, security and defence of the British West Indies, providing an effectual substitute for the African slave trade. (London, 1807).

This pamphlet contains a full statement on Layman's views on Chinese immigration to the West Indies which were the basis for the experiment initiated in Trinidad in 1806.

J.B. Philip, *An Address to the Right Hon. Earl Bathurst, His Majesty's Principal Secretary of State for the Colonies Relative to the Claims which the Coloured Population of Trinidad have to the Same Civil and Political Privileges with their White Fellow-subjects.* (London, 1824).

An able and informative exposition of the free coloured case.

(John Sanderson), *A Political Account of the Island of Trinidad, from its Conquest . . . in the year 1797, to the Present Time, in a letter to His Grace the Duke of Portland.* (London, 1807).

Published anonymously there can be no doubt that Sanderson was the author of this work. He admitted as much in his subsequent book, *An Appeal,* p. 36. Also, *The Times* (London) of Wednesday December 7, 1808, contains an account of his trial on an accusation of libel brought against him by Messrs. Begorrat and Black as a result of publication. See also C.O. 295/20 which contains a copy of the summons issued against him.

(John Sanderson), *An Appeal to the Imperial Parliament upon the Claims of the Ceded Colony of Trinidad, to be Governed by a Legislature and Judicature, Founded on Principles Sanctioned by Colonial Precedents and Long Usage . . .* (London, 1812). Both these works, though replete with distortions, are invaluable for a study of the constitutional struggles of the period.

Another work, *Emancipation in Disguise. . . ,* (London, 1807).

James Stephen, *The Crisis of the Sugar Colonies: or, An Enquiry into the Objects and Probable Effects of the French Expedition to the West Indies; and their Connection with the Colonial Interests of the British Empire. To which are subjoined, Sketches of a Plan for Settling the Vacant Lands of Trinidada. In Four Letters to the Rt. Hon. Henry Addington. . .* (London, 1802).

An important statement of abolitionist views on the future cultivation of Trinidad.

V. Contemporary Histories.

W.H. Burnley,
Observations on the Present Condition of the Island of Trinidad and the Actual State of the Experiment of Negro Emancipation, (London, 1842).

Mrs. Carmichael,
Domestic Manners and Social Condition of the White, Coloured, and Negro Population of the West Indies. Two volumes, (London, 1834).

Thomas Clarkson,
The History of the Rise, Progress, and Accomplishment of the Abolition of the African Slave Trade by the British Parliament. Two volumes, (London, 1808).

Bryan Edwards,
The History, Civil and Commercial, of the West Indies. Five volumes, (London, 1819 edition).

E.L. Joseph,
History of Trinidad, (Trinidad, 1837).

J.J. Dauxion Lavaysse,
A Statistical, Commercial and Political Description of Venezuela, Trinidad, Margarita and Tobago. . . from the French of M. Lavaysse: with an introduction and explanatory notes by the editor (i.e. Edward Blaquiere), (London, 1820).
Voyage aux Iles de Trinidad, de Tabago, de la Marguerite et Dans Diverses Parties de Vénézuéla dans l'Amerique Méridionale. Two volumes, (Paris, 1813). Volume I is devoted entirely to Trinidad. A very attractive edition of this work, in Spanish, was published by the Universidad Central de Venezuela in 1967. Earlier editions in English were published in London in 1820 and 1821.

David Macpherson,
Annals of Commerce, Manufactures, Fisheries and Navigation with Brief Notices of the Arts and Sciences connected with them. Four volumes, (London, 1805).

F. Mallet,
Descriptive Account of the Island of Trinidad, (London, 1797).

R. Montgomery Martin,
History of the British Colonies. Five volumes, (London, 1835).

Baron de Montlezum,
Souvenirs des Antilles: Voyage en 1815, et 1816, aux Etats-Unis, et dans l'Archipel Caraibe. . . . Two volumes, (Paris, 1818).

Hon. George Pellew,
The Life and Correspondence of the Right Hon'ble Henry Addington, First Viscount Sidmouth. Three volumes, (London, 1847).

George Pinckard,
Notes on the West Indies. Two volumes, (London, 1816, second edition).

William Walton,
Present State of the Spanish Colonies. Two volumes, (London, 1810).

Robert Isaac and	
Samuel Wilberforce,	*The Life of William Wilberforce,* (London, 1838). A companion volume, published much later, can be included here: *Private Papers of William Wilberforce,* collected and edited by A.M. Wilberforce, (London, 1897).
John Williamson,	*Medical and Miscellaneous Observations Relative to the West India Islands.* Two volumes, (Edinburgh, 1817).
Sir William Young,	*The West India Common-Place Book; Compiled from Parliamentary and Official Documents. . . ,* (London, 1807).

VI. Newspapers.

There are no collections of Trinidad newspapers for this period in Trinidad or in England. The volumes of original correspondence at the Public Record Office do, however, contain clippings and excerpts from both the *Trinidad Weekly Courant* which, during the constitutional struggle, round about 1808, became the *Trinidad Weekly Courant and Commercial Gazette;* and from *The Independent Trinidad Gazette* which was a late starter in the field.

Some references to affairs in the Island have been found in the London papers of the period but references are sketchy and marginal. Those consulted with some success were:

The Times;
Morning Chronicle; and the
Morning Post.

VII. Periodicals.

Anti-Jacobin Review.
Edinburgh Review.
Gentleman's Magazine.
Except for the Picton-Fullarton controversy there was very little relating to the Island.

VIII. Modern Printed Works - Books and Articles

Eleanor B. Adams,	"An. English Library at Trinidad", *The Americas,* Vol. II, No. 1, July 1955.
H.H.S. Aimes,	*"Coartación:* A Spanish Institution for the Advancement of Slaves into Freedmen", *Yale Review,* February 1909.
A.S. Aiton,	"Spanish Colonial Reorganization under the Family Compact",

	Hispanic American Historical Review, Vol. XII, No. 3, 1932.
Anonymous,	*A Narrative of the Proceedings Upon the Complaint Against Governor Melvill,* (London, 1770).
Josefina Perez Aparicio,	*Perdida de la Isla de Trinidad,* (Escuela de Estudios Hispano-Americanos, 1966).
Frances Armytage,	*The Free Port System in the British West Indies: A Study in Commercial Policy, 1766-1822,* (London 1953).
Augier, Gordon, Hall and Reckord,	*The Making of the West Indies,* (London, 1960).
Roy Augier,	"Before and After 1865: The Consequences of Morant Bay", *New World Quarterly,* Vol. 2, No. 2. 1966.
C.A. Banbuck,	*Histoire politique, economique et sociale de la Martinique Sous l'Ancien Regime, 1635-1789.* (Paris, 1935).
Henri Bangou,	*La Guadeloupe, 1492-1848,* (No date, Editions du Centre).
Roger Bastide,	"Race Relations in Brazil", *International Social Science Bulletin,* IX, No. 4, 1957.
Alfred B. Beaven,	"Canning and the Addington Administration in 1801", *English Historical Review,* XXVIII, January 1913.
G.L. Beer,	*The Origins of the British Colonial System,* (New York, 1908).
	The Old Colonial System. Two volumes, (New York, 1912).
F.L. Benns,	*The American Struggle for the British West India Carrying-Trade. 1815-1830,* (Indiana, 1923).
Pierre-Gustave-Louis Borde,	*Histoire de L'Ile de La Trinidad Sous le Gouvernement Espagnol.* Two volumes, (Paris, 1882).
Lloyd Braithwaite,	"Social Stratification in Trinidad", *Social and Economic Studies,* Vol. 2, No. 2, 1952.
J.N. Brierley,	*Trinidad: Then and Now,* (Trinidad, 1912).
Allan S. Brown,	"The Expedition to the St. John's River and the Lake of Nicaragua, 1779-80", *Caribbean Historical Review,* No. II, December 1951.
V.L. Brown,	"Contraband Trade: A Factor in the Decline of Spain's Empire in America", *Hispanic American Historical Review,* Vol. VIII, 1928.
W.L. Burn,	*Emancipation and Apprenticeship,* (London, 1837).
	The West Indies, (London, 1951).
W.H. Burnley,	*Opinions on Slavery and Emancipation,* (London, 1833).

Cambridge History of the British Empire.
Cambridge History of British Foreign Policy.

George Canning,	*The Speeches of the Right Honourable George Canning; with a Memoir of His Life,* by R. Therry. (3rd Edition, Six volumes, London, 1836).
Gertrude Carmichael,	*History of the West Indian Islands of Trinidad and Tobago,* (London, 1961).
Arturo Morales Carrion,	"Eighteenth Century Puerto Rico in Diplomacy and War", *Caribbean Historical Review,* No. 1, December 1950.
E.M. Carus-Wilson (Ed.),	*Essays in Economic History.* Three volumes, (London, 1954).
C.E. Castañeda,	"The *Corregidor* in Spanish Colonial Administration", *Hispanic American Historical Review,* Vol. IX, 1929.
Eugenio Rodriguez Chang,	"Chinese Labor Migration into Latin America in the Nineteenth Century", *Revista de Historia de America,* No. 46, December 1958.
Hector Garcia Chuecos,	*La Capitania General de Venezuela: Apuntes para una Exposicion del Derecho Politico Colonial Venezolano,* (Caracas, 1945).
	Hacienda Colonial Venezolana, (Caracas, 1946).
Allan Christelow,	"French Interest in the Spanish Empire during the Ministry of the Duc de Choiseul, 1757-71", *Hispanic American Historical Review,* Vol. XXI, 1941.
	"Great Britain and the Trades from Cadiz and Lisbon to Spanish America and Brazil", *Hispanic American Historical Review,* Vol. XXVII, 1947.
	"Contraband Trade between Jamaica and the Spanish Main, and the Free Port Act of 1766", *Hispanic American Historical Review,* Vol. XXII, 1942.
Sir Cecil Clementi,	*A Constitutional History of British Guiana,* (London, 1937).
E.W. Cohen,	*Growth of the British Civil Service, 1780-1939,* (London, 1941).
Juan Comas,	"Recent Research on Race Relations in Latin America", *International Social Science Journal,* XIII, No. 2, 1961.
R. Coupland,	*Wilberforce,* (Oxford, 1923).
	The Quebec Act, (Oxford, 1925).
	The British Anti-Slavery Movement, (Oxford University Press, 1933).
Hewan Craig,	*The Legislative Council of Trinidad and Tobago,* (London, 1952).
Philip Curtin,	*Two Jamaicas: The Role of Ideas in a Tropical Colony, 1830-65,* (Harvard University Press, 1955).
R.C. Dallas,	*The History of the Maroons. . . (in) Jamaica.*

	Two volumes, (London, 1803).
David Brian Davis,	*The Problem of Slavery in Western Culture*, (Cornell University Press, 1966).
Noel Deerr,	*The History of Sugar.* Two volumes, (London 1949-50).
	"The Early Use of Steam Power in the Cane Sugar Industry", *Paper read at the Chartered Institute of Patent Agents,* London, October 9, 1940.
Carl N. Degler,	"Slavery and the Genesis of American Race Prejudice", *Comparative Studies in Society and History,* II, October, 1959.
S. de Madariaga,	*The Rise of the Spanish American Empire,* (London, 1947).
	The Fall of the Spanish American Empire, (London, 1947).
	Spain, (Second edition: London, 1931).
	Englishmen, Frenchmen, Spaniards: An Essay in Comparative Psychology, (Third edition, Oxford University Press, 1931).
Francois Raymond Joseph de Pons,	*Travels in South America during the Years 1801, 1802, 1803, and 1804 etc.,* (London, 1807).
Sheila Duncker,	*The free Coloured and their fight for Civil Rights in Jamaica, 1800-1830,* (London M.A. thesis, 1960).
C.R. De Silva,	*Ceylon Under the British Occupation, 1795-1833. Two volumes, 1953.*
R.P. Devas,	*Conception Island: or the Troubled Story of the Catholic Church in Grenada, B.W.I.* (London, 1932).
	The History of the Island of Grenada, (Grenada, 1964).*
L. de Verteuil,	*Trinidad,* (London, 1856).
O.M. Dickerson,	*The Navigation Acts and the American Revolution,* (Philadelphia, 1951).
Gordon Donaldson,	*The Scots Overseas,* (London, 1966).
H.E. Egerton,	*A Short History of British Colonial Policy, 1606-1909,* (London, 1950).
Stanley M. Elkins,	*Slavery: A Problem in American Institutional and Intellectual Life,* (New York, 1963).
Erich Eyck,	*Pitt versus Fox Father and Son, 1753-1806,* (London, 1950).
Eduardo Arcila Farias,	*Economía Colonial de Venezuela,* (Mexico, 1946).
J. Halcro Ferguson,	*Latin America: The Balance of Race Redressed,* (Oxford University Press, 1961).
W.F. Finlason,	*The History of the Jamaica Case: Being an Account Founded upon documents, of the Rebellion of the Negroes in Jamaica etc.,* (London, 1869).

	Justice to a Colonial Governor; or, some considerations on the Case of Mr. Eyre containing the substance of all the documents, discussions, and proceedings relating thereto, (London, 1869).
Archibald S. Foord,	*His Majesty's Opposition, 1714-1830,* (Oxford, 1964).
J.W. Fortescue,	*A History of the British Army.* Thirteen volumes, (London, 1899-1930).
	The British Army, 1783-1802, (London, 1905).
José Gil Fortoul,	*Historia Constitucional de Venezuela,* (B e r l i n, 1907).
L.M. Fraser,	*History of Trinidad, 1781-1839.* Two volumes, (Trinidad, 1891-96).
Holden Furber,	*Henry Dundas, First Viscount Melville 1742-1811,* (London, 1931).
W.J. Gardner,	*A History of Jamaica,* (1st published 1874; London, 1891).
Eugene D. Genovese,	*The Political Economy of Slavery,* (Vintage Books, 1967; first published 1961).
D.B. Goebel,	"British Trade to the Spanish Colonies, 1796-1823", *American Historical Review,* Vol. XLIII, 1938.
Elsa V. Goveia,	"The West Indian Slave Laws of the Eighteenth Century", *Ciencias Sociales,* Vol. 12, No. 1, March 1960.
	Slave Society in the British Leeward Islands, 1780-1800, (Yale University Press, 1965).
G.S. Graham,	*British Policy and Canada, 1774-91; A Study in 18th Century Trade Policy,* (London, 1930).
	Sea Power and British North America, 1783-1820: A Study in British Colonial Policy, (Harvard University Press, 1941).
W.L. Grant,	"Canada versus Guadeloupe", *American Historical Review,* Vol. XVII, 1912.
J.R.W. Gwynne-Timothy,	"The Role of Overseas Colonies in the European Power Balance, 1793-1815", *Canadian Historical Association Annual Report,* 1953.
Douglas Hall,	*Free Jamaica, 1838-65,* (Yale University Press, 1959).
Harley Ross Hammond,	"Race, Social Mobility and Politics in Brazil", *Race,* IV, No. 2, 1962.
Earl J. Hamilton,	*American Treasure and the Price Revolution in Spain, 1501-1650,* (Havard University Press, 1934).
Lewis Hanke,	*Bartolomé de Las Casas: An Interpretation of His Life and Writings,* (The Hague, 1951).
	The Spanish Struggle for Justice in the Conquest of America, (Philadelphia, 1949).
	Aristotle and the Indians, (London, 1959).

M.L. Hansen,	*The Atlantic Migration, 1607-1860,* (Harper Torchbook edition, 1961).
W. Hardman,	*History of Malta, 1798-1815,* (London, 1909).
C.H. Haring,	*The Spanish Empire in America,* (New York, 1947).
	Trade and Navigation between Spain and the Indies in the Time of the Hapsburgs, (Harvard University Press, 1918).
V.T. Harlow and A.F.M. Madden,	*British Colonial Developments, 1774-1834: Select documents,* (Oxford, 1953).
V.T. Harlow,	*A History of Barbados, 1625-1685,* (Oxford, 1926).
	The Founding of the Second British Empire. Two volumes, (London, 1952-64).
Lawrence A. Harper,	*The English Navigation Laws,* (New York, 1939).
D.R. Harvey,	*Economic Aspects of the Historical Geography of Trinidad since 1802.* (London University M.Sc. thesis, 1955).
John Hay,	*A Narrative of the Insurrection in the Island of Grenada, which took place in 1795. By John Hay, An Inhabitant of the Colony and one of the prisoners taken by the Insurgents. With an Introduction by a Military Man Resident for Thirty years in the West Indies.* (Said by Devas, *History of Grenada,* p. 154, n. 1, to be General Maitland). (London, 1823).
E. Hayot,	*"Aux Antilles, sous la Revolution: Marins francais au service de l'Espagne",* Annales des Antilles, No. 12, 1965.
	"Noblesse des Iles: les Anoblis à la Martinique avant 1789", Annales des Antilles, No. 12, 1965.
Eli F. Hecksher,	*Mercantilism,* (Two volumes, 1934).
M.J. Herskovits,	*The Myth of the Negro Past,* (New York, 1941).
Bernard Holland,	*Imperium et Libertas,* (London, 1901).
Sir Claud Hollis,	*A Brief History of Trinidad under the Spanish Crown,* (Trinidad, 1941).
E.M. Howse,	*Saints in Politics,* (Second edition, London, 1960).
José M. Piernas Hurtado,	*La Casa de Contratación de las Indias,* (Madrid, 1907).
Roland D. Hussey,	*The Caracas Company, 1728-1784,* (Harvard University Press, 1934).
C.L.R. James,	*The Black Jacobins,* (First published 1938; second edition New York, 1963).
(G.W. Jordan),	*Copies of a letter containing Queries Respecting the State of the Silver and Copper Coins in Barbados and of an Answer Describing the Same and Recommending measures necessary to be adopted for furnishing a full and perfect supply to all the*

	Colonies. By the Agent for Barbados. (London, 1816).
Winthrop D. Jordan,	"The Influence of the West Indies on the Origin of Negro Slavery", *William and Mary Quarterly*, XVIII, April 1961.
G.P. Judd,	*Members of Parliament, 1734-1832,* (New Haven, 1955).
Arthur Berriedale Keith (ed.),	*Selected Speeches and Documents on British Colonial Policy, 1763-1917,* (Oxford University Press, 1918).
J.F. King,	"Evolution of the Free Slave Trade Principle in Spanish Colonial Administration", *H i s p a n i c American Colonial Review,* Vol. XXII, 1942.
Herbert S. Klein,	*Slavery in the Americas,* (London, 1967).
F.J. Klingberg,	*The Anti-Slavery Movement in England,* (Oxford University Press, 1926).
Klaus E. Knorr,	*British Colonial Theories, 1570-1850,* (First published 1944; reprint, London, 1963).
L.W. Labaree,	*Royal Government in America,* (New Haven, 1930).
M. Lacour,	*Histoire de l'Ile de la Guadeloupe, 1635-1830.* Four volumes, (Basseterre, 1835-60).
Sir Norman Lamont,	*Burnley of Orange Grove,* (Port-of-Spain, 1947).
John Le Riverend,	*Economic History of Cuba,* (Havana, 1967).
H. Lemery,	*La Revolution Francaise à la Martinique,* (Paris, 1936).
Sir George Cornewall Lewis,	*An Essay on the Government of Dependencies,* (Oxford, 1891).
J.G. Leyburn,	*The Haitian People,* (New Haven, 1941).
Patrick C. Lipscomb,	"Party Politics, 1801-1802: George Canning and the Trinidad Question", *The Historical Journal,* Vol. XII, No. 3, 1969.
John Lynch,	*Spanish Colonial Administration, 1782-1810: The Intendant System in the Viceroyalty of the Rio de La Plata,* (London, 1958).
A.T. Mahan,	*The Influence of Sea Power upon the French Revolution and Empire.* Two volumes, 1892.
Anthony Maingot,	*The Role of the French Creole in 19th Century Trinidad,* (Unpublished Ph.D thesis, University of Puerto Rico, 1962).
Helen Taft Manning,	*British Colonial Government after the American Revolution 1782-1820,* (Yale University Press, 1933).
	The Revolt of French Canada, 1800-35, (London, 1962).
J. Marryat,	*Thoughts on the Abolition of the Slave Trade etc.,* (London, 1816).

	More Thoughts etc., (London, 1816).
Dorothy Marshall,	*The Rise of George Canning,* (London, 1938).
W.L. Mathieson,	*British Slavery and Its Abolition, 1823-1838,* (London, 1926).
	British Slave Emancipation, 1838-1849, (London, 1932).
J.R. Mc Cullough,	*A Dictionary of Commerce.* Three volumes, 1834.
G.R. Mellor,	*British Imperial Trusteeship, 1782-1850,* (London, 1951).
R.B. Merriman,	*The Rise of the Spanish Empire in the Old World and in the New.* Four volumes, (New York, 1918-34).
J.C. Miller,	*Origins of the American Revolution,* (Stanford University Press, 1943).
Arthur Mills,	*Colonial Constitutions,* (London, 1856).
James Millette,	"The Civil Commission of 1802: An Account and an Explanation of an Issue in the Early Constitutional and Political History of Trinidad", *Jamaica Historical Review,* Vol. VI, 1966.
Ludwell Lee Montague,	*Haiti and the United States,* (Duke University Press, 1940).
Bernard Moses,	"The Casa de Contratacion of Seville", *American Historical Association, Annual Report,* 1894.
	South America on the Eve of Emancipation, (New York, 1908).
Guillermo Morón,	*A History of Venezuela,* (London, 1964; edited and translated by John Street).
D.J. Murray,	*The West Indies and the Development of Colonial Government, 1801-1834,* (Oxford University Press, 1965).
Jerome Nadelhaft,	"The Somersett Case and Slavery: Myth, Reality and Repercussions", *The Journal of Negro History,* Vol. LI, No. 3, 1966.
J.C. Nardin,	*"Tabago, Antille Francaise, 1781-1793",* *Annales des Antilles,* No. 14, 1966.
Oracy Nogueira,	"Skin Color and Social Class", *Plantation Systems of the New World,* (Research Institute for the Study of Man, 1959).
Francisco Morales Padron,	"Trinidad en el Siglo XVII", *Anuario de Estudios Americanos,* XVII.
	"Descubrimiento y Papel de Trinidad en la Penetración Continental", *Anuario de Estudios Americanos,* Vol, XIV, 1957.
R. Pares,	*A West India Fortune,* (London, 1956).
	Yankees and Creoles, (London, 1956).
	Merchants and Planters, (Economic History Review

Supplement, No. 4, 1960).

C. Northcote
Parkinson (ed.),
The Trade Winds: A Study of British Overseas Trade During the French Wars, 1793-1815, (London 1948).

J.H. Parry,
The Audiencia of New Galicia in the Sixteenth Century: A Study in Spanish Colonial Government, (Cambridge, 1948).
The Sale of Public Office in the Spanish Indies Under the Hapsburgs, (Berkeley and Los Angeles, 1953).
"The Patent Offices in the West Indies", *English Historical Review*, 1954.

J.H. Parry and
P.M. Sherlock,
A Short History of the West Indies, (London, 1956).

Orlando Patterson,
The Sociology of Slavery, (Mc Gibbon and Kee, 1967).

L.M. Penson,
The Colonial Agents of the British West Indies, (London, 1924).

Sir Charles Petrie,
Life of George Canning, (London, 1932).

Mariano Picón-Salas,
De la Conquista a la Independencia, (Mexico, 1944).

William W. Pierson, Jr.,
"La Intendencia de Venezuela en el Regimen Colonial", *Boletin de la Academia Nacional de la Historia*, (Caracas, 1941).
"Some Reflections on the *Cabildo* as an Institution", *Hispanic American Historical Review*, Vol. V, 1922.

F.W. Pitman,
The Development of the British West Indies, (New Haven, 1917).
"Slavery on British West India Plantations in the Eighteenth Century", *Journal of Negro History*, Vol. XI, 1926.

F. Pridmore,
The Coins of the British Commonwealth of Nations to the Reign of George VI, (Spink and Son Ltd., 1965).

Herbert Ingram
Priestley,
José de Galvez: Visitor-General of New Spain, 1765-1771, (Berkeley, 1916).

L.J. Ragatz,
The Fall of the Planter Class in the British Caribbean, 1783-1833, (New York, 1928).
Absentee Landlordism in the Caribbean, 1750-1833, (London, 1931).

F.P. Renault,
"*L'Odysée d'un Colonial sous L'Ancien Regime: Phillipe-Rose Roume de St. Laurent*", *Revue de L'Histoire des Colonies Francaises*, Vol. 9, Huitième Année, 1920.

Charles Reis,
A History of the Constitution or Government of Trinidad. Two volumes, (Trinidad, 1929).

C. Reith,
The Police Idea: Its History and Evolution in England in the 18th Century, (London, 1938).

William Renwick
Riddell,
"Le Code Noir", *Journal of Negro History*, Vol. X, No. 3, July, 1925.

Wilhelm Georg Friedrich Roscher,	*The Spanish Colonial System,* (translated from the German by E.G. Bourne, New York, 1904).
J. Holland Rose,	*The Life of Napoleon I,* (London, 1901).
	William Pitt and the Great War, (London, 1911).
	"British West India Commerce as a Factor in the Napoleonic Wars", *Cambridge Historical Journal,* 1929.
Betty Russell,	*The Influence of the French Revolution upon Grenada, St. Vincent and Jamaica,* M.A. thesis in preparation, University of the West Indies, Mona Jamaica.
José Antonio Saco,	*Historia de La Esclavitud de la Raza Africana en el Nuevo Mundo y en especial en los paises Américo-Hispanos* (Havana, 1938).
Moreau de Saint-Méry,	*Description Topographique, Physique, Civile, Politique et Historique de l'Isle Saint Domingue.* Three volumes, (Philadelphia, 1797; Paris, 1958).
H. Salandre et R. Cheyssac,	*Les Antilles Francaises,* (Fernand Nathan, 1962).
Ernest Samhaber,	*Merchants Make History,* (published Germany, 1960, translated and published London, 1963).
Maurice Satineau,	*Histoire de la Guadeloupe sous l'Ancien Régime, 1635-1789,* (Paris, 1928).
Sir R.H. Schomburgk,	*The History of Barbados,* (London, 1848).
R.L. Schuyler,	*The Fall of the Old Colonial System, 1770-1870,* (New York, 1945).
	Parliament and the British Empire, (Columbia University Press, 1929).
Bernard Semmel,	*The Governor Eyre Controversy,* (London, 1962).
W.G. Sewell,	*The Ordeal of Free Labour in the West Indies,* (2nd edition London, 1968; 1st published 1861).
R.B. Sheridan,	"The Commercial and Financial Organization of the British Slave Trade 1750-1807", *Economic History Review, 1958.*
Arnold A. Sio,	"Interpretations of Slavery: The Slave Status in the Americas", *Comparative Studies in Society and History,* April 1965.
Ronald V. Sires,	"Governmental Crisis in Jamaica, 1860-1866", *Jamaican Historical Review,* Vol. II, No. 3, December 1953.
	"Constitutional Change in Jamaica, 1834-1860", *Journal of Comparative Legislation and International Law,* Vol. XXII, November 1940.
M.G. Smith,	"Some Aspects of Social Structure in the British Caribbean About 1820", *Social and Economic Studies,* Vol. I, No. 4, 1953.
	"Slavery and Emancipation in Two Societies", *Social and Economic Studies,*Vol. 3, No. 4,1954.

Adam Smith,	*The Wealth of Nations.* Two volumes, (Everyman edition, 1958).
Raymond T. Smith,	*The Negro Family in British Guiana,* (London, 1956).
Luis M. Diaz Soler,	*Historia de la Esclavitud Negra en Puerto Rico, 1493-1890,* (Madrid, no date).
F.G. Spurdle,	*Early West Indian Government,* (New Zealand, no date).
Kenneth M. Stampp,	*The Peculiar Institution: Slavery in the Ante-Bellum South,* (New York, 1956).
C.E. Stephen,	*The First Sir James Stephen,* (Gloucester, 1906).
Roume de St. Laurent,	"Reclamation du Citoyen Roume sur le Remboursement que lui doit le Gouvernement Espagnol", *Trinidad and Tobago Historical Society, Publication* No. 739.
José Sucre-Reyes,	*Le Système Colonial Espagnol dans l'Ancien Venezuela,* (Paris, 1939).
E.P. Tanner,	"Colonial Agencies in England D u r i n g the Eighteenth Century", *Political Science Quarterly,* XVI, 1901.
Frank Tannenbaum,	*Slave and Citizen: The Negro in the Americas,* (New York, 1946).
H.W.V. Temperley and L.M. Penson,	*The Foundations of British Foreign Policy, from Pitt to Salisbury,* (Cambridge, 1938).
(G. Turnbull),	*A Narrative of the Revolt and Insurrection of the French Inhabitants in the Island of Grenada,* (Edinburgh, 1795).
Carl Ubbelohde,	*The Vice Admiralty Courts and the American Revolution,* (Chapel Hill, 1960).
Alexander von Humboldt,	*The Island of Cuba,* (translated by J.S. Thrasher; New York, 1856).
J. Steven Watson,	*The Reign of George III, 1760-1815,* (Oxford University Press, 1959).
C.H. Wesley,	"The Emancipation of the Free Coloured Population in the British Empire", *Journal of Negro History,* 1932.
Martin Wight,	*The Development of the Legislative Council, 1606-1945,* (London, 1946).
Curtis A. Wilgus (ed).	*Hispanic American Essays,* (Chapel Hill, 1942).
Eric Williams,	"The Intercolonial Slave Trade After its Abolition in 1807", *Journal of Negro History,* Vol. XXVII, April 1942.
	Capitalism and Slavery, (Chapel Hill, 1944).
	The Negro in the Caribbean, (Manchester, 1946).
	Documents on British West Indian History, 1807-1833, (Port-of-Spain, 1952).
K.S. Wise,	*Sketches of Trinidad and Tobago.* Four volumes,

	(Trinidad, 1934-1938).
Donald Wood,	*Trinidad in Transition*, (Oxford University Press, 1968).
H.I. Woodcock,	*The Laws and Constitutions of the British Colonies in the West Indies, having Legislative Assemblies*, (London, 1830).
Hume Wrong,	*Government of the West Indies*, (Oxford, 1923).
H.A. Wyndham,	*The Atlantic and Emancipation*, (London, 1935).
	The Atlantic and Slavery, (London, 1937)
D.M. Young,	*The Colonial Office in the Early Nineteenth Century*, (London, 1961).
Phillip Zeigler,	*Addington: A Life of Henry Addington, Viscount Sidmouth*, (London, 1965).

INDEX

A

Abercromby, General Sir Ralph, 35, 47, 49, 52, 68, 101, 169

Acton, Lord, xii

Act of Parliament of 1795, 29

Addams, seizure of, 216, 217

Adderley, George, 148, 162ff

Addington, Henry, (U.K. prime minister, 1801-4), 67, 79ff, 84, 97, 129ff, 159

Addresses, of 1803 to Picton and Fullarton, 152, 192-3
    of 1805, 206
    of 1810, 249

alcaldes, 41ff, 50, 145, 244

alcalde del monte, 42

alcalde de la Santa Hermandad, 42

alcalde de primer voto, 41

alcalde de segundo voto, 41

alcalde mayor provincial, 43

alcaldes ordinarios, 41, 158

alcalde provincial, 42

alférez real, 40

alguaçil, 40, 57

alguaçil mayor, 40, 58

Alleyne, Sir John Gay, 90

Angeles, Father Joseph Maria, 195-6

Apodaca, Admiral, 116

Aranguez, 116

Aristotle, xii

Articles of capitulation, 35

Asesor, 36ff, 48, 50, 53

Asiento, 2

Audiencia, 37ff, 52ff, 232-3

Auditor (see *Asesor*)

A View of the English Interests in India, 174

B

Baker and Dawson, 15, 17, 115

Balcarres, Lord, 91, 92, 93, 94, 95ff

Barbados, opposition to formation of Black Regiments, 90ff

barrios, 114

Barry, Edward, 115

Beckford, William, 171, 181

Begorrat, St. Hilaire, 37, 45-6, 116, 142, 151, 154, 194, 198, 211, 231

Berbice Slave Rebellion of 1763, xii
Black, John, 151, 154, 158, 194, 211

Black Regiments, 90ff

Bobb, Lewis, vii

Hartman, Isaac, 87

Hastings, Warren, 175

Higham, Thomas, 102, 104, 194

Hippisley, John Coxe, 172

Hislop, Governor Thomas, 111, 197
    assumes government of
      Trinidad, 158
    conflict with Briarly, 216ff
    conflict with Dickson, 214ff
    conflict with George Smith, 240ff
    absence from Trinidad, 244-9
    returns to Trinidad, 249
    espouses the British party, 251ff
    his conversion explained, 253
    takes action against the free
      coloured in 1810, 261ff

History of Trinidad, 160

*History of the People of Trinidad
and Tobago,* vii

Hobart, Lord (Secretary of State for
    War and the Colonies, 1801-4),
    67, 97, 105, 131, 133, 156, 159
    despatch of 16.10.1802, 70, 71
    relationship with Fullarton, 162
    attitude to development in Trinidad,
      178-82
    on the role of the commissioners,
      188-9

Holmes, Captain William, 219

Hood, Commodore Samuel, 128, 137,
    145ff

Hope, Colonel, 153

Hugues, Victor, 23

I

India, 171ff
    government in India, 174-5

Inglis, 241-3

Irving, General, 89

J

Jacobs, John Henry, 58

Jamaica
    slave population in 1795, 80
    opposition to Black Regiments, 91ff
    conflict with the Executive, 94ff

James, C.L.R., viii

Joseph, E.L., 24, 112, 160

jusqu'à nouvel ordre, 145

K

Kingston, Col. J.P., 107-8

Knox, George, 217, 242

L

Langton, Philip, 151, 196

Las Casas, Bartolomé de, 63

Layman, Capt. W., 134, 224

Littlepage, John Burnley, 117

Liverpool, Earl of (Secretary of State
    for War and the Colonies, 1809-12),
    70, 264-66

Lockheed, William, 104, 258-9

London Corresponding Society, 102

Lynch, Dr. Frederic, 160

M

Macartney, Lord, 172

Maitland, Brig. Gen., 153

Maling, John, 97, 223

Malouet, Baron Pierre Victor, 28-9

Malta, 128, 130-2

Mansfield, Lord, 77

maravedis, 44

Marryat, Joseph, 97, 209, 227-8,
    241-2, 246

Martinique, 11, 23, 24, 27, 29, 32
    constitutional government in, 72

M'Callum, Pierre, 115, 150, 224, 233-4

Merchants vs Planters
    on debts, 119-126
    on the constitution, 206-7,
       208-11

Modeste affair, 194

N

Negro troops (see Black Regiments)

Nihell, John, 35, 46, 47, 49, 50,
    53, 151, 154, 195, 198, 209,
      211, 217ff, 235

Nihell, Lawrence, 209

Noel, Monsieur, 145

North, Lord, 73

North American trade, 224-6

Nugent, John, 209

O

Ogé, 23

Ogle shootings, xii

oidor, 63

P

Painter, Ephraim, 104

Payne, William, 144

Peace of Amiens, 3, 102, 129-30

Philip, J.B., 110

Philip II, 2

Picton, Lt. Col. Thomas, 35, 46, 49,
    54ff, 68, 113, 137, 140ff, 145ff
    154ff, 159, 160ff, 192ff, 205-6
    instituted as military commandant, 35
    instituted as civil governor, 67
    attitude to British party, 103ff
    attitude to free coloured, 106ff
    attitude to colonial government, 107ff
    leaves Trinidad, 153
    trial, 160
    on his assailants, 164-6
    strength of position in Trinidad, 166
    biography of, 168-70
    difficulty of his early years, 168-9
    prosperity in Trinidad, 170
    attitude to social development, 178-82
    conduct in Trinidad investigated,
      197, 199
    views on constitutional change, 205
    on George Smith, 231

"Pictonians", 190, 192ff

Piggott, Sir Arthur, 219

Piggott, James, 219

Pinckard, George, 181

292

financial difficulties in, 222-6
support for British laws in 1810, 254ff

Trinidad Courant, 138

Trinidad Gazette, 65

Trinidad in Transition, v

*Trinidad Weekly Courant and Commercial
Gazette,* 245

Turnbull, Forbes & Co., 118

V

Vaughan, Capt., 27-8

Vaughan, Sir John, 169

Venezuela, 4

W

Warner, Thomas, xiv

West Indies,
French revolution in, 23ff, 86ff
Black Regiments in, 89ff

Wharton's Tavern Affair, 102ff, 126

What is History?, xviii

Wilberforce, William, 79, 84

Williams, Eric, vii

Williams, Dr. Alexander, 242

Wilson, Andrew, 154, 194

Winterflood, 104

Wood, Donald, v

Woodford, Governor, 110

Worswick, Thomas & Sons, 115

Y

York, Frederick, Duke of, 92